TO BE
A MAN

. . . .

This *New Consciousness Reader*
is part of a new series of original
and classic writing by renowned experts on
leading-edge concepts in personal development,
psychology, spiritual growth, and healing.

TO BE A MAN

*In Search of the
Deep Masculine*

EDITED BY

KEITH THOMPSON

JEREMY P. TARCHER, INC.
Los Angeles

For my first nephew
Keith Arthur Thompson
Born January 23, 1991

The long day wanes: the slow moon climbs: the deep
Moans round with many voices. Come, my friends,
'Tis not too late to seek a newer world.
Alfred, Lord Tennyson

Library of Congress Cataloging-in-Publication Data

To be a man: in search of the deep masculine/edited by Keith Thompson.
  p. cm.
Includes bibliographical references.
ISBN 0-87477-637-6
  1. Men—Psychology.   2. Masculinity (Psychology)   I. Thompson,
Keith, 1954—
HQ1090.T59   1991
305.32—dc20   91-28741
                                                    CIP

Jeremy P. Tarcher, Inc.
5858 Wilshire Blvd., Suite 200
Los Angeles, CA 90036

Distributed by St. Martin's Press, New York

Copyrights and Permissions appear on pp. 287–93, which constitute a con-
tinuation of the copyright page.

Manufactured in the United States of America
10 9 8 7 6 5 4 3 2

CONTENTS

. . . .

PART 3

Through the Eye of the Wound:
Images of Male Pain, Fear, Anger,
Loss, and Grief

ACKNOWLEDGMENTS

. . . .

I want to acknowledge the many individuals who have contributed in different ways to this book, to my work as a writer, and in some cases to my sense of what it means to be a man.

Special thanks to the contributors whose works grace these pages. At times when assembling this volume grew impossibly difficult, I turned to your writings in their protective manila folders and came away refreshed. At other times I imagined you as guests on a variety program and myself as host; I knew the show had to go on. I bow to all of you.

Stephen Aizenstat offered valuable assistance by organizing a preliminary group of writings for the book. My stepbrother Brett Shingledecker made many helpful suggestions concerning issues of intimacy between men. With welcome dispatch Franklin Abbott helped me pinpoint the whereabouts of several contributors; so did Sy Safransky, editor of the marvelous Chapel Hill monthly *The Sun: A Magazine of Ideas*. Aaron Kipnis brought to my attention several contributions that appear in these pages. In the final weeks of the project Mary Wickwire descended from angelic realms to offer crucial administrative support and intellectual stimulation.

I am indebted to you all, as well to numerous individuals at literary agencies and publishing houses for expediting my requests for permission to include various writings in this book.

Particular gratitude goes to my editor Connie Zweig for her critical and aesthetic insight, generous spirit, spacious heart, and delightful humor throughout the life of this work; to Jeremy Tarcher for sharing his vision at the outset of my labor and supporting my vision as it steadily emerged; and to my agent, Fred Hill, who has understood and backed my interest in men's studies for several years.

I am deeply grateful to Laurance S. Rockefeller for his generous support of my work in recent years. Similarly, I thank Jean Lanier, George Lamb, and Elizabeth McCormack.

Heartfelt appreciation to Howard Metzenbaum, Michael Murphy, and Robert Bly: mentors and friends with whom, spanning a period of many years, I shared the pleasures of inspired work.

In the early 1970s Marjorie Grey Reid introduced me to the *New Yorker* and *I.F. Stone's Bi-Weekly* and otherwise fostered in me a love of ideas that grows as the years pass. As the poet wrote: "And that has made all the difference."

At an early age I gained a lasting appreciation for the dignity of physical work from three kind and devoted men: Albert Bobson, Jack Thomas, and a man whom I remember only as Mr. Mize.

Because we were together from the start, through uncounted storms and clearings, I honor the spirit of the men in my immediate bloodline: my father, Reed, and his sons, my brothers, Jeff, Tom, and George. Someday the depths of our bonds may be more clear—to me, to all of us.

Finally, to Kathryn, loving partner, worthy adversary, generous friend: my deep appreciation for your support and apologies for my extended absence during the odyssey of this work. The book is done. Tell Tyler and Yoshi I'm on my way home.

· · · · · · · ·

PROLOGUE

KEITH THOMPSON

"The apparent individual conflict of the patient is revealed as a universal conflict of his environment and
epoch. Neurosis is thus nothing less than an individual
attempt, however unsuccessful, to solve a universal
problem."

C.G. JUNG

When I accepted the invitation to prepare this anthology of writings on what
it means to be a man I realized it was probably inevitable that I would end up
questioning prevailing assumptions about masculinity, mine included. How
could it be otherwise, in this post-feminist age when experts on *Oprah, Dona-*
hue, Geraldo, and *Sally* assert with drumbeat regularity that masculinity is not
merely in transition but faces a crisis of unprecedented proportions?

Even so, it never occurred to me that composing this volume would lead
me to a conclusion far more radical than the collective diagnosis of talk-show
clinicians: namely, *masculinity does not exist.*

I realize this is a bold assertion, so let me say more.

In the weeks after beginning work on *To Be a Man,* I embarked on a
search—an increasingly beleaguered search—for an all-encompassing "master context" for unifying and integrating a remarkable diversity of view-
points on men, masculinity, and manhood. When this big picture didn't
emerge, I redoubled my efforts to find it, citing the accompanying mental
strain as clear evidence that the new framework was on the verge of revealing
itself to my psyche in a sudden intuitive flash—at any moment.

Or so I imagined. The closest I came to a bona fide epiphany was when I
decided that I (not to mention my fledgling anthology) would be better
served by turning my attention to other projects for a while, preferably those
that didn't depend on visionary states. I needed a break. In the weeks that followed I came to see that my struggle to find a comprehensive, monolithic perspective was fundamentally at odds with the fact that I no longer believed in
masculinity as a comprehensive, monolithic phenomenon. Clarifying this
discrepancy allowed me to appreciate how my very search for such a framework effectively masked my loss of faith. *Masculinity does not exist,* I found
myself saying; *there are* many *masculinities, multiple ways to be a man.*

xv

This came as no flash but rather as the culmination of a dialogue that had been brewing in the recesses of my psyche ever since I failed to make my high school track team, or perhaps since Mary Bibbins dispatched one of her girlfriends to tell me she didn't want to go steady anymore. I doubt that in either case my pain would have been less if a man I trusted had counseled me that there are as many *masculine* ways to fail as there are *masculine* ways to succeed, each involving multitudes of payoffs and tradeoffs. But who knows? Maybe understanding would have helped me retain some of the adolescent courage and confidence that seemed to bleed away quietly.

Many years later, something had shifted, something of magnitude. It was a shift that had been edging closer to consciousness for a long time. I returned to work on this anthology knowing I had surrendered most if not all of the last vestiges of adolescent faith in the fantasy of masculinity as a one-note recital, a definitively coded program that all men everywhere need only "get with."

This is not to say that I believe there's no common ground among the many masculinities that men embody today and the masculinities men have embodied in times past. It is to say, instead, that masculinity, taken literally as a *singular anything,* invariably obscures the richness, complexity, and multiplicity of male experience, fostering the supposition that one or another model of male ways is "correct" in some absolute sense, as if masculinity could not be big enough to include Sly Stallone and David Bowie, James Earl Jones and Peewee Herman, George Patton and Mohandas Gandhi, Superman and Homer Simpson, all at once.

In a sense, *masculinity* (one) is *not* big enough, whereas *masculinities* (many) *is* big enough *and* deep enough. Many years ago, in an interview reprinted in this book, Robert Bly introduced me to the image of the "deep masculine," which connotes ancient modes of adult manhood characterized by emotional richness and spiritual intensity. I have chosen this phrase as the organizing image of this volume because it links masculine experience with positive qualities associated with depth: *dimension, range, concentration, substance, strength, authenticity,* and *stimulating, visceral, instinctive, soulful, penetrating.* Also because I find "deep" and "depth" compelling for the *cloudier* associations they call forth: *latent, archaic, hidden, disguised, buried, remote, silent, fallen, unavailable, distorted from lack of use, inert, bottomless.*

In the pages that follow I have attempted to include writings that capture these two sets of images in varying combinations: sometimes surprising, often gratifying, frequently disturbing. Rather than being somehow opposed to one another, the differing moods or tones of these image groups actually appear closely related.

For instance, the very title of Aaron Kipnis's piece, "Forgotten Images of Sacred Masculinity," draws from both pools of depth imagery: something *significant* has been *lost.* Robert Bly ("What Men Really Want") finds the mythic wildman a compelling image of male strength and substance. Yet Bly also urges caution, for the wildman has only recently been released from a long period of silent solitude at the bottom of a remote forest pond. In "At What Price?" Sam Keen confesses both to loving his work and to being haunted by doubt: "How often, doing work that is good, have I betrayed what is better in myself and abandoned what is best for those I love?" Listen closely as James Hillman ("Fathers and Sons") restores value to the very qualities of fathers— absence and abuse—that typically receive only condemnation from sons.

Many other contributors invoke the "deep masculine" as decidely mixed, complex, ambiguous. Their diverse writings offer welcome ground for my emerging view of masculinity as intrinsically plural.

I realize this view is rather at odds with conventional assumptions about manhood. To be sure, most males in our culture are taught early and often to eradicate ambiguity and ambivalence from their lives; to walk, talk, stand up, and act "like a man"; to suppress traces of wavering and wandering, lest they impede steely-glint clarity and decisive forward-moving action. Yet most of us in fact *live with* considerable ambiguity at many levels; most of us waver in ways that make us uncomfortable, but so often enhance our creativity, flexibility, and soulfulness.

I simply am not interested in reinforcing the cultural prejudice against masculine variety, contradiciton, shading, and nuance. Indeed, because I see these as defining characteristics of masculine depth, as editor I have sought at every turn to honor and give place to the "god" Ambiguity (not at the expense, however, of clarity and conviction, whose place is also granted in a cosmos of masculine multiplicity).

But, of course, I engaged this book as man as well as an editor. It comes as no surprise to me that I feel a personal affiliation with "cloudier" images of male depth (*latent, disguised, remote, fallen, bottomless,* and the like), for it was a gut sense of these images that precipitated my pilgrimage many years ago to find a definition of manhood that I could live *for myself.* In the spirit of those men who tell their personal stories in the pages that follow, I offer the following brief chapter from my own.

Nearly ten years ago a close friend called to urge me to go with him that night to hear a presentation in San Francisco by a Minnesota poet, essayist, editor, storyteller, philosopher, and spiritual provocateur named Robert Bly. Having attended a previous Bly event, my friend insisted that I cancel whatever I had planned and join him. "It's crucial," he added. Everything was *crucial* in those days.

Sure, I responded, why not? I loved poetry and had no other plans.

Bly recited his beautiful translations of Rainer Maria Rilke's poems, while accompanying himself on dulcimer before an audience of several hundred in San Francisco. I remember that evening feeling perplexed, then curious, then inexplicably moved by the subtext of Bly's remarks: a loosely connected pattern of fragments, tangents, asides, and implications with which (I would discover over time) he regularly punctuated his workshops and lectures, no matter what his formal topic.

In the broadest sense, this subtext highlighted the emotional lives of men. Specifically, Bly was addressing men's pain in relationship to women, grief between fathers and sons, peculiarly male modes of feeling, and rites of passage crucial to male "soul-making." I was in my mid-twenties and searching; for what I was not sure, though the anxiety Bly's ideas stirred in me suggested clues. So I wrote this man a rather audacious letter saying I knew he had more to tell and he should let me interview him for publication. Yes, he responded; let's do just that.

To our mutual surprise, the resulting conversation (*New Age* magazine, May 1982) became one of the most widely discussed and photocopied articles in recent years, prompting letters from men and women from the Americas to Europe to New Zealand to South Africa. To say that Robert and I were both astonished by this response is a considerable understatement. In the week before the interview hit the newsstands, we spoke by phone about our just-finished collaboration.

"I wonder whether the interview will speak to anyone else," I remember saying to Robert. "Maybe the issues we've raised are of interest primarily to us." Robert said the same doubts had occurred to him. "It's a sobering thought that the ideas we've discussed could be personal," he said. He meant: personal to us alone. In an important sense, Robert chose the right words— the ideas *were* personal for men and women throughout the world whose hunger for insight into "male mysteries" had been whetted by a print conversation between two men of two different generations. Eight years later, Robert published *Iron John: A Book About Men,* in which he extends the ideas he began to develop in our interview which is reprinted here in several parts.

To Be a Man is very much an outgrowth of a process set in motion by that interview. *Something was missing* for men in our times. As is well revealed in my conversation with Robert, my particular wound lay in the realm of the Father, involving my personal father yet something larger; a domain including mentorship, initiation, connection with ancestors, and my own generativity. My heart longed for a sense of confidence connected with these, though my words were inadequate to express that longing. That isolation began to change when I received dozens of letters from men my age saying they were as moved by the interview format as by the ideas discussed. "I never considered that a man my age could sit down with a man my father's age and have a heartfelt talk about 'what men really want,'" wrote a South Carolina man who ended with: "P.S. Today as a man I feel less *desperate*. I know that someday my son (now age 5) and I will read the interview together."

This letter and others like it helped me realize that the significance of my questions and Robert Bly's answers was not personal in the narrower sense of the word. Something *universal* (as Jung used the word in the opening epigraph) had been touched—but what? The writings in this volume attest to a richness of thought about men, masculinity, and manhood that was "in the air" well before Robert Bly turned his attention to the subject—a richness that has continued to unfold in the years afterwards.

While working on *To Be a Man,* I became keenly aware that some leaders of the embryonic "men's movement" do not take kindly to the suggestion that their campaign is a response to the women's movement. I find this sensitivity somewhat perplexing. If the point is that the men's movement can't simply be reduced to a blind reflex to the hard knocks of feminism, I emphatically agree. Yet some "men's movement men" insist with considerable vigor that men's growing interest in rethinking masculinity bears no relation to women's changes in recent decades—as if "men's work" loses significance when seen as a response to "women's work."

When I search my thesaurus for synonyms of *respond,* this is what comes up: *answer, reply, acknowledge, come back, rejoin.* When either gender undertakes a collective reappraisal of its commitments—as history will record women did in the years following the tumultuous appearance of Betty Friedan's book *The Feminine Mystique*—how can the other gender *not* respond, *not* be effected? One part of me wishes we men had blazed the trail. But then we'd be open (again) to the charge of always needing to lead the way! As it is, by *acknowledging* and *rejoining* the feminist challenge to long-standing arrangements between the sexes, we're in a position to nullify the insidious myth that men, by virture of being men, are incapable of being in relation to anything.

No less important, we're also then able to evaluate *for ourselves* a myriad of feminist claims, separating the obviously nonsensical ("All men as *men* sufffer from terminal testosterone poisoning") from the obviously sensible ("Men are as hampered in particular ways by simplistic sex-role stereotypes as women are hampered in particular ways") from those that invite prolonged reflection ("There are certain crucial differences between men and women that must be honored if men and women are ever to meet on true common ground").

In the long run, the stimulus-response metaphor falls short in explaining interactions between the collective masculine and the collective feminine, especially in recent years. The relationship seems more dialectical, a matter of responses to responses to responses. For instance, rather than taking as gospel or simply repudiating feminist observations, Warren Farrell, in his 1974 book *The Liberated Male,* insisted that attempts to discuss women's changes are futile without discussing corresponding changes for men. Farrell, who came to be known as the "Gloria Steinem of the Men's Movement," also introduced the provacative image of male polygamy: "a man married to his job and wife (but barely to the latter)."

"In another 1974 book, *Male Survival,* author Harvey Kaye urged men to embrace sources other than their work to support personal identity and to validate new avenues of relationship (deepening connections with family and community, for instance). Stephen Koch, in an *Esquire* article called "The Guilty Sex," informed fathers that they could no longer simply stand by, watering the grass, "wooden as a dead post while inside the household lived that real life in which he didn't count." By 1979, Muskingham College history professor Joe L. Dubbert, in his book *A Man's Place: Masculinity in Transition*, gave this account of preliminary efforts toward a New Male:

> By the mid-1970's, men's conferences were being held and organizations formed to respond to a growing list of male concerns, ranging from divorce and alimony rights, parenting, and job situations to sexual fulfillment and, especially, gay rights, which dominated the early movement. A men's liberation movement had been born. The basic focus was a recognition of the shortcoming of playing the traditional masculine role of always getting ahead and staying cool. Men were thinking about how they treated associates, competitors, and women and how they chose to spend their leisure time. Men were encouraged to evaluate their physical and mental health in a new light. Although the movement was mostly campus-based, it appealed to men everywhere who felt the need to discuss their masculine identity. Robert Gould [quoted in "Now Men's Lib Is the Trend," *U.S. News & World Report*, March 18, 1974] stated that the liberation movement was just beginning, and he predicted that it would have far-ranging consequences comparable to the civil-rights movement.

The jury is still out of Robert Gould's prediction about the likely social impact of the still-emerging men's movement—or, rather, men's *movements*. In keeping with my earlier suggestion that the term *masculinity* should be understood as inherently plural, it seems wise to avoid trying to compress the depth and breadth of several nascent men's movements into a single gray collective. Here I value the spirit of storyteller and men's teacher Michael Meade:

> I prefer to imagine something that isn't a single movement, because that suggests an ideology or a dogma. And I don't think that's what's going on. I think there are a number of movements; there's a lot of exploration going on, but not one coalescing movement. . . . We're only just emerging from a historical period in which the royal king archetype, or the storm god archetype, has been dominant. That energy causes large, unified movements. But now that kind of energy has dissipated, and what's coming in is more varied.

During the past year I have scanned hundreds of essays, articles, poems, and works of fiction, far more of which deserve inclusion in these pages than limits of space permit. Most of the pieces included here are excerpted from larger works, owing to my desire to feature more shorter rather than fewer longer contributions (in keeping with my premise that our focus is best trained on *masculinities* and *movements*).

To Be a Man is by no means intended as the definitive or exhaustive chronicle of what it means to be a man. Such an account would necessarily involve a shift from one form (anthology) to another (encyclopedia), and would require not one but many volumes. Such a creature would also probably incite mass narcolepsy.

From the outset mine has been a different goal, namely to feature provocative works representative of multiple tributaries feeding contemporary masculine thought, vision, and practice. Even when for ease of expression I employ the deceptively singular term *masculinity,* as I do throughout this volume, I intend for the term to be understood as plural (similar to the way *color* indicates a continuum of possibilities).

Many pieces didn't make it into this book because they lost coherence when excerpted; others because my efforts to locate authors for reprint permission went unrewarded; still others because satisfactory arrangements could not be reached with copyright-holding agents. In no case was a perspective refused for ideological reasons. I take final responsibility for the choices I've made *tam facti quam animi* (as much in deed as in intention).

"Drop the Latin, kid," Humphrey Bogart just whispered in my ear. "A man's gotta do what a man's gotta do . . ."

PART 1

· · · · · · ·

TO BE
A MAN:
QUESTIONS
OF IDENTITY

I have always disliked being a man. . . . Even the expression "Be a man!" strikes me as insulting and abusive. It means: Be stupid, be unfeeling, obedient and soldierly, and stop thinking. Manliness . . . is a hideous and crippling lie, . . . it is also by its very nature destructive—emotionally damaging and socially harmful.

PAUL THEROUX

There are continuities of masculinity that transcend cultural differences.

THOMAS GREGOR

INTRODUCTION

· · · · · · ·

Is masculinity, an innate, primordial essence, universal at its very core; or is it a social construction, an evolving improvisation that can and does assume many apparently contradictory forms?

If the *genetic* facts associated with the word *male* could be shown to be synonymous with the *cultural* facts associated with the word *manhood,* this question might lend itself to simple, undisputed answers—at last! But for now, the safest response to this either/or query is: *Both.* Masculinity does appear to be embedded in—and to be the expression of—certain elementary, rudimentary "deep structures." Even so, these pathways clearly provide for a remarkable degree of variety, diversity, and "natural drift" in masculine expression in cultures throughout the world.

In light of this, the old debate about whether masculinity is based on nature *or* nurture seems decidedly tired. I find a different question more compelling: *How much* and *what kinds* of nature and nurture make for being a man? Though not expressly stated, this question fuels a provocative conversation among several lively thinkers, all focused in this opening section on masculine identity—and identifying masculinity.

Cooper Thompson, who leads workshops and trainings revisioning masculinity, argues that although biological factors obviously shape masculine behavior, "there is undeniable evidence that cultural and environmental factors are strong enough to override biological impulses." In his essay "We Should Reject Traditional Masculinity," Cooper says the task faced by today's males is fundamentally a social one: moving beyond traditional masculine modes (especially courage, physical strength, and independence) while opening to traditional feminine qualities (such as gentleness, nurturance, and vulnerability).

Author and men's movement pioneer Warren Farrell agrees—somewhat. Yes, men have much to gain from transcending narrow limits of identity, but there is also much that is valuable in traditional masculinity. "Praise of men is an endangered species," he writes in an excerpt from *Why Men Are the Way They Are.* "But the good about men is not. And when something good is endangered it needs special attention." The traditional male role should be embraced, not simply rejected, Farell proposes.

Enter Robert Bly, poet, author, and convener of and participant in men's gatherings throughout the United States. In "What Men Really Want," adapted from my 1982 interview with him by the same name, Bly affirms Cooper Thompson's challenge to traditional masculinity ("the Fifties male") while also joining Warren Farrell's affirmation of traditional male ways ("the deep masculine"). Bly accomplishes this by turning to imagination for new insight and to mythology for fresh ground. "The male in the past twenty years has become more thoughtful, more gentle," Bly states. "But by this process he has not become more free." Today's "soft males" find themselves unhappy, Bly notes. "They are life-preserving but not exactly life-giving."

Aaron Kipnis, a Northern California psychotherapist and men's group leader, enters with a spirited call for recognition of a newly-emerging image of sacred masculinity: "Creative, fecund, generative, nurturing, protective, compassionate . . . existing in harmony with the earth and the feminine . . . yet also erotic, free, wild, playful, energetic, and fierce." Kipnis warns that men who seek to reconnect to soul solely through the feminine place themselves "in danger of reentering a son-lover-victim relationship with the goddess."

Our written symposium on male identity is rounded out with Thomas Moore's beautiful essay "Eros and the Male Spirit." It is a pleasure to follow this artistic psychologist (and psychological artist) as he insists "that we will not deal with gender in depth until we recover a sense of the sacred." This involves, Moore says, abandoning the frustrating attempt to *be* the male spirit and learning instead to be its priest.

· · · · · · ·

1 · WE SHOULD REJECT TRADITIONAL MASCULINITY

COOPER THOMPSON

I was once asked by a teacher in a suburban high school to give a guest presentation on male roles. She hoped that I might help her deal with four boys who exercised extraordinary control over the other boys in the class. Using ridicule and their status as physically imposing athletes, these four wrestlers had succeeded in stifling the participation of the other boys, who were reluctant to make comments in class discussions.

As a class we talked about the ways in which boys got status in that school and how they got put down by others. I was told that the most humiliating put-down was being called a "fag." The list of behaviors which could elicit ridicule filled two large chalkboards, and it was detailed and comprehensive; I got the sense that a boy in this school had to conform to rigid, narrow standards of masculinity to avoid being called a fag. I, too, felt this pressure and became very conscious of my mannerisms in front of the group.

Partly from exasperation, I decided to test the seriousness of these assertions. Since one of the four boys had some streaks of pink in his shirt, and since he had told me that wearing pink was grounds for being called a fag, I told him that I thought he was a fag. Instead of laughing, he said, "I'm going to kill you."

Such is the stereotypical definition of strength that is associated with masculinity. But it is a very limited definition of strength, one based on dominance and control and acquired through the humiliation and degradation of others.

A NEW IMAGE OF STRENGTH

Contrast this with a view of strength offered by Pam McAllister in her introduction to *Reweaving the Web of Life:*

> The 'Strength' card in my Tarot deck depicts, not a warrior going off to battle with his armor and his mighty sword, but a woman stroking a lion. The woman has not slain the lion nor maced it, not netted it, nor has she put on it a muzzle or a leash. And though the lion clearly has teeth and long sharp claws, the woman is not hiding, nor has she sought a protector, nor has she grown muscles. She doesn't appear to be talking to the lion, nor flattering it, nor tossing it fresh meat to distract its hungry jaws.
>
> The woman on the 'Strength' card wears a flowing white dress and a garland of flowers. With one hand she cups the lion's jaws, with the other she caresses its nose. The lion on the card has big yellow eyes and a long red tongue curling out of its mouth. One paw is lifted and the mane falls in thick red curls across its broad torso. The woman. The lion. Together they depict strength.

This image of strength stands in direct contrast to the strength embodied in the actions of the four wrestlers. The collective strength of the woman and the lion is a strength unknown in a system of traditional male values. Other human qualities are equally foreign to a traditional conception of masculinity. In workshops I've offered on the male role stereotype, teachers and other school personnel easily generate lists of attitudes and behaviors which boys typically seem not to learn. Included in this list are being supportive and nurturant, accepting one's vulnerability and being able to ask for help, valuing women and "women's work," understanding and expressing emotions (except for anger), the ability to empathize with and empower other people, and learning to resolve conflict in non-aggressive, non-competitive ways.

LEARNING VIOLENCE

All of this should come as no surprise. Traditional definitions of masculinity include attributes such as independence, pride, resiliency, self-control, and physical strength. This is precisely the image of the Marlboro man, and to some extent, these are desirable attributes for boys and girls. But masculinity goes beyond these qualities to stress competitiveness, toughness, aggressiveness, and power. In this context, threats to one's status, however small, cannot be avoided or taken lightly. If a boy is called a fag, it means that he is perceived as weak or timid—and therefore not masculine enough for his peers. There is enormous pressure for him to fight back. Not being tough at these moments only proves the allegation. . . .

Ultimately, violence is the tool which maintains what I believe are the two most critical socializing forces in a boy's life: *homophobia,* the hatred of gay men (who are stereotyped as feminine) or those men believed to be gay, as well as the fear of being perceived as gay; and *misogyny,* the hatred of women. The two forces are targeted at different classes of victims, but they are really just the flip sides of the same coin. Homophobia is the hatred of feminine qualities in men while misogyny is the hatred of feminine qualities in women. The boy who is called a fag is the target of other boys' homophobia as well as the victim of his own homophobia. While the overt message is the absolute need to avoid being feminized, the implication is that females—and all that they traditionally represent—are contemptible. The United States Marines have a philosophy which conveniently combines homophobia and misogyny in the belief that "when you want to create a group of male killers, you kill 'the woman' in them."

The pressures of homophobia and misogyny in boys' lives have been poignantly demonstrated to me each time that I have repeated a simple yet provocative activity with students. I ask them to answer the question, "If you woke up tomorrow and discovered that you were the opposite sex from the one you are now, how would you and your life be different?" Girls consistently indicate that there are clear advantages to being a boy—from increased independence and career opportunities to decreased risks of physical and sexual assault—and eagerly answer the question. But boys often express disgust at this possibility and even refuse sometimes to answer the question. In her reports of a broad-based survey using this question, Alice Baumgartner reports the following responses as typical of boys: "If I were a girl, I'd be stupid and weak as a string"; "I would have to wear makeup, cook, be a mother, and yucky stuff like that"; "I would have to hate snakes. Everything would be miserable"; "If I were a girl, I'd kill myself."

THE COSTS OF MASCULINITY

The costs associated with a traditional view of masculinity are enormous, and the damage occurs at both personal and societal levels. The belief that a boy should be tough (aggressive, competitive, and daring) can create emotional pain for him. While a few boys experience short-term success for their toughness, there is little security in the long run. Instead, it leads to a series of challenges which few, if any, boys ultimately win. There is no security in being at the top when so many other boys are competing for the same status. Toughness also leads to increased chances of stress, physical injury, and even early death. It is considered manly to take extreme physical risks and voluntarily engage in combative, hostile activities.

The flip side of toughness—nurturance—is not a quality perceived as masculine and thus not valued. Because of this boys and men experience a greater emotional distance from other people and few opportunities to participate in meaningful interpersonal relationships. Studies consistently show that fathers spend very small amounts of time interacting with their children. In addition, men report that they seldom have intimate relationships with other men, reflecting their homophobia. They are afraid of getting too close and don't know how to take down the walls that they have built between themselves.

As boys grow older and accept adult roles, the larger social costs of masculinity clearly emerge. Most women experience male resistance to an expansion of women's roles; one of the assumptions of traditional masculinity is the belief that women should be subordinate to men. The consequence is that men are often not willing to accept females as equal, competent partners in personal and professional settings. Whether the setting is a sexual relationship, the family, the streets, or the battlefield, men are continuously engaged in efforts to dominate. Statistics on child abuse consistently indicate that the vast majority of abusers are men, and that there is no "typical" abuser. Rape may be the fastest growing crime in the United States. And it is men, regardless of nationality, who provoke and sustain war. In short, traditional masculinity is life threatening.

NEW SOCIALIZATION FOR BOYS

Masculinity, like many other human traits, is determined by both biological and environmental factors. While some believe that biological factors are significant in shaping some masculine behavior, there is undeniable evidence that cultural and environmental factors are strong enough to override biological impulses. What is it, then, that we should be teaching boys about being a man in a modern world?

- Boys must learn to accept their vulnerability, learn to express a range of emotions such as fear and sadness, and learn to ask for help and support in appropriate situations.

- Boys must learn to be gentle, nurturant, cooperative, and communicative, and, in particular, learn non-violent means of resolving conflicts.

- Boys must learn to accept those attitudes and behaviors which have traditionally been labeled feminine as necessary for full human development—thereby reducing homophobia and misogyny. This is tantamount to teaching boys to love other boys and girls.

Certain qualities like courage, physical strength, and independence, which are traditionally associated with masculinity, are indeed positive qualities for males, provided that they are not manifested in obsessive ways nor used to exploit or dominate others. It is not necessary to completely disregard or un-learn what is traditionally called masculine. I believe, however, that the three areas above are crucial for developing a broader view of masculinity, one which is healthier for all life.

These three areas are equally crucial for reducing aggressive, violent be-havior among boys and men. Males must learn to cherish life for the sake of their own wholeness as human beings, not just *for* their children, friends, and lovers. If males were more nurturant, they would be less likely to hurt those they love. . . .

SCHOOLS AND ATHLETICS

Where will this change in socialization occur? In his first few years, most of a boy's learning about masculinity comes from the influences of parents, sib-lings, and images of masculinity such as those found on television. Massive efforts will be needed to make changes here. But at older ages, school curric-ulum and the school environment provide powerful reinforcing images of traditional masculinity. This reinforcement occurs through a variety of channels, including curriculum content, role modeling, and extracurricular activities, especially competitive sports.

School athletics are a microcosm of the socialization of male values. While participation in competitive activities can be enjoyable and healthy, it too easily becomes a lesson in the need for toughness, invulnerability, and dominance. Athletes learn to ignore their own injuries and pain and instead try to injure and inflict pain on others in their attempts to win, regardless of the cost to themselves or their opponents. Yet the lessons learned in athletics are believed to be vital for full and complete masculine development, and as a model for problem-solving in other areas of life.

In addition to encouraging traditional male values, schools provide too few experiences in nurturance, cooperation, negotitation, non-violent con-flict resolution, and strategies for empathizing with and empowering others. Schools should become places where boys have the opportunity to learn these skills; clearly, they won't learn them on the street, from peers, or on tele-vision.

Despite the pressures on men to display their masculinity in traditional ways, there are examples of men and boys who are changing. "Fathering" is one example of a positive change. In recent years, there has been a popular emphasis on child-care activities, with men becoming more involved in providing care to children, both professionally and as fathers. This is a clear shift from the more traditional view that child rearing should be delegated to women and is not an appropriate acitivity for men.

For all of the male resistance it has generated, the Women's Liberation Movement has at least provided a stimulus for some men to accept women as equal partners in most areas of life. These are the men who have chosen to learn and grow from women's experiences and together with women are creating new norms for relationships. Popular literature and research on male sex roles is expanding, reflecting a wider interest in masculinity. Weekly news magazines such as *Time* and *Newsweek* have run major stories on the "new masculinity," suggesting that positive changes are taking place in the home and in the workplace. Small groups of men scattered around the country have organized against pornography, battering, and sexual assault. Finally there is the National Organization for Changing Men which has a pro-feminist, pro-gay, pro-"new man" agenda, and its ranks are slowly growing. . . .

BOYS WILL BE BOYS

I think back to the four wrestlers and the stifling culture of masculinity in which they live. If schools were to radically alter this culture and substitute for it a new vision of masculinity, what would that look like? In this environment, boys would express a full range of behaviors and emotions without fear of being chastised. They would be permitted and encouraged to cry, to be afraid, to show joy, and to express love in a gentle fashion. Extreme concern for career would be replaced by a consideration of one's needs for recreation, health, and meaningful work. Older boys would be encouraged to tutor and play with younger students. Moreover, boys would receive as much recognition for artistic talents as they do for athletics, and, in general, they would value leisure-time, recreational activities as highly as competitive sports.

In a system where maleness and femaleness were equally valued, boys might no longer feel that they have to "prove" themselves to other boys; they would simply accept the worth of each person and value those differences. Boys would realize that it is permissible to admit failure. In addition, they would seek out opportunities to learn from girls and women. Emotional support would be commonplace, and it would no longer be seen as just the role of the female to provide the support. Relationships between boys and girls would no longer be based on limited roles, but instead would become expressions of two individuals learning from and supporting one another. Relationships between boys would reflect their care for one another rather than their mutual fear and distrust.

Aggressive styles of resolving conflicts would be the exception rather than the norm. Girls would feel welcome in activities dominated by boys, knowing that they were safe from the threat of being sexually harassed. Boys would no longer boast of beating up another boy or of how much they "got off" of a girl the night before. In fact, the boys would be as outraged as the girls at rape or other violent crimes in the community. Finally, boys would become active in efforts to stop nuclear proliferation and all other forms of military violence, following the examples set by activist women.

The development of a new conception of masculinity based on this vision is an ambitious task, but one which is essential for the health and safety of both men and women. The survival of our society may rest on the degree to which we are able to teach men to cherish life.

· · · · · · · ·

2 · WE SHOULD EMBRACE TRADITIONAL MASCULINITY

WARREN FARRELL

Every virtue, taken to the extreme, becomes a vice. For the past twenty years I have critiqued traditional masculinity because masculinity has been taken to the extreme. And taken to the extreme it creates anxiety, homicide, rape, war, and suicide; not taken to the extreme it has many virtues not to be tossed out with the bathwater.

Praise of men is an endangered species. But the good about men is not. And when something good is being endangered it needs special attention. And so, for a rare moment in recent history, here is special attention to what's good about male socialization. . . .

GIVING/GENEROSITY. Why do we think of women as giving of themselves and men as giving gifts? Because women's socialization teaches direct giving—as listening nurturers, cooks of men's meals, and doing more of his wash than he does of hers. He may give by working in a coal mine and contracting black lung so his child can attend college as he never could, but his giving is done at at the mine—where we don't see it. The result of his giving is a check. With women's giving we appreciate more than the result, we appreciate the process: we see her cook the meal, serve it, and usually clean it up. We don't see him wading through water in a dark and damp mine shaft, or driving a truck at 2 A.M. on his fourth cup of coffee, behind schedule in traffic and with no time to nap. We see him at home withdrawing from the coffee.

He may spend much of his life earning money to finance a home his wife fell in love with, but we don't think of him as giving when he's away from home nearly as much as we think of her as giving when she cleans up his dishes.

Sometimes a man's giving is reflexive and role-based, such as when he reflexively picks up a tab at a restaurant. We forget this is also giving: fifty dollars for dinner and drinks may represent a day's work in after-tax income. Theater tickets, gas, and babysitters are another day's work. We don't think of his picking up these tabs as being as giving as when a woman spends two days preparing a special meal for him. Both forms of giving are role-based; hers are just more direct. . . .

FAIRNESS. The best thing emerging from sports, games, work rules, winning, and losing is fairness. Not necessarily honesty—fairness. In Little League, when I trapped a ball in my glove just after a bounce, the umpire credited me with catching a fly. I volunteered to the umpire that I hadn't. The umpire, embarrassed, changed the decision. The angry coach bawled me out. The other coach bawled out my coach for bawling me out. They disagreed on honesty. But neither would have disagreed with the fairness of a neutral umpire making the decision.

Male socialization teaches the value of a careful system of rules, within which anyone can work to gain advantage, and some of which can be gotten around (with possible consequences). Once mastered, the rules give everyone a much more equal chance than they would have had without the rules. To men, mastering these rules feels like survival—survival of themselves and their family. A lifetime of practicing these rules gives many men a sixth sense for fairness. Groups of men and women who have disregarded these rules as "too male" or "too establishment," as did the Students for a Democratic Society in the sixties and seventies, soon evolve into backstabbing elites which self-destruct.

MALE ACTION

NURTURING. Carl wasn't great at expressing feeling. And he didn't understand fully that sometimes Cindy just needed a listening ear. His way of supporting her was to volunteer to help Cindy with the problem that was making her upset. For Carl, taking Cindy seriously meant taking Cindy's problem seriously, and taking Cindy's problem seriously meant trying to find a solution. To him this was an act of love. Anything less, like just standing around when she was hurting, was an act of cruelty. "If Cindy's bleeding," he'd say, "find a solution. . . . Don't just stand there with that sickening supportive smile on your face while the woman I love is bleeding to death!" *Solutions are male nurturance.* . . .

LEADERSHIP. Accusations that "men have the power" have appeared more frequently in the past decade and a half than appreciation for the billions of hours sacrificed by men to give themselves the leadership training to get that power. Or the benefits of the leadership itself. For example, few articles explain how male socialization has trained millions of leaders to lead thousands of businesses that are now providing millions of women with opportunities for leadership that might not exist were it not for male leadership.

OUTRAGEOUSNESS. While women are socialized to get male attention by being "good girls" or not offending male egos, men are being socialized to get female attention by standing out. One way a man can stand out is to be outrageous. The best part of outrageousness is the barriers it breaks to allow all of us more freedom to experiment with discovering more of ourselves. The Beatle's hair, considered outrageous at the time, permitted a generation to experiment with their hair; Elvis the Pelvis allowed a generation to experiment with their sexual selves; the Wright Brothers were told it was scientifically impossible to fly—and suicidal to try; and Salvador Dali, Picasso, and Copernicus looked at the world in ways considered outrageous in their time; in retrospect, we can see that they freed us to live in a way we could not have dreamed of before.

MALE PSYCHOLOGY

TO KEEP EMOTIONS UNDER CONTROL. Although in relationships this tight lid leads to a "male volcano" after months of repressed emotions, the flip side is our dependence on this male trait in crisis situations. Dirk recalls a head-on collision. "Five cars crashed. There was glass and blood everywhere. Four of us guys ran from car to car, following the screams and preparing tourniquets. We stopped two cars to recruit passengers to redirect traffic, called the police, and removed a woman and her son from a car that burst into flames a minute later."

The newspapers reported the accident. But no headlines read, "Men Control Their Emotions in Order to Save Lives of Women and Children." They ran a picture—not of four men standing next to the women and children they saved, but of the five cars that collided.

EGO STRENGTH. When women reevaluate what goes wrong in a relationship the unspoken assumption is that this takes ego strength. When men compete fiercely to be number one, we see it as a reflection of their fragile egos (which it can be) and call it strategizing, *rather than recognizing the ego strength required to conduct a self-reevaluation immediately after a loss.* A man needs to ask, "What did *I* do wrong?" And then, when he finds the answer, rather than credit himself with his introspection, he must focus immediately on correcting it before the next game. . .

TO EXPRESS ANGER. "One minute we were shouting and calling each other names. A minute later we were concentrating on the next play." The male tendency to take sports seriously combined with the willingness to express feelings intensely leads many adult men to say, "I lose my temper for a minute, then it's done with." The positive side of male anger is the quick, intense release of emotions, with the subsequent calm that follows the storm. If the intensity is understood, and not exacerbated, grudges are rarely held. The intensity, like all powerful energy, can be harnessed—and channeled into powerful lovemaking . . .

MALE STRENGTH

TO SAVE HER LIFE AT THE RISK OF HIS OWN. I described in the introduction [of my book] how my younger brother Wayne died in an avalanche as he ventured ahead to check out a dangerous area alone rather than have his woman friend share the risk or do it herself. No news account of his death discussed this as an example of men's willingness to forfeit their lives for the women they love. We read of accounts of women lifting automobiles to save the life of a child, but not to save the life of a husband. Frequently, a woman who hears about this difference gets defensive even though she says she wants to appreciate men more.   •

There is nothing to be defensive about. It is not a statement that men are better. Members of each sex do what they are socialized to do both to give themselves the feeling of being part of a whole and to deviate a bit to feel like an individual. This makes both sexes equal—with different programming. A man's dying for a woman he loves doesn't make him better at all, but part of his socialization leaves him vulnerable. My brother was quite vulnerable.

TO GIVE UP HIS LIFE FOR HIS BELIEFS. Some men give up their lives at war because they believe in their country; others do it because if they cannot be a hero they'd rather not live; others do it to support families. Others risk their lives in war so that if they live, they will earn enough money and status to "earn" a wife. Men with different class or ethnic backgrounds do the same in the CIA, FBI, State Department, and Mafia: their beliefs or their willingness to support their families are as important as their entire existence.

For these men, these are not empty words. While the worst part of this is an extraordinary statement of male insecurity and compensation for powerlessness, the best part is the extraordinary conviction men have for their beliefs and their families. It is a statement (within their value system) of the importance of values, responsibility, and quality of life: theirs and their family's. . . .

MALE RESPONSIBILITIES

SELF-SUFFICIENCY. We don't call men "career men," because the word *career* is built into the word *man*. Self-sufficiency is built into masculinity. . . .

Male socialization is an overdose in self-sufficiency. There are no fairy tales of a princess on a white horse finding a male Sleeping Beauty and sweeping him off to a castle; no fairy tales glorifying a man who is not self-sufficient. When the going gets tough, he doesn't talk it through, he gets going.

How do these fairy tales translate into reality? Liberation has been defined as giving women the "right to choose": to choose the option of being at home or being at work. *Men do not learn they have the right to choose to be at home. That would imply someone else would have to take care of him at home.* A man doesn't learn to expect that. He learns, instead, "The world doesn't owe you a living." Self-sufficiency implies *earning* rights. The right to choose, he learns, comes from choosing, for example, to take a job that pays a lot so he has more choices when he is away from the job. As a result of a man's training to take care of himself, millions of women have been freer to look at their own values—and to criticize men—than they would be if they had to support them. . . .

RISK TAKING. The male socialization to take risks on the playing field prepares a man to take risks investing in stocks, businesses, and conglomerates. To invest in his career with years of training, and then extra training. A plastic surgeon may have risked from age five to thirty-five as a student or part-time student, underpaid and overworked, in order, during the second half of his life, to be able to earn a half million dollars a year. . . .

On numerous levels, male socialization teaches men to risk a lot and be willing to fail a lot—and all for the hope of being rewarded a lot. (Conversely, if he doesn't risk, he doesn't expect the rewards.) If he survives, he will then be able to provide a security for his wife and children that he never had for himself. . . .

TO DEVELOP IDENTITY. The pressure on men to be more than self-sufficient, which forced them to take risks and self-start, to sort out their values quickly, to learn how and when to challenge authority, and to invent, resulted, at best, in the development of *identity.* Identity arises out of seeing both how we fit in and how we don't fit in—but especially how we don't fit in. The foundation of society is here before we arrive and after we pass. Identity is discovering our uniqueness in that continuity. As we take risks, and challenge what exists, the friction between ourselves and society makes all the boundaries clearer. Which is how we develop identity, and why the best parts of male socialization are helpful in developing identity. Of course, most men sell a good portion of their identity out to institutions just as most women sell out to a man. But the part of a man true to the values he has sorted out still challenges, still takes risks, still benefits from the development of identity. . . .

RESPONSIBILITY. Male socialization is a recipe book of taking responsibility. From the responsibility of getting a job at age fourteen so he can pay for his first date's food and tickets, to performing adequately within view of the girl he wants to ask out to increase his chances of acceptance, to actually asking his first date out, to arranging for his parents to drive, then, in later years, to borrowing the car, then driving himself, then taking initiatives—all of these are responsibility. . . .

My study of male-female language-pattern differences reflects the male training to take responsibility. Men are much less likely to use phrases like "This happened to me," and much more likely to use phrases like "I did this."

WHAT MALES CAN DO

SENSE OF EFFICACY. In the process of learning to take risks, men get especially strong training in learning what is and what is not effective—a sense of efficacy. In the process of trying a wide variety of jobs, we learn what we are effective at. We are socialized with a different attitude toward lost investments—as experiences that fine-tune us to the questions we must ask to prevent the next loss. We see the loss as an investment in investing. Tinkering for hours under a hood teaches him by trial and error how to be effective with a car (I said teaches him—it hasn't taught me!).

Once again, this is reflected in male-female language differences. Men are much less likely to say, "Maybe we can get Bill to do that," and much more likely to say, "Maybe if I try. . . ."

DOING RATHER THAN COMPLAINING. To become effective, men learn to make the unarticulated distinction between two types of complaining: "I'm helpless" versus "This is the complaint, now here's the solution." Men are not tolerant enough of other men complaining, "I'm helpless." But the best part of this intolerance is the pressure it exerts on a man to get rid of the problem that created the complaint.

PUSHING THE LIMITS OF ONE'S TALENTS. Doing may be better than complaining, but doing is not enough. A man's pressure to earn as much as he can with his talents means a constant pushing of the limits of each and every talent to discover which one can support him best. When people hear "pushing the limits of one's talents" they think of talents as raw capability; they feel that job advancement involves an expansion of talents and an application of talents toward an appropriate job and frequent promotions. Successful people learn that pushing the limits of one's talents also means balancing the politics of everyone else's egos while making themselves shine; balancing facade with personal integrity; and selling themselves repeatedly without appearing as if they're selling. The struggle to master the complex politics of advancement is the real pushing of the limits of one's talents.

The recent focus on discrimination has made us feel that the formula for success is qualifications plus lack of discrimination. That one-two approach has limited our appreciation of the extraordinary subtlety and range of talents required for advancement. . . .

MALE FLEXIBILITY

SENSE OF HUMOR. Whether it's Woody Allen's ability to laugh at the schlemiel in himself or George Carlin's ability to laugh at masculinity itself, one of the best things that emerges from men's training to see life as a game is the ability to laugh both at our own roles in the game and at the game itself. Even the most traditional and serious of male systems are mocked, such as Bill Murray in *Stripes* mocking the military. It is difficult to find movies similarly mocking the traditional female role—for example, a movie mocking motherhood. . . .

CHANGE WITHOUT BLAME. Although men have made fewer changes than women, what changes they have made—as in fathering—have occurred without movements that blamed women. Fifteen years ago, few men were sensitive to orgasms or clitorises. Few had heard of the ERA. Few fathers-to-be joined their wives in the delivery room, in the preparation for the birth of their child. But soon, men had changed in all these ways.

The changes that occurred happened without attacking women with equal-but-opposite rhetoric, such as "Women hold a monopoly of power over the child," or "Women have a fragile mothering ego perpetuated by a quiet matriarchy that sends men into the field to die while women conspire to sleep in warm beds at home." Nor did men respond to blame by labeling it psychological abuse.

When we hear the phrase "the battle between the sexes," there is an unspoken assumption that both sexes have been blaming equally. The battle, though, could easily be called "the female attack on men," not "the male attack on women." There is a distinction between responding to blame and initiating it. Men have changed less, but they have also blamed less.

· · · · · · ·

3 · WHAT MEN REALLY WANT

ROBERT BLY

KEITH THOMPSON:
After exploring the way of the goddess for many years, lately you've turned your attention to the pathways of male energy—the bond between fathers and sons, for example, and the initiation of young males. You're also writing a book relating some of the old classic fairy tales to men's growth. What has your investigation turned up? What's going on with men these days?

ROBERT BLY:

No one knows! Historically, the male has changed considerably in the past thirty years. Back then there was a person we could call the '50s male, who was hardworking, responsible, fairly well disciplined; he didn't see women's souls very well, though he looked at their bodies a lot. Reagan still has this personality. The '50s male was vulnerable to collective opinion: if you were a man, you were supposed to like football games, be aggressive, stick up for the United States, never cry, and always provide. But this image of the male lacked feminine space. It lacked some sense of flow, it lacked compassion, in a way that led directly to the unbalanced pursuit of the Vietnam War, just as the lack of feminine space inside Reagan's head now has led to his callousness and brutality toward the poor in El Salvador, toward old people here, the unemployed, schoolchildren, and poor people in general. The '50s male had a clear vision of what a man is, but the vision involved massive inadequacies and flaws.

Then, during the '60s, another sort of male appeared. The waste and anguish of the Vietnam War made men question what an adult male really is. And the women's movement encouraged men to actually look at women, forcing them to become conscious of certain things that the '50s male tended to avoid. As men began to look at women and at their concerns, some men began to see their own feminine side and pay attention to it. That process continues to this day, and I would say that most young males are now involved in it to some extent.

Now there's something wonderful about all this—the step of the male bringing forth his own feminine consciousness is an important one—and yet I have the sense there is something wrong. The male in the past twenty years has become more thoughtful, more gentle. But by this process he has not become more free. He's a nice boy who now not only pleases his mother but also the young woman he is living with.

I see the phenomenon of what I would call the "soft male" all over the country today.

Sometimes when I look out at my audiences, perhaps half the young males are what I'd call soft. They're lovely, valuable people—I like them—and they're not interested in harming the earth, or starting wars, or working for corporations. There is something favorable toward life in their whole general mood and style of living.

But something's wrong. Many of these men are unhappy. There's not much energy in them. They are life-preserving but not exactly life-giving. And why is it you often see these men with strong women who positively radiate energy? Here we have a finely tuned young man, ecologically superior to his father, sympathetic to the whole harmony of the universe, yet he himself has no energy to offer.

KEITH THOMPSON:

It seems as if many of these soft young men have come to equate their own natural male energy with being macho. Even when masculine energy would clearly be life-giving, productive of service to the community, many young males step back from it. Perhaps it is because back in the '60s, when we looked to the women's movement for leads as to how we should be, the message we got was the new strong women wanted soft men.

ROBERT BLY:

I agree. That's how it felt! The women did play a part in this. I remember a bumper sticker at the time that read "WOMEN SAY YES TO MEN WHO SAY NO." We know it took a lot of courage to resist or to go to Canada, just as it took some courage also to go to Vietnam. But the women were definitely saying they preferred the softer receptive male, and they would reward him for being so. "We will sleep with you if you are not too aggressive and macho." So the development of men was disturbed a little there; nonreceptive maleness was equated with violence, and receptivity was rewarded.

Also, as you mention, some energetic women chose soft men to be their lovers—and in a way, perhaps, sons. These changes didn't happen by accident. Young men for various reasons wanted harder women, and women began to desire softer men. It seems like a nice arrangement, but it isn't working out.

KEITH THOMPSON:

How so?

ROBERT BLY:

Recently I taught a conference for men only at the Lama Community in New Mexico. About forty men came, and we were together ten days. Each morning I talked about certain fairy tales relating to men's growth, and about the Greek gods that embody what the Greeks considered different kinds of male energy. We spent the afternoon being quiet or walking and doing body movement or dance, and then we'd all come together again in the late afternoon. Often the younger males would begin to talk and within five minutes they would be weeping. The amount of grief and anguish in the younger males was astounding! The river was deep.

Part of the grief was a remoteness from their fathers, which they felt keenly, but part, too, came from trouble in their marriages or relationships. They had learned to be receptive, and it wasn't enough to carry their marriages. In every relationship, something fierce is needed once in a while; both the man and the woman need to have it.

At the point when it was needed, often the young man didn't have it. He was nurturing, but something else was required—for the relationship, for his life. The male was able to say, "I can feel your pain, and I consider your life as important as mine, and I will take care of you and comfort you." But he could not say what he wanted, and stick by it; that was a different matter.

In the *Odyssey*, Hermes instructs Odysseus, when he is approaching a kind of matriarchal figure, that he is to lift or show Circe his sword. It was difficult for many of the younger males to distinguish between showing the sword and hurting someone. Do you understand me? They had learned so well not to hurt anyone that they couldn't lift the sword, even to catch the light of the sun on it! Showing a sword doesn't mean fighting; there's something joyful in it.

KEITH THOMPSON:

You seem to be suggesting that uniting with their feminine side has been an important stage for men on their path toward wholeness, but it's not the final one. What is required? What's the next step?

ROBERT BLY:

One of the fairy tales I'm working on for my *Fairy Tales for Men* collection is a story called "Iron John." Though it was first set down by the Grimm Brothers around 1820, this story could be ten or twenty thousand years old. It talks about a different development for men, a further stage than we've seen so far in the United States.

As the story starts, something strange has been happening in a remote area of the forest near the king's castle; when hunters go into this area, they disappear and never come back. Three hunters have gone out and disappeared. People are getting the feeling that there's something kind of weird about that part of the forest, and they don't go there anymore. Then one day an unknown hunter shows up at the castle and says, "What can I do around here? I need something to do." And he is told, "Well, there's a problem in the forest. People go out there and they don't come back. We've sent groups of men to see about it and they disappear. Can you do something about it?"

Interestingly, this young man does not ask for a group to go with him—he goes into the forest alone, taking only his dog. As they wander about in the forest, they come across a pond. Suddenly a hand reaches up from the pond, grabs the dog, and drags it down. The hunter is fond of the dog and he's not willing to abandon it, in this way. His response is neither to become hysterical, nor to abandon his dog. Instead, he does something sensible, he goes back to the castle, rounds up some men with buckets, and then they bucket out the pond.

Lying at the bottom of the pond is a large man covered with hair all the way down to his feet. He's kind of reddish—he looks a little like rusty iron. So they capture him and bring him back to the castle, where the king puts him in an iron cage in the courtyard.

Now, let's stop the story here a second. The implication is that when the male looks into his psyche, not being instructed what to look for, he may see beyond his feminine side, to the other side of the "deep pool." What he finds at the bottom of his psyche—in this area that no one has visited in a long time—is an ancient male covered with hair. Now, in all of the mythologies, hair is heavily connected with the instinctive, the sexual, the primitive. What I'm proposing is that every modern male has, lying at the bottom of his psyche, a large primitive man covered with hair down to his feet. Making contact with this wildman is the step the '70s male has not yet taken, this is the process that still hasn't taken place in contemporary culture.

As the story suggests very delicately, there's a little fear around this ancient man. After a man gets over his initial skittishness about expressing his feminine side, he finds it to be pretty wonderful, he gets to write poetry and go out and sit by the ocean, he doesn't have to be on top all the time in sex anymore, he becomes empathetic. It's a beautiful new world. But Iron John, the man at the bottom of the lake, is quite a different matter. This figure is even more frightening than the interior female, who is scary enough. When a man succeeds in becoming conscious of his interior woman, he often feels warmer, more alive. But when he approaches what I'll call the "deep male," that's a totally different situation!

Contact with Iron John requires the willingness to go down into the psyche and accept what's dark down there including the sexual. For generations now, the business community has warned men to keep away from Iron John, and the Christian Church is not too fond of him either. But it's possible that men are once more approaching that deep male. Freud, Jung, and Wilheim Reich are three men who had the courage to go down into the pond and accept what's there, which includes the hair, the ancientness, the rustiness. The job of modern males is to follow them down. Some of that work has already been done, and in some psyches (or on some days in the whole culture) the Hairy Man or Iron John has been brought up and stands in a cage "in the courtyard." That means he has been brought back into the civilized world, and to a place where the young males can see him.

Now, let's go back to the story. One day the king's eight-year-old son is playing in the courtyard and he loses his beloved golden ball. It rolls into the cage, and the wildman grabs it. If the prince wants his ball back, he's going to have to go to this rusty, hairy man who's been dying at the bottom of the pond for a very long time and ask for it. The plot begins to thicken.

KEITH THOMPSON:
The golden ball, of course, is a recurrent image in many fairy stories. What does it symbolize in general, and what is its significance here?

ROBERT BLY:
The golden ball suggests the unity of personality that we have as children—a kind of radiance, a sense of unity with the universe. The ball is golden, representing light, and round, representing wholeness, like the sun, it gives off a radiant energy from inside.

Notice that in this story the boy is eight. We all lose something around the age of eight, whether we are girl or boy, male or female. We lose the golden ball in grade school if not before; high school finshes it. We may spend the rest of our lives trying to get the golden ball back. The first stage of that process I guess would be accepting—firmly, definitely—that the ball has been lost. Remember Freud's words? "What a distressing contrast there is between the radiant intelligence of the child and the feeble mentality of the average adult."

So who's got the golden ball? In the '60s, males were told that the golden ball was the feminine, in their own feminine side. They found the feminine, and still did not find the golden ball. That step that both Freud and Jung urged on males, and the step that men are beginning to undertake now, is the realization that you cannot look to your own feminine side, because that's not where the ball was lost. You can't go to your wife and ask for the golden ball back. She'd give it to you if she could, because women are not hostile in this way to men's growth, but she doesn't have it anyway and besides, she has lost her own. And heaven knows you can't ask your mother!

After looking for the golden ball in women and not finding it, then looking into his own feminine side, the young male is called upon to consider the possibility that the golden ball lies within the magnetic field of the wildman. Now, that's a very hard thing for us to conceive the possibility that the deep nourishing and spiritually radiant energy in the male lies not in the feminine side, but in the deep masculine. Not the shallow masculine, the macho masculine, the snowmobile masculine, but the deep masculine, the instinctive one who's underwater and who has been there we don't know how long.

Now, the amazing thing about the "Iron John" story is that it doesn't say that the golden ball is being held by some benign Asian guru or by a kind young man named Jesus. There's something connected with getting the golden ball back that is incompatible with niceness. And the frog only turns into a prince when it is thrown against the wall in a fit of what New Age people might call "negative energy." New Age thought has taught young men to kiss frogs. That doesn't always work. You only get your mouth wet. The women's movement has helped women learn to throw the frog against the wall, but men haven't had this kind of movement yet. The kind of energy I'm talking about is not the same as macho, brute strength which men already know enough about; it's forceful action undertaken, not without compassion, but with resolve.

KEITH THOMPSON:

It sounds as if contacting the wildman would involve in some sense a movement against the forces of "civilization."

ROBERT BLY:

It's true. When it comes time for a young male to have a conversation with the wildman, it's not the same as a conversation with his minister or his guru. When a boy talks with the hairy man, he is not getting into a conversation about bliss or mind or spirit, or "higher consciousness," but about something wet, dark, and low—what James Hillman would call "soul."

And I think that today's males are just about ready to take that step, to go to the cage and ask for the golden ball back. Some are ready to do that, others haven't gotten the water out of the pond yet, they haven't yet left the collective male identity and gone out into the wilderness alone, into the unconscious. You've got to take a bucket, several buckets. You can't wait for a giant to come along and suck out all the water for you; all that magic stuff isn't going to help you. A weekend at Esalen won't do it either! You have to do it bucket by bucket. This resembles the slow discipline of art; it's the work that Rembrandt did, that Picasso and Yeats and Rilke and Bach all did. Bucket work implies much more discipline than many males have right now.

KEITH THOMPSON:
And of course, it's going to take some persistence and discipline, not only to uncover the deep male, but to get the golden ball back. It seems unlikely that this "un-nice" wildman would just hand it over.

ROBERT BLY:
You're right; what kind of story would it be if the wildman answered: "Well, OK, here's your ball—go have fun." Jung said that in any case, if you're asking your psyche for something, don't use yes or no questions—the psyche likes to make deals. If part of you for example is very lazy and doesn't want to do any work, a flat-out New Year's resolution won't do you any good; it will work better if you say to the lazy part of yourself, "You let me work for an hour, then I'll let you be a slob for an hour—deal?" So in "Iron John," a deal is made, the wildman agrees to give the golden ball back if the boy opens the cage.

At first, the boy is frightened and runs off. Finally, the third time the wildman offers the same deal, the boy says, "I couldn't open it even if I wanted to because I don't know where the key is." The wildman now says something magnificent, he says, "The key is under your mother's pillow."

Did you get that shot? The key to let the wildman out is lying not in the toolshed, not in the attic, not in the cellar—it's under his mother's pillow! What do you make of that?

KEITH THOMPSON:
It seems to suggest that the young male has to take back the power he has given to his mother and get away from the force field of her bed. He must direct his energies away from pleasing Mommy and toward the search for his own instinctive roots.

ROBERT BLY:
That's right, and we see a lot of trouble right there these days, particularly among spiritual devotees. A guru may help you skip over your troubled relations with your mother, but one doesn't enter the soul by skipping; one's personal history is also history in the larger sense. In the West our way has been to enter the soul by consciously exploring the relationship with the mother—even though it may grieve us to do it, even though it implies the incest issue, even though we can't seem to make any headway in talking with her.

KEITH THOMPSON:
Which would explain why the boy turns away twice in fright before agreeing to get the key from his mother's bed. Some longtime work is involved in making this kind of break.

ROBERT BLY:

Yes, and it also surely accounts for the fact that, in the story, the mother and father are always away on the day that the boy finally obeys the wildman. Obviously, you've got to wait until your mother and father have gone away. This represents not being so dependent on the collective, on the approval of the community, on being a nice person, or essentially being dependent on your own mother because if you went up to your mother and said "I want the key so I can let the wildman out," she'd say, "Oh no, you just get a job" or "Come over here and give Mommy a kiss." There are very few mothers in the world who would release that key from under the pillow because they are intuitively aware of what would happen next—namely, they would lose their nice boys. The possessiveness that some mothers exercise on sons—not to mention the possessiveness that fathers exercise toward their daughters—cannot be overestimated.

And then, we have a lovely scene in which the boy succeeds in opening the cage and setting the wildman free. At this point, one could imagine a number of things happening.

The wildman could go back to his pond, so that the split happens over again; by the time the parents come back, the wildman is gone and the boy has replaced the key. He could become a corporate executive, an ordained minister, a professor, he might be a typical 20th-century male.

But in this case, what happens is that the wildman comes out of the cage and starts toward the forest and the boy shouts after him, "Don't run away! My parents are going to be very angry when they come back." And Iron John says, "I guess you're right; you'd better come wth me." He hoists the boy up on his shoulders and off they go.

KEITH THOMPSON:

What does this mean, that they take off together?

ROBERT BLY:

There are several possible arrangements in life that a male can make with the wildman. The male can be separated from the wildman in his unconscious by thousands of miles and never see him. Or the male and the wildman can exist together in a civilized place, like a courtyard, with the wildman in a cage, and they can carry on a conversation with one another, which can go on for a long time. But apparently the two can never be united in the courtyard, the boy cannot bring the wildman with him into his home. When the wildman is freed a little, when the young man feels a little more trust in his instinctive part after going through some discipline, then he can let the wildman out of the cage. And since the wildman can't stay with him in civilization, he must go off with the wildman.

This is where the break with parents finally comes. As they go off together the wildman says, "You'll never see your mother and father again," and the boy has to accept that the collective thing is over. He must leave his parents' force field.

• • • • • • •

4 · FORGOTTEN IMAGES
OF SACRED MASCULINITY

AARON R. KIPNIS

The first man is of the earth, earthy.

I CORINTHIANS

Something is stirring in the hearts of men. We're beginning to come up hard against many painful limitations in our traditional role models. We are now seeking new images of masculinity that support us in a return to feeling, aliveness, connection to nature, our bodies, our children, women, and other men.

A few prominent mythological images have served as our Western cultural foundations for masculinity. These characters have been the major actors in the play of men's psyches for the last few millennia. One has been the image of the youthful, conquering, invincible hero—such as Hercules. The strong, dominant, elder male—such as Moses or Abraham—is another pervasive ideal of manhood. He leads his tribe with absolute authority, ruling in the name of an all-powerful god in the sky. Another major image is that of a superhuman healer. He becomes a suffering, victimized, wounded, and murdered man nailed to a cross—the martyred Christ. He, too, is related to and derives his power from a distant father-in-the-sky.

Even though omnipotent, this sky-god is also capricious, wrathful, possessive, jealous, dominating, and devaluing of the feminine. He was known as Kronos, Zeus, and Uranus by the Greeks; Jupiter or Jove by the Romans; Indra or Brahma by the Indians; Jehovah by the Israelites; Allah by Islam; and by many other names in different cultures. Patriarchy evolved from these mythologies.

In Genesis, the Old Testament proposes that we are made in God's image. In depth psychology, this belief is mirrored in the theory that our individual ego reflects an archetype—a universal pattern that shapes life—or more precisely, a complex of archetypal forces in relationship with one another. Our lives may reflect the story of a particular myth or a collection of stories, instead of one single, archetypal god or goddess. Men who draw *only* from images of "solar" deities for their inspiration of sacred masculinity are condemned to conceive of their own divine nature as distant, abstract, erratically wrathful, and superior.

On the positive side, the solar image presents an ideal of warmth and light. It helps things grow. But problems arise when there is *too much* sun. That is the condition of many men in our culture: too hot, too dry, too distant, too brittle—disconnected from the body and the earth. At this time, a masculine sort of moisture is needed to balance this "global warming of the psyche."

The male initiation process, through which young men once were connected with the masculine powers in the earth, is for the most part lost to modern culture. In the absence of male initiation, many men have sought reconnection to soul through the feminine. However, femininity is not the primary cure for the drought in the masculine psyche.

Indeed, the modern trend to personify the earth as a feminine entity effectively perpetuates the divorce of the male psyche from its own fecund, inner-masculine, life-affirming nature. This perspective ignores many ancient myths that depicted the masculine as earth- or lunar-based and the feminine as solar. To envision nature or soul as only feminine does the same injustice to men as the sky-father myth did to women through exiling and degrading the sacred image of the goddess.

Men who seek the "inner-feminine" are often in danger of re-entering a "son-lover-victim" relationship with the goddess, as may have been the case in ancient matriarchal times. Old goddess icons often show a mature goddess with her young son/lover, but rarely depict her in relationship with an adult and equally powerful male.

In his book *Phallos,* Jungian analyst Eugene Monick argues that when men are disconnected from "phallos" (primordial earth-based masculinity) then "castration has begun . . . the feminization process in a male is inimical to his psychological connection with phallos . . . a fundamental differentiation must take place." A man's individuation is in danger if he bases his development solely on a return to the mother—whether through worship of a female earth or a goddess image, idealizing women, or trying to cultivate his "inner femininity." Men require initiation into the field of archetypal masculinity before they can coexist with women in partnership, neither dominating nor being dominated by them.

The newly emerging image of sacred masculinity is of a creative, fecund, generative, nurturing, protective, and compassionate male, existing in harmony with the earth and the feminine, yet also erotic, free, wild, playful, energetic, and fierce. This image is a far cry from the invincible, rigid, patriarchal, war-making hero, the silently suffering martyr, or the feminized "soft" male who serves the goddess.

One of the many tasks men now face is to return awareness of the earth-god archetypes to our psychology, philosophy, and spiritual lives. In *The Dream and the Underworld* James Hillman says, "We are able to recall that oceans and rivers belong to Oceanos and Poseidon; that Eros is also a male figure and force; that a lord of vegetation and zoetic life, and of childhood too, is Dionysus; and that even the earth itself can have, as in Egypt at the historical roots of our symbolisms, a masculine personification." A multitude of earth-based masculine dieties, from various cultures and epochs, reflects images of masculinity quite different from those presented by the archetypes of our Judeo-Christian culture.

Dumuzi, for example, is an agricultural god from ancient Sumer. He is a husband of the earth who as a shepherd protects the flocks. He is also the juicy, erotic lover of the goddess Inanna, who fondly calls him the Wild Bull. He presents an image of masculinity that protects and generates life, yet is still wild and undomesticated. Also from Sumer is Enki, an earthy, fluid, magical god of depth and wisdom who aids Inanna on an epic journey to the underworld. Both sacred male figures are directly connected to the earth, depth, and feeling, while maintaining a powerful relationship in alliance with the goddess.

From Africa comes Ogun, the Dragonslayer. Like Iron John of whom Robert Bly speaks, Ogun is a wildman of the woods. With the advent of urban culture, however, he transforms into a toolmaker—a traditional occupation of men. The African Elleggua is a trickster like Native American Coyote and Kokopeli. Like the Greek Hermes and Min, the phallic god of Coptos who was a protector of travelers, Elleggua is also a messenger and magician associated with the penis and the crossroads. Obatala, who is most revered in the African Yoruba tradition, is an androgynous creator god associated with the high mountains.

Many pre-Christian, Greek masculine dieties are connected to the earth. Hephaestus works deep beneath mountains creating wondrous works upon his forge. Orpheus is associated with music and wild animals, as is Pan. Hades dwells deep beneath the earth in the place of souls. Fertility and riches spring from the depths of Pluto, the Roman name for Hades. Poseidon is an oceanic god of deep, fluid, passionate feeling. Hermes, the great communicator and transformer, can go deep into the underworld and return to the world above. He also brings down the word from the Olympian gods on high.

From Egypt comes Osiris, son of earth-father Geb and sky-mother Nut. He is associated with the Nile River. The overflowing of the river deposited fresh alluvium, which fertilized the crops each year. This was depicted in several ancient paintings as Osiris' ejaculate fluid flowing directly from his phallus into the mouths of the people. He represents a fluid, cyclic style of earth-based masculinity that engenders and supports life.

Why is it valuable to embrace earth-based masculinity? The heroic, solar, heavenly model, taken alone, is dominating and oppressive. The solar gods are abstract and often inaccessible to our imagination—the very image of the remote or disembodied father. Christ, for example, was not a father or a husband. His heavenly father was also without a feminine consort or partner. What can these images communicate to us as men concerned about issues as important as raising our children, relating to women, and preserving the earth?

The earth-god is not a Lord of the Universe. He is a more personal god who is a progenitor of life on *this* planet. He is concerned with life's evolution and preservation. He presents a sacred image of masculinity that is life-generating, erotic, nurturing, connected to the earth and the body. These fundamental qualities and sacred images of men are in our collective unconscious and our mythological heritage, and in our bones.

In pretechnological, polytheistic cultures, the gods were associated with many different domains, interacting with one another as a council, a family, or a tribe. There was usually no chief executive officer who ruled over all worlds with absolute power. Men enjoyed a *personal* relationship with these dieties who were close to their lives. There were gods of the sea, forest, rivers, mountains, desert, sun, sky, and moon.

Like the earth, the moon has not always been the exclusive symbol of femininity that it is today. There was once a *man* in the moon. In ancient Egypt there were numerous inscriptions referring to Osiris as Lord of the Moon. His son Horus, also known as Old Man Who Becomes a Child Again, has the moon as his left eye. Thoth, a god of wisdom and spokesman for the gods, is also a lunar-related diety.

In ancient Sumer, in the city of Ur, the Moon Father was worshiped as Nanna. He is known in Serbian myth as Myesyats, the Bald Uncle. He is in the far-flung outreaches of Greenland and Malay, and among the Maoris as well. In India he is referred to as Soma and Chandra, great liberators from ignorance. In Australia he is still called Japara. In ancient Babylonia he was known as Sinn. Among the ancient druids of Ireland he was called St. Luan, Dugad, and Moling. The Eskimos of Baffin Island speak of Brother Moon who wears the black handprints of his sister, the sun.

Why is it valuable to understand lunar masculinity? Consider the consistency of the heroic, solar model. The sun rises and falls every day, always the same. It is a model of the man who remains the same throughout time. This has its value in establishing a model of discipline and consistency in our lives. However, that consistency can smother other aspects of our being. The ebb and flow of the moon, in contrast, reminds us that only sometimes do we feel completely full and luminous. Sometimes our brightness is on the wane. Sometimes we want to be completely dark, withdrawn, and alone. Other times our light starts to grow again; we feel expansive and move outward.

If we envision masculinity as changeless, like the sun, then we become alarmed when we get moody, when we fluctuate. We may try to modulate our behavior with substance abuse or other obsessive behaviors in an attempt to numb out "unmasculine" feelings. Lunar masculinity provides a male model that gives place to emotional flux. We ebb and flow. We don't have to be hard, brave, or outward all the time. Sometimes we can be soft, vulnerable, and inward.

There are countless examples of masculine deities more related to the earth, moon, sea, or forest than to the sky, stars, or sun. Any of these old gods can be reknown, reclaimed, remembered, and reintegrated into our consciousness. They may also suggest how new gods can be born or invited into our collective consciousness—in *this* time, for *this* culture. As men and women rediscover these ancient powers in the earth, we may then also find our common ground as allies committed to preserving the Earth Parent and stimulating creation of a new culture that holds the lives of men and women as equally sacred.

· · · · · · ·

5 · EROS AND THE MALE SPIRIT

THOMAS MOORE

I am in the hands of the unknown God, he is breaking
me down to his own oblivion to send me forth on a
new morning, a new man.

D. H. LAWRENCE

Gender is one of the grand metaphors for the human condition and for the nature of the cosmos, used by visionaries and poets in all places and in all times. Like all metaphors, this one participates in the concrete reality that gives rise to the image: differences between men and women. However, it takes a poetic sensibility to appreciate the metaphor, and the metaphor is primary. Without a taste for image, the mind slips quickly into literalism. Not catching the poetry in gender, we tend to place all our gender talk onto actual men and women; so that no matter how hard we try to resolve the war of the sexes, antagonism and polarization remain.

The Latin people of the time of Cicero, for example, understood that the male spirit is not the same as a male person. They called the male spirit "animus," a word that suggests a male element in the breath. This spirit was present in a family, in a place, in a marriage, and in an individual. Shrines were set up to honor the male spirit or genius of the family. This spirit, they believed, was conveyed from generation to generation when a young person kissed the dying father and received the family spirit from his breath. They believed that adultery dishonored the spirit of the marriage bed, not the marriage partner. Masculinity was not identified with men.

Jung picked up on this Latin idea and wove the notion of animus into his psychology; however, he tied it more concretely to actual gender. For Jung an animus or male spirit is felt in thinking, judging, acting, and valuing. But even in Jung's thought, where gender is treated less metaphorically than it could be, the male spirit has a life of its own. Because women adjust themselves to a split-gendered society, they, Jung said, have to work extra hard to accommodate this male spirit, just as men have trouble aligning themselves with the feminine anima.

Jung thought that one of the most pressing psychological needs of every person is to reconcile these two figures of the psyche: anima and animus, or soul and spirit. That is to say, so as not to be at war within oneself, one has to find a way to befriend the female and male figures within oneself and out in the world. This implies that male is not simply a man's way of being. Man is the source of the metaphor, but the male spirit is something needed by men and women, by both societies and individuals.

We don't realize how deep existential secularism runs in our approach to everyday life. We tend to take everything onto ourselves. There is no room for spirit and soul. Peoples of other times and places have taken for granted that all of life cannot be squeezed into conscious, controlling, intentional subjectivity. In moods, enthusiasms, fantasies, obsessions, depressions, and addictions spirits flow through and captivate us. Only a secular attitude tries to deal with these encounters literalistically with medications and exercises of will. A sensibility attuned to the sacred can respect larger-than-human factors without denying them in a spirit of modernism and without reifying them in an attitude of religious fundamentalism.

I am saying, therefore, that we will not deal with gender in depth until we recover a sense of the sacred. I am not talking about a sectarian or even New Age belief, but simply an awareness of a spiritual dimension. With D. H. Lawrence I would define renewed manhood by saying: "I am in the hands of an unknown God, he is breaking me down to his own oblivion." I find my manhood and masculinity not by identifying with some faddish notion of what a male is, but by letting this male spirit course through my being. I am male through my participation in *him*.

Cicero said that it is the animus that gives a sense of identity and character. We tend to think that identity is persona, self-image. Therefore, much gender talk gets its feet stuck in the surface linoleum of image and role. An alternative would be to understand that what gives character and identity is the spirit that drives and motivates a person. In Renaissance times this spirit was called the *daimon,* the more than rational source of fate and special destiny. I am what I am because of the powerful forces that well up within me and which place me in history.

The secular life that denies the world its animism places the full cosmic weight of gender upon the shoulders of the mere human being. Men are expected to embody masculinity, women femininity. Naturally, we all fail. It is too much to expect of us. In Renaissance times a writer having trouble getting the words out didn't talk about *his* writer's block, he worried that the spirit of Mercury, the daimonic source of a writer's inspiration, might not pass by. This is more than simple rhetoric. It is a way of being in the world, a way of imagining experience that allows for the nonhuman elements in the face of which human life defines itself.

Therefore, one of the symptoms of loss of masculinity or the male spirit is the frustration of trying to *be* it instead of being its priest. But the symptomatic manifestations only begin there. They become quite outrageous.

SYMPTOMATIC MASCULINITY

For example, because the animus grants power, creativity, authority, and drive, its symptomatic forms exaggerate all of these. With no real animus, power turns into tyranny, creativity into productivity, authority into authoritarianism, and drive into manic impulsiveness. Women struggling for equality with these exaggerated substitutes for masculinity run the risk of establishing their own gender neuroses. They also, of course, have to dare the blind reactions of bogus authorities who, ultimately void of power, have no limits on the extent of their tyranny. True power enjoys its own inherent inhibitions, but inauthentic power is capable of atrocity.

Symptoms of any kind tend toward literalism, exaggeration, and destructiveness. Where ordinarily a quality should be quite subtle and interior, symptomatically it takes absurd external forms. Power becomes the display of instruments that suggest power. Armies march in stiff profile, bayonets and barrels raised in caricature of the phallus. Nations hoard stockpiles of weapons. If an individual were to do this, he would be arrested and hauled off to the local mental hospital. It is obvious to most that the more weapons a person carries or hoards, the less secure and stable that person is.

The male spirit is creative, but producing great numbers of things with no regard for quality and no sense of inhibition in the proliferation indicates symptomatic creativity. The creative drive can go wild in spasms of production in which there is no genuine creation. It is not the male spirit that values only growth: economic, psychological, territorial, financial. It is not the male spirit that measures a man's success by his W-2 form. And it is not the male spirit that conquers and collects women.

We know from religions that the male and female factors in all of life— yin and yang, lingam and yoni, creator and wisdom, Zeus and Hera, Jesus and Mary—live a certain tension and yet complement each other and nourish each other. Keeping them together is not always an easy task. We see these tensions lived out among men and women. Zeus and Hera do not symbolize the man and woman in matrimony. The man and woman in their struggles toward marriage represent and provide an instance of the cosmic couple. Every coming together of a man and woman is the *hieros gamos,* the sacred mingling.

Sex has nothing to do with biology. The love or lust between a man and a woman only set up the altar on which the Gods and Goddesses mate. Physiology is the sacred technology of the Gods. That is both a limitation on human personal love—it's not all about me and the other person—and it is a wondrous exaltation of human love and a great gift from one person to the other. Renaissance psychologists recognized this aspect of love when they applied their Neoplatonic world-view to the love between people. Marsilio Ficini, intellectual advisor to the Medicis, writes of human love: "It descends first from God, and passes through the Angel and the Soul as if they were made of glass; and from the Soul it easily emanates into the body prepared to receive it." Then this love returns to its divine source. Bodily love is a point on the circuit of the soul, and from that transpersonal circulation it takes its nobility and its sacredness.

The male spirit, so full of vision and creative promise, longs for a female soul to impregnate. The world needs the audacity and daring of the male spirit. But it also needs the receptive, reflective feminine alchemy of the soul to give spirit its context, its material, and its vessel. Naturally, the two seek each other out.

But what happens in a time like ours in which the male spirit is elusive, supplanted by its surrogate, hyperactive male? Then there is no movement toward inner marriage. Human marriage cannot hold together. The whole society becomes captivated by the daring of the titanic male and undervalues the female. It is not women, precisely, who are oppressed in this culture; it is the feminine. Women suffer this oppression to the extent they are identified with the feminine, but the oppression is aimed at the feminine. Simple proof of this is male acceptance of the woman who honors the plastic phallus of commercial success and power. The masculine, too, is oppressed in a secular, ego, and will-centered culture. It is axiomatic that as long as one gender is debilitated and undervalued, the other will also suffer complementary wounds.

Jung described the animus as "spermatic." It impregnates. Women look for this engendering spirit because the feminine soul requires it. Women look to men, but often they find the fetish of male potency, unqualified growth, instead of true fertility. They look for drive and strength and instead find muscles and machines. The male spirit, if it were the real thing, would fertilize the imaginations and lives of women. It would offer security, not brutality. A man doesn't lord it over a woman or treat her violently if he has the male spirit pumping through him. He turns to violence in a desperate search for the lost spirit. These are not strong men who have to possess and bind women. They are the weakest, the least masculine, those most lacking in masculine spirit.

Confusion about this distinction between flaunting men and the male spirit keeps the breach wide between men and women. As a result, women often fall too much into the feminine. Neither men nor women thrive when the gender in them is lopsided. Men have the opportunity, being male, to radiate ritually the male spirit needed by both men and women. Women need the male stuff from the man. Men also need it from each other.

Women abused by men become attached to the abuse because they crave that spirit, finding it only in its twisted, emaciated manifestation. They are attached, too, because they are only-feminine. We always become destructively attached to that which we give over fully to another or to the world. On their part, men require the woman's opening, the eternal wound, the flow of blood, the moon-friendship, the vegetative strength that comes from vulnerability to the rhythms of the stars and seasons. But those very things ardently desired by the male are also a threat to his spirit. The male spirit, animus, can survive the encounter. But the symptomatic male, non-animus gender, has nothing to fall back on, nothing behind the facade of masculinity to stand up to the feminine mystery. He can only puff up and thrash that feminine being he needs, loves, and cannot abide.

The marriage sought after in every affair, every dalliance, every flirtation, every spat, and every matrimony is the union of these spirits. We know this in part from the dreams of those contemplating such actual unions. In these dreams partners may vary, circumstances change, moods fade, outcomes vary. Gender and its marriage are in no way literal. All gender is dream gender, except when it falls disastrously into literalism.

The male spirit that hovers in the heart longs for the feminine, not to be completed—it is as complete as it ever will be—but to find fulfillment in its reaching out to lattice itself in that other different, responding, echoing, resonant partner. The man's radiance of femininity in the subtle airs of his soul plays the overtones of the women's fundamental womanhood, and the woman sings the upper partials of the man's familiar male spirit. Marriage is a consonance, a vertical harmony. Men, of course, in their loves with each other sound rich overtones of the harmony as well.

A woman is not always befriended by a female nymph. She may be as remote from the feminine spirit as a man who feels the longing for female stuff. Women sometimes resent and reject the feminine sphere. Often their dreams are filled with women's mystery rites. An anorexic woman dreams of many old women washing her and presenting her with long tables of food. The dream offers her the healing services of archaic womanhood. A man may not know the male spirit that is his brother, yet in his dreams an unknown male companion walks by his side sharing in his adventures. The soul has its own homoerotic desires that may or may not find themselves breaking into life.

EROS AND AGGRESSION

For the Greeks, Eros is one of the male spirits. Masculinity is erotic by nature. It is male to be erotic, erotic to be male. The rush of desire for another soul is the male spirit doing his job, taking us along, making connections. He mingles and unites. He makes friendships. He hammers out unions. He keeps us within certain orbits. In art, Eros is adolescent, brash, active, uncontrollable. He has wings. He shoots arrows. This is the natural aggression of the male: to bring things together, to join what is joinable.

To be masculine, therefore, is to tolerate the rush of eros, to live by desire. One gets masculine strength from the strength of the desire. It is Eros who has power, and the individual becomes powerful in a deep way through participation in that erotic power. William Blake says that desire that can be suppressed is not true desire. Centuries before Christ, Hesiod sang that Eros breaks the strength in the arms and legs of Gods and humans. By all accounts, Eros is a source of immense power.

There is a fundamental difference, however, between the power that Eros brings and the manipulative opportunity created by the abuse of Eros. A man can enslave another person who is in love (in eros) with him. But he does that only as a defense against the true power of eros that stirs in himself. All false, inhumane loves betray the abuse of eros: addictions, obsessions, fetishes. We are in love with the nuclear bomb because explosive, powerful eros has been blocked. The bomb is our fetish.

But Eros is not only powerful, he is also beautiful, full of life and grace. He is brilliant. He shines. His erection is not an emblem of blunt power, it is his showing. The pornographic imagination, repressed wherever Eros is abused, wants to see the display of Eros.

The name "Zeus," the high God, means "shining." He is known in his brilliant displays of lightning. According to Jung, phallos among other things means "light." To be phallic, the great emblem of the male spirit, is to shine. When we don't shine, we swing our fists and butt our chests. People become violent when their male spirit cannot shine forth. When we can't shine, we expect our metallic missiles and our military shoes to shine, as fetishes. Shining is the ultimate aggressive act; anything else is symptomatic and therefore deeply unsatisfying. Isn't the satisfaction of boxing in the shining and not the bruising? In the bravura, the exaggeration, the show? Doesn't the ice hockey free-for-all manifest the latent male force that wants to shine?

I don't shine; the male spirit shines through me. My passions burn and glow in my maleness. When the male spirit is vibrant, my character, my daimon, my archon, my angel shines its halo of spirit in my slightest gesture. There is no need for violence when the spirit radiates. The glint of the steel gun barrel replaces the glow of the angel who is the guardian of light—Lucifer, Light-Bearer.

Lucifer is a dark angel. Sometimes the male spirit shines with an Underworld aesthetic, with the beauty of dark mystery. Only a sentimental misunderstanding of religion believes an angel to be superhumanly good. The male spirit has to shine sometimes in his mischief, like the great God Hermes, archetypal thief and liar.

Light and desire are almost indistinguishable, like the penis of sex and the phallos of shining. Desire, the aura of eros, is warm and phosphorescent. It shines. To let desire shine is to heal that man who beats the woman whom he thinks has smothered his desire. When desires are not allowed to glow, they turn into addictions and odd loves. There is love within all those things to which we are madly attached: alcohol, sex, money, home, wandering, oneself. These odd loves are the egos of the male spirit. The Greek Orphics said that eros arises from a a great egg. We might look for eros in the eggshells that render life brittle and concealed as phobias, depressions, and dysfunctions. We need not get rid of these eggshell complaints. We have only to look closely into their interior spaces.

We carry our desires around like eggs, going from romance to romance, orgy to orgy. But eros appears only when the egg is incubated, when it opens and reveals its inside. The heaviness of eros we feel in love and desires is its own maturing nature, its burden, its pregnancy, which is not revealed from the beginning. The true objects of eros sometimes appear only after a long period of engagement with its decoys. Our crazy loves and attachments may be destructive, but they are important as unique embryos of authentic love.

The egg from which eros appears is often a long-standing obsessive love. It is a truism that in loving another we are in love with love. Love is the object of our love, and the other gives us love that he or she has been holding for us as in a shell. Aphrodite, the great Goddess, the awesome and profound mystery of love and sex, was recognized for centuries in the scallop shell.

Part of the mystery of Aphrodite, for a man, is the ironic truth that his sexual fantasy, drive, and emotion are feminine. It is she, the shell, Venus the sea, Aphrodite whose name means "foam-Goddess" or perhaps, the scholars say, "the Goddess who shines," who grants the wet and sea-surging tides of sex to a man. Sex itself is a union, then, of male Eros and female Venus. In some ancient stories, she is his mother. But Apuleius, the second-century writer of the *Golden Ass,* shows her giving her son a passionate kiss. The world of Eros is never contained in the rectangular boundaries our morals and customs and expectations built to fence him in. Eros, the Orphics said, is a maker of worlds. We know that he makes relationships, friendships, families, communities, even nations. He also inspires poetry, letters, stories, memories, shrines. In short, erotic sex makes individual and social culture. Or, it makes soul. As James Hillman has said, where Eros stirs, soul is to be found. Soul is a sign that eros is truly present. If there is no sign of soul, then the sex is symptomatic on the path toward eros, but not yet out of its shell.

The mystery of male sexuality, therefore, is not to be found and lived in literal gender or literal sex. The other can only be loved and pleasured when one has discovered the cosmic couple, inside oneself and in the world at large. Only when the male and female have coupled in our buildings and economics and schools and politics will the God and Goddess take their long night together with us, like Zeus and Hera on their three-hundred year honeymoon, radiating the truth of sex into all our lives. Then the act of sex would be what it is meant to be: a ritual act epitomizing and celebrating the marriage of heaven and earth. Only when the genders of culture enhance their love can two human beings find the fullness of sexuality.

Of course, it works the other direction, too. Culture is us. Our rediscovery of eros in our own microcosmic lives is the beginning of the cosmic union. When we realize what the Orphics understood, that desire is the fundamental motive force of life and soul, that its power is true aggression, its action authentic creativity, then sex can be released from its captivity in literalism. At the moment our world is frightened by desire, knowing that its limits are not the limits of heroic will and Promethean secularism. But perhaps we can risk the pleasures of desire and glimpse the new worlds it engenders. Then we may discover sex for the first time.

PART 2

. . . .

MALE
INITIATION:
IMAGES OF
MASCULINE
RITES
OF PASSAGE

Initiation is equivalent to a basic change in existential condition; the novice emerges from his ordeal endowed with a totally different being from that which he possessed before his initiation; he has become *another*.

MIRCEA ELIADE

Many of those male groups that do remain intact have lost their purpose. They no longer serve as secret societies where masculine mysteries are shared and learned. Many have degenerated into hiding places where men gather to socialize as they hide from the Devouring Mother . . .

JEROME S. BERNSTEIN

INTRODUCTION

· · · · · · ·

The dictionary defines the verb *initiate* as "to begin, start, commence, enter upon, set going, give rise to, originate."

For centuries, cultures throughout the world provided specific rituals through which boys become men, rites that *set going, give rise to,* manhood. To *be* a man meant to *become* a man. How is this work going today? According to most of the authors in this section, inadequately, haphazardly, badly, if at all.

It must be noted that modern men and women alike carry the legacy of the absence of adequate rites of passage. Christianity triumphed as a universal religion in large part by separating itself from the milieu of Greco-Oriental initiation-based mystery religions, declaring itself a religion of salvation accessible to all. The democratic appeal of this shift is obvious, yet a new dilemma appears: The withdrawal of initiatory pathways enhances the psyche's *hunger for*, while diminishing the psyche's *access to*, initiation.

When a culture ceases to provide specific, meaningful initiatory pathways, the individual male psyche is left to initiate *itself*. And therein lies a great danger, visible in the kinds of initiation to which many men turn: street gangs, drug and alcohol abuse, high-risk sports, militarism, discipleship to charismatic cult leaders, obsessive workplace competition, compulsive relocation of home and job, serial sexual conquests, pursuit of the "perfect" (and thus unattainable) older male mentor, and so forth.

In another excerpt from our wide-ranging conversation, Robert Bly cites Hopi and African Kikuyu initiation rituals that, he believes, bear witness "that a boy becomes a man only through ritual and effort . . . it doesn't happen just because he eats Wheaties." The problem as Bly sees it is that elder men aren't doing their job, thus disrupting continuity between generations of men and also saddling women (specifically mothers) with tasks that are not rightly theirs to perform.

Men's need and unconscious desire for initiation refuse to go away, says Michael Meade, gifted storyteller and teacher of men's work, because "the old initiation forms . . . were set up to be repeated, in the sense that different parts of ourselves go through the experience, time and again." Without clear rites of passage, modern culture faces a "crisis in masculine ritual process" because, say psychologist Robert Moore and mythologist Douglas Gillette, the male psyche finds no true substance in "pseudo-rituals" such as street gangs. Social psychologist Peter Marsh, author of *Tribes*, follows with an examination of the initiatory structure of youth gangs and British football fans. Ray Raphael pays tribute to the growing impulse of men to fashion their own personal rites of passage. But Raphael, author of *The Men from the Boys: Rites of Passage in Male America*, also wonders how these men will achieve the social validation so crucial to traditional initiatory rituals.

No author is more clearly identified as a "man's man" than Ernest Hemingway. For many who came of age between the two world wars, Hemingway's writing conveys the epitome of traditional manly virtues: virility, courage, honor, and passionate engagement with nature. It is clear from Hemingway's contribution to this section (excerpted from his classic book *Death in the Afternoon*) that he saw these values as the very essence of bullfighting—and of true manhood. And it is just as clear from syndicated columnist Christopher Matthews's essay that he considers Hemingway's account hopelessly, even dangerously, idealized. I've placed these two perspectives side by side by way of illustrating how two American journalists of two different generations came away from bullfights with very different impressions—and therefore different masculinities.

Next, Jungian analyst Allan B. Chinen urges a turn to fairy tales for compelling images of masculine depths available to men at mid-life. Clinical psychologist Frederic Wiedemann gives a touching account of his own personal search for modern male initiation, undertaken with his father and brother: "the Wiedemann men."

. . . .

6 · THE NEED FOR MALE INITIATION

ROBERT BLY

KEITH THOMPSON:

In the ancient Greek tradition a young man would leave his family to study with an older man the energies of Zeus, Apollo, or Dionysus. We seem to have lost the rite of initiation, and yet young males have a great need to be introduced to the male mysteries.

ROBERT BLY:

This is what has been missing in our culture. Among the Hopis and other Native Americans of the Southwest, a boy is taken away at age twelve and led down into the kiva (down!): he stays down there for six weeks, and a year and a half passes before he sees his mother. He enters completely into the instinctive male world, which means a sharp break with both parents. You see, the fault of the nuclear family isn't so much that it's crazy and full of double binds (that's true in communes, too—it's the human condition), the issue is that the son has a difficult time breaking away from the parents' field of energy, especially the mother's field, and our culture simply has made no provision for this initiation.

The ancient societies believed that a boy becomes a man only through ritual and effort—that he must be initiated into the world of men. It doesn't happen by itself, it doesn't happen just because he eats Wheaties. And only men can do this work.

KEITH THOMPSON:

We tend to picture initiation as a series of tests that the young male goes through, but surely there's more to it.

ROBERT BLY:

We can also imagine situations as that moment when the older males together welcome the younger male into the male world. One of the best stories I've heard about this kind of welcoming is one which takes place each year among the Kikuyus in Africa. When a young man is about ready to be welcomed in, he is taken away from his mother and brought to a special place the men have set up some distance from the village. He fasts for three days. The third night he finds himself sitting in a circle around the fire with the older males. He is hungry, thirsty, alert, and frightened. One of the older males takes up a knife, opens a vein in his arm and lets a little of his blood flow into a gourd or bowl. Each man in the circle opens his arm with the same knife as the bowl goes around, and lets some blood flow in. When the bowl arrives at the young male, he is invited in tenderness to take nourishment from it.

The boy learns a number of things. He learns that there is a kind of nourishment that comes not from his mother only, but from males. And he learns that the knife can be used for many purposes besides wounding others. Can he have any doubts now that he is welcome in the male world?

Once that is done, the older males can teach him the myths, the stories, the songs that carry male values, not fighting only, but spirit values. Once these "moistening myths" are learned, they lead the young male far beyond his personal father and into the moistness of the swampy fathers who stretch back century after century.

KEITH THOMPSON:

If young men today have no access to initiation rites of the past, how are they to make the passage into their instinctive male energy?

ROBERT BLY:

Let me turn the question back to you: as a young male, how are *you* doing it?

KEITH THOMPSON:

Well, I've heard much of my own path described in your remarks about soft men. I was 14 when my parents were divorced, and my brothers and I stayed with our mom. My relationship with my dad had been remote and distant anyway, and now he wasn't even in the house. My mom had the help of a succession of maids over the years to help raise us, particularly a wonderful old country woman who did everything from changing our diapers to teaching us to pray. It came to pass that my best friends were women, including several older, energetic women who introduced me to politics and literature and feminism. These were platonic friendships on the order of a mentor-student bond. I was particularly influenced by the energy of the Women's Movement, partially because I had been raised by strong yet nurturing women and partially because my father's absence suggested to me that men couldn't be trusted. So for almost ten years, through about age 24, my life was full of self-confident, experienced women friends and men friends who, like me, placed a premium on vulnerability, gentleness, and sensitivity. From the standpoint of the '60s and '70s male, I had it made! Yet a couple of years ago, I began to feel that something was missing.

ROBERT BLY:
What was missing for you?

KEITH THOMPSON:
My father. I began to think about my father. He began to appear in my dreams, and when I looked at old family photos, seeing his picture brought up a lot of grief—grief that I didn't know him, that the distance between us seemed so great. As I began to let myself feel my loneliness for him, one night I had a powerful dream. I was carried off into the woods by a pack of she-wolves who fed and nursed and raised me with love and wisdom, and I became one of them. And yet, in some unspoken way, I was always slightly separate, different from the rest of the pack. One day after we had been running through the woods together in beautiful formation and with lightning speed, we came to a river and began to drink. When we put our faces to the water, I could see the reflection of all of them but I couldn't see my own! There was an empty space in the rippling water where I was supposed to be. My immediate response in the dream was panic—was I really *there*, did I even *exist*? I knew the dream had to do in some way with the absent male, both within me and with respect to my father. I resolved to spend time with him, to see who we are in each other's lives now that we've both grown up a little.

ROBERT BLY:
So the dream deepened the longing. Have you seen him?

KEITH THOMPSON:
Yes. I went back to the midwest a few months later to see him and my mom, who are both remarried and still live in our hometown. For the first time I spent as much, if not more, time with my dad than with my mom. He and I took drives around the country to places we'd spent time during my child-

hood, seeing old barns and tractors and fields which seemed not to have changed at all. I would tell my mom, "I'm going over to see dad. We're going for a drive and then having dinner together. See you in the morning." That would *never* have happened a few years earlier.

ROBERT BLY:

The dream is the whole story. What has happened since?

KEITH THOMPSON:

Since reconnecting with my father I've been discovering that I have less need to make my women friends serve as my sole confidantes and confessors. I'm turning more to my men friends in these ways, especially those who are working with similar themes in their lives.

What's common to our experience is that not having known or connected with our fathers and not having older male mentors, we've tried to get strength secondhand through women who got *their* strength from the Women's Movement. It's as if many of today's soft young males want these women, who are often older and wiser, to initiate them in some way.

ROBERT BLY:

I think that's true. And the problem is that, from the ancient point of view, women *cannot* initiate males, it's impossible.

When I was lecturing about the initiation of males, several women in the audience who were raising sons alone told me they had come up against exactly that problem. They sensed that their sons needed some sort of toughness, or discipline, or hardness—however it is to be said—but they found that if they tried to provide it, they would start to lose touch with their own femininity. They didn't know what to do.

I said that the best thing to do when the boy is twelve is send him to his father, and several of the women just said flatly, "No, men aren't nourishing, they wouldn't take care of them." I told them that I had experienced tremendous reserves of nourishment that hadn't been called upon until it was time for me to deal with my children. Also, I think a son has a kind of body-longing for the father which must be honored.

One woman told an interesting story. She was raising a son and two daughters. When the son was fourteen or so he went off to live with his father but stayed only a month or two and then came back. She said she knew that, with three women, there was too much feminine energy in the house for him. It was unbalanced, so to speak, but what could she do?

One day something strange happened. She said gently, "John, it's time to come to dinner," and he knocked her across the room. She said, "I think it's time to go back to your father." He said, "You're right." The boy couldn't bring what he needed into consciousness, but his body knew it. And his body acted. The mother didn't take it personally, either. She understood it was a message. In the United States there are so many big muscled high school boys hulking around the kitchen rudely, and I think in a way they're trying to make themselves less attractive to their mothers.

Separation from the mother is crucial. I'm not saying that women have been doing the wrong thing necessarily. I think the problem is more that the men are not really doing their job.

. . . .

7 · WE MUST ASK WHAT
THE CRAZINESS IS

MICHAEL MEADE

I think initiation is built into the human experience. The form is going to be there no matter what. For instance, sports have a kind of initiatory framework, though it's dealt with unconsciously. The military has the remnants of the warrior initiations. These old forms reside in the psyche, but nowadays, people lack the awareness of what the form is for, so the initiation lacks direction.

We live in a monolithic culture, based on one god, one country, one mother, one father, and one marriage—that used to be the idea—or one great love. Sadly, because of that, there tends to be the notion that there's one initiation. And the feeling of having missed it is very widespread. But actually initiation is repetitive; it's a way of experiencing life over and over, not one time. The old initiation forms, as I understand them, were set up to be repeated, in the sense that different parts of ourselves go through the experience, time and again. Sometimes we're on the initiate side, and sometimes on the initiating side. The idea, I think, is to initiate all aspects of one's humanity fully into life. Part of the initiation is physical, and that still happens to some degree in sports and other activities; part of it is emotional, in which ordeals and trials are used to intensify the emotional experience; and part of it is mystical, in which one is initiated into the world of spirit. We can't get away from this; it has to happen to some degree. But mythos is what gives it form and style and makes us conscious of the process; through mythos, we can describe it in a coherent way. That is why I talk about a collapsed mythology.

There is something in us that wants to get initiated; the initiatory desire in men is extremely strong. To complain that it's crazy for young men to drive around in cars at ninety miles an hour is useless. We need to ask what the craziness is. To say that it is foolish for young men to want to hurl their bodies against each other in sports or to practice intricate physical routines is to say nothing. We need to ask why. What's pulling men and boys into that?

. . . .

8 · THE CRISIS IN
MASCULINE RITUAL PROCESS

ROBERT MOORE AND DOUGLAS GILLETTE

We hear it said of some man that "he just can't get himself together." What this means, on a deep level, is that so-and-so is not experiencing, and cannot experience his deep cohesive structures. He is fragmented; various parts of his personality are split off from each other and leading fairly independent and often chaotic lives. A man who "cannot get it together" is a man who has probably not had the opportunity to undergo ritual initiation into the deep structures of manhood. He remains a boy—not because he wants to, but because no one has shown him the way to transform his boy energies into man energies. No one has led him into direct and healing experiences of the inner world of the masculine potentials.

When we visit the caves of our distant Cro-Magnon ancestors in France, and descend into the dark of those otherworldly, and inner-worldly, sanctuaries and light our lamps, we jump back in startled awe and wonder at the mysterious, hidden wellsprings of masculine might we see depicted there. We feel something deep move within us. Here, in silent song, the magic animals—bison, antelope, and mammoth—leap and thunder in pristine beauty and force across the high, vaulted ceilings and the undulating walls, moving purposefully into the shadows of the folds of the rock, then springing at us again in the light of our lamps. And here, painted with them, are the handprints of men, of the artist-hunters, the ancient warriors and providers, who met here and performed their primeval rituals.

Anthropologists are almost universally agreed that these cave sanctuaries were created, in part at least, by men for men and specifically for the ritual initiation of boys into the mysterious world of male responsibility and masculine spirituality.

But ritual process for the making of men out of boys is not limited to our conjectures about these ancient caves. As many scholars have shown, most notable among them Mircea Eliade and Victor Turner, ritual initiatory process still survives in tribal cultures to this day, in Africa, South America, islands in the South Pacific, and many other places. It survived until very recent times among the Plains Indians of North America. The study of ritual process by the specialist may tend toward dry reading. But we may see it enacted colorfully in a number of contemporary movies. Movies are like ancient folktales and myths. They are stories we tell ourselves about ourselves—

about our lives and their meaning. In fact, initiatory process for both men and women is one of the great hidden themes in many of our movies.

A good, explicit example of this can be found in the movie *The Emerald Forest*. Here, a white boy has been captured and raised by Brazilian Indians. One day, he's playing in the river with a beautiful girl. The chief has noticed his interest in the girl for some time. This awakening of sexual interest in the boy is a signal to the wise chief. He appears on the riverbank with his wife and some of the tribal elders and surprises Tomme (Tommy) at play with the girl. The chief booms out, "Tomme, your time has come to die!" Everyone seems profoundly shaken. The chief's wife, playing the part of all women, of all mothers, asks, "Must he die?" The chief threateningly replies, "Yes!" Then, we see a firelit nighttime scene in which Tomme is seemingly tortured by the older men in the tribe; and forced into the forest vines, he is being eaten alive by jungle ants. He writhes in agony, his body mutilated in the jaws of the hungry ants. We fear the worst.

Finally, the sun comes up, though, and Tomme, still breathing, is taken down to the river by the men and bathed, the clinging ants washed from his body. The chief then raises his voice and says, "The boy is dead and the man is born!" And with that, he is given his first spiritual experience, induced by a drug blown through a long pipe into his nose. He hallucinates and in his hallucination discovers his animal soul (an eagle) and soars above the world in new and expanded consciousness, seeing, as if from a God's-eye view, the totality of his jungle world. Then he is allowed to marry. Tomme is a man. And, as he takes on a man's responsibilities and identity, he is moved first into the position of a brave in the tribe and then into the position of chief.

It can be said that life's perhaps most fundamental dynamic is the attempt to move from a lower form of experience and consciousness to a higher (or deeper) level of consciousness, from a diffuse identity to a more consolidated and structured identity. All of human life at least attempts to move forward along these lines. We seek initiation into adulthood, into adult responsibilities and duties toward ourselves and others, into adult joys and adult rights, and into adult spirituality. Tribal societies had highly specific notions about adulthood, both masculine and feminine, and how to get to it. And they had ritual processes like the one in *The Emerald Forest* to enable their children to achieve what we could call calm, serene maturity.

Our own culture has pseudo-rituals instead. There are many pseudo-initiations for men in our culture. Conscription into the military is one. The fantasy is that the humiliation and forced nonidentity of boot camp will "make a man out of you." The gangs of our major cities are another manifestation of pseudo-initiation and so are the prison systems, which, in large measure, are run by gangs.

We call these phenomena *pseudo*-events for two reasons. For one thing, with the possible exception of military initiation, these processes, though sometimes highly ritualized (especially within city gangs), more often than not initiate the boy into a kind of masculinity that is skewed, stunted, and false. It is a patriarchal "manhood," one that is abusive of others, and often of self. Sometimes a ritual murder is required of the would-be initiate. Usually the abuse of drugs is involved in the gang culture. The boy may become an acting-out adolescent in these systems and achieve a level of development roughly parallel to the level expressed by the society as a whole in its boyish values, though in a contracultural form. But these pseudo-initiations will not produce men, because real men are not wantonly violent or hostile. Boy psychology is charged with the struggle for dominance of others, in some form or another. And it is often caught up in the wounding of self, as well as others. It is sadomasochistic. Man psychology is always the opposite. It is nurturing and generative, not wounding and destructive.

In order for Man psychology to come into being for any particular man, there needs to be a death. Death—symbolic, psychological, or spiritual—is always a vital part of any initiatory ritual. In psychological terms, the boy Ego must "die." The old ways of being and doing and thinking and feeling must ritually "die," before the new man can emerge. Pseudo-initiation, though placing some curbs on the boy Ego, often amplifies the Ego's striving for power and control in a new form, an adolescent form regulated by other adolescents. Effective, transformative initiation absolutely slays the Ego and its desires in its old form to resurrect it with a new, subordinate relationship to a previously unknown power or center. Submission to the power of the mature masculine energies always brings forth a new masculine personality that is marked by calm, compassion, clarity of vision, and generativity.

A second factor makes most initiations in our culture pseudo-initiations. In most cases, there simply is not a contained ritual process. Ritual process is contained by two things. The first is sacred space and the second is a ritual elder, a "wise old man" or a "wise old woman" who is completely trustworthy for the initiate and can lead the initiate through the process and deliver him (or her) intact and enhanced on the other side.

Mircea Eliade researched the role of sacred space extensively. He concluded that space that has been ritually hallowed is essential to initiations of every kind. In tribal societies this space can be a specially constructed hut or house in which the boys awaiting their initiation are held. It can be a cave. Or it can be the vast wilderness into which the would-be initiate is driven in order to die or to find his manhood. The sacred place can be the "magic circle" of magicians. Or, as in more advanced civilizations, it can be an inner room in the precincts of a great temple. This space must be sealed from the influence of the outside world, especially, in the case of boys, from the influence of women. Often, the initiates are put through terrifying emotional and excruciatingly painful physical trials. They learn to submit to the pain of life, to the ritual elders, and to the masculine traditions and myths of the society. They are taught all the secret wisdom of men. And they are released from the sacred space only when they have successfully completed the ordeal and been reborn as men.

The second essential ingredient for a successful initiatory process is the presence of a ritual elder. In *The Emerald Forest* this is the chief and the other elders of the tribe. The ritual elder is the man who knows the secret wisdom, who knows the ways of the tribe and the closely guarded men's myths. He is the one who lives out of a vision of mature masculinity.

With a scarcity in our culture of mature men, it goes without saying that ritual elders are in desperately short supply. Thus, pseudo-initiations remain skewed toward the reinforcement of Boy psychology rather than allowing for movement toward Man psychology, even if some sort of ritual process exists, and even if a kind of sacred space has been set up on the city streets or on the cell block.

The crisis in mature masculinity is very much upon us. Lacking adequate models of mature men, and lacking the societal cohesion and institutional structures for actualizing ritual process, it's "every man for himself." And most of us fall by the wayside, with no idea what it was that was the goal of our gender-drive or what went wrong with our strivings. We just know we are anxious, on the verge of feeling impotent, helpless, frustrated, put down, unloved and unappreciated, often ashamed of being masculine. We just know that our creativity was attacked, that our initiative was met with hostility, that we were ignored, belittled, and left holding the empty bag of our lost self-esteem. We cave in to a dog-eat-dog world, trying to keep our work and our relationships afloat, losing energy, or missing the mark. Many of us seek the generative, affirming, and empowering father (though most of us don't know it), the father who, for most of us, never existed in our actual lives and won't appear, no matter how hard we try to make him appear.

. . . .

9 · TRIBAL INITIATIONS:
YOUTH GANGS AND FOOTBALL

PETER MARSH

Some youth cultures have evolved their own initiation rites—although we should note at the outset that these are often surrounded by myths generated by prurient media interest. In U.S. street gangs potential new members are sometimes required to show what they are made of before they are admitted to the tribe. Often the requirements amount to no more than the commission of a fairly minor criminal offense. In this way the new recruit is bound to the group through his shared complicity in illegal activities. In other cases he will be admitted as a "brother" only after his blood has been mingled with that of his fellows. This usually involves making minor cuts to the hand, but the symbolic significance is quite considerable. Hell's Angels are reputed to have more dramatic initiation ceremonies, involving such acts as biting the heads off live pigeons or chickens.

These are, however, exceptions to the general rule. In most cases young people attach themselves to a subculture simply by dressing in appropriate ways, adopting prescribed patterns of adornment, and subscribing actively to the values, attitudes, and general style which characterize the tribe's distinctiveness. Nevertheless, although they avoid the rigors of initiation, youth cultures provide for orderly transition and the achievement of status within their alternative social framework. This sense of "career" structure is particularly apparent in the British football [soccer] subculture and in the street gangs of the United States.

British football-fan tribes share some common elements with youth gangs in the United States. The football culture provides an umbrella framework for the various groups of supporters of particular teams. Football fans, whether from Liverpool, Birmingham, or anywhere else, have similar styles of dress and behavior and subscribe to the same general set of values and attitudes. Each particular tribe, however, comes into conflict from time to time with the others it encounters when two teams meet on the football field. Similarly, U.S. youth gangs share a common cultural framework, but each defends its own territory with considerable aggressive determination.

The youth gang is organized in a clearly hierarchical way, with formal titles for members—President, Vice-President, Armorer, and so on down the line. The football-fan tribe is much more loosely structured, partly because its members usually meet only once a week in the ceremonial territories of the football terraces. However, closer inspection reveals a distinctive social network, with three main tiers based around age sets.

Football fans tend to enter this alternative culture at an age of about 9–11. Being small, these children occupy the front parts of the rows behind the goals, where their view of the game is not obscured by others in the crowd. Yet the progress of the game is often not their primary concern: for much of the time they can be seen facing back toward the upper rows, closely observing the activities of the older boys behind them.

These "novices" in the fan tribe are engaged in a process of social learning, acquiring knowledge of the ritual chants and songs and the occasions on which it is appropriate to use them. Their style of nonverbal behavior, including posture, facial expressions, and gestures, gradually changes in response to the influences around them. Moreover, they begin to internalize the various attitudes and ideas expressed by their older role models.

This "novice" period lasts for up to 3–4 years, its end being marked by a sudden shift of position on the rows and incorporation into the main body of vociferous fans. This usually happens at the beginning of a new football season, and thus marks a distinct transition from the status of "little kid" to that of "one of the boys." The main group that they have joined is essentially the core of the soccer culture. The individuals involved are commonly referred to as "thugs," "savages," or "mindless hooligans" in the popular media. A more neutral term to describe them is Rowdies, for this more accurately describes their routine patterns of behavior.

Being accepted as a Rowdy represents a second tier within the tribe. It involves constant displays of loyalty and commitment to the team that the tribe supports. The opposing fans are required to be ritually denigrated and certain standards of courage, or "bottle," are expected. A Rowdy should not run from encounters with rivals, but neither should he act in such a way as to attract the attention of the police or incite levels of violence that result in serious injury. To aid his sense of career development, a number of informal role positions are available to which he might aspire.

Most tribes of football fans have identifiable, although not formally selected, leaders whose functions vary considerably. There are Chant Leaders whose task is to initiate singing and chanting at appropriate points throughout the match. This might sound relatively easy, but there are certain hazardous features in the enactment of this role. If a fan raises his arms and shouts out the first few words of a chant, but finds that nobody else is prepared to join in with him, then distinct loss of face results. The Chant Leader must therefore have the confidence of those around him and understand the subtle rules governing the use of chants.

Aggro Leaders are those who initiate fighting in and around the football grounds. Their role within the grounds is now quite limited, due to the installation of various security measures, but opportunities arise for minor skirmishes outside the grounds and on journeys to matches away from home. The nature of the violence in which they are involved, however, has particular tribal features that render conflicts relatively bloodless.

Other recognizable roles include various kinds of Organizers. These fans are responsible for coordinating travel to away matches, liaising with club officials, disseminating information, and generally helping to maintain group cohesion. A particularly interesting position, however, is that of the Nutter (or Headbanger). Nutters are individuals with a reputation for being quite mad and doing things that no sane fan would ever do. They are deviants within their own culture, but their presence is tolerated because they serve a useful function. By breaking the unstated rules of the tribe, they remind others of what the rules really are. Also, like officially tolerated jesters and clowns, they provide amusement. While they can sometimes be a danger to themselves and the group by, for example, issuing challenges to large groups of rivals, they are usually prevented by their fellow tribe members from going too far.

It is in the Rowdies' status-level that a fan's tribal activities are at their most intense. Like his counterpart in traditional African culture, it is at this stage that his displays of warrior potential and his wearing of the tribal dress and insignia will be most marked. Such constant symbols of commitment and loyalty, however, are difficult to maintain over a long period: there are, after all, other considerations that he has to keep in mind, such as finding and retaining a regular job and getting married. An additional problem is that routine fan activity brings those involved to the attention of the police, who are generally keen to put an end to their rituals. For these reasons, a further stage of transition—the third tier—is provided within the football culture. Once an individual's reputation has been firmly established, he can safely abandon some of the more onerous requirements and become a Graduate.

To talk of football fans graduating may seem a little odd, but the term is very appropriate. They have done the equivalent of attending lectures and writing essays. They have been examined by their peers and elders, and now they rest on their laurels. They remain, however, firmly within the tribe, taking on a role of sagelike aloofness, but coupled with this is an unchallenged sense of commitment and influence. They rarely engage in the chants and the issuing of ritual insults and challenges; such things they leave to the young warriors. They may even stand in a part of the ground not specifically designated as part of their tribe's home territory. Yet, like the elders of traditional tribes, they are the guardians of their culture.

Patterns of transition like those of the football tribes are found in other youth cultures. There are few specific rites and the rules are rarely formulated in any fixed way, but the basic process is very much in evidence, providing for those who seek the special rewards of tribal bonding a sense of true worth through progression and the attainment of status in the eyes of their peers.

* * * * * * *

10 · FREESTYLE INITIATIONS AND THE QUEST FOR MALE VALIDATION

RAY RAPHAEL

Does a youth always need a formalized structure, complete with separation, transition, and incorporation? Why should he have to depend upon community ritual if he can somehow manage to prove his manhood, pure and simple, all by himself?

Today, many young men prefer to undertake their initiations all by themselves. From the standpoint of an avowedly individualistic culture, this seems like the most admirable way to proceed. A youth would appear to be more manly, not less, if he can not only *endure* his rite of passage but also *create* it; such an approach is certainly more in keeping with the frontier ethic of rugged independence still closely linked with the masculine mystique in modern America.[1]

But where can a young man go, in this technological and interdependent world with no more frontiers, to prove he can stand alone? Roger G. chose to travel by himself in an exotic foreign land—and he also chose to retreat into the wilderness:

> After I left home I started experiencing the real disjuncture between civilized life and wilderness life. I liked the danger out in the wilderness, the sense that anything could happen and I had to be constantly aware. I also felt that I achieved a kind of animalness, a kind of wildness, when I walked by myself for a long time, when I wasn't in touch with other human beings. I became increasingly sensitive to the signs. Like five days out, I started seeing animal trails a lot more than I did at first. I started seeing disturbed places where things had been. I started smelling deer. I started fishing in the streams with my bare hands, catching trout by trapping them underneath the rocks in the little pools and pulling them out. At one point I got so crazed that I actually ate it raw out of my hands. It was a spontaneous act, an unconsidered act, one continuous motion. I caught the fish with my bare hands and pulled it out and bit it. It tasted very alive, the freshest fish imaginable. That kind of connection . . . like running across a bear face-to-face because we both came around from the rock at the same time, with mutual surprise and respect. That kind of aloneness and contact with wildness.

Out in the wilderness, separated from both comfort and culture, a young man can experience the primal experiences, the life-and-death realities, that are obscured in civil society. He can prove himself to himself without the interference of social distortions; he is a man apart, and he must make it through on his own. He convincingly frees himself from the strongest yet most confining of all social units—his family—by abandoning the entire edifice of human society. By sacrificing the security of home in favor of the uncertainty of the wilds, he dramatically negates his prior status as a weak and dependent creature.

And while repudiating his childish past, a youth simultaneously affirms his archetypal image as man-the-survivor. He declares himself wild, not tame. Instead of being continually nurtured within the safe and secure confines of modern civilization, he recreates the presumed vitality of the primitive hunt:

> When I was younger I worked at some very sedentary jobs; middle-management, the service department, sales. About three or four nights a week I would go out after work with my bow. I put a lot of effort into it, good enough to where I took quite a few deer with a bow and one bear and lots of small game. If I was in Orange County I'd go out in the orange groves and shoot jackrabbits. If I was in New Jersey I'd go chasing woodchucks, jackrabbits, squirrels. Here in the Bay Area I'd hunt brush rabbits and jackrabbits up in the hills. Almost every night I'd take two or three arrows out and prowl the hills and hunt rabbits. I'd eat the young ones and the older ones I'd give to my dog. I always used almost everything I took. I'd make leather articles out of animal skins. I'd take home possum and cook it up—not the best food in the world, either. I enjoyed using it, but I

didn't really need the meat. It was mainly for recreation. It was what I had to do for my own emotional needs. Hunting helped me keep focus.

It took a lot of fine tuning, physical tuning and spiritual tuning, to get with it for a hunt. I never really felt quite with it until I rubbed the charcoal on my face and hands to cut the shine. I also liked to take a cold bath in the lake or river the night before. The Indians frequently did that. You get rid of the body odor, but it's also neat just to do it. I've taken some cold ones. It's stimulating. It's a way of knowing you're alive.

This last summer I discovered that apparently I have a great-grandmother who was Indian. It was a neat thing to discover that, that I probably do have some Indian blood in me. When I was a kid sometimes I'd get lost in a store and people would say, "Whose little Indian boy is this?" I looked very much like a little Indian fella, dark-complected, straight black hair. My brothers are all lighter haired, some of 'em almost blonde. I had a reading one time, and the mystic decided that in my prior life I was an Indian. That was kind of an affirmation of some things about me; I didn't come by my interests artificially. (Dick Byrum)

Dick Byrum's hunting was clearly a matter of style, not necessity. He used charcoal "to cut the shine," but its real purpose was certainly more symbolic and personal: It made Dick *feel* like a hunter. Even if all he killed was possum, he still managed to put meat on the table. Through hunting, the most traditional of all masculine activities, Dick formed an important bond with his alleged Indian ancestors.

As one of the ultimate male traditions, hunting constitutes an ideal form of self-initiation. Although hunting can be, and often is, performed in groups, all it really takes is a party of one. In this sense the hunt is more accessible than war for a youth who wishes to initiate himself by rediscovering his primal masculine role. A youth cannot simply decide, all on his own, to go off and become a warrior—there might not be any wars to fight at the moment—but he can, if he so chooses, go out to the wilds and pretend he's a primitive hunter.

The problem of public validation seems inherent to any self-styled initiation that takes place off in the wilderness, far away from the watchful eyes of human society. Surely there is personal power to be gained by these experiences, but by removing the initiations from any social context a youth makes it harder for that power to be sustained. It is therefore quite understandable that many young men try to refabricate the context which is lacking: they compete with others, they brag, they publicize their private events in any way they can. If the arguments on their own behalf sometimes seem a bit forced, that is only because they have no choice but to sing their own praises when the rest of society refuses, or at least neglects, to sing their praises for them.

Perhaps the task of public validation is more difficult when our freestyle initiations occur in the wilds, but any youth who creates for himself a personalized initiation has to deal in one way or another with the interplay between the private and public affirmation of his manly status. By their very nature, freestyle initiations can occur in any location, situation, or context; the only requirement is that a youth set for himself a series of goals which, once achieved, will prove to his own satisfaction that he's a man. The question is: How will he define success? *Who* will define success? If he's unable to validate the results exclusively by himself, then what other forms of validation will he seek? How can he translate his personal achievements into socially recognized events?

The most important and sweeping function of a primitive initiation was to provide a youth with a sense of his own personal significance within the context of a greater world. In becoming a man he took his place alongside his father and forefathers; by discovering his tribal heritage he became connected with the ongoing flow of life. He was transformed into a spiritual being as he joined his ancestors in a universal brotherhood that cut through time.[2]

Fraternities, in their own inimical manner, manage to simulate this function. They offer a true initiation in its classical form, where the power of the tribe is paramount and personal growth is carefully engineered. The ancestors—the football stars of yore, the names on the tub room wall—gaze down upon the neophytes, encouraging them to shape up and belong. The members sleep together, eat together, sing together, suffer together as they learn what it means to be a man among men.

As with the primitives, these modern-day novitiates must deny and transcend their prior and separate identities before they are allowed to join the tribe. To accomplish this monumental task, the fraternity barrages and assaults their individual egos until they acquiesce. The youths are ridiculed for their personal idiosyncracies, their ears, and their foreskins, which set them apart. Their privacy is mercilessly denied as they are stripped of their clothes and ordered to perform all sorts of ridiculous acts. They are humiliated at every turn. They are given new names, as if their old names were not good enough. And of course they are frightfully hazed. They are deprived of sleep and incessantly harassed. They are forced to endure extremes of hot and cold. Their minds and their bodies are tossed about till they almost shatter.

How are the initiands taught to cope with such duress? In true classical form, they are given two invaluable aids. First, they are actively discouraged from giving up: "They didn't want you to run, they didn't want you to get away, they didn't want you to try to quit." The fraternity is not merely testing the pledges to see if they are strong enough to endure; it wants and *needs* them to make it through, for without new members it has no reason to exist.

Second, the pledges are encouraged to help each other out in times of stress. By volunteering to suffer individually on behalf of their brothers, they can become true heroes at nobody else's expense. They prove their courage not by aggressive displays of personal superiority but rather by coming to the aid of the group. The ideal of interpersonal competition is superseded by that of service. Group loyalty and personal caring—these are the values that the fraternity wishes to foster through its communal hazing as well as through such powerful rituals as the passing of the "Loving Cup."

All this is done, of course, with an abundance of traditional male image-ry. There's cigar smoking and tobacco chewing and communal drinking and the telling of sexual tales. There's a focus upon genitals to the point of obsession. Pulling on onions which are tied to cocks—the symbolism here is blatantly reminiscent of the genital mutilations practiced in primitive initiations.[3] Then of course there's the Mystic Dragon, the *beast*, the primordial challenge to male *homo sapiens*. These symbols are not chosen randomly; they are powerful references to the most obvious and dramatic aspects of primitive masculinity.

And somehow it all seems to work. The whole process, admittedly bizarre and occasionally even obscene, really does accomplish the desired goals. Joseph A. feels better about himself—and, presumably, so do his fellow pledges. He no longer feels encumbered by the burden of proof. Now that he has endured he is free to be himself, but this time the image of "himself" has more of a group context. He is a Beta. He can paint his name on the tub room wall. He is one with the ancestors.

But who are these ancestors, anyway? Just a bunch of college boys from the early twentieth century who saw fit to create theatrical representations of a traditional male culture. The drama they fashioned is rich in symbols from other people's history, but it is strangely out-of-synch with our own. In part, the Beta initiation must remain secret because its various and sundry antics might be construed as reprehensible in the context of more public mores. Indeed, our self-conscious body politic often tries to stop these fraternal activities as soon as it learns what is really going on. The only event which does not remain secret is the day of service, a perfectly normal and acceptable offering to respectable society. All the rest of it—well, it's more than a little risqué.[4]

The success of these fraternal orders is due to their inherently social fabric. Not only do they offer particular images of manhood, but they also provide viable settings in which those images can be realized. This is no small feat in an individualistic culture where young males are often left to their own devices to prove they are men. When a group—*any* group—offers a well-defined set of norms and goals, along with a method for living up to those norms and meeting those goals, we are given at least a semblance of structural support for our transition into manhood.

Fraternal fellowships therefore help us place our personal struggles in a larger context. By joining a group we move beyond our individual limitations and share in the collective power of a body of men. And the groups themselves generally try to exceed their own narrow boundaries, claiming access to the universal power of *all* men. The symbolism used by the various fellowships is replete with archetypal images. At least through ritual, each group wants to extend its scope, to connect with life's most fundamental realities, to gain a sort of ceremonial power over the world.

To affirm for itself this transcendent sense of self-importance, each fellowship tries to establish its historical roots, to tie itself to a significant tradition. Beta Theta Pi takes its name from the ancient Greek alphabet, while it self-consciously attempts to turn its own founding fathers into important historical figures. Jokingly but meaningfully, it even refers back to the era of dragons, a time when a man in search of honor and glory could supposedly find for himself a challenge to meet all challenges. The Masons refer all the way back to the Old Testament, and they ceremoniously conduct their rituals in Middle English. Each with its own theatrical style, our modern-day fellowships use the sheer weight of history to transform apparently petty antics into emotionally significant events.

When viewed from the outside, however, the nostalgic imagery of these various rituals seems at best only quaint. If bar mitzvahs or confirmations appear today as merely trivial, the initiation ceremonies of college fraternities or the Masons can be perceived as contrived and contorted. Unless we can somehow manage to suspend our disbelief, we are likely to interpret all this mustering-up of tradition as a futile attempt to return to archaic images which have little or nothing to do with contemporary realities. Dragons, the Greek alphabet, Middle English—what, we might ask, does all this have to do with a man's coming-of-age in the late twentieth century? But when we cast about for a group to join in our attempts to gain access to the brotherhood of men, these strange adaptations of ancient imagery are about all we will find. Our forced and unnatural air belies desperation. We reach back to other people's history precisely because our own contemporary lifestyles seem to be lacking in resonance or appropriate meaning.

· · · · · · ·

11 · DEATH IN THE AFTERNOON, 1932

ERNEST HEMINGWAY

The principle of the bullfight, the ideal bullfight, supposes bravery in the bull and a brain clear of any remembrance of previous work in the ring. A cowardly bull is difficult to fight since he will not charge the picadors more than once if he receives any punishment. . . . No one can be sure when a cowardly bull will charge. . . . All brilliance is impossible unless the matador has the science and valor to get so close to the bull that he makes him confident and works on his instincts . . . and then, when he has gotten him to charge a few times, dominates him and almost hypnotizes him. . . .

A great killer must love to kill; unless he feels it is the best thing he can do, unless he is conscious of its dignity and feels that it is its own reward, he will be incapable of the abnegation that is necessary in real killing. The truly great killer must have a sense of honor and a sense of glory far beyond that of the ordinary bullfighter. In other words he must be a simpler man. Also he must take pleasure in it . . . must have a spiritual enjoyment of the moment of killing . . . but above all he must love to kill. Killing cleanly and in a way which gives you aesthetic pleasure and pride has always been one of the greatest enjoyments of a part of the human race.

· · · · · · ·

12 · DEATH IN THE AFTERNOON, 1990

CHRISTOPHER MATTHEWS

Barcelona, Spain—In his famous guide to the Spanish bullfight, "Death in the Afternoon," Ernest Hemingway wrote of a classic, if tragic, struggle between man and bull.

This is not what I saw here last Sunday at the capital Placa de Toros. Expecting to see a one-on-one contest, I witnessed a series of gang attacks on a half dozen extremely confused animals.

As is the custom six bulls were killed that Sunday. I saw none die in the quick and dramatic fashion celebrated in "Death in the Afternoon." I can assure you none died "swaying on his legs before going up on his back with four legs in the air." No, it was different than that.

The bulls killed in last Sunday's Corida de Toros here met their ends neither quickly nor dramatically. The first bull to enter the ring died the fastest. After taking the full length of the matador's sword in his back, the huge animal wandered dismally around the edge of the ring for several minutes before collapsing. It was not clear what reaction was expected from the crowd during this death walk. My own initial impulse, which I did not follow, was to bolt for the exit stairs mouthing my opinion all the way about this pastime the Spanish consider a sport.

I was wrong to judge the bullfight by a single killing. Each of the other five bulls to enter the ring Sunday died even more grotesquely than the first. The second to take the matador's blade roamed the full diameter of the ring after being stabbed, all the while spewing blood through his mouth like a fire hose.

The death of the other four bulls was more complicated. Not being an aficionado, I assumed this was due to the clumsiness of the matadors. Instead of their doing their work with the single thrust of the sword, they spent the afternoon sticking as many as three separate swords into their assigned bulls. Each time the huge wounded animal would run madly for its life—like a chicken with its head cut off or like the Saturday morning cartoon character who runs off the cliff but fails to fall because he doesn't look down.

Hemingway was right about one thing. You know nothing of your true reaction to a bullfight until you have seen one of these once ferocious animals, a first or second or even third sword run clear through him, still managing to challenge the bullfighters surrounding him. You know nothing of your reaction to the bullfighters until you have watched the matador and his coterie of banderilleros pursuing and harassing these dying bulls until they can run no more.

Then there is the real dirty work of the modern Spanish bullfight— the coup de grâce. This is when one of the banderilleros takes out a pen knife, stabs the wounded bull between the eyes and then sticks the blade into the animal's ear and gouges him to death as if he were a young boy cutting the core from an apple.

There is something else I saw and learned in the greatly sunny Placa de Toros Monumental last Sunday.

The bullfight is not as it is so often advertised in movies and literature some great heroic test of wits between man and beast. The whole tragedy of the bullfight—the animals charging into the ring, the teasing by the banderilleros, the brutal lancing by the mounted picadors, the insertion of the painful banderillas, the capework by the matador and the slow, final butchering—is less a one-on-one affair and more a gangland-style execution. From the time the bull enters the scene he is relentlessly harassed and confused by the banderilleros, either standing in the ring itself or teasing him and taunting him from behind the wooden barerra, the fence which surrounds it.

Even when the matador stood alone in the ring, his banderilleros regularly worked to distract the bull. The second the matador got in trouble, every time a bull turned too abruptly on him or failed to follow his cue, the matador's claque of banderilleros would emerge from behind the fence to lure the bull away and their boss to safety. Even after the sword or several swords had been plunged full length into the animal the matador's lieutenants continued to harass and distract the bull. This confusion and humiliation of the bull gives some support I suppose to the tragedy of how much easier it is to butcher a beast once he had been made to look stupid.

But if the bull were so stupid, why is so much effort made to keep him confused throughout this so-called sporting activity? If he is so lacking in basic intelligence why is the fighting bull kept from the sight of a dismounted man until he enters the ring to be killed in the first place?

And if the bull requires so much effort to be confused and subdued, why is he the worthy object of so much of our torture?

• • • • • • • •

13 · MEN'S MID-LIFE INITIATION INTO THE DEEP MASCULINE

ALLAN B. CHINEN

Fairy tales and myths about heroes are well-known. These stories present young men battling evil enemies, winning a great victory, and then becoming king. The dramas reflect the traditional heroic and patriarchal paradigm of masculinity. Fairy tales, though, are not just the stuff of fantasy. Society expects young men in real life to be brave, aggressive—and victorious. So young men struggle to fit the heroic and patriarchal image. However, a large group of fairy tales that are mostly neglected today present an entirely different picture of manhood. These stories focus on men wrestling with mid-life crises and, ultimately, arriving at a new vision of masculinity. The tales portray men's mid-life initiation into the deep masculine.

The plot of these fairy tales is similar, no matter what country the stories come from. The tales include "Brother Lustig" from Germany, "The North Wind's Gift" from Italy, "Go I Know Not Whither" from Russia, and "The King and the Ghoul" from India, among others. Fairy tales should be told fully and enjoyed slowly, but space does not permit me to recount all the stories. So the bare plot must suffice here.

These fairy tales open with a middle-aged man exercising patriarchal power. He suffers some sort of calamity, but is rescued by his wife or another feminine figure. The experience forces the man to honor and accept the feminine in his life. The man then meets a divine male companion, who offers him further help and guidance. Through this male companion, the middle-aged man finds healing, inspiration, and renewed masculine energy. This pattern—moving from heroic masculinity to the feminine, and then to a divine masculine figure—can be found in literary classics, such as the *Odyssey* by Homer, *The Golden Ass* by Apuleius, and *The Divine Comedy* by Dante.

Men's mid-life encounter with the deep masculine constitutes a second initiation. Men's first initiation is usually the puberty rite, in which young men prove their heroism. Ironically, the initial task of the mid-life initiation is to give up youthful heroism. Only then can men come to terms with their feminine side. Jung was one of the first to discuss this process. Young men, he observed, normally repress their feminine side, their feeling, sensitivity, and relatedness, so they can be competitive, aggressive, and tough. This repressed feminine side breaks out at mid-life, and is symbolized in dreams by mysterious women, whom Jung called "anima figures." Systematic research in several cultures confirms men's turn to the feminine.

The mid-life initiation includes another step. Men must move from the inner feminine to the deep masculine. And stories from around the world specifically depict the deep masculine as a Trickster Spirit. The suggestion is astonishing, because the Trickster is usually considered immature, impulsive, foolish, and nasty. Recent anthropological and mythological research, however, reveals a different picture. The Trickster is complex, elusive, paradoxical, creative, and generative. Unlike the Hero and the Patriarch, who fight to dominate others, the Trickster avoids battle and power. He is the patron of communication and mediation, instead. Like the Greek Hermes, or the Brazilian Exu, the Trickster acts as a messenger and negotiator, not a warrior or ruler. Besides, the Hero and Patriarch secretly disdain women and fight women's authority, as feminists argue. But the Trickster treats women as equals. He mediates between opposites—masculine and feminine, gentle and cruel, light and dark.

The Trickster emerges from hunter-gatherer societies. Tricksters, for example, are prominent among the folklore of the Plains Indians of America and the Bushmen of Africa, both hunting societies. The importance of the Trickster to hunters is practical and religious. Before the invention of guns, or even bows and arrows, hunters had to approach their quarry closely. This meant they had to disguise themselves, usually by wearing animal skins. So hunters had to be Tricksters. On a religious level, the Trickster is the spirit behind shamanism, which is characteristic of hunting cultures. The shaman's main activity is entering a trance through ecstatic dancing or drumming. In these trances, shamans say they travel to the gods or to the spirits of the dead, asking for help in curing the sick or ensuring a successful hunt. Carrying such messages is exactly what Tricksters do in mythology. The Greek Hermes, the Hindu Narada, and the African Legba all shuttle back and forth between heaven, hell, and earth. Tricksters mirror in mythology what shamans claim to do in real life.

Tricksters, I suggest, animate hunting cultures the way the Great Goddess governs agricultural societies, the Hero inspires warrior cultures, and the Patriarch dominates city-states and empires. Humans, of course, were originally hunters and remained so for thousands of years before agriculture and warfare appeared. So the Trickster-Shaman is literally the deep masculine— the first paradigm of manhood, antedating the Hero and the Patriarch.

Perhaps the most dramatic example of the deep masculine comes from the spectacular prehistoric cave sanctuaries of France and Spain. The figures and animals in these caves follow a definite order. The entrance usually has male figures or male symbols. Further in, animals dominate, with female figures and feminine symbols. At the very rear of the cave, or in remote places difficult to reach, male figures reappear, typically as dancing shamans. The same pattern appears in cave art as in fairy tales—masculine themes first, followed by feminine ones, and ending with masculine symbols. The parallel with fairy tales is remarkable and emphasizes the ancient roots of the archetype of the deep masculine.

An excellent example of a mid-life initiation into the deep masculine can be found in Jung's life. After breaking with Freud, Jung suffered a painful mid-life crisis. In the middle of his turmoil, he dreamed that he killed Seigfried, the archetypal hero from Germanic tradition. The dream, Jung realized, symbolized the death of the heroic spirit that had inspired him in youth. Shortly afterward, a series of female figures appeared in Jung's dreams and fantasies. He puzzled over these women, and finally interpreted them as symbols of his repressed feminine side. (Thus was born his theory of the anima.) A little later, a dramatic masculine figure emerged in Jung's reveries— Philemon, a man with the horns of a bull and the wings of a bird. Earthy, yet spiritual, Philemon became Jung's inner guide and teacher. Philemon, of course, is another form of the Trickster-Shaman. Surprisingly, Jung did not write as much about Philemon or the Trickster-Shaman as he did about the anima. But this neglect of the deep masculine is common among men. The deep masculine is even more unconscious than men's feminine side. Men usually do not question the roots of their masculinity, but quickly begin to reflect when a feminine aspect of themselves emerges in public!

In practical terms, what does the Trickster-Shaman mean to men at mid-life? I can make only one suggestion here. As mentioned before, the Trickster-Shaman uses dance to produce trances and spiritual visions. This divine "madness" contrasts with the Hero's war frenzy, or a man going "berserk" with rage. In fact, the Trickster-Shaman's ecstatic dancing offers another way of expressing male energy. Instead of using masculine power to dominate men and women, the Trickster uses it to enter a numinous realm. In psychological terms, the Trickster sublimates aggression into spirituality. But the Trickster came before the warrior in prehistory, so it is more accurate to say that spiritual frenzy is the basic state, not war madness. That is, aggression is really a degenerate form of spirituality. The Trickster's spiritual frenzy, I might add, is the primordial energy behind intoxication and addiction. Like the warrior's battle frenzy, inebriation is a distortion of the deep masculine. By consciously reclaiming the deep masculine, men can avoid destructive aggression and drunkenness. The Trickster-Shaman thus offers a model for men and society, beyond the violence of the heroic and patriarchal tradition. Ironically, the most ancient image of masculinity is also a hope for a better future. This is the paradox—and power—of the Trickster-Shaman, hidden in the masculine soul.

· · · · · · ·

14 · IN SEARCH OF A
MODERN MALE INITIATION

FREDERIC WIEDEMANN

Bly's article arrested me immediately; even the title [*The Need for Male Initiation*] stopped me in my tracks. My God, have I been naive, passive, and numb in my life: the money I have lost; the women I have needed to show me my emotions. But now I know I have my own feelings about things. I started a men's group a year ago. Six of us meet every other Friday morning for two hours. We give each other strength to go into places we have never been before without a woman.

Bly cries out that our male emotional bodies are not active because the male initiation was interrupted. I have some concerns about the naivete of this idea—some tribes with full-blown male-initiation rites produce violent men, for example. Mostly, however, I sense the power that initiation could play in activating our emotional bodies.

But what initiation? Where do men go for this initiation? How do we undergo it?

I believe the male initiation is being taken into the Mystery by a man, or men. It is feeling the Mystery together with other men, without recourse to a woman. When we men are in Mystery, we don't know how to be. That is the Mystery and the initiation. One day recently my father, two brothers, and I set off into this Mystery. Let me tell you what we discovered about initiation:

We set off together, the four of us—a father and his three sons, three brothers and their father. Heading for the Pecos wilderness. Jonathan (31) the youngest brother was driving. Dad (67) was in the front seat, studying the maps. Harden (36) the middle brother and I (40) sat in back. We joked and tossed our high expectations back and forth. We left unsaid our fears of the intimacy. Could we be intimate with each other? What did we have to say to one another? What was this Father-Son thing all about? What were brothers?

I had first proposed an outdoor wilderness trip with Dad when I was 27. Wanting to connect with him, I wrote him proposing that we go on a weekend trip. He wrote back inviting me on a trek in Nepal. The adventures on that trek started our long, slow journey back toward being able to get real with each other.

It was late afternoon when we shouldered our packs to enter the beautiful canyon that threaded up and around the 3,000-foot granite walls guarding our goal, Hermit's Peak. It was said that an old hermit lived up there who lived on wild mushrooms. The trail hesitated as to which side of the stream would grant us more immediate penetration into the wilds. We crisscrossed the same stream 21 times. We were spooked by a snake slithering up the underbrush with a fish in its mouth. Setting up camp, we ribbed each other about who had the latest gear. Jonathan had been an Outward Bound instructor, so he wrought small miracles over the campfire. We ate fresh guacamole, risotto rice, marinated sirloin, and chocolate mint cookies.

Like driftwood floating effortlessly around the top vortex of a whirlpool, we enjoyed unwinding from making marriages work, making kids grow up, and making money. Around the dying fire, we mixed memories, stories, and coffee with peppermint schnapps. We were not yet willing to be sucked down deeper into the whirlpool of who we really were to each other. We were just easing into the initiation.

We weren't a mile up the trail the next morning when Dad said that he had forgotten the pills for his heart. This medicine kept his heart from beating too fast under exertion. We were carrying 100-pound backpacks, about to ascend a four hour trail at a 60-degree incline rising 4,000 feet of elevation. He told us to pound on his chest if he had a heart attack. My God! We brothers swallowed and looked at each other. Out of his earshot we decided to divide his gear between us, leaving him with a light daypack. Dad was told he had no veto in the matter. Surprisingly for the Patriarch, he accepted this rather gracefully, as if he welcomed our support as much as a light pack. How many years had he carried our burdens?

Hiking up the steep switchbacks, we took frequent rests. We monitored our pulse. Dad was doing great; he was in splendid shape, clocking in at 105 beats per minute. My heart was pounding the fastest. I was the most out of shape! In my mind, I designed and scheduled elaborate exercise programs for myself upon return.

We passed a spot where swarming ladybugs completely covered baby pine trees and dead aspen logs.

In typically male aggressive fashion, we mounted the summit by 1:00 P.M. We pitched camp, gathered firewood, drew water from the spring. We were in the male organizing mode. Why, we had every size of wood a fire could want. Then we were done organizing, done doing. The sun was still high. The whole afternoon undressed before us. We had arrived, and prepared everything. There was no place else to go. There was nothing left to do. Now we could be. Now that we were in the wilderness, we had to enter the wilderness. Now the initiation.

A black raven cruised the edge of the cliffs. The summit fell off thousands of feet, down sheer rock walls. We looked out, out, out—from 11,000 feet to the wilderness below at 7,000 feet, and beyond to the plains of the Texas panhandle. The clouds created and destroyed themselves several hundred yards out from us at eye level. We talked as a foursome, we broke into subgroups, we went off alone, we found ourselves back together endlessly recombined. The afternoon suspended itself in midair. Sun rays smashed through a cloud bank, and dazzled the wilderness forest a mile below us.

In single file we prowled back and forth on the very edge of the precipice. With arms held behind our backs we were monks treading the eye of the world in the Himalayas. With silent padding of steeled legs, we were panthers marking territory in the wilds of Africa. With silent sitting, we were the gnarled trees shouting their branches into the intense silence below, as if aching to hurl their energies through the spaces. Suddenly it was evening. We talked, we laughed. We disappeared into silence. The forces worked us over. I fell to the ground. I left my head. Wave after wave of emotion welled up. I traveled past my wife's defenses into her hurt. I traveled past her hurt into her goodness. How much I loved—and I didn't even let myself know it. My God!

My father was old. What intense feelings I had for this man whose spasming loins produced me 40 years ago. This man had husbanded a 41-year marriage, fathered 3 successful sons, captained his own profitable business, amassed wealth, and trekked the world. Despite his love, his bouts of generosity, he was a self-contained man. He did not like to submit to things outside of his control. Yet he had softened over the years. He had opened sectors of his heart. He was trying to court surrender. He even had sayings on his bathroom cabinet doors he opened everyday reminding him to let go. But the only way past the grip of a man like my father was through the door of his health. He had heart trouble. Along with daily medicine, his treatment was to trust. He forgot his heart medicine. Oh my God. Now he had to trust. He wanted us to see his old age. His rite of passage—he had left the trailhead a man, now he was an old man. He was walking through that gnarly gate gracefully. I admired that. I was proud to be one of the Wiedemann men.

Me and my brothers—the Wiedemann men. I slung that feeling around like a man high on brandy. There is something in "The Wiedemann Men" that mixed blood with pride. There was a gleam in our eyes, I could see it. A call to maleness; we were men. We are the ones left. The other male generations had been mowed down. Except us. Dad stood on the front line. We brothers were the next line back. Someday Dad would die in battle. Are you at peace, Dad? We brothers would have to advance to the front line. Before that befell us, we celebrate our solidarity. Back at home, we will again face the relentless grind of life. Soon we would face death. But now the male bonding. For this initiation today, we have momentarily thrown aside our responsibilities, our families, our obsessions. We were naked in the wilds, intoxicated on our own sense of self, and awed by the Now, the Here.

I came back to my senses. I sprang from the earth. My god, where was time? Where were the others? I wanted to dance. I had been too inhibited before. But now, over here, alone, I felt the great race haunch muscles stirring. I danced the ancient mating dance. The vista below was my prey. I stalked her, proving how virile I was. I teased, dominated, and seduced her. Before I mounted her, I raised her to heights of ecstacy, worshiping her every sinew. And finally I overpowered her, just as she overpowered me. And our mating flowed into the streaming sunset, all whirled in a rush of storm clouds, distant rain, and beautiful black smeared over pink and gold. We were all there watching the sunset as if we had never left each other's side. Our silence was our indestructible bond. My father and my brothers all ravished by the same moment. My God.

And in the aftermath, we found ourselves around the stone pit where the evening fire was being born. The hot food bled strength and warmth directly into our veins. Our hands were dirty with earth. The stars peered down at us; the rest of the world was now dark. How could we not break through the walls surrounding our chests? We passed the talking stick. The day had woven its spell, had conspired to ply our wounds and soften our fears. Each of us spoke from our heart. Of old wounds, of struggles, of love, of the difficulty of loving. Our Patriarch spoke of his kingdom and how it would be divided. We brothers spoke of finding our way in the multitude of the worlds we faced. The Mystery wrapped us gently in its embrace.

PART 3

· · · · · · ·

THROUGH THE EYE OF THE EYE OF THE WOUND: IMAGES OF MALE PAIN, FEAR, ANGER, LOSS, AND GRIEF

There is an empty place
in my metaphysical shape
that no one can reach:
a cloister of silence
that spoke with the fire of its voice muffled.

On the day I was born,
God was sick.

CÉSAR VALLEJO

We may imagine our deep hurts not merely as wounds
to be healed but as salt mines from which we gain a pre-
cious essence and without which the soul cannot live.

JAMES HILLMAN

INTRODUCTION

· · · · · · ·

Hypothesis: Each wound that a man experiences at any point in his life is but a localized instance of the One Male Wound.

In a sense this hypothesis is obviously false—clearly there are as many kinds of masculine wounds as there are kinds of masculinity. But in another sense—a lived, felt, emotional sense—"all wounds are one" carries an unmistakable truth. For when a man is wounded, Nietzsche declared, "it is that very wound which forces him to live."

This part of *To Be a Man* illustrates some of the myriad ways in which, wounded, a man is *forced to live*. He is forced to encounter something forbidden, lost, stolen, destructive, destroyed; something *all-powerful* (when in its grip); yet something also *necessary* (from the perspective of hindsight) for the deepening of male soul.

If these stories of wounded masculinity begin to sound like a litany, remember that a litany is a prayer in which the congregation recites responses—a *public* prayer. After centuries of overly-heroic, silent, "characteristically male" suffering, we men are due to give voice to our burdens. I say, let the litany grow loud!

Of course, there are dangers in men giving new volume to complaints, among them self-pity and a foolish belief that "my griefs as a man are greater than hers as a woman." But surely there are equal risks in not speaking our wounds and consequently enacting them blindly, repetitively, at the expense of others. We've had much too much of that already.

"The pain I have has no explanations," writes the great Peruvian-born poet César Vallejo. "Today I am simply in pain." Listen to the rhythms of Vallejo's language; feel these rhythms in your body and then move on to the psychotherapist Francis Weller's "Ashamed to Be Male," and men's rights activist Fredric Hayward's "Male-Bashing." Different tones, converging messages. Don Hanlon Johnson, a philosopher who probes the meanings of embodied experience, asks in "The Loneliness of the Male Body" that we begin measuring the price exacted by the distances we men keep even as we ache for contact. Franz Kafka's brief remarks, "The Misery of Bachelors," echo Johnson's theme of painful male isolation, or "exile" as Michael Meade puts it. "The male spirit or soul doesn't feel that it has a home," Meade writes in "Lamenting the Loss of Male Spirit." Thus Pablo Neruda's grieving words in "Walking Around" come as no surprise:

> It so happens that I am sick of my feet and my nails
> and my hair and my shadow.
> It so happens I am sick of being a man.

Many of us long for Neruda's direct access to feeling, especially because we know our feelings are *there* and *deep*. Psychologist Robert Hopcke, author of *Men's Dreams, Men's Healing*, writes of an encounter with a male client who is just beginning to close this gap. The work of restoring feeling, especially feelings of utter betrayal, is the focus of Stephen Grubman-Black's essay on childhood sexual abuse ("Forgetting But Remembering"). It's also the focus of Tav Spark's account of his life as an addict ("To Hell and Back"). Massachusetts psychotherapist John Weltner chronicles how a young Japanese male's sensitivity to "ancestral ghosts" symbolized his family's emotional numbness, and how the boy and his family came to new insights together.

In a conversation about the masculine casualties of feminism, men's movement activist Chris Brazier asserts that feminism's piercing wounds to traditional notions about masculinity will eventually serve men well. No way, responds Richard Haddad, who argues that feminism per se holds masculine experience per se in contempt. Arguing that "male feminist" is an oxymoron, Haddad insists that men must chronicle their *own* griefs and healing.

· · · · · · ·

15 · I AM GOING TO TALK ABOUT HOPE

CÉSAR VALLEJO

I do not feel this suffering as César Vallejo. I am not suffering now as a creative person, or as a man, nor even as a simple living being. I don't feel this pain as a Catholic, or as a Mohammedan, or as an atheist. Today I am simply in pain. If my name weren't César Vallejo, I'd still feel it. If I weren't an artist, I'd still feel it. If I weren't a man, or even a living being, I'd still feel it. If I weren't a Catholic, or an atheist, or a Mohammedan, I'd still feel. it. Today I am in pain from further down. Today I am simply in pain.

The pain I have has no explanations. My pain is so deep that it never had a cause, and has no need of a cause. What could its cause have been? Where is that thing so important that it stopped being its cause? Its cause is nothing, and nothing could have stopped being its cause. Why has this pain been born all on its own? My pain comes from the north wind and from the south wind, like those hermaphrodite eggs that some rare birds lay conceived of the wind. If my bride were dead, my suffering would still be the same. If they had slashed my throat all the way through, my suffering would still be the same. If life, in other words, were different, my suffering would still be the same. Today I'm in pain from higher up. Today I am simply in pain.

I look at the hungry man's pain, and I see that his hunger walks somewhere so far from my pain that if I fasted until death, one blade of grass at least would always sprout from my grave. And the same with the lover! His blood is too fertile for mine, which has no source and no one to drink it.

I always believed up till now that all things in the world had to be either fathers or sons. But here is my pain that is neither a father nor a son. It hasn't any back to get dark, and it has too bold a front for dawning, and if they put it into some dark room, it wouldn't give light, and if they put it into some brightly lit room, it wouldn't cast a shadow. Today I am in pain, no matter what happens. Today I am simply in pain.

· · · · · · ·

16 · ASHAMED TO BE MALE

FRANCIS WELLER

We have a difficult time in this culture appreciating the wounds that a man carries. For the most part, men's wounds remain invisible, guarded by sentinels of denial, heroism, and isolation. The lessons began early and the teachings were clear: Do not expose your pain, for if you do you will be seen as weak and a failure. This type of branding can reduce a man's sense of himself to rubble.

Men are taught to triumph, be victorious, and rise above the failings of body and emotion. We suffer from what psychologist James Hillman calls the "Hercules Complex," in which we never surrender to the fates of life. We secretly fear failure, grief, surrender, loss, aging, and death; we feel ashamed that we cannot triumph over them so we deny them, showing no signs of defect or wound.

But what happens to a man when he is not allowed the humanizing experience of failure and defeat? He loses soul and becomes a "prisoner of perfection."

The men I see in my psychotherapy practice suffer from a common wound: the shame of being male, or more accurately, the shame of being raised male. The distressing absence of pride in these men reflects the reality that men have lost a basic sense of "ground" in which failure is tantamount to worthlessness. They have little feeling of the sacred and often even less of a sense of what it is that moves them, what they long for, or what it is that weighs on them so heavily. They live according to prescription and find no meaning in their lives. These men are lonely—shame keeps them silent and prevents them from connecting with the men and women who could help heal their pain.

THE EXPERIENCE AND NATURE OF SHAME

Shame is a bodily based, archetypal response to experiences that rupture a man's sense of adequacy and worthiness. In those moments of painfully binding self-consciousness, he senses himself as inferior in some critical way. He desires during those moments of exposure to hide from the view of others. He withdraws into an interior world and searches for the flaw.

Shame is experienced as an expression of our core worth. When in the grip of shame, *who we are* is defective and wrong. We feel powerless to change the condition and this leads to the hopelessness that is so characteristic of the shame-bound life.

Internal dialogues characterized by self-contempt and self-hatred carried on unrelentingly remind us of our past, present, and future failures. There is a loss of heart and compassion, and we measure everything by comparisons in which we inevitably come up short. *To live with shame is to be in despair.*

SOURCE OF SHAME IN MEN

The sources of shame in men are varied. I will discuss four of them. They are characterized by loss (1) of the father, (2) of archetypal ground, (3) of passion and the body, and (4) of masculine community. These losses comprise a near total collapse in the beauty and radiance of the masculine psyche.

The first and earliest source of shame is the loss of the father. As young boys we feel a pull to the father, a desire to be touched, held, and contained within his psychic field. What we met more often was a wounded man unable to provide these emotional needs. When we experience a failure of bridging with the father we feel shame; what's more, we feel we are to blame for the failure.

In *Finding Our Fathers,* Samuel Osherson suggests that one of the fundamental male vulnerabilities lies in the fantasies devised to explain the father's absence. These fantasies almost always reflect self-blame. What is wrong with me that my father is not closer with me, does not touch me, does not love me? This shame is internalized over time and, in an attempt to shape a self that is acceptable to our fathers, some of us try to become perfect sons. Others push away and secretly deny our desire of his approval, only to play it out with countless other "fathers."

One man that I worked with in therapy revealed that he stopped fifteen feet from his father's door for fear that he would reject him again. He had not seen his father in fourteen years. Nor had he male friends with whom to share his pain.

The second source of shame is less obvious. It involves the erosion in the imagination of the masculine that has occurred over the last several hundred years. What was once a rich and varied depiction of the masculine psyche is now reduced to flattened billboards and gross simplifications of what it means to be male. We have effectively moved from an archetypal configuration of the masculine, which included images of the sacred king, warriors, and lovers, to stereotyped representations. The result of such a loss is that we move from images that connect and resonate within the souls of men to images that invite comparison and, consequently, shame.

Comparison is a form of shaming that provides fuel for endless competitiveness among men. With the culture's edicts of success, wealth, possessions, and status, men are driven to compete for power and position, often forsaking friendships, family, and partners. Strict taboos discourage openly sharing feelings of self-doubt, pain, isolation, or sorrow. Men that I see who are caught in this driven-ness feel totally alone and unable to make substantial connections with other men. This individualism is valued as indispensable and essentially masculine, but it is rooted in power, not in relationship.

The third loss is that of passion and the body. This loss alienates men from the living experience of their existence. Early in our lives this impulse was deemed unacceptable in the family, church, and culture. We were expected to demonstrate control of our passions and to rid ourselves of "wildness." As a result, we had to disown our vitality.

William Blake captures the feeling of this loss in his poem *The Garden of Love*. The last two lines read:

And priests in black gowns were walking their rounds,
And binding with briars my joys and desires.

Men are struggling with this very loss of passion. The impulse of desire reaches out and toward another and feels gratified when the bridge is made. When the instinctual desire for erotic connecting is shamed, it is disowned and the movement toward the other is arrested. The possibility of intimacy, vulnerability, and connectedness is lost. To cover our shame, sexuality often becomes fixated within the world of power, which objectifies our partners and diminishes the possibility of contact.

The final loss is the dissolution of the masculine community. This loss does not shame men directly, but rather maintains the isolation in which shame breeds. With the breakdown of the community of men, we no longer have access to relationships that restore a feeling of connectedness and belonging. We are left with the perception that it is up to us to endure alone, without the solace of male friendship. Shame originates in the failure of relationships; it is also there that we can begin to heal.

HEALING THE WOUNDS OF SHAME

Shame is without doubt a "sickness of the soul," a sickness that is maintained through self-contempt, self-hatred, and isolation. To restore the vitality of the masculine we must effect fundamental changes in our relationships to ourselves and to the world.

Three shifts are necessary in order to initiate healing: We must move from feeling worthless to seeing ourselves as wounded, because we will not attend to our pain until this primary shift is effected. We must move from holding contempt for the self to feeling compassion. And we must move from concealing our shame in silence to revealing ourselves in sharing. These shifts are fundamental requirements in the restoration of "the self's relationship to the self." Inherent in these three movements is the recognition of oneself as worthwhile and as connected to the world.

Carl Jung said, "There appears to be a conscience in mankind which severely punishes the man who does not somehow and at some time, at whatever cost to his pride, cease to defend and assert himself, and instead confess himself fallible and human. Until he can do this, an impenetrable wall shuts him out from the living experience of feeling himself a man among men."

The willingness to relate compassionately to the wounds we carry aids us in providing what has been needed all our lives. Establishing a relationship with ourselves that cares for and honors the wounds allows us to move out of shame and into connection with the world. To feel ourselves a "man among men" requires a masculine community that can restore the sense of value and wholeness that we seek in our lives. And through restoring the imagination we can remember what it is that hold us in the vast configuration that is the masculine spirit.

As we heal and the feelings of isolation give way to the experience of connectedness, we begin to feel our stewardship for the world. As men we carry a particular responsibility that concerns us with protecting the sacred in all things. To recognize the sacredness of life, together with women, puts us in partnership at a time when the planet faces extraordinary challenges. Healing our shame thus becomes not only a personal challenge, but a transpersonal one as well. To bring about such a transformation requires that we receive a strong sense of validation and recognition that allows us to drop the cloak of shame and be seen for who we are—men of soul.

Let us begin this work, together.

• • • • • • •

17 · MALE-BASHING

FREDRIC HAYWARD

By far, "Male-Bashing" is the most popular topic in my current talk shows and interviews. Reporters and television crews have come to me from as far away as Denmark, Australia, and Germany to investigate this American phenomenon. What is going on, they ask? Why do women want it? Why do men allow it?

The trend is particularly rampant in advertising. In a survey of 1,000 random advertisements, one hundred percent of the jerks singled out in male-female relationships were male. There were no exceptions. That is, whenever there was a husband-wife or boyfriend-girlfriend interaction, the one who was dumped on was the male.

One hundred percent of the ignorant ones were male. One hundred percent of the incompetent ones were male. One hundred percent of the ones who lost a contest were male. One hundred percent of the ones who smelled bad (mouthwash and detergent commercials) were male. One hundred percent of the ones who were put down without retribution were male. (Sometimes, the male would insult the female, but she was always sure to get him back in spades before the commercial ended.) One hundred percent of the objects of rejection were male. One hundred percent of the objects of anger were male. One hundred percent of the objects of violence were male.

In entertainment, the trend is similarly raging. Some television shows are little more than a bunch of anti-male jokes strung together. Deciding to count the phenomenon during one episode of "Golden Girls," I found thirty-one women's insults of men compared to two men's insults of women. Family sitcoms like "The Cosby Show" or "Family Ties" have an unwritten rule that mothers are *never* to be the butt of jokes or made to look foolish.

As to literature, just glance through the recent best-seller lists. There is no anti-female literature that matches the anti-male tone of *Smart Women, Foolish Choices, Women Who Love Too Much, Men Who Can't Love, Men Who Hate Women and the Women Who Love Them.* Two authors told me about pressure from their editors to create anti-male titles as a way of increasing sales. The closest thing to a female flaw that one can publicly acknowledge is that women tend to "love too much."

Products also reflect the popularity of hating men. One owner of a greeting card store reported that male-bashing cards are her biggest selling line. 3M sells a variety of Post-it notes such as "The more I know about men, the more I like my dog," and "There are only two things wrong with men . . . everything they say and everything they do." A 3M spokesperson added that they have no intention of selling similarly anti-female products. Walk through any T-shirt store and compare the number of anti-female slogans to the number of anti-male slogans. Women might take offense at sexual innuendos, but there is a qualitative difference between something that is interpreted as insulting and something that is intended to be insulting.

With news coverage and school curricula fanning the flames, it is no surprise that judges and legislators also punish men. Most people seem to buy the common assumption that the man is always wrong. For example, I have had almost identical discussions with several people recently. Each person first told me that divorce laws should be harsher toward men for, they maintained, it is too easy for men to abandon their families.

Statistics would imply, however, that if divorce is too easy on anyone, it is too easy on women. When I informed them that it is women who currently initiate the overwhelming majority of divorces, they revised their logic: Each one of them concluded that men are so bad that women must leave a marriage in order to liberate themselves from these "oppressive men." In other words, no matter who leaves whom, the conclusion will always be that the man is at fault.

The result is that we encourage women not to improve themselves. So-called "self-help" books simply "help" women adjust to an inferior pool of men. When every problem can be blamed on male inadequacy, women lose the motivation to examine critically their own patterns of behavior. As a result, women lose out on one of the most rewarding experiences of human life: genuine self-improvement.

Very few women have even been aware of what Female Chauvinism is, let alone made any progress toward overcoming it. Articles telling women that they are more communicative, more empathetic, more prepared to be intimate and committed, more liberated, etc., than men, combined with the still common assumption that a man is not eligible unless he is even older, wiser, taller, more successful, and wealthier than a woman, have produced an aura of fear in women. A spate of articles on a mythical "shortage of eligible men" graces current literature.

Unfortunately, sexism teaches us to think of men as one giant organism that has been dominant for thousands of years, and that can handle (or even deserves) a generation or two of abuse. The reality is that men have the same human insecurities as women, and the generation of abuse has already had dire consequences for male mental health. Boys, struggling with maturation and never knowing anything but the current age of abuse, suffer even more. Relationships suffer as well. In male-bashing times, disagreements lead to the man feeling blamed and the woman feeling oppressed.

Since the dawn of history, the male-female relationship has been able to survive evolutionary traumas by remaining a perfectly balanced system. Both men and women had their own sets of privileges and power. Both men and women had positive and negative stereotypes. Feminist activists were the first to recognize that the system was obsolete, but seem to be the last to recognize that the system was, at least, in balance. They disrupted the system, and that was good, they disrupted the balance, and that was dangerous.

The current male-bashing trend appeals to the female consumer, upon whose whims our economy depends. It is comforting for women to think that men are always at fault, while women are always innocent. Interestingly, male-bashing even appeals to the male mentality. Forced to compete with each other, in contrast to the way women are allowed to empathize with each other, men enjoy male-bashing (as long as the bashee is another male). Males have long had negative self-images, and every man has a deep fantasy that he can be better than all the other men . . . the hero who will earn women's love by rescuing them from all the other rotten men.

For society's sake, however, and for the health of future male-female relationships, we better start to curb the excesses of male-bashing. It does not take many angry letters before an advertiser withdraws an offensive commercial or before a businessperson changes an offensive product.

The alternative, allowing male-bashing to continue its momentum, can only lead to a men's movement as angry with women, and far more violent, than the women's movement has been toward men. It is time to speak out. It is time to recognize that male-female dynamics have been far more reciprocal than feminist theory portrays. To those who insist that the female perspective is the only perspective: Your day has come and gone.

· · · · · · ·

18 · THE LONELINESS
OF THE MALE BODY

DON HANLON JOHNSON

A man, we are told, is to stand on his own two feet, apart from the crowd, unbent either by the opinions of others or by untrustworthy feelings. "I never found a companion as companionable as solitude," wrote Henry David Thoreau, a sentiment echoed in works of countless male thinkers: Plato, Lao-Tze, the Buddha, St. Augustine, Kierkegaard. The isolation of such places as

Walden Pond, St. Anthony's cave, Robinson Crusoe's island, Gauguin's Tahiti, or Paul Bowles's Sahara has always seemed to be more attractive to men's imaginations than the hurly-burly worlds of cities and families. For many of us it seems easier to be hiking alone in mountain wilderness or writing in a quiet room than to be engaged with other people.

But, of course, that is only part of the story: alone, we ache for contact. That ache, we now know from various medical studies, is a major factor in male patterns of illness, addiction, and death.

Even in groups working, hunting, drinking, or playing cards, we men often feel alone. We talk a lot, but from a distance. With only a handful of men do I experience the presence of eyes, transparency of facial expression, and punctuating touch that show that we are truly listening to and interested in each other. We also write a lot, but the styles of writing and research we have created rarely, except in the work of poets and novelists, tell the reader about our personal concerns and passions; we like to think that we are talking about "objective reality."

Male bonds are often tenuous. In a not uncharacteristic breakup of a male friendship, Freud wrote in response to a conciliatory letter from Jung: "I propose that we abandon our personal relations entirely. I shall lose nothing by it, for my only emotional tie with you has long been a thin thread." Although they had been intimate friends for years and partners in assaulting society's illusions, although Freud had named Jung his dearest son and heir, the connections they had woven together were so flimsy that they easily unraveled under the strain of petty arguments about psychoanalytic ideas.

Freud's seemingly easy dismissal of Jung evokes a haunting image of a world controlled by groups of men who are connected to each other like those little bump cars in amusement parks. In such a world, we men are typically separated from each other by hard edges and dead spaces of abstraction; we achieve a sense of contact by knocking up against each other in competition and argument.

Our loneliness is not just a loneliness attitude, or the "natural" state of being an adult male. It results from how we learn to sense (or not sense) the world and to feel (or not feel) our movements in space. Becoming what our culture identifies as a "man" requires learning to gesture and speak in predictable ways, to identify with certain parts of our bodies to the neglect of others. Many of the rough edges we find in our contacts with other men and with women are rooted in this learned sense of our bodies, which manifests in such forms as the glaze in our eyes when a friend is talking to us, a shrinking away as someone comes too close, a breathless rush to get in the last word in a conversation, an angry glare at an imagined opponent, and a rush of feeling from the penis as we begin to feel too much intimacy.

A man's sense of self is delineated by his feelings about where his body ends and another's begins. When that sense is ill-developed, even distorted, it can lead to a mistaken extension of the boundaries of self beyond the skin surface into his favorite armchair, car, house, nation, and philosophical world-view. Damage to any of these feels like a blow against himself.

To become a "real man," one must learn to construct a self apart from other people and the sensible world. That construction begins in the family. The flashy, sensual relationship to the mother is intimate, immediate: womb, birth, nursing, nurturing. Compared to it, his sensual relationship to the father is, in most families, tenuous at best. The radical difference between the mother's and father's relation to the child's body anchors in that child's earliest perceptions—a felt difference between the immediate perceptual world associated with women, and the more abstract, unperceived world associated with men.

For a traditionally raised male, the journey to manhood can be viewed as a struggle to leave our mothers to find our fathers. From the standpoint of body-image, that constitutes an attempt to define our physical boundaries as clearly separated from our nurturing mothers, and as truly connected with distant fathers. In intimate relations with women we often seem to find ourselves falling into their world of feelings and perceptions. To maintain a sense of self with them often involves drastic separations, running away. With male intimates, by contrast, we maintain a sense of self by a clearly felt sense of distance, knocking up against, arguing, competing. The boundaries are clear, but the felt connections are not resilient enough to hold against strain.

The family passes on bodily techniques developed within more comprehensive institutions, religion being one of the oldest and most pervasive. Jesus, like his Asian counterparts the Buddha and Lao-Tze and his Jewish predecessors the prophets, wandered alone, disconnected from wives, children, parents, and material possessions. Jewish ascetics and their early Christian heirs developed a wide variety of postures, movements, fasts, and self-inflicted tortures to embody their belief that reality is divided into two essentially distinct realms. What is said to be the true world is "supernatural," imagined to contain God, Satan, angels, demons, saints, and the soul. The ephemeral natural world, including the body and women, is said to hide the real. To penetrate its masks, a man has to be trained to keep from being captivated by the needs of his body for food, beauty, rest, and sexual delight.

Those ancient body-shaping methods have been consistently effective in producing men who are literally out of contact with the sensible world and other persons. The instincts of the spiritual adult are deflected from their sensuous objects and turned within. He lives encased within a world of images and ideas, anxious and alone with his god.

Such practices are not unique to monks. Such body-oriented practices, stripped of religious and moral content, came to characterize the appropriate shaping for the modern man in many different areas. The Reformers, for example, renounced the monastic traditions of physical penance and meditation postures while they retained the denigration of bodily impulses, preaching sobriety, self-control, and discipline as key virtues for the Protestant bourgeoisie. The physical disciplines of manners, sport, dance, and posture-training taught in the upper-class schools of Europe and the United States are secular versions of the older mystical techniques. In training for military service, the workplace, and intellectual work, men are characteristically encouraged to become so indifferent to their own perceptions and needs that they are ready in a moment to follow the directions of their commanders or bosses. The soldier and the worker are disciplined to detach themselves from their bodily feelings so that they can carry out their tasks obediently, without the distraction of those human impulses that might counter the needs of war and profit. The scientist is thought to require freedom from the sway of bodily impulses that might contaminate his experimental conclusions. While advocates of biomedicine asserted the authority of empirical reason against religious authority, they retained religion's detached attitudes toward the natural world of the body, the physical environment, and women.

The problems typically addressed by modern philosophers are intimately bound up with an image of the body as the atomistic "extended thing," divided by an unbridgeable gulf from the thinking self: How can one know external reality, live peacefully in a society of individuals, understand or love another atomistic self, if selves are separated by rigid boundaries? The human community is imagined to be an artificial construct, which has to rely on effort, even force, for cohesion.

Standing alone can be an admirable posture. Winning personal and political freedoms has often required men to detach themselves from the comforts of close-knit societies that are dominated by unquestioned religious and political dogmas. But the need to adopt a firm stance apart from others has been allowed to permeate our lives in pathological ways. The world in which we live now demands more supple responses. More men are standing up together for brothers and sisters of ethnic minorities, learning to walk beside, instead of two paces ahead of, women and children.

During this century, many factors have been chipping away at the ideal of the lonely male. A succession of wars has produced a generation of men disillusioned with the glorification of the military image. The explosion of world travel and information exchange have brought in a rich variety of alternative male images from other cultures. Feminism has demonstrated the necessity of involving fathers with their infant sons, creating a new generation of men who do not link sensuality exclusively with mother-enmeshment. By its theory as well as its behavior, the gay community has challenged the supposed naturalness of traditional models.

Within this larger cultural matrix, there have evolved a number of approaches to the body designed to educate men in a non-alienated sense of self: new approaches to sports emphasizing body-awareness and flexibility, some building on the older Asian traditions of martial arts; new body-therapies such as Rolfing, the Alexander Technique, and Feldenkrais; more reflective methods of sexual stimulation drawing from ancient traditions; and a variety of body-oriented psychotherapies. Sophisticated touch, manipulation of limbs, guided imagery and awareness, and refined forms of body movement help create a more comprehensive map of the fleshy self: the precise shapes and locations of bones, muscles, and organs, the true size of shoulders and hips, the topography of the skin. Within this more accurately defined body image, a man can learn how to discern those critical moments when that image interferes with his values: when his skin dulls in defense against an imagined attack by another person; when his eyes begin to fade in avoidance; when he blocks his breath to stifle an expression of affection that feels too dangerous; when he restricts his hip and shoulder movements out of old fears. In the moment of being noticed, those artificial boundaries lose their grip.

At the most profound level, these new approaches to the body help a man see through the artifice of alienation by giving him the sense of how we exist in connection—breathing the same atmosphere, seeing each other, able to contact with touch, hearing each other's voice, and responding to each other's movements. Hypnotized by abstract ideas, we live dissected into isolated communities and individuals; in our bodily sensitivity, we are one species.

. . . .

19 · THE MISERY OF BACHELORS

F R A N Z   K A F K A

The unhappiness of the bachelor, whether seeming or actual, is so easily guessed at by the world around him that he will curse his decision, at least if he has remained a bachelor because of the delight he takes in secrecy. He walks around with his coat buttoned, his hands in the upper pockets of his jacket, his arms akimbo, his hat pulled down over his eyes, a false smile that has become natural to him is supposed to shield his mouth as his glasses do his eyes, his trousers are tighter than seem proper for his thin legs. But everyone knows his condition, can detail his sufferings. A cold breeze breathes upon him from within and he gazes inward with the even sadder half of his double face. He moves incessantly, but with predictable regularity, from one apartment to another. The farther he moves away from the living, for whom he must still—and this is the worst mockery—work like a conscious slave who dare not express his consciousness, so much the smaller a space is considered sufficient for him. . . . When he dies the coffin is exactly right for him.

· · · · · · ·

20 · LAMENTING THE LOSS
OF MALE SPIRIT

MICHAEL MEADE

THE SUN:
Do you see anything encouraging about being at the end of a historical period?

MEADE:
The opportunities for change are incredible. When things collapse there's a lot of fresh air, a lot of openness. So, yes, I think there's a lot of good in it. Sometimes I focus on what's lost, because it helps me understand why we all seem to feel the way we do. People, for the most part, seem to be suffering a sense of loss.

THE SUN:
In the men's groups that you've been involved with, how does the loss express itself? What are the more common laments?

MEADE:
Oh, that's a nice word, *lament*. There are many things that have been seen as losses. Isolation has become a common experience. I often think of it as exile. Sons feel exiled from their fathers, father feel exiled from their sons. It's as if there were huge chasms between them reinforced by sex roles. The father is supposed to act like a father, the son is supposed to act like a son. Sometimes, when people try to conform to those behaviors, the interactions get lost altogether.

Men feel a loss of home. The male spirit or soul doesn't feel that it has a home. The man goes to work and deals with that set of responsibilities and difficulties. Then he goes home and deals with that set of responsibilities and difficulties. He doesn't have a sense of home—as in a dwelling place, where he gets to dwell within himself.

There's also a loss of connection man to man. At a men's conference, it's clear that everybody's afraid—rightfully so, I think. Nobody knows what the dance is. So, men wind up working on how to connect with one another, how to get together. Men feel a great loss for some fluid way of being with one another. They are often tired of working so hard: you have to work hard to find meaningful work; you have to work hard to stay in a relationship; you have to work hard to stay connected to children.

Men have inherited a great depth of sorrow; so have women. It's what we used to call "the sorrow of the world." But the tone for grieving, or dealing with sorrow, is different for a man than it is for a woman. Grief is grief, but as the grief ascends or descends, moves through a particular body with a particular psychic shape, it takes the tone of that body. So the tone of a man's grieving is a little different, just like the tone of a man's voice is different from a woman's. Somehow men have lost those forms of grieving together, and lamenting. People used to sit down, and take turns lamenting—just being the sorrow of the world. Men do it very well together. It's one of the great joys, interestingly enough, of working with men—seeing how men grieve and express sorrow together. Men activate each other's emotions. And when men have some purpose and some depth of meaning that they're dealing with, and they get together in a safe environment, then the feelings will deepen tremendously. That kind of opportunity is generally missing in men's lives.

· · · · · · ·

21 · WALKING AROUND

PABLO NERUDA

It so happens I am sick of being a man.
And it happens that I walk into tailorshops and movie houses
dried up, waterproof, like a swan made of felt
steering my way in a water of wombs and ashes.

The smell of barbershops makes me break into hoarse sobs.
The only thing I want is to lie still like stones or wool.
The only thing I want is to see no more stores, no gardens,
no more goods, no spectacles, no elevators.

It so happens I am sick of my feet and my nails
and my hair and my shadow.
It so happens I am sick of being a man.
Still it would be marvelous
to terrify a law clerk with a cut lily,
or kill a nun with a blow on the ear.

It would be great
to go through the streets with a green knife
letting out yells until I died of the cold.

I don't want to go on being a root in the dark,
insecure, stretched out, shivering with sleep,
going on down, into the moist guts of the earth,
taking in and thinking, eating every day.

I don't want so much misery.
I don't want to go on as a root and a tomb,
alone under the ground, a warehouse with corpses,
half frozen, dying of grief.

That's why Monday, when it sees me coming
with my convict face, blazes up like gasoline,
and it howls on its way like a wounded wheel,
and leaves tracks full of warm blood leading toward the night.

And it pushes me into certain corners, into some moist houses,
into hospitals where the bones fly out the window,
into shoeshops that smell like vinegar,
and certain streets hideous as cracks in the skin.

There are sulfur-colored birds, and hideous intestines
hanging over the doors of houses that I hate,
and there are false teeth forgotten in a coffeepot,
there are mirrors
that ought to have wept from shame and terror,
there are umbrellas everywhere, and venoms, and umbilical cords.

I stroll along serenely, with my eyes, my shoes,
my rage, forgetting everything,
I walk by, going through office buildings and orthopedic shops,
and courtyards with washing hanging from the line:
underwear, towels and shirts from which slow
dirty tears are falling.

· · · · · · · ·

22 · A DREAM
OF ANTS AND SPIDERS:
MEN AND FEELINGS

R O B E R T   H.   H O P C K E

I am asleep on my bed, which is beneath the window at the back of the house. Then I feel something on my chest—light, almost tickling. I open my eyes and see that ants and spiders are crawling across me. It's strange—I observe them calmly and make no move to brush them off or kill them. I simply watch them go their way as they walk across my chest, down onto the bed, then up the wall and out the back window. Watching them I notice that they are in orderly columns, in formation, like soldiers. The ants are large, like big fire ants, but these don't sting at all. The spiders are smaller and more delicate, and it strikes me that some of these are carrying others piggyback—don't ants do this? Still not moving but simply observing, I let my eyes follow their trail backward and notice that they are coming through the front door of the house, marching in a straight line through the living room, dining room, and then into my bedroom, up the bed, across me, then out the back window. The whole thing has a strange calmness to it—it is very early in the morning.

I asked Pete, after he had finished describing the dream, what he thought about the dream, which was the first he had reported in our sessions for at least six months. Unlike past responses in which he had dismissed dreams by simply saying, "I have no idea," this time he answered me quickly and directly, "I think the ants and spiders are my negative feelings."

Of course, negative feelings had been the latest topic of our meetings for at least the month prior to this dream, but not for the reasons the outside observer might suppose. For Pete, like many men, negative feelings had become the topic of his twice-a-week therapy sessions, not because of an abundance of such feelings, but rather, unfortunately and typically, because negative feelings were so rarely felt and Pete found himself quite unable to even identify such a feeling. Tellingly, feelings, negative feelings, had become merely the topic of our discussions, not yet the living presence in therapy. My intuition was that the dream, as dreams often do, was functioning to point out to the two of us precisely what Pete's relationship was to these much-discussed but as yet still abstract negative feelings he only very dimly perceived himself having.

But before we go on to examine Pete's dream in more detail, a little background is in order. I met Pete when he came to me for therapy at age twenty-five, a short, stocky gay man who found himself now three years past the time when he should have graduated from college. He seemed clear on the reasons for this delay: though an architecture major, he found himself often unable to draw. "Well, not really unable to draw," he told me in what I would find was a characteristic pattern of self-qualification. "I am able to draw; it's just that I'm not ever happy with what I do, so I find myself endlessly correcting it, trying to make it better, but what usually happens is that I end up somehow ruining the project, or having to start over. Well, I mean, sometimes I start over. Sometimes I am unable even to begin. When I start, I usually can't finish it, though. And when I do finish it, I usually hate the project and start over anyway."

For this reason, Pete decided to enter psychotherapy and, again in the words of many of my other male clients, "get the problem fixed" so he could at long last graduate. When we began our work together, he still had quite a few classes to take before he could graduate; he told me that academically he was considered a junior. Since his university no longer considered him eligible for student loans, he was forced to find part-time work as a word processor at a wage high enough to support himself. His need to work obviously cut down even further on his time for school, and, as he described his dilemma, I felt a sense of entrapment and desperation. Knowing men, I wondered if he was at all aware of these feelings.

"So it sounds as if you're coming here feeling kind of stuck and anxious, looking for a solution," I ventured.

"Exactly, a solution. It just can't go on like this."

After a short pause, I said, "You sound as if you're feeling kind of desperate."

"I just need to be able to draw and get my projects done." He looked at me with brown eyes wide.

"I'm wondering what you feel when you say that to me."

"I feel as if this has gone on too long and I need to get my act together. That's why I am coming to you."

Trapped in a situation with no clear out. Anxious about his ability to perform, to succeed, to produce. Desperate, as he grew older and as former classmates graduated and began their careers. As I listened to him and sensed the mood in the room, the urgency of his speech, and the directness of his stare, I conjectured further. Afraid perhaps, afraid of failure? Certainly needy; he was coming for help, having found no solution on his own for years. Panicky? This I dismissed. He seemed quite controlled, well-dressed, actually very professional-looking and sounding, a clean-shaven young man who paid meticulous attention to his hair and nails; his shoes were shined, his shirt cuffs ironed.

What other feelings did I pick up from him? Oddly I felt no uncertainty from him about my ability to help him. He seemed from the very first to trust my ability to "fix the problem" and "get him working" again, as he put it. I

wondered if his faith in my abilities might not be due to the good recommen-
dation I had received from the colleague who had referred him to me.

"You seem to be pretty sure that therapy with me is the answer."

"Marty said you have helped a lot of students with this kind of problem,
so here I am."

"Do you have any feelings about coming here for help? Sometimes, people have feelings about going to someone for something they feel they can't do
on their own." I felt myself push him a bit here, in order to evaluate whether
he would be the exception or the rule.

Again, there was no pause or hesitation. His response came back to me
quickly and articulately. I was to find that silence would be a stranger in the
room with us. "Feelings about coming here? Not at all. I just want to solve
this ridiculous procrastination problem and get on with my life."

I nodded my head and merely said, "Oh." I had gotten the answer to my
tacit question and felt a familiar sadness. Once again, like nearly every man I
had ever seen as a therapist, like nearly every male patient any of my interns
had seen, Pete found himself unable to identify much, if anything, of what he
was feeling.

. . . .

23 · FORGETTING BUT REMEMBERING: BOYHOOD SEXUAL ABUSE

STEPHAN D. GRUBMAN-BLACK

There are the original offenses against the young boy. Whether they involved
exhibitionism, fondling, or penetration, the perpetrator usually acted in a
series of steps that lead to the offense. There was a kind of softening or preparing for the kill, finding a mark, looking for a likely victim. A perpetrator
of sexual abuse is a careful observer, skillfully using conversation, feigned interest, or gifts to gain the trust of the unsuspecting child. Most offenders have
had much practice: those arrested have reported as many as 70 or 80 victims.

As a young boy, I was carefully and slowly seduced by a man in the neighborhood. He ended up becoming friends with my family, but his contacts were
through me first. It's like I brought him home, if you follow.

Well, over a period of months, he worked his thing on me. He was good
company. I learned to trust him. I could go in and out of his house, and since my
parents were out a lot, he was a convenient thing for them too. They never questioned anything about him because he was well respected and he didn't act
"funny."

He was great fun to be with, and I looked forward to him so much. I even stopped seeing some friends because I wanted to be with him. I would run over to his house after school sometimes and he would even get me to do my homework. So he was even considered a good influence over me! Over time though he's kind of testing me, I think, although I didn't think anything at the time. Little secrets between us. A secret handshake. A magic coin. Treats before dinner as long as I would eat my whole dinner at home.

The events preceding the first intimate contact between perpetrator and victim are usually lighthearted. The boy is lured into a situation in which he progressively loses control over himself. This stage has been termed "engaging the victim." We often think of this stage as involving someone outside the child's family, seeking to establish a bond.

After all, he was the adult, and he was so sure of everything. The way he drove, the way he moved, he was really masculine. He brought me farther and farther away from the safety of my parents (with their permission) and I became more dependent on him, for transportation and food on these day trips, so when it happened, I had no choice, no escape hatch.

The male perpetrator may be threatened or challenged by some aspect of the boy; he wants to "straighten him out." Or, he may be attracted to a young boy's vulnerability or sensitivity, yet react to it violently or destructively. If the perpetrator is a female, she too may be motivated by the power issues of the male perpetrator, using her sex to control the young boy.

When I was growing up, I was sickly. Lots of problems with my stomach and bowels, for example, so I was used to my mother taking me to doctors and being in the examining room with me. My father was never with us on those visits, and when I'd get sick in the middle of the night, even when I was 13 or 14, it was she who would come to my room and help clean me up. Sometimes she would even give me a rubdown while she laid in my bed next to me, rubbing my back and shoulders, and I can remember times when my stomach was so sore she had me lay on my back and she would rub my belly. Sometimes I'd get a hard-on, and she would tell me not to worry, it was perfectly natural, and she would hold me and rock me in her arms. She never touched my cock though.

One time I was really hurting, and the pain was in my groin. I was about 15 or 16 at the time. She told me to let her see, and I was really shy, so I said no, but she sat down on the bed next to me, and told me she was my mother, that she loved me, that she had seen me naked before (no matter that it was years and years ago!), and she gradually lowered the blankets to my thighs.

I was really embarrassed but she was so convincing, saying she just wanted to make sure I was all right, that she wanted to see if I was swollen or if the color was different. So I agreed, but when I started to undo my pants she said no because I must be so tired and weak (after all I was in bed still dressed), let her take care of me, and she undid my pants, and slid them down. I can still feel her hands resting on my hips and it was her eyes that really got to me. She was pulling down my shorts and she was kneeling on the bed because she said she had to get them all the way down so she could see everything, and her eyes never left that area.

She said don't worry about having an erection, we would just wait for it to go down, and then she started asking me to show her where it hurt, and telling me to tell her what part and she would touch me all over there saying, "here?" And I couldn't help it. All of a sudden I came and she just said that was okay, it was natural, and she would leave me alone now. But she said she bet I was feeling much better. And I was. And she would ask me how I was feeling a lot since then, and I would always say fine, and she would say, "Are you sure?" She said that my father was too busy to tell about the changes real men go through, but that she as a woman knew too, and she could help me.

And one other time, when she had waited up for me to come home from a date and I was in a really pissy mood because this girl was a real pain, we sat on the sofa and she (my mother) laid on my lap as I told her everything. When we both noticed that I had a hard-on, she patted me and said that was okay because we knew about it and why didn't I go get ready for bed (she knew I slept in my shorts) and she'd fix us something nice to drink.

I was standing in my room in just my shorts when she came in with some Pepsi or something and told me it was okay; it was like I was wearing swim trunks. We sat on my bed and she kept eyeing my crotch, watching me get harder and harder. We were talking, and then she curled up next to me and then leaned against my chest. She admired the way I had grown, and although she never again came in contact with my cock, I felt like she was making love to my body. Then she got up and said good-night.

I was so horny, I shoved my hands inside my shorts and started jerking off. The door swung open, she smiled and said she forgot to take the glasses from our drinks back to the kitchen. Then she smiled again and said good-night. I started trying to avoid her a little although we were always very close.

I started college and her office was nearby, so I would stop over to visit her, and discovered that one of my buddies was spending a lot of time in her office. I found out later she was screwing him. And I thought that's what she wanted to do with me. I've had numerous affairs with married women, all ending after a few rolls in the hay.

The hurt is deep and painful. Many victims lose trust, and in its place come fear and disloyalty.

I avoided team sports because I would never trust anyone. I just figured my team-mates wouldn't protect me. And I was so afraid of being caught, I would want to bolt and not follow the planned play.

Lack of trust may manifest itself in later relationships as a lack of commitment or unfaithfulness. It may occur both as a response by the former victim or reappear in the responses of those around him. He may seek relationships that require loyalty but repeat the offense by disappointing partners. He may seek and find relationships in which he apparently demands complete loyalty or monogamy, but choose partners for whom these expectations are unreasonable or unrealistic.

So often I would feel I was losing some part of me when I would start to get close to someone. It wasn't limited to a sexual thing, either. I just used to feel that if I gave, I wouldn't get back, that people don't reciprocate.

I was the pleaser. It was my job to always make sure that everybody else was happy. I know that this is true of my early abuses. My mother always had to be pleased, so that I was not allowed to do or say anything that upset her. So, I never told her what was happening to me. And the man who was abusing me wanted only for himself to be satisfied. And if I didn't do it right, he'd get upset, like I was really hurting and failing him. And it never seemed to be good enough, but I was so confused I kept trying.

In my work, I still take it very hard when somebody voices displeasure or disappointment. It's easier for me to do just what has to be done, and get out, and that's the way I've been in relationships.

The offenses may have ceased, yet they continued in different forms. The victim represses the abuse, usually because of disbelief, fear, confusion, or pain, so that numbness and amnesia replace recall. The boy still hurts and he hides, trying to avoid those who might hurt again as well as those who might know.

Some parts of me really did remember while other parts forgot. The latter saved me while the formed shaped me in so many inexplicable ways.

Not remembering is different from forgetting. The young boy has little choice other than to forget. The perpetrator orders him to forget and so do adults who just don't want to acknowledge that something is wrong. As more former victims disclose what happened to them, the cycle of self-protectiveness and defensiveness is broken.

When I first began to realize what had happened to me, I remember telling people that I thought that was what had happened, that it all seemed like a dream. Imagine trying to convince adults, when as a child, those are the kinds of impressions and perceptions one has! Those might be the only kinds of feelings one has. As the realities grew, and as an adult I felt more inner strength and support from others, I was better able to discuss details. Still, I was like a reporter, giving the details, with little emotion. I was both remembering and forgetting. How could that have happened to me? Why did it happen? Where was everyone else? And perhaps most important: Was he right in saying and doing those things to me because I took it instead of fighting back and winning? So, second-best, I kept quiet, showing little if any feeling. Yet there were the signs.

People need to know what those signs are so that love, support, understanding, and trust may be applied like salves to the soul.

Inconsistencies in the victim's stories, when they do describe what happened, are usually due to the cycle of remembering and forgetting rather than lying. It is unfair to allow the clever adult mind of the perpetrator/defender to argue against the victim/plaintiff. The perpetrator is trying to make his victims forget while he tries to remember his lies. The victim is trying not to remember the realities of the attack while he tries not to forget that he is a victim of a crime that he does not understand except through the filters of adults.

· · · · · · ·

24 · TO HELL AND BACK: ONE MAN'S RECOVERY

TAV SPARKS

As an addict I have spent time in hell. It is a strange mixture of curse and blessing that for some of us the circumstances of our lives are so dramatic that their mythic nature immediately hits us in the face. But the addict as epic hero does not exactly fill the classic bill. His story is not just about courage, but also about fear. More than being a victory epic, addiction is an odyssey in which the deepest loss reveals the greatest gift.

It is not easy to describe the pure suffering of absolutely unfulfilled desire. Nor is it easy to talk about the freedoms and blessings of recovery. For me, among the greatest gifts has been a new sense of what it means to be a man. Recovery has been about discovering this sense in the healing of old wounds.

My childhood and adolescence were times of fear and insecurity. I have always felt as though I had been washed up on some strange shore or had come from another galaxy. Both my parents were alcoholic, and expression of love came hard for us. I remember the pain of aloneness, the coldness, and a constant sense of impending doom. Somehow I took on the weight of the family's sorrow, and then, like Atlas, the world's as well. Had I been "man enough," I reasoned, maybe I could have saved us all. In my shame I set out to do atonement—alone.

My first drink of alcohol was a spiritual experience because it let me feel part of humanity. Finally, I was a man among men. I could be with a girl, and hold my own in all the ritual contests we males created in order to prove ourselves. Over time, alcohol became my ally, as necessary to me as breath itself.

Through psychedelics, my life perspective shifted profoundly in the Sixties. I began to realize that there was another search that lay not in outside conquests, but in the exploration of my psyche. In inner realms I fought my greatest battles, lost and died, and knew rebirth. Through experiences of real wholeness and compassion, I and my fellow journeyers began to feel that we were actually creating a new reality. Among these insights there were hints that surrender was the key not to ignominy and defeat as the culture insisted, but to a victory for which there were no recognized accolades in our society. This was a golden age of inspiration between the pain of my childhood and the wounds of addiction to come.

My drinking continued to escalate, but now the world of drugs was opening up to me as well. The drama of addiction was not just played out within my psyche; the disease is much more pervasive. Like monsters of myth, it eats up self and world.

As the light of the LSD years faded, I entered the very different universes of cocaine, amphetamines, heroin, morphine, and barbiturates. The sense of unity and compassion that had emerged in the Sixties was lost in obsession and compulsion. I was overwhelmed by the power of want and transformed into one who would stop at nothing to get high. I lived on the riverbank and under bridges, with the insane in psyche wards and, through delirium tremens, I knew real insanity. I felt the paranoia of being watched by narcotics agents and of standing in front of grand juries. Because drugs came first, I became known for breaking promises, and I left a path of shattered friendships behind me. I was ashamed of feeling powerless—of being somehow forced to think, feel, and behave in a totally self-centered way, in stark contradiction to the realizations about self and humanity that had emerged through psychedelics.

In retrospect, I realize there was a logic to my embrace of the drug culture. Part of my early life pain was a sense of failure and shame about being unable to find my place in a world that I felt was dominated by our fathers' dreams of relentless glory. Then, in the upheaval of the Sixties, it was exciting to believe I could forge a new destiny for myself based on new ideals.

Yet in active addiction, I unwittingly played out many of the themes that I had sought to disinherit. I changed the trappings, yet somehow the core patterns remained the same. There was still the old pride of "one-upmanship." When everybody else took one hit, I took two—sometimes three. There was still an attempt at honor and glory. I had a reputation to uphold—the longest hair, prettiest female companion, rock and role cronies. Then there was that deadly obsession—the needle—a masculine mystique that, in a perverse way, embodied a sense of the gladiator, the knight, and the sorcerer.

Embracing the counterculture was an answer for many, but for addicts like myself it offered just one more opportunity to fail. In this brave new world that stood for compassion and connectedness, the helpless craving and self-centeredness of the addict has no place. So once again I was bereft of identity.

This was the stuff of tragedy. I played out the hero with the tragic flaw, the rampant, raving ego. The final chapter to this story is always some kind of death. One leads to the coffin; but by some fate I took the other—ego death. I will never forget what I call my "wasteland experience"—my last binge. Severed from self, God, and humanity, totally powerless to help myself, I was hiding out in an old haunt. After being drunk for two days, I injected PCP for the tenth time that episode. I crawled outside to look at the stars—to feel the old magic of the Sixties. But it was gone. Instead of the heavens opening up, the sky devoured me. I had never been so afraid.

This was the turning point. I know now that I had hit bottom. I went back to my clean and sober friends who, through the years, had always tried to help me. For the first time in a decade, however, something felt different.

My surrender experience was accompanied by no great realizations. I do not know how this surrender happened. It was not caused by anything that I did. My conceptual reality as I knew it was gone. There had been no heroic act of will on my part. All vestige of will had been consumed in the craving. There had been only the experience of absolute powerlessness. Then, in the vacuum of no will and no mind, I was graced with surrender.

It took the profound crisis of the addictive experience, the surrender to powerlessness, to "clear the decks," so to speak, to ultimately destroy any vestige of hope that some old identity might rescue me. This very absence, this void, was the requirement for a new image of self.

In a sense, after "the wasteland experience" I became the focus of myths in collision. From powerlessness and death a new masculinity began to emerge. It took me a few years to see this. But I gradually came to understand that for me the foundation of manhood was a bewildering force that confounded every idea I had held about heroism. It seemed to threaten the old order and contradict the relentless grasping nature I had grown to know—our cultural norm. This power was the mystery of surrender. My recovery depended on it, and, what's more, I knew that it had been a gift.

Thus I began the most intimidating yoga of all—learning to live on planet Earth. No battle with demons I had ever fought on a psychedelic journey can compare with the intensity of my struggle to be fully, simply human—to live one day at a time. I found tremendous help waiting for me in fellowships of recovering addicts who worked hard in putting their lives back together.

Through rigorous inner work, I gradually began to make sense out of some of the old childhood wounds. I came to realize I had lived my whole life in search of a myth to connect my story with the heroic journey of my ancestors. Its hero was an impossibly brave warrior who lived to win, and who saw little honor in defeat. This perspective fueled my addiction, and in the end nearly killed me.

But creating a new image of the masculine is not about rejecting altogether the inheritance of the past. It includes salvaging what is valuable. Courageous questing has proven to be indispensable, but I can also see a place in manhood for honor, duty, and even humility. To these timeless attributes, the surrender experience adds a deeper, more fulfilling sense of the masculine. And I can begin to derive a sense of power in choosing *new* attributes to fight for. These may be the ideals of my ancestors. Yet they can be uniquely mine as well.

For me and many like me, the journey toward the true heroic has been about finding the courage to honor fear, not obliterate it. It has been about the power of the masculine that emerges from the darkest hour of personal destruction. Through surrender there emerges a self of power, which truly lives life as the myths can only sing of it. Among the many apparent contradictions in the surrender metaphor, foremost is the mystery of grace itself. I experience surrender not as something that I accomplish, but something that manifests in emptiness, beyond doing and grasping. It happens not *because* of me, but *in spite* of me. It is a grace because it is a gift.

Surrender has introduced me to a new type of warriorship and new meanings for fear and courage. I invoke courage in my life by honoring and welcoming fully the extent of my fear. Recovery seems to be about facing fear. Every decision to confront the unfaceable—entering therapy, willingly exposing the raw places of my psyche, this is warriorship. I have even begun to celebrate fear. Courage is not about *not* being afraid. It is about welcoming the fact that I fear.

This new warriorship requires that I also reexamine every idea I hold about power. I understand that I have tyrannized others and myself by rampantly wielding personal power in order to be at least *some* kind of man. I can also see how the culture has always fostered these destructive forms of the masculine.

I have encountered other paradoxes in recovery as well. For instance, I have found a strength and wisdom in giving up the need to know, and in surrendering to not knowing. Allowing my self to be defined—not constantly *doing* the defining—results in a very real outpouring of creative power that I could never have wrested from the world through sheer force of ego alone.

Again and again, I champion my own path, even though it may contradict much of what we commonly call masculine. In the wake of the emerging men's movement, when so many are celebrating new definitions of the masculine, I feel the mystery even more. Yet now I can dare *not* to know. I am most brave when I can accept the power that emerges from an experience of powerlessness.

I do not have to rush to some new metaphor to define myself. I can stand still or dance, be shaman or ascetic, father or fool. I can have faith that I am being defined not by giving up my power, but by courageously surrendering to something greater within myself.

My recovery is an unfinished odyssey. In this new poem, I have come to honor the curse that is a blessing. I am grateful for hell as well as heaven, and for deep wounds. Out of death, out of powerlessness and surrender, I have found a new strength, health, and wholeness. I can celebrate the deep masculine that I am discovering, even as the fullness of it still unfolds. There is much I have to learn, but it is the mystery that makes the journey rich. And it is good not to have to know.

· · · · · · ·

25 · THE LOST GENERATION OF JAPANESE MEN

JOHN S. WELTNER

A father, mother, and their 18-year-old son came into the clinic in Kyoto where I was teaching family therapy. The father had been transferred to a job far from home two years before, and only returned now for a visit once a month. His wife temporarily brightened during these visits, but was otherwise depressed. For five years, their son had refused to leave the house. Interested only in the "death world" and ancestor worship, he was silent and uncommunicative except when he fought with his mother. The therapist who came to me for a consultation reported that the son acted somewhat bizarre and seemed lost in his thoughts, as if current reality had no interest for him. Nonetheless, it was the son who finally brought his family into therapy. During the first session, he complained angrily about being the one holding the family together.

This family resembled many other families in post-World-War-II Japan. Traditionally, Japanese marriages have always been arranged, with little expectation of intimacy between husband and wife. The strength of family ties has been carried in alliances along ancestral blood lines. The loyalty of both husband and wife flows to his parents and to their children rather than being centered in a tightly-knit nuclear family. Since the war, ties binding men to their companies have further weakened the connection of fathers to their immediate families.

During the last forty-five years, however, the infusion of Western expectations about marriage and family life among younger generations has created disappointment and bewilderment for both husbands and wives who have no cultural models for functioning together as affectionate partners. Because of these contradictory social patterns—Western-influenced desire for close nuclear families and traditional mores favoring the extended, patriarchal family line—marital therapy is often difficult, an act of faith and courage rather than common sense.

The boy's father had been only four years old when his own father had died in combat during World War II. Now the father concentrated on business and avoided his home, not knowing how to be a father or a husband. Like many Japanese men, he felt suspended, without a clear sense of what his role was, either in his family or in society.

Japanese men I have spoken with all agree that their society has profoundly changed since the war. Men can no longer do or be what their culture traditionally demanded. Militarism and patriarchy have been thoroughly discredited, and centuries of male role models of invulnerability and authority have been swept away, leaving no clear alternative. Many men would like to be more available and involved with their families and in society, but there are no role models to emulate, not even popular male characters on television or in the movies. Men do not know how to act, and feel twice weakened—once for not having seen their own fathers in action; second, because no social consensus still exists about what a man should be.

Together with my Japanese colleagues, I speculate that the boy feels this weakness. In the absence of a strong father, and with his mother depressed, he truly does need to "hold the family together." He feels burdened and overwhelmed; his interest in the spirit world represents his search for strength from his ancestors, specifically from a grandfather even his father never knew. The boy is reaching back to a more secure time, when men, steeped in a tradition centuries old, knew who they were and what was expected of them.

During the first session, the son reproached his father for allowing his father's stepmother to keep the grandfather's ashes instead of burying them in the family gravesite. In a brilliant and simple intervention, the therapist helped the son convince the father to demand some of the ashes for their own gravesite. In the assigned task, father and son were told to get the ashes and take them to the family grave.

Two months after completing the task, during the third therapy session, the son was alert, going out regularly with friends, and planning his return to school. At that time, the father announced to his unsuspecting family that he was considering retiring so that he could come home to live again.

. . . .

26 · MEN SHOULD EMBRACE FEMINISM

CHRIS BRAZIER

"Masculinity" itself is something of a taboo area in our culture. True, it is a culture dominated by men, and we will sound off endlessly about most things under the sun. But, as Simone de Beauvoir once pointed out, men are always the subject rather than the object of the discussion. We never talk about what it is actually like to be a man. Instead we simply react when forced to by the urging of our female partner or a feminist at work. We wait for women to raise the issue and then adjust accordingly. This is why almost all heterosexual men who have thought seriously about masculinity have been obliged to do so by entering a relationship with a feminist—at which point they are doing it for the sake of their own comfort.

This is understandable but it is time we stopped seeing "women's concerns" as being only relevant to us when they smack us in the face. Women have enough trouble dealing with their own problems in a sexist world without having to take all the responsibility for changing me, too. . . .

Back in the 1970s some men concluded . . . that they were just as much victims of their "sex role" as were women. They conceived the idea of "men's liberation," when there can't really be any such thing. What they forgot is that men have power over women and not the reverse. It is men who have constructed a world for their own benefit—and men who must be prepared to relinquish their power by supporting women's rights in the home, the workplace, and society at large.

But at least these men were putting some serious thought into what had made them men. Most men are still light-years away from understanding the issues, let alone from embodying the newly-popular marketing image of "the new man." We could all come up with depressing evidence that we have a long way to go. My own mind goes back to the bar at Johannesburg's Jan Smuts airport. I was joined by a white man keen to engage me in conversation. As most of us will, he chose what he thought would be uncontentious shared ground for his opening comment. He said: "There are some tasty pieces of meat on this flight, aren't there?" What he meant, since you may well be in need of an interpreter, was that he found some of the women sexually attractive.

I should perhaps have answered that I was a vegetarian. I should certainly have done more than splutter apologetically into my orange juice and then pointedly ignore him. But, like most men, I am often weak when it comes to telling other men that their sexism is unacceptable to this one, at least, of their brothers. I've had some successes along the way, too. But somehow it's always easiest to opt for a quiet life and keep your head down than to confront that sexist joke at work, that casual aside about a woman's appearance.

I'm sure you know the pressures I mean. Ever since adolescence, socializing with other men has meant being drawn into this kind of banter. Yet another part of learning to be "a regular guy" in this society is learning the codes of conduct that are acceptable between men, knowing the right prejudiced levers to pull. We joke about straight sex to prove we're healthy red-blooded males who lust after women. We joke about gay sex to prove we're not homosexual—and so scared are we of being thought so that when we're in a public toilet we stand in lines, eyes straight ahead in case that man in the next urinal might think we have an abiding interest in his lower anatomy.

I'd be surprised if there was a single man reading this who is genuinely free of complicity in this kind of sexism. We have to be brave and leap in there to pull up other men on their sexist witticisms and remarks, no matter how much social discomfort this causes us. Taking responsibility for our own sexism and that of other men is a bottom line—but it has positive spin-offs too. By accepting responsibility for other men we are holding out the hope of another kind of communication and relation with them, beyond the backslapping banter. At the moment our male friendships too often subsist on a ritualized level—we rarely expose in them our deeper feelings and anxieties, saving those instead for one or two selected women. But our male friends should be worth more to us than this.

There may be a long way to go, but I think there are still grounds for hope. Men are already experiencing some of the beneficial effects of feminism, whether they realize it or not. They are finding themselves in more equal relationships with strong, independent women. Such relationships may require painful compromise at first but they ultimately provide a mutual understanding undreamed of in the past.

. . . .

27 · FEMINISM HAS LITTLE RELEVANCE FOR MEN

RICHARD HADDAD

I argue that men do not enjoy a life of privilege. Far from it, a look at the life of the average man is a fairly depressing sight. What kind of privilege is it that bestows on men a ten-year-shorter life span than women, and a higher incidence of disease, crime, alcoholism, and drug addiction? What kind of privilege is it that blesses men with a frequently self-destructive need to achieve? What kind of privilege is it that honors a man with the duty to spend a lifetime supporting others, more often than not at an unsatisfying job?

Whether or not we choose to look, the effects of sexism are all around us, in plain sight. What the feminists, in their proper concern for women, have neglected to point to our attention is that for every women who is discouraged from working (by the whole of society, not just its economic or political components) there is a man forced by social convention to work; and for every bored and unfulfilled woman, there is a man burdened with the responsibility that only a primary wage-earner knows, who will die early, in part, from sex-role poisoning. . . .

ANGRY AT WOMEN

. . . I am angry because of the sometimes defensive and sometimes self-righteous denial of most of the women in my life that they had anything at all to do with my conditioning and the reinforcement of my conditioning to think, behave, and react in certain prescribed ways, and that they have bene-fitted as well as suffered by my conditioned reactions.

I am angry because women have been blaming and dumping on men for close to fifteen years now, harping on the privilege and power we theoretically have and have used to exploit them and keep them subservient, forgetting and overlooking that our so-called privileges and powers were foisted on us by social customs that *they also* helped to maintain, and that these same customs have exacted from us an outrageous price for a very questionable male advantage.

I am angry that in the name of eliminating sex-stereotyping, feminism has reinforced some of the most fundamental and devastating stereotypes of all: the man as predator . . . stalking . . . powerful . . . base and insen-sitive . . . exploitive and untrustworthy . . . driven by uncontrollable and animalistic urges; the woman as victim . . . noble . . . pure . . . car-ing . . . selfless . . . loving . . . trusting . . . sensitive . . . suffering . . . used, battered, and reused for man's unspeakable purposes.

I am angry over the hypocrisy of too many women I know—their asser-tion of strength and independence *except when it is convenient* to be weak and dependent; their insistence that I and other men change, but *only* in ways and to a point that will please them; cries for affirmative action in employment but not in the domestic relations court; a thousand press releases from NOW on abortion but "Let's not press the draft issue because that's 'politically unwise.'"

I am angry because of the broken bodies and spirits of good men who spend their lives locked in a death dance, driven by compulsions they do not understand, filled with fear of not meeting the masculine ideal, buffeted by the frequently contradictory expectations of the women whose approval they desperately need. . . .

So the men's movement in which I am involved will have none of the nonsense about oppressed and victimized women; no responsibility for the conditions of women, whatever that condition might be; none of the guilt or the self-loathing that is traditionally used to keep men functioning in harness. . . .

The men's movement is rooted in the male experience, not the female ex-perience or the female perception of the male experience.

It is positive, not negative, on the subject of men, and is supportive of men who dare to break out of self-destructive roles. . . .

The men's movement, however, is most certainly *not feminist*—that would be a contradiction in terms. Feminism will have nothing of the male experience and will not recognize it as valid. It downplays the relative importance of male concerns and insists that women's problems and struggles be given top priority. . . .

We need to listen to each other for the cries of pain and to recognize the fear we all have. We need to approach each other cautiously but steadily, holding out a hand of understanding and trust and support. We need to acknowledge our anger and help each other turn it into a source of energy for positive change. We need to talk with each other openly and stop worrying about how "cool" or knowledgeable we will appear. We need to forget what women will have us be, and to figure out first *what we are* and what *we* want to be and how *we* choose to live our lives, and that—and only that—is what will make for a genuine men's liberation movement.

. . . .

PART 4

THE BODY OF HIS SOUL: PASSION, DESIRE, IMAGINATION, SEXUALITY, AND SPIRIT

Why should I flail about with words, when love has
made the space inside me full of light?

KABIR

And then it was that Hanley, loved, desperate to
possess and be possessed, staring into the green and
loving eyes of the saint, saw that there can be no
possession, there is only desire. He plucked at his
empty skin, and wept.

JOHN L'HEUREUX

INTRODUCTION

. . . .

W*hat does woman want?* Freud asked many decades ago. Let's invert and expand the question: What does *man* want? What does he desire? Hunger for? Dream of? Lust over? Obsess about? Action, *what a man's gotta do*, is widely considered the essence of masculinity. But before the act comes the itch; before the itch, the desire. *Desire!* The very word conjures compulsions, inhibitions, and prohibitions too numerous to name, forever pressing their claims on our attention, comprising in their very essence the body of the masculine soul.

It's not that life before puberty is uncomplicated; it only seems that way when puberty's peculiar complications make the scene. "Adolescence is the birth of the body hairs," writes legendary artist Salvador Dali, who by plucking one of his first pubic hairs, thus opposing the onslaught of puberty, created for himself a unique rite of passage into manhood. The narrator in David Cale's essay ("So This Must Be What the Fuss Is All About") chanced upon sexual awareness through a puberty rite of his own, involving eggs—raw eggs—lots of them. Milwaukee poet Antler's awakening takes the form of an unambiguous demand: "Show me anything that's not an ejaculation!"

California writer David Goff ("In Praise of Masturbation") seeks to separate the perennially taboo subject from "connotations of dirtiness, self-absorption, and empty longing." Prize-winning author Norman Mailer ("Against Masturbation") declares himself against the practice, fearing that masturbators end up unable "to fight the good fight."

The next piece is an exchange of letters between Greg (an anonymous author) and his parents about the fact that he is gay. It reveals a degree of family acceptance that most gay men only dream about.

D. H. Lawrence, long an opponent of English censors for daring to ban writings as pornographic, is always ready for a good fight. In "Rivers Flowing On," Lawrence chides a young man's dismissal of sexual desire and then offers a characteristically lyrical praise of the possibilities for union between man and woman.

Oregon writer David Koteen ("The Lucy Syndrome") gives a wonderfully honest account of playing the edge between devotion and obsession in his passionate affair with "Lucy . . . You beautiful creature!" In "Ditching the Bewitching Myth," British Columbia writer and teacher Robert Augustus Masters takes men to task for assuming that they are "bewitched" by women when, he says, we're really under the spell of our own narcissistic greed to be pleasured.

L.A. Weekly columnist Michael Ventura, in "Coming," excerpted from his book *Shadow Dancing in the USA*, insists that if the new dialogue about masculinity is to have any social force, "it will have to have at its core a discussion of male sexuality." Such a dialogue must attend to the religious dimension of the subject, specifically the primordial image of *phallos*, writes Jungian analyst Eugene Monick, in a fine essay from his book *Phallos: Sacred Image of the Masculine.*

We close with "The Drunkards," a lively invocation to "lovers, singing from the garden, the ones with/brilliant eyes," by the ecstatic thirteenth-century Sufi poet Rumi.

· · · · · · ·

28 · THE FIRST HAIR OF MANHOOD

SALVADOR DALI

Adolescence is the birth of the body hairs. In my case this phenomenon seemed to occur all at once, one summer morning, on the Bay of Rosas. I had been swimming naked with some other children, and I was drying myself in the sun. Suddenly, on looking at my body with my habitual narcissistic complacency, I saw some hairs unevenly covering the very white and delicate skin of my pubic parts. These hairs were very slender and widely scattered, though they had grown to their full length, and they rose in a straight line toward my navel. One of these, which was much longer than the rest, had grown on the very edge of my navel.

I took this hair between my thumb and forefinger and tried to pull it out. It resisted, painfully. I pulled harder and, when I at last succeeded, I was able to contemplate and to marvel at the length of my hair.

How had it been able to grow without my realizing it on my adored body, so often observed that it seemed as though it could never hide any secret from me?

A sweet and imperceptible feeling of jealousy began to bud all around that hair. I looked at it against the sky . . . brought it close to the rays of the sun; it then appeared as if gilded, edged with all the colors, just as when, half shutting my eyelids, I saw multitudes of rainbows from between the hairs of my gleaming eyelashes.

· · · · · · ·

29 · THIS MUST BE
WHAT THE FUSS IS ALL ABOUT

DAVID CALE

When I was a kid. When no one was in the house. I would go over to the cupboard under the stairs and take out the vacuum cleaner. Plus all the attachments. I'd plug the vacuum cleaner into the wall. Attach the long metal tube to it. The one you add all the attachments to. Then I'd place the tube's hole against my neck. Switch the vacuum cleaner on with my foot. Hold the tube so it sucked my neck for about ten minutes. Then I'd change sides and repeat the whole operation. Then I would put the vacuum cleaner and the attachments back under the stairs. Go over to the mirror. And sure enough I'd have hickeys. Or lovebites as we used to call them. Then I would go out and meet my friends and pretend nothing had happened. Pretty soon they'd notice the marks on my neck and they'd say, "He's had sex again! How does he do it? What's his secret?" And I'd give them a knowing look and not say anything.

Then we'd go and look at the *H & E* magazines. *H & E* was this magazine specially for nudists. The H & E part stood for Health and Efficiency. It was full of pictures of nude families playing volleyball. In special camps where people who didn't want to wear clothes could go and just take them off.

There'd be a sentence under each photograph: "Here's Christopher. Age 6. Nude. Playing gin rummy with his Aunt Trixie. Age 47. Two people enjoying their nudity." Nude aunts. Nude uncles. Nude nephews. Nude nieces. All these nude grandmothers sitting round campfires eating chickens.

You didn't have to be a certain age to buy *H & E* because it was officially a health magazine. Anyone could buy it. The only trouble was most of the people in *H & E* were really overweight. They'd have big bellies that would hang low, so you couldn't really see anything.

Sometimes Kevin White would come and look at the *H & E*'s. Kevin White lived up the street. He was always trying to get me to do things. After a lot of persuasion Kevin convinced me that if I showed him mine he would show me his. This all happened behind the shed. Well it was a big success. So we started exposing ourselves to each other on a regular basis. Then I don't know what happened. It must have started to be too much for him 'cause after a while Kevin started playing hard to get. That ended that.

Then one day I was riding my bike in the countryside. I saw this package in a ditch. I jumped down and pulled it open. It was full of magazines. Nude magazines. Real nude magazines. Not the *H & E* kind. All the magazines had their covers torn off. The women in the pictures looked really mean. Most of them had their tongues sticking out. There was a page where readers could send in photos of their wives and the magazine would print them. It was really peculiar. All the wives were wearing boots and holding bull whips. There was another section called "Erotic Tips: What You Can Do with Eggs."

It had instructions:

Lie in an empty bath.
Take a dozen raw eggs.
Crack the eggs over your body.
Then rub them in.
—A delightful erotic experience.

Suddenly this car started coming toward me. I was convinced it was the people who owned the magazines coming to get them back. Panic set in. I got back on my bike and sped off.

When I got home no one was in. I couldn't get my mind off the eggs. So I went to the refrigerator to see if we had any. We did. There were three dozen. At first I thought, "How many eggs can I take without anyone noticing that any are gone?" Then I must have forgotten about that because I ended up taking all of them up to the bathroom. I took off all my clothes and climbed into the empty bath. It was really cold against my back. Took a long time getting used to it. Then I started cracking the eggs over my body. They looked awful. The yolks were breaking and sliding off me. But nothing was happening. No delightful erotic experience. So I started in on the second carton. Then the third. By this point I was about six inches deep in eggs. Every time I moved a wave of eggs would wash up over my chest.

I was rubbing them in when something started to happen. So I kept rubbing them in. The eggs were splashing everywhere. Sloshing over the side of the bath. There were eggs up the wall. I got egg in my eye. But something was happening. Maybe I was having it. A delightful erotic experience. There were eggs everywhere. I didn't care.

Something was happening.
Something was definitely happening.
Something was happening.
Something was definitely happening.
Something was happening.
Something was definitely happening.
Then I realized,
THIS MUST BE WHAT ALL THE FUSS IS ABOUT!

· · · · · · ·

30 · EJACULATION

ANTLER

Every Universe is an ejaculation!
Every sun is an ejaculation!
Every earth is an ejaculation!
Every being is an ejaculation!
Women ejaculate babies!
Girls ejaculate breasts!
Boys are ejaculations that ejaculate!
Men ejaculate six million ejaculations per orgasm!
Everyone alive ejaculates their corpse!
Everything we eat is an ejaculation!
Fruit and vegetables are ejaculations!
Trees are ejaculations—they burst up and collapse
    in a speeded-up movie of time!
Every leaf is an ejaculation!
The earth ejaculates wildflowers every spring!
The sea is a continual ejaculation!
Look at the youth surfboarding the orgasms!
Every cloud is an ejaculation!
Every lightning is an ejaculation!
Every drop of rain or snow is an ejaculation!
Every sunrise is an ejaculation!
Every waterfall is an ejaculation!
Every meteor is an ejaculation!
Every mountain is an ejaculation!
Every grain of sand is an ejaculation!
Every second that passes is an ejaculation!
This Universe has been ejaculating 100 billion years!
Scientists listen by radio telescope
    to the Big Bang's orgasmcry!
Every word spurts from our mouth!
Every book, symphony, statue, painting, film,
    house, car, plane, ship, train
    ejaculates from some brain!
Every exclamation point is an ejaculation!
Every inhalation and exhalation
    is an ejaculation!

Every shit is an ejaculation!
Every spaceship is an ejaculation!
Every nation is an ejaculation!
Every religion is an ejaculation!
Every Bible is an ejaculation!
Every Savior is an ejaculation!
I calculate ejaculate ululate through All!
Show me anything that's not an ejaculation!

. . . .

31 · IN PRAISE OF MASTURBATION

DAVID GOFF

One afternoon in early spring two years ago, I touched myself in a new way. Looking back on that afternoon I am now amused to realize that despite having masturbated since I was five or six years of age this was like the very first time. Through the magically transformative power of emotional crisis I had the opportunity to rediscover and repossess my self through the simple act of making love to, and pleasing, myself. This simple hour I spent in bed exploring my own passionate longing, erogenous zones, and expanding sensitivity to love, changed my love life totally.

What I experienced that day, and in the months that followed, was a unique and powerful sense of love and caring for and from "something" in myself that fulfilled and healed me. After two years of examining this ongoing intra-psychic, erotic, love affair, I have come to believe that masturbation contains the potential for something of greater significance to well-being than simple sexual release. I believe that autoerotic love provides an opportunity for the inner feminine and masculine to merge in an act of harmony that diminishes the emotional charge associated with projecting the Beloved upon men and women in our external lives. This creates a freer internal atmosphere from which to express ourselves and engage others. I want to share with you how this process came about in me, and why I think it meaningful, and replicable, for those who might be seeking greater fulfillment in their relationships and love lives.

I started "playing with myself" consciously around the age of six. By eight years of age it became part of morning and evening rituals. Somehow, I had already developed the good sense to keep this delicious activity to myself.

I found great solace in the warm tickling sensations that both excited and re-laxed me, and assured me that wherever I was, I always had a secret friend with whom I could play. By the time my mother and the church began their urgent warnings about the dangers and corruption of self abuse, I was already addicted to myself. They never succeeded in getting me to abandon my first lover. But, they did succeed in making me feel guilty, dirty, and very paranoid that anyone (especially my mother) should find out about my "disgusting" habit. The pleasure, however, got ever so slightly more delicious.

I have masturbated more or less regularly ever since those early years. Touching myself provided a necessary pressure release valve that helped me survive adolescence. Later it got me through times of loneliness and comple-mented the times of plenty in my life. The guilt remained, but declined sig-nificantly after I darted out from the heavy-handed wing of the church. I re-member one priest telling me in confessional that no woman would ever want to marry me if I continued.

In my early adulthood I kept my autoerotic activity a closely guarded secret. As I became capable of deeper and more intimate relationships with women I found that they were often open-minded about masturbation as a phenomenon, but none too pleased to know that I practiced it despite the quality of our relationship. My observation was that it was cool to acknowl-edge that we "normal" people did it, as long as there was no discussion about the hows, whys, and the frequency. It seemed that what one did with one's self was much more private and taboo than what one did with others. I have since come to wonder why in a sexually liberated age, masturbation, now consid-ered a normal behavior, still carries the stigma of being associated with un-satisfied passion, sexual insatiability, and self-absorption?

Having reflected on that question for some time, it occurred to me that masturbating always provided the physical release from sexual frustration that I wanted, but it frequently left me feeling empty and lonely. This feeling of emptiness seemed inherent in the experience and resulted in my feeling less than complete. This feeling of being incomplete translated into unwhole-someness, and contributed directly to my unwillingness to openly and freely discuss masturbation and its attendant rituals. As a man acknowledging my feelings of being less than whole remains a difficult task. Despite all that I know about my self, admitting that I am missing something still seemingly threatens the self-image that permits me to function as a man in the world.

I am reluctant to generalize from my own early experiences a widely-held male belief system around masturbation. In the last two years, male friends willing to discuss their experiences with masturbation have reiterated my experience. I have no doubt the popular euphemisms, "jerking off" and "whacking off" are indicative of attitudes that are widespread. There is an aura of derision and inauthenticity surrounding masculine self-love. Refer-ences to people as "jerk-offs" or to experiences of being "stroked" by untrustworthy neighbors or manipulative business associates are consistent with such attitudes. The hand motions associated with masturbation occasionally crop up as a means of putdown, implying someone is inferior. I believe that for men, masturbating, something we almost all do, still too frequently is experienced as a failure of our manhood, and as a testimony to our unwholesome sexuality.

My experience with women suggests that their attitudes are similar but perhaps less virulent. The women's movement, and the relatively new (last twenty years) demand for sexual satisfaction and orgasmic fulfillment has tended to bring women into a more endearing relationship with their bodies. Women are encouraged by sex therapists and popular women's magazines to touch themselves, to get to know their bodies, and their erogenous zones. For many women the road to becoming orgasmic includes a great deal of self-love. Still, by and large, the women with whom I have discussed masturbation admit to infrequent practice and solely as a means of release.

So it is with some wonder that I look back on my experience two years ago, and marvel at the circumstances that constellated a whole new approach to, and deeper respect for, self-loving. I was two months into a very painful separation from my wife. I was experiencing agonizing feelings of being rejected and abandoned. Our twelve-year relationship had totally capsized. Emotionally, I was deeply wounded and enduring incredible doubt about my self. Additionally, for the first time in my life I was suffering from prostitus, an inflammation of the prostate gland that can result in painfully swollen testicles. The urologist I consulted suggested regular intercourse as the best available treatment for what was essentially a stress-related ailment. Sexual intimacy with another was impossible. The pain and discomfort could only be relieved by regular masturbation. The only sexual fantasies I had were about my wife and these were emotionally painful. Arousal itself was intensely painful physically. I was faced with an incredible dilemma. I had to masturbate, but I could not do so, as I always had. My initial attempts were so painful and difficult that I simply could not continue. I was very unhappy.

I persevered through those difficult days thanks to the support of some loving and nurturing men friends, and a real determination to accept and be transformed by this experience. Without my wife to love, I soon wisely chose to give that love to myself and to explore new ways of loving my self. A man friend told me of a feminist adage he had heard. "A woman should become the man she wants to marry." I decided that made sense for me as a man, and that I could become the woman I wanted to love. The desire to heal myself physically and emotionally, combined with the stimulus of thinking about, and experiencing the feminine I embodied, culminated in my creating a whole new masturbatory ritual, organized more around my need to love and be loved than around sexual release.

At last I arrived, that spring afternoon, in my bed with time to be with myself. I created an environment rich with textures, music, incense, and massage oil that would stimulate and please the one I chose to be with. Very slowly I began to touch and explore my body, as if I were the woman I had longed for, loved, and now had the opportunity to experience and express those feelings with. With the excitement of discovery I ventured into my erogenous zones and found feelings and sensations that were sometimes familiar and sometimes new. I became quickly aroused and anxious. It was painful, but instead of driving myself over the threshold of orgasm, I slowed my breathing and pace and reexplored my body, connecting all of myself with the excitement I felt. For nearly an hour I repeated this drama of approaching release and retreating. My body sang to me in ways that I had known only in my most incredible moments with a lover. As I let myself slip over that threshold I was released into a full-bodied orgasm that washed away all my fears of lost and unrecoverable love. In the afterglow I knew myself as well-loved and as complete as I had ever felt.

With this experience I noticed that I felt loved as if I had been with my beloved. I found that I was a lot less obsessive in thinking about my wife. I needed to masturbate less frequently as time went along because my physical condition improved. I got greater satisfaction out of the times I did touch myself. And, surprisingly, I needed to put less energy into creating a fantasy to catalyze my excitement. The care-full touching and loving attention I gave my self seemed quite enough.

This experience of self-love seems to encapsulate the real and virtually undiscussed potential that masturbation carries for each of us. I do not believe masturbation must remain an experience needlessly encumbered by connotations of dirtiness, self-absorption, and empty longing. I believe my experience calls into question the attitudes and rituals that we men perpetuate in our self-love. What do our goal-oriented and abbreviated autoerotic rituals say about our relationships with our own bodies, our internal lovers? And how do we play these attitudes out in our relationships? I believe the quality of masturbatory rituals is indicative of the love we hold for ourselves.

There is much talk these days about the importance of our inner relationship between our masculine and feminine sides. Much has been written about how our healthy development depends upon the success of this inner merging. Elaborate theories about this inner courtship and its impact upon our relationships in the world have emerged from psychotherapists and spiritual teachers alike. I believe conscious masturbatory rituals that align the erotic power of our instinctual sexuality with a desire to explore, know, and love our total being can help increase our well-being and self-fulfillment. By focusing a greater degree of regard upon our intra-psychic opposite we access and reinforce communication of the most healing, nurturing, and intimate sort.

The equation of love that seems to govern and regulate our capacities for unconditional relatedness remains "Love Thy Neighbor as Thyself." A conscious, passionate, and full-bodied experience of self-love then becomes an affirmation of love for all. The quality of relatedness within is reflected without. The richness of my internal marriage enlarges the spectrum of experiences and emotions I can embrace in my relationships with others. I am much more capable of loving and supporting the emergence of masculine and feminine attributes in others.

In one sense it seems almost trite to say that masturbation itself is self-love. We see it unfold unself-consciously in children and then it goes underground. When it reemerges in adulthood it is understood as normal and quasi-acceptable but is framed in mechanistic terms of providing release of pent-up instinctual energy. And, it is precisely this reason that the gift we give ourselves sexually remains so unsatisfying. It fulfills our physical criteria for satisfaction but usually ignores the psychospiritual instinctive urge to merge. When I followed that instinctive urge to merge it led me to internalizing an I-Thou relationship with my beloved. What had been intuited and understood now became dynamic and soul-satisfyingly real. Masturbation became procreative. What is born of this intra-psychic coupling? Love has its own chemistry in each of us. My guess is that when it takes, what emerges is a deeply individuated and authentic manifestation of our truest sexual identity. I offer that possibility as incentive enough for considering and recreating masturbation and its attendant rituals.

· · · · · · ·

32 · AGAINST MASTURBATION

NORMAN MAILER

Q. Do you think you're something of a puritan when it comes to masturbation?

A. I think masturbation is bad.

Q. In relation to heterosexual fulfillment?

A. In relation to everything—orgasm, heterosexuality, to style, to stance, to be able to fight the good fight. I think masturbation cripples people. It doesn't cripple them altogether, but it turns them askew, it sets up a bad and often enduring tension. I mean has anyone ever studied the correlation between cigarette smoking and masturbation? Anybody who spends his adolescence masturbating generally enters his young manhood with no sense of being a man. The answer—I don't know what the answer is—sex for adolescents may be the answer, it may not. I really don't know.

. . . .

33 · ON COMING OUT

GREG AND HIS PARENTS

Dear Greg,

I have been thinking a lot of you lately and have some thoughts that I feel must be said. So I will try to put them in this letter.

We have thought for some time now that you were a homosexual. That you have decided to make a definite choice for your lifestyle. That, in itself is no big problem for us. But we do feel it has put a strain on our relationship, sort of an uncomfortable feeling. Probably because you did not know what we would think? How would we accept this? Well you are not a parent. "Parent Love" is a strong and mysterious thing. But it can become weakened if it isn't nurtured once in a while. So this is the point of this letter, to revitalize our feelings.

Now some thoughts:

1st—It seems a shame you felt you had to move thousands of miles away, but we understand. It gave you a feeling of the space you needed and you were protecting us in a way. Besides, for generations, kids have been up and going off and leaving home for adventure or seeking a new life, fortunes, etc. We think it's great how well you have done, and we are very proud of you.

2nd—It is good to know you have come to like yourself more, and feel right about yourself. We can only believe you will think clearly and live a good life.

3rd—Now as for complete happiness . . . 24 hours worth . . . day after day. This is not a reality. This we will all never have. You sound pretty happy to me, except when you cried at Christmas it made me feel sad and I cried too. But that is always good for us all, once in awhile. It shows our humanness. Christmas can be a very blue time for many people. It has been for me for many years. We have been blessed with many happy times. You are blessed with a wonderful sister. So be good to her, for she is your family, after we are gone.

4th—I hope you find someone to share your life with for that can be a rich experience for anyone. Uncle Jack had Carl. Carl was a very kind, gentle and especially nice person. I saw Gordon last week at McDonalds and we chatted awhile. He said he thought he would head back to California soon. Well now you probably will not like this part—but I must be honest yet be delicate. I feel at this time, for you and Gordon to be together would not be the best thing. I can't say why, it's just a gut feeling. Of course it's none of my business. It's your life and you're old enough to make your own decisions.

I hope this letter will help to make us all feel better and help you to realize that we are trying to understand. I would be fooling us all if I did not say it isn't easy for us. But we are all separate and individual human beings unto ourselves. We are all different in God's creation of us. And the bottom line in the strange scheme of things is that we love one another. Life is not easy—so be happy with the life you have. (Hey that ain't half bad!!!) Get it laminated!!!

Love Always,
Mom & Dad

From Greg, age 32, California

Dear Mom and Dad (and Nancy too),

All I can say is a heartfelt thanks. Thanks for caring and trying to understand. Thanks for having the courage to bring things out in the open and for lifting a burden off my back. And thanks especially for now allowing us to become closer.

I can understand your probable concern and confusion. It's not hard to imagine with all the misunderstanding and myths that are perpetrated by a society that fosters conformity instead of appreciating diversity.

I'm sure you are full of questions, so I'll try to anticipate some of them and attempt to answer them here.

Yes, I am Gay. "Gay" is a word we like to use to describe our different lifestyle. The word "homosexual" is more appropriately used as an adjective to describe some *thing* and not a *person*. Besides, it puts too much emphasis on sex and says little of feelings and a way of "being."

To me, Gay means an ability to fully love, in both an emotional and sexual capacity, someone of my own gender. I'm very proud and unashamed to be Gay. I consider it a special gift that I'm a little bit different than most. I relish being able to see things in a different light and not being bound by traditional views of how life should be. I enjoy being able to cut my own path and determine what's best for me. I enjoy the sense of "community" with my Gay friends; the supportive consolation that this "family" provides in a world that can sometimes feel hostile. And finally, I cherish being a stronger individual, who, in the face of great pressure to the contrary, has made up his mind to be who I am.

I have wanted to tell you for some time now, particularly since I have become more comfortable and proud of myself. I have felt for awhile that hiding this aspect of myself could imply that I think it's wrong or bad to be Gay, and this is certainly not the case. But I shied away from confronting you because I did not know how you would take the news. I didn't know if you would understand that I really am the same person you've known all my life—that the disclosure can only improve our communication and relationship. But as you've said, "parental love" is a strong and mysterious power that I probably underestimated.

I've always had a fairly close relationship with Nancy, and I wanted to be totally honest with her, so with my ever-increasing self-respect I "came out" to her last summer during your visit to California. She handled it wonderfully, thanking me for having the courage to confide in her what she had already half-suspected for awhile anyway. Although it wasn't in one of the most appropriate of settings (we were in a Burger King parking lot), the sudden freedom and closeness I felt when we embraced and expressed our love is something I will always remember. The same feeling occurred when I read your letter.

Probably the first questions a non-Gay person has are to the effect, "When did you become Gay?" "Why are you Gay (what 'caused' it)?" And "When did you realize you were Gay?" They are really quite different questions. First, the "when" and the "why."

I don't know when I *became* Gay. I think that, at birth, there is a certain disposition toward being Gay (or assertive or passive or introverted or extroverted or any number of other qualities or characteristics). I believe being Gay is just a natural phenomenon of normal variation. A certain percentage (estimated at 10% nationwide) will be Gay just like a certain percentage of people will be tall.

There are probably influencing factors in very early childhood, but in such a complex world, with its myriad influences, one would be hard-pressed to identify a "cause." Nor does it matter much unless one believes that Gay means inferior. Because the "cause" is indeterminable, you are not entitled to feel guilty ("What did we do wrong?"). If it were attributed to child rearing, then why do children raised in a household with a Gay parent and his/her lover invariably turn out to be non-Gay?

As to when I *realized* I was Gay, this was really an ongoing gradual process. As far back as I can remember, I have always felt I was a little different—that I was attracted to other males. I can remember certain "crushes" I had on guys while I was in grade, and later high school. I went through all the usual denials—"I'm not one of those 'queer' people"—"I'll grow out of it," etc.

When I moved to University Park to attend Penn State, I suddenly began to really think and question things. It was in my junior year that I finally "came out" to myself. A lot of people go through a great deal of trauma at this point. After they can no longer deny their feelings, they begin to see themselves as "bad." Certainly society does not present any "good" Gay role models to emulate. Fortunately, I skipped over this phase and considered my Gayness matter-of-factly. "So I'm Gay . . . it doesn't have to be a limiting thing . . . I'll make the best of my life," etc. I've been growing ever since and am now quite comfortable with who I am and very happy with the way things turned out. I wouldn't want it any other way.

Almost all Gay people will report similar experiences of "knowing" quite early in life—that they were not recruited (unlike the myths spouted by the 'Moral?' Majority along with their "fire Gay teachers or who ever else we don't like" campaigns).

In your letter you mentioned my move to California. It really has been one of the best decisions I've made. Not only are the job opportunities in my career much better, but it has had a positive effect on my individual growth (not to mention my tan too!). In addition to the generally more tolerant society, the Gay people here are more self-liberated and feel good about themselves.

I didn't know too much about Gay life before I moved. At that point I thought, except for Gordon and I, that there weren't other people (i.e., "nice" people) that were Gay. Society leaves one with the impression that Gay people are unhappy, immoral perverts and freaks. After all, that's all the media usually shows—the effeminate men, a guy in drag, or the 'butch' lesbian. I wouldn't identify with that. Where were the normal ones—the Gays that work normal jobs and live respectable lives? I got my answer when I moved.

After stopping at Jack's, everything was brought out in the open and I began to see that there were plenty of "nice" Gay people. In fact, I was shocked by the numbers. We went to a gay disco, and instead of the 10 old men I expected to find, to my surprise there were over 300 mostly young people—all having a terrific time. And that was only one place in one city.

A real eye-opener occurred this year when I attended the L.A. Gay Freedom Day Parade. Similar parades are held annually in major cities across the country in June. As far as I could see, up and down the street (it was packed) were one hundred thousand Gay brothers and sisters along with our supporters. I was especially impressed by the local chapter of the national organization called Parents and Friends of Gays. They held up signs that read "We love our Gay sons and daughters." It's nice not to feel alone.

Let's see . . . I've covered how I feel about being Gay, the Whats, Whys, and Whens, and my "coming out" experiences . . . What's next? Ah, about my roommate. Jon is not gay. He knew I was before we moved in. He and his girlfriend are very supportive and occasionally go to Gay discos and restaurants with me and my friends. We all get along great.

In your letter you mentioned crying at Christmas. I was a little keyed-up because I had just returned from a wonderful Christmas celebration at my friend's home. His mother and brother and several guys and their families were there. We all exchanged gifts together. Everything was out in the open. One mother remarked how wonderful it was to spend Christmas with these nice boys. Even a 70-year-old grandmother was there telling her grandson, while he was opening his gift, that she really wanted to get him a 'husband' for Christmas but didn't know what size to get! When I talked to you after opening those nice gifts, I was a little sad that I couldn't be myself with my family. Now I can.

I haven't said too much about Gordon. I guess you pretty well figured out that we were lovers. It was a strong love, as deep, caring, and meaningful as any others', that we shared for almost two years. It was a valuable experience and would still be ongoing were it not for changes (growth) that occurred to both of us and my desire to meet more people and experience a richer life.

Well, that about leads us up to today. After Gordon and I parted ways, I began to meet a lot of people and today have a number of really good friends. We do a lot of socializing—dinner parties, get-togethers, theatre, etc. I have been dating a guy, Michael, for the past six months and things are going really good. Michael has introduced me to some very nice successful and influential professional people.

. Well, I suppose that about covers it—my whole (hidden) life's story in these few pages. We have a lot of catching up to do. I've tried to convey a sense of what it has been like all these years that we had trouble relating to one another. Hopefully, with your support, that is all behind us now. I'm not about to pretend that there won't be uncomfortable times or that this letter answers all your questions. However, our new openness will surely help eliminate these.

I've enclosed a copy of the book *Loving Someone Gay* that I hope you all will take the time to read. Even though there are specific sections written to parents and brothers/sisters of Gays, I hope you'll read it from the beginning because it describes the subjective experience of growing up and being Gay better than I can.

In summary, again I say thanks for your understanding. I know parts of this letter may have tended to run on (that's what happens when it's composed over several days), but the first two pages really say it all.

I love you all,
Greg

· · · · · · ·

34 · RIVERS FLOWING ON

D. H. L A W R E N C E

A young man said to me the other day, rather sneeringly, "I'm afraid I can't believe in the regeneration of England by sex." I said to him, "I'm sure you can't." He was trying to inform me that he was above such trash as sex, and such commonplace as women. He was the usual vitally below par, hollow, and egoistic young man, infinitely wrapped up in himself, like a sort of mummy that will crumble if unwrapped.

And what is sex, after all, but the symbol of the relationship of man to woman, woman to man? And the relation of man to woman is wide as all life. It consists in infinite different flows between the two beings, different, even apparently contrary. Chastity is part of the flow between man and woman, as is physical passion. And beyond these, an infinite range of subtle communication which we know nothing about. I should say that the relation between any two decently married people changes profoundly every few years, often without their knowing anything about it; though every change causes pain, even if it brings a certain joy. The long course of marriage is a long event of perpetual change, in which a man and a woman mutually build up their souls and make themselves whole. It is like rivers flowing on, through new country, always unknown.

. . . .

35 · THE LUCY SYNDROME

DAVID KOTEEN

Time, a pallid fiction; a courteous sycophant come to prate of future reward. And yet, the only vibrant thread visible throughout the entire tapestry. Lucy. A cousin of one of my college professors; he drove her over to the house we (four others and I) rented. Everyone else left for the dance and I was waiting on the third floor in our common room. Jerry, our pet squirrel monkey, sat on the window ledge eating peanuts, throwing the shells at whoever walked by, or nobody. The kindly prof brought her up the wobbly fire escape, our habitual ingress. Lucy Olinsen: rosy-haired, blue of eye, straight nose, round cheeks, beautiful smile. Honestly feminine. The apparition of my choice. She walked like a duck. Whatever my shortcomings were, she forgave them. We drank something for a while, the three of us. Jerry got drunk, tried to jump to the lampshade, and fell to the floor. Lucy laughed and the monkey bit her thumb, which caused a few drops to come down her cheeks. I was immediately in love. The way her hair curled around her Scandinavian neck, the fullness of her nineteen–odd years in hips and breasts, the way her cotton skirt clung to her thighs. Young and hot and exceedingly loose to begin with, how was I to know that this was the beginning of an inconspicuous sequence that was to follow me like a tail of lead? A little alcohol and a lot of youth; all I could feel was this intense vortex, effluxing from Lucy's woman center, sucking me to where I wanted to go. And, she was there the whole time. We were dancing and I fell back on the couch. Happenstance. Abruptly, her goodness came tumbling after, duck legs and all. With her rump in the air our friendly monkey seized his chance, and leaped on it, chattering all the while, sniffing and scratching at her undergarments. Then in counterpoint to the previous movements came a taut whisper: "When I was seventeen I got raped, and pregnant; and I wanted to have the baby. I was rejected by my parents who made me give it up for adoption. (Jerry ejaculated.) My friends condemned me. (Now a rain of tears were falling on my face.) So, please understand this; you're wonderful, but I can't let you come inside of me. I'm too afraid!"

Later, after graduation, I moved to New York, Lower East Side of Manhattan; very cheap apartment—sixty dollars a month. I lived with Robert, one of my college roommates, whose sister resided in Brooklyn. He was very Jewish, and not surprisingly, so was the sister: Lucy Hemmen. Also very uptight. Slender, angular with high cheekbones, light brown eyes, cropped red hair. The two of them had a long-standing flirtation going—touching, innuendos, lots of tongue-on-the-lips action. He told me that all her experiences with men were cut short and unfulfilling. With a Ph.D. in English literature, she was a recluse, eking out dollars proofreading for *Reader's Digest*. She was contracted and in permanent hibernation. Immaculate two rooms, blue and gray. Of course, my heart went out to her. When you're the way I was—three months of rent in the bank, no responsibilities except to give the day everything you've got, floating and flowing, back to the wind, sails billowed with tasting and touching and seeing, alive with give-and-take, skimming the cream and licking my fingers, always higher and higher—no thought entered of why I was interested in this cold woman. Robert was very jealous of his relationship with Lucy, but one weekend while he was gone, around eleven at night, I wandered over to Brooklyn, saw the light on, rang the buzzer, and got a reticent invitation up. She knew why I was there, and greeted me as warmly as she could (like the string beans do when you open the freezer). Same tight and trim outfit; not that I expected a negligee or something. Coffee, she offered, at 11:30. Somewhere down in my subconscious cellar, behind the aging red wines, there was knowledge that before me stood a debt to be paid. Preferable would be passionate frolicking on the kitchen floor. Un-uh. Strictly business. So when she went to the toilet, I raced quietly around her cupboard like a mongoose, finally uncovering some scotch and brandy. Took a long draught from each bottle, returned the scotch and asked her through the door if I could have a drop of brandy. She would sip a little too. At last she led me at 2 A.M. to her bed where "I made love to her." Only due to the double Taurus in my astrological chart was I able to arouse enough emotion for both of us. About an hour trudged by, guilty and sober. I asked her did she feel all right? Could I get anything for her? She invited me to sleep on the couch.

So, Hell has many vestibules. Teacups of flaming brimstone can be a relatively potable beverage. The couch was comfortable; but listening to Lucy's wide-eyed pathetic thoughts, cacophonically ticking with the kitchen clock, left me empty as an abandoned tortoise shell. And not hungry. "Would you like to go out for breakfast?" I asked, several hours later. Nothing like a hot pastrami sandwich when your intestines are knotted up, and nausea has backed up your esophagus to the base of your throat. Maybe there'll be some flaming brimstone tea?

When I bumped into Lucy Olinsen in the Glass Department of Macy's, it was north and south poles of two magnets approaching each other. It was as if we had gone to sleep that night and were just awaking, still in embrace. My hands were on her buttocks and her legs were spreading, only restrained by the tightness of her skirt and social propriety. Waiting for 5 o'clock, I walked through the muddy Winter city in shirtsleeves. Snow-mush around my sneakers. We drank Spanish wine on the subway downtown. Then slaloming through the overflowing cans of trash in front of the Ninth Street apartment building, rose up the stairs on passionate vapors. Avoided the many who frequented our small flat, gathered cozily around the electric stove oven. Did the landlord ever turn on the heat? It didn't matter. I led her into the back storage room, six-and-a-half by eight feet, curtained, frost on the soot-fouled window, facing the next blackened brick building. Still a virgin. Except once. (She had snuck up to Massachusetts and climbed an old wisteria vine to peep at her sleeping child without adopted parents knowing.) More than I, Lucy O. understood why we had re-met. I never quite saw the ramifications of my actions, splashing out along the curved side to return one day; one day not too far off. Heating the room as we went, until from a hollow distance came that little voice: "Don't let it go inside of me! I'm still scared!" Iron echo. So with a mixture of conflicting feelings, she lifted my twisting auger onto her belly as it was at the end of its course. When the liquid heat hit the soft flesh she screamed like a panther breaking loose from its manacles. In the background the soothing laughter of my friend Robert, saying, "Don't worry. We keep it chained up to frighten burglars." I took her home uptown, where she had a room with her better-to-do relatives. I never saw her again. Lucy called me the next day to say she had been severely reprimanded, as her carnal sin radiated boldly from her face. A good lesson: don't show happiness. Her aunt and uncle asked her to be gone by the end of the month. What did that have to do with me?

When Spring emerged in NYC, it was time to go; thumb in hand I landed in Berkeley, California, which offered plenty of stimuli, and 3,000 miles from the Atlantic Coast. One adventure faded into the next; the less you remembered, the better off you were. I was writing a little but mostly chasing the sun. Whatever was of import, day or night, this year or the next, was not it. Lucy Whitman was five or six years my senior, a dance teacher who bounded about the streets of Berkeley, leaping and lunging where she would. She was some kind of queen, who exuded regality with every step. She asked me to her modern dance class which was an hour and a half of incessant transformation from rigorous exercise into improvisational, whatever works movement. Married, but living alone. The morning after the second class, she stopped by where I was staying, invited me to the beach—a picnic. I was surprised and elated; we went off in her Rambler station wagon. She was very West Coast; I held her in awe. Below my curly black hair there was a great deal of fear, which I kept at bay with the whip and prod of faith. California beaches around Point Reyes are magnificent. I was honored by the invitation and delighted with the sunny sands of the Pacific. Lucy and I ran and played along the shoreline. We climbed a steep cliff to eat; I sensed a change in the weather; with malevolent fingers the sea spray reached toward us; sharp rocks scraped my skin as I climbed; as we went higher up the sheer ocean side of the cliff, Lucy's features hardened. I shivered slightly. The ocean was leering and a voice came out of it, and said, "Why don't you dive on to these rocks? I will protect you from being injured, you know. Try it." Such a clear and seductive Voice. Squatting, I gazed into the crashing waves below, wondering whether I should jump or not. Lucy asked me if I wanted some yogurt; I looked up at her; she was huge. Her face was very far away; blouse wet; her nipples were little tongue tips beckoning me. Waist-length hair, blowing and winding about her sensual body; I thought it was seaweed and she, some kind of evil mermaid—part of the plan to get me to jump into the sea. She wore loose-fitting sailor pants with a large hole right above the left knee. She was the Temptress all right, and I knew it! At the end of her extremely long arm was this small purplish container. My jaw was set as I took it from her (now she was the witch from Hansel and Gretel, fattening me up for the oven—or in this case, to hurl me on the sharp rocks below). I lifted up the lid and spun it into the sea, and stuck my middle three fingers into the fruit at the bottom of the yogurt—boysenberry. And very slowly, gazing continuously into her green eyes, I slipped my hand full of yogurt through the slit in her bell bottoms, slid it up the inside of the thigh and began working it into her woman's opening. Back and forth like a house painter; and then I came back for more, up through the slit again, working it much more vigorously, always with eye contact, until finally, the spell was broken; the ocean let go of its menacing ways, and Lucy returned to being a woman. On the thirty-inch rock ledge we made love so deep, so intense, that the sound of the sea was silenced.

Lucille, Louise, Louis, Lulu, Lucifer, Lucy. Because we come from such a stiff-necked race (as Moses puts it), the cycles of our self-debilitating behavior—the ones that keep us firmly rooted to anxiety and frustration, year in, year out—to us are always subtly obscured. All the passing show, the glittering patina, possessions and wealth, and what-have-you remain on the earth when we drop off. What we take with us when we traverse the veil is awareness—a slight shift in consciousness. The whole story may be for a single hard lesson. The petite orgasms along the path act to keep us on task. Everyone has his own signs, sarcastic quips that demarcate the turns at the crossroads, reminders of our shortcomings. For me the trail has been blazed with Lucys. This excruciatingly lucid bit of information has barely penetrated my mind after fifteen years. It has nothing to do with the individual females who don the name; it has only to do with my genetic, personal, and historical derivation. Well, perhaps a little more. There are two aspects of the Lucy Syndrome. The classic double-edged scimitar. In the Judeo-Christian tradition they are personified by Lucifer—the bearer of light; i.e., Venus before the sunrise. Lucifer, also, is the fallen angel, he who rebelled against God. He is of colossal pride. Lucifer—the cross of *light* and *pride*.

Another shape to this dualism comes out of a pair of Lucys who haunted the Sixties. B. B. King, the monarch of hard blues, has a guitar named Lucille, which he makes love to; rather she is the female sexual persona—the body of woman. When I first heard him sing, "I got a sweet little angel/I love to see her spread her wings," I knew he was singing to me. I gotta get me some Lucy! For those leaning on the intellectual came the Beatles with their portrayal of the same angel, only more abstracted—Lucy in the Sky with Diamonds. Unlike B. B. King's Lucy, this one is not a sex-object, but the ideal partner or helpmate that is promised to every son by his parents.

My father hated my grandmother, his mother-in-law. "A selfish bitch!" was his favorite epithet. The major manifestation of the schism in my parents' marriage was this loathsome creature: Louise or Lulu. Not only was the active detestation of Lulu present in my upbringing, but both my sisters were named after her (how far we bend to break our back): the elder was Louise; the second, Lucy. Thus, it is readily comprehensible to see why the Lucy Syndrome pervaded my being; I am its natural heir.

Not long after I finished my first book, I went to France. Too cold. To Spain, and eventually, the romantic and traumatic island of Ibiza. From there a motorboat would take you to the serene isle of Formentera. I was on it. As was a red-haired Irish Lass, freckled and pug-nosed: Lucy Reirdon. When we docked, she took me home. Formentera is flat and rocky. Rocks piled in rectangular fashion for fences and to form small agricultural plots and pastures. A few roads and mossy labyrinths of rock walls. Lucy was strong of arm and will. After we wound through the maze and arrived, she insisted that she wash my hair, which desperately needed it. (I hadn't realized that this lady was the fourth nonfamilial Lucy in my life; nor that all of them had red hair. When you're me, you're pretty dense!) "Strip!" she commanded. From the cistern she pulled up a bucket of icy water and methodically poured it over my head. As the water reached my loins, whatever flickering was occurring there was immediately squelched. Lucy Reirdon was her own woman; talked very little; knew what she wanted. She had some type of intense Irish shampoo and sharp fingernails. I asked her if she had considered torture as a profession. Then came the icing on my scalp—about two gallons of cold water. I was in shock; one large mass of goose bumps. She took pity and wrapped a towel around me. And then some strong tea with milk and honey; and goat cheese and bread. Then a little onyx pipe with smokeable matter within. I hardly knew where I was in the first place, and what she offered in this burning vessel took care of the remaining fragments of my memory. She led me inside the whitewashed house, which was really an altar—pictures of Christ, Krishna, Buddha, and many-armed goddesses with lotus flowers. Pillows and fragrance everywhere. A fever of fear shot up my spine: I was to be sacrificed! Quickly, I turned, expecting to see her with an ornate, sacrificial knife . . . but no. She had disappeared for a moment, dropped her army pants, and returned in an emerald green satin robe. As we sat quietly together on an assortment of sheepskin and Moroccan rugs, I perceived very clearly that Lucy Reirdon was a goddess. At the base of my skull a surging of energy gathered and was steadily rising like a thermometer over an open flame. Lucy unmoved, eyes closed, lips barely parted. Throughout the room a vague, undulating orange glow. Then that old distant Voice: "Welcome home, lost one. You were right the first time; you are the sacrifice. Sacrifice yourself. It takes a long time; begin now. Now!"

Five years squeeze through the hour glass. Lucy went her own way. For me marriage and children and a farm in Oregon. What is begun is always completed. Sooner or later. As my marriage deteriorated, sexual frustration mounted. It became a malignant tumor in my head that grew and grew. It was cut out. You always get what you deserve. In this case I certainly did. Lucifer wields a decisive scalpel. But still my consciousness lay unaltered. One night around 3 A.M.—the hour of Lucy—I found myself in a deep cavern. There were three cots; on the left was an old emaciated friend of mine, named Louis, rapidly demising. On the right, a bull-necked, bulging-muscled man. In the middle was the succulent-bodied Ms. Lucy, her backside raised up like a cat in heat. And I—the ego of this vision—was floating above her in conspicuous coition. The heavy duty male leans over and in a gruff, throaty voice says, "Lucy. Louis is dead. Nothin' can stop me now. I'm coming to get ya!" Lucy weeps out, "You fucking coward! You're too chicken to do anything!" "Don't say that about me! I'm coming to get ya, right now! Look out honey! I'm comin'!" He leaps from the cot toward Lucy, who turns in fright. And what of our hero? I see the dead Louis and the raspy-throated bull, snorting fire. So still deep inside of Lucy, just as he lunges, I shove my foot in between his neck and shoulder. With the thud of foot against neck, I sit up in bed and look over at my wife, curled up asleep. My eyes close and that familiar Voice starts up: "You proud and lustful fool! Lucy. Lust. Lulu. Lucifer. You know how language works! I've warned you many times before! A word to the wise! You fool! This is the last time! We'll take this body from you, if you can't use it properly! Remember! Remember well!" And with that I was awake, staring into the chilly, dark room, sweating profusely. With the speed of a computer all the fragments of this story raced through my mind. Slivers from my childhood and my parents' relationship—thousands of translucent slivers. The letters *L* and *U*. Grandma Lulu, the wedge. The quartet of redheaded Lucys. Why are we cast in this incessant drama? We stare at it and don't see it.

And so, like Adam of the earth, I cry out, "Lord. Here am I, eater of apple." And in the palm of my hand a single seed of understanding. Not much, after all these years, since I first met Lucy. The inexorable pride that haunts me, the fever of gluttony, and lust that would forego God for an ecstatic moment are the gas, grease, and oil that lubricate this hell-bent vehicle. They are tears, the sperm that race up the tube; they excite and terrify but they will never, never save me. This jot of being who I am is a poor student. On the great scale the drop of awareness truly balances the vast weights of pain and frustration. Hours on the operating table pass; decades of unconscious days, they too pass. The moist dark gem awaits its proper season. And finally like a thin shaft of light I am ready to nurture it. Finally. Ah! Lucy. You beautiful creature! Beautiful, beautiful creature! Good-bye.

. . . .

36 · DITCHING THE
BEWITCHING MYTH

ROBERT AUGUSTUS MASTERS

Sexual excitation, or erotic buildup, is not just something that happens to us, but actually is something that we, however unconsciously, generate in our-selves, often to the point where some sort of corresponding release is obses-sively sought, fought, or funnelled into screwed-up thought. The unwilling-ness to take responsibility for engineering one's own sexual charge is even more common in men than in women, or at least more glaringly common. Most men automatically blame women for whatever erotic interest arises in them toward women, as so succinctly illustrated by declarations like: "She put a spell on me" or "She makes me hard" or "She's an enchantress" or "She turns me on." Women are still frequently viewed as being responsible for their own rapes, regardless of how liberally such cases are treated in the courts—all too easily, many man still get righteous about their supposed helplessness in the presence of feminine allure, while simultaneously overcompensating elsewhere in terms of their image as a powerful, nonhelpless person.

Even more to the point, many fathers' cruelty or psychoemotional with-drawal from their daughters, especially their postpubescent daughters, is but a neurotically self-protective reaction to the budding (or heated) arousal they feel (or entertain thoughts of) with their daughter(s), a punishment whose unacknowledged core would seem to be along the lines of: "It's your fault that I'm feeling these feelings that I shouldn't be feeling." To make matters even worse, many women have, for reasons ranging from pure survival to self-aggrandizing ambition, tended to exploit their capacity to "turn on" men, re-ducing themselves to unillumined seductresses, ever reinforcing the tired old myths of Eve tempting Adam, Helen enchanting Paris, the Sirens luring Odysseus, a raped woman "drawing" her violators to her, Mr. Everyman being swept off his feet. (Yes, Eve's, Helen's, and the Sirens' "actions" have a deeper, more Life-affirming meaning, full of succulent metaphor, but their shallower, and much more common, imprint on the usual human psyche is one wherein women are to blame for men's arousal.) Whether the lure is per-sonal or transpersonal, it usually carries the same crude misrepresentation of human dynamics—Woman as negative Enchantress, Archetypal Feminine Juiciness and Radiance as a Spell before which men are helplessly lascivious, lost in the soft pornography of masturbatory fantasy, or in the brutal pornography of antisexual fervor, as epitomized by the inquisitorial period of Christianity.

No one arouses us. We arouse ourselves, no matter how convincingly we project such a capacity onto another. Men are not bewitched by women, but are bewitched by their own hoping-to-be-engorged appetites, or, more precisely, by their unwitting animation of and submission to such appetites, particularly those that promise some pleasurable numbing.

Back to fathers and daughters: Infants and young girls cannot help but register whatever erotic interest emanates from their fathers, either shying away from their own sexuality as they mature, or overoccupying themselves with it as a Daddy-ensnaring or Daddy-controlling device. So "Daddy" easily becomes somebody to avoid, or somebody to seduce. Consider how many men call women they're hot for "Baby"—"My baby left me" and similar statements, usually laced with false emotion, form the tinsel heart of many a popular tune, pointing not only to the distancing of men from the virginal purity and depth of Woman (both in females *and* in themselves), but also to the estrangement of almost all men from their own primal innocence, which of course they view as having left them, rather than as them having left it.

Once we've marooned ourselves from our core of Being, nothing truly satisfies us, but sex, especially romantically heated sex, provides probably the best satisfaction we can get in our fragmented, Ecstasy-absent condition— such pleasuring distracts us from our self-imprisonment, weakening our impulse to free ourselves. In this context, which characterizes all too much of our culture, sex is but a narcotic, and Woman is but a spell-maker, a conniving witch, a mere temptress, a magnet for pornographic yearning, as ubiquitous and sleazily banal as a Madonna music video.

• • • • • • •

37 · COMING

MICHAEL VENTURA

There has been much talk of late about masculinity and about the possibility of a masculine movement through which men would begin describing themselves in a more full, more vital way than they yet have during the reign of Christianism. If this dialogue or movement is going to have some social force, it will have to have at its core a discussion of male sexuality, as feminism had at its core a discussion of female sexuality.

For certainly the weakest, silliest aspect of feminism—which for the most part has been an overwhelmingly beneficial movement—has been its description of male sexuality. It was a description that assumed a monolithic, monointentioned erection; it was a description that equated the ejaculation of sperm with coming. But there are many secret passageways within an erection. As far as the question of male "coming"—it is an immense and untried question. Ejaculation is a muscle spasm that many men often feel with virtually no sensation but the twitch of the spasm. To ejaculate is not necessarily to come. Coming involves a constellation of sensations, physical, psychic, emotional, of virtually infinite shadings. Coming may *sometimes* or *often* occur at the moment of ejaculation, when it occurs at all. *But many ejaculations for many men happen without any sensation of coming*.

Until a woman understands this she doesn't know the first thing about male sexuality.

Nor do many men. There is ample evidence in face after face that, as there are women who have never come, so there are men who have often ejaculated but never come. And they likely don't know it, as many women never knew it until a few began to be vocal about such things. These men live in a terrifying and baffling sexual numbness in which they try the right moves and say the right things but every climax is, literally, an anticlimax. It is no wonder that in time they have less and less connection with their own bodies, and are increasingly distant from the women they want to love.

Feminism has also gotten a lot of mileage out of the mistaken notion that men can't fake coming the way women can. Men can't fake the ejaculation of sperm, of course, but we can fake muscle-spasms, hip-jerks, and moans as well as any woman can. During an agonizing period of premature ejaculation, I ejaculated almost instantly upon entering but, remaining hard, I didn't let on but kept right on going through the motions, faking the muscle spasms and moans of orgasm when the woman had (or faked) her own. Several male friends, when questioned, admitted having had similar experiences.

How are men and women to know of these things when they're never spoken of, and when even in literature you can search far and wide for a worthy, complex description of what it may be for a man to come. You don't find it, for instance, in Henry Miller. He describes brilliantly how it feels to be a cock inside a cunt, to truly enter and *be* there; he describes his perceptions of women coming; and he is truly brilliant at writing of the shaman's dreaming erection—often he seems to write out of the center of those dreams themselves; but he never, in all my reading of him, gets inside his own coming. Nor does D. H. Lawrence, who is so fine at expressing the longing of the phoenix-like, winged erection. Their narratives stop before the ejaculation, pass over the experience of coming with some summary phrase, and continue after it.

Mailer gets close, once, but not in one of his novels—where, considering his aesthetics, his glossing over the issue is unconscionable. But he did it in an essay, a brief passage in his thought-sparking book *The Prisoner of Sex*. After chiding feminist writers (a brave move in 1971) for their "dull assumption that the sexual force of a man was the luck of his birth" he writes of "orgasms stunted as lives, screwed as mean and fierce and squashed and cramped as the lives of men and women whose history was daily torture . . . comes as far away as the aria and the hunt and the devil's ice of a dive, orgasms like the collision of a truck, or coming as soft as snow, arriving with the riches of a king in costume, or slipping in the sneaky heat of a slide down slippery slopes."

A few sentences onward he gives one of the sentences of his life: at orgasm, he says, "the eye of your life looked back at you then. Who would wish to stare into that eye if it was poorer than one's own?"

Who indeed. We are all paying the price of such moments. We pay for our own and for each other's. Men and women alike. Yet there are times when the eye of your orgasm, the eye staring back at you, matches your own; and times when it is richer than your own, leading you on to what you may yet be.

A single suggestive passage about male orgasm in years of sexually explicit literature is a poor showing. Doubtless there are more floating about, but not many, and they're hardly known and apparently unremembered.

We men, who have never spoken of such things, are squarely to blame for the consequences of our constipated silences. What more than spasms is to be expected of our entire culture of adult men who are frightened to wear colors during business hours? The neatly knotted tie is all that's left of our desert shawl and shaman robe. Most American and European businessmen, aped by businessmen all over the world now, still walk around in the black-and-white and brown-and-white color variations of celibate monks who spent a thousand years frightened of nothing so much as of all the imagery that might rise out of an erection.

One example of a reaction to the color fear are rock stars like Prince who, for all his childish and sexist lyrics, is on the cutting edge of these issues right now because he is bringing colors back to men. Or at any rate, back to boys who will one day be men. The hot-colored styles Prince inspires reflect the spectrum of the psyche much better than gray flannel.

There are many who would like the needed innovation and advances to occur on a more sophisticated and enlightened level than, say, Prince works on. But that is a luxury we can hardly afford. We are desperate people, and must take our signs as they come, whether from a rock star, or a sullen statue on Ocean and Wilshire, or a painting in a cramped cave, or a mural in a Mexican bar. They are the work of men, and so they are ours.

The body is such an immense place. We take so long to find our ways across it. And each of us has so many bodies. Sometimes they drag behind us, and we feel encumbered and earth-laden. Sometimes they race before us, making huge decisions in our name, while we scramble to catch up—and sometimes we call that "sex." And we know so little about these things. And one of the only ways we can test the little we know is to speak of it.

. . . .

38 · PHALLOS AND RELIGIOUS EXPERIENCE

EUGENE MONICK

PHALLOS AS GOD-IMAGE

As a child of about seven, in the early days of the psychosexual period that Freud called latency, I crawled into my parents' bed one summer morning. We had moved to our summer cottage on White Bear Lake, now a suburb of St. Paul but then two hours' journey by back roads from the city. Mother had left the bed to prepare breakfast. Father lay there asleep, naked. I went under the covers to explore. I may have had a flashlight with me, which would indicate an intention to investigate. Or, sensing there was a discovery to be made, I left the darkness of the blankets to find one. In any case, crouched in the darkness next to my father's body, I came upon his genitalia. I focused the light and gazed upon a mystery. How long I remained there I have no idea; the particulars of the experience have faded. There were no words, then or afterward. As far as I know, my father was not aware that I was there.

What I do remember is the powerful effect the incident had upon me. I think now that I looked upon my father's maleness as a revelation. Certainly at the time I could not articulate what it was; I have difficulty doing that even now. I do know that maleness was unequivocally present before me. There, in those organs, was a picture I had not known before. The picture intimated another world. It was a world I somehow knew existed but until that exposure I had no tangible image to embody my fledgling inner sense. Suddenly, in those naked parts, it faced me.

The other world surely was the potential within me for a sexual life of my own in the future, then only dimly perceived. I also think it was much more. It was the beginning of transpersonal awareness, presented to me as connected with masculine sexual organs. The organs were my father's, and through them I came into being. They were also archetypal in essence— something more, even, than my father. He and I were united within a masculine identity having its roots beyond us both.

My relationship to my father in subsequent years was one of guarded, arm's-length closeness. As I grow older, I discover increasingly that I am much like him, more so than I thought possible in earlier years. I catch glimpses of him occasionally, out of the corner of my eye, as I see my reflection in a shop window. When I shave, I sometimes think for a moment that I see him looking at me in the mirror. My smoking habit is certainly his, and I am beginning to hunch over as he did, a telltale sign of his emphysema. I laugh at odd times as he did: I worry about money as he did. Often I think that I am as afraid of my feelings as he was, even after my years of psychoanalysis. I am indebted to him in many ways, not the least being his presence for me on that morning in that bed. He gave me something he did not know he was giving. He had no way of knowing how much I needed it; even if he had, there is no way to give such an experience. It happens. In many ways, that initial exposure of my father's sex was a paradigm of our relationship through the years. What I learned by observing him had less to do with him as a person than with my amazing discovery, and with my search through the fifty years since then for an understanding of what I experienced on that morning.

George Elder of Hunter College writes:

> Phallus, like all great religious symbols, points to a mysterious divine reality that *cannot be apprehended otherwise*. [Emphasis mine] In this case, however, the mystery seems to surround the symbol itself. . . . It is not as a flaccid member that this symbol is . . . important to religion, but as an erect organ.

Carl Jung understood psyche in the original Greek sense of soul, that part of human experience which comes to one from within. Psyche is entwined in mystery and enriched by nuance and meaning, constantly interacting with the outer world but in no sense an epiphenomenon of it. Jung understood religion, generally, as an activity of psyche sui generis, irreducible to any other explanation. He held to this conviction in the face of ridicule and rejection, inevitably cutting himself off from the mainstream of psychoanalysis. By so doing, he made it possible for me to have the tools needed to investigate my experience in my father's bed. Chances are that without Jung and his perspective on psyche, I would be trapped by my experience, bereft of images and a worldview within which to place it. As it is, when I mention to people that I am interested in the sacred nature of phallos, they tend to smile benignly and change the subject.

People are uneasy with the correlation of sexuality and religion. Christianity, especially, has separated the two in a way that would make them appear to be irreconcilable. Psychiatry continues the disjuncture, emphasizing it with pathological labels. The church elevates religion, devaluing sexuality. Psychiatry does the opposite—elevating sexuality and devaluing religion. The union of sexuality and religion is like an electrical connection. Wrong joining leads to disaster. No joining produces no energy. Proper joining holds promise.

Jung is to be celebrated because he held to his conviction that the invisible soul is at least as important a psychological phenomenon as the visible ego—which can be seen, measured, and superficially changed. Jung understood that soul is an individual's entrée to a realm of psyche that is universal and eternal, transcending the finite limitations of the ego. He held that psychology is the study of the soul and the discipline of its care. This cannot be done without the inclusion of a world other than that of the ego.

In what sense might my experience in my father's bed be called a religious experience, an encounter with soul? It is a difficult question to answer head-on.

Recently a young man, much in love with the woman he had dated for four years, came into my office. His fiancée had called off their wedding just days before it was to take place. He feared family pressure had been put on her; he felt rejected, abandoned, angry, and hurt. Above all, hurt. I saw that his masculine pride was damaged. He was handsome, basically confident, well-positioned to make something of himself educationally and professionally, sure of his desire for the woman, almost precocious in his possession of himself. Left fatherless at an early age, he had fathered himself. His hurt was a wounding of soul. The potential loss of his sweetheart was a strongly emotional sting to him. But his hurt was also related to a threatened loss of his self-respect, a questioning of his manhood, a challenge to his sense of direction. These qualities are intrinsically related to phallos. Young or old, males suffer when their phallic identity is threatened.

One can understand this as castration anxiety. That is one way of speaking about what I observed, but it only partly tells the story. Nuance and mystery are gone when one speaks clinically, diagnostically, of castration anxiety. Why is the diminishment of one's masculinity equated with the loss of the male sex organ, while the attainment of manhood is equated with its active use? This question brings one closer to the revelatory quality of phallos. Psyche emerges: phallos carries the masculine inner god-image for a male. The young man was experiencing a threat to this god-image when he felt hurt at the loss of his self-respect. Damage to phallos was at the bottom of his suffering.

This is what Elder means when he refers to phallos as "a mysterious divine reality that cannot be apprehended otherwise." In his intimate relationship with his fiancée the young man knew her generosity, her love, her giving nature. Intimacy was his way of comprehending the feminine, in his partner and in himself (his anima, to use Jung's word). And it was more. His inner reality as a man was tied to the relationship; it informed the young man's sense of who he was. The problem was not only the loss of his woman. Loss of masculine identity was also at stake. Such a loss—or gain as I experienced with my father—is a religious experience, as Jung used the term. It is the crushing of soul or the making of soul as psyche, the invisible reality that supports and gives meaning to existence.

In other words, as phallos enters a situation, an apprehension of masculine divinity takes place that could not take place without phallos. That is the horror of castration. It has always been so. The young man did not consciously create his passion for his fiancée, any more than I created the revelation in my father's bed. Both were visitations. Phallic visitations come as surprise, as grace, time after time, generation after generation, in much the same way, in all cultures. Jung felt that archetypal patterns have coalesced in the psyche through just such constant and similar repetition. Phallos became, over eons of masculine identification with its inner-directed comings and goings, its outer success and defeat, the god-symbol for males. I was able to connect with the young man because I too have felt the devastation of phallic loss. I was able to stay with him because I have also known the glory of phallic resurrection.

Phallic resurrection has to do with the capacity of the male member to return to life, time and again, after defeat and death. Each time phallos explodes in orgasm, it dies. Energy pours forth from phallos as the fountain of life in great excitement, and its time is over. A man is spent. Quiet returns, a desire for rest falls upon a man as though he were falling into the grave—his need for sleep. As Elder points out, phallos is erection, not flaccid penis. Physical phallos has become a religious and psychological symbol because it decides on its own, independent of its owner's ego decision, when and with whom it wants to spring into action. It is thus an appropriate metaphor for the unconscious itself, and specifically the masculine mode of the unconscious.

Penis is phallos *in potentia*, whether or not it is apparent outwardly. In both the interchange with the young man in my consulting room, and my experience with my father, phallic potential was present, though phallos was not. I can imagine saying to myself then, "So this is what I will look like when I am a man. Not only will I grow tall, but all of this will grow too." I can imagine it now because within me still is the seven-year-old boy who wonders at the drawing back of that curtain.

This is religious experience, viewed from the standpoint of psychology. An experience that is also a revelation—such as my childhood discovery, or the young man's trauma in love—permanently affects one's life. If it does not do this, it is not religious. What we take for granted is secular—common, without much meaning, without numinosity, without thrall. The potential for numinosity might be present, but depth is not experienced. That is the case when one merely urinates with his penis, oblivious to the storehouse of energy in one's hand, the cosmic tool, the great sword of heroism. In the course of growing into young adulthood, my experience was forgotten as I went about my boyish business. A functioning ego acts to obstruct awareness of early religious experience so that the grass can be mowed and the arithmetic done. But religious experience returns in the dead of night, between the fine crazing in one's ego-pottery, in intimations and erotic tugs, when one least expects an intrusion. Then one knows that a god is sneaking in, its presence first hinted at in early years.

In the ensuing years I resisted accepting my childhood revelation as a manifestation of the masculine god-image. Phallos was repressed in the cultural structures of my socialization—schooling, good citizenship, profession. In that world, there is no place for phallos as god-image; it is not permitted to participate in everyday life. Physical phallos is acknowledged in asides—in the secrecy of motel rooms and pornography stands, in joking with the boys, in endless fantasies and in the gay world—but furtively, under cover of darkness. Nowhere is phallos out in the open; it sneaks in, since we are embarrassed by its presence. In my early experience, the cover of blankets, the dim light, and the unconscious quality of the encounter were paradigmatic.

Men hide their source of authority and power, not exposing their sexuality, their genitalia, in a way similar to the cultural evasion of phallos as god-image. Men substitute phallic surrogates for the thing in itself—family authority, job superiority, institutional construction, female ownership, physical prowess, wealth, religion, politics, intellect, and social conformity. This may be a way of protecting the god, as if the inhibition of direct exposure were a way of avoiding an invasion of the sacred tabernacle and diminishing seminal potential. The physiological phenomenon of the drawing of the testes closer to the trunk of the body in time of danger mirrors psychological protective tendencies. The god is revered in the collusion of male secrecy. Men know something they do not speak about directly. They laugh about it together, they implicitly understand one another, but they do not speak openly. A world of mutual knowledge is shared by males without any explicit effort to communicate what is known. Here also one gets close to the religious quality of phallos and to the depths from which it emerges into masculine life. Men have no way to speak about that which is simultaneously known and unknown.

Males expose their phallic member in private, when they are comfortable with their capacity for prowess, when the secret can be shared with another person in intimacy, or when they permit themselves to acknowledge potency alone. They do it when the power of the secret is too strong for containment, when the god demands expression. Men are naked together only within a mutually understood masculine frame of reference, as in athletic shower rooms. Even then, men are careful not to expose phallos. A conflict ensues. Males have genitalia outside the trunk of the body, difficult to hide. Phallos by nature is extraverted, while female organs are introverted. Phallos is external; it desires to show itself in an outward, even blatant way. Phallos stands up, as if to be noticed. A way is required to deal with the double bind: the need to hide what demands to be exposed. Masculine surrogate behavior and constructions, as mentioned above, serve to resolve the conflict. In modern Western societies, however, males must stumble into an accomplishment of this by themselves. Cultural awareness of the importance of phallos is so low that adequate means are not provided for young men to find a way into adult manhood. There is a male desire for participation in brotherhood—masculine veneration of the god—but hardly any way to attain it. Initiation does not take place. The result, often, is exaggerated exposition or exaggerated protection.

Twenty-five years ago, just after my marriage, I was sent to Uganda by the Episcopal Church to teach for a semester in a theological college near Mbale. The students of the college were males preparing for ordination to the

priesthood. All but two had undergone the ritual of circumcision in their native tribes some years before, in early adolescence. In Uganda at the time,
male circumcision was cause for great tribal celebration. Ritual circumcision
was the manner in which a boy became a man, and it was necessary that the
young male undergo the ordeal without flinching or drawing back. The two
uncircumcised males in our student body at Buwalasi were different from the
others. They may have been the only two that were not married, and they
were distinctly inferior to the others in stamina, demeanor, and in masculine
presence. One of the two had been absent when his time came to be circum-
cised because his distant grandmother had died. No matter—he had missed
his date, and his life was changed. He was not a man.

Male initiation rituals do sneak through in spite of modern ignorance
of their importance. In my case, in addition to my fortuitous exposure to my
father's maleness, there was membership in a close-knit Boy Scout troop
which had use of an isolated and undeveloped campground on a northern Minnesota river. Each boy was ritualistically taken to a country cemetery at night,
stripped bare, and deserted. He was required to find his way back to the
campground, perhaps a mile distant, through the forest. Clearly he could
not ask for directions should he come across a farmhouse or a chance car on
the road. Eventually such ordeals were stopped, as fraternity hazings have
been; for good reason, perhaps, but their purpose is not being served in other
ways. The problem is not easy to solve. It is clear, nonetheless, that phallos ab-
hors a vacuum.

For me, the conflict between inner god and outer society as regards
phallos finally came to this: either I took seriously the importance of that revelatory experience in my father's bed or admitted to myself that my acceptance of the reality of the unconscious was inadequate. Avoidance of the phallic god-image was avoidance of the unconscious in the service of ego adaptation. The unconscious was offering and phallos was demanding. I was forced
to the conclusion that phallos is wondrous and at the same time very odd as a
taskmaster. That is what religious people have always said about gods.

· · · · · · ·

39 · THE DRUNKARDS

R U M I

The drunkards are rolling in slowly, those who hold to wine
   are approaching.
The lovers come, singing, from the garden, the ones with
   brilliant eyes.

The I–don't–want–to–lives are leaving, and the I–want–to–lives
   are arriving.
They have gold sewn into their clothes, sewn for those who
   have known.

Those with ribs showing who have been grazing in the old
   pasture of love
are turning up fat and frisky.

The souls of pure teachers are arriving like rays of sunlight
from so far up to the ground–huggers.

How marvelous is that garden, where apples and pears, both
   for the sake of the two Marys,
are arriving even in winter.

Those apples grow from the Gift, and sink back into the Gift.
It must be that they are coming from the garden to the garden.

. . . .

PART 5

LOVING, LOSING, LEAVING, LONGING: ENCOUNTERS WITH WOMEN AND THE FEMININE

All men do hate women. . . . We have to turn our individual awareness and energies into an active, collective political struggle to destroy sexism and patriarchal society which makes all men misogynists, all men rapists, and all men emotionally crippled.

LEONARD SCHEIN

Forget all that woman-as-the-nigger-of-the-world talk. Because it isn't true: You know it, I know it, and even most feminists know it; they just keep using it because it works, and because not enough people have blown the whistle yet.

JOHN GORDON

INTRODUCTION

· · · · · · ·

That these passages reveal two men's responses to feminism is self-evident. Less immediately obvious is the sense in which the polarized perspectives speak to an ever-present (if periodically dormant) ambivalence within the male psyche toward women and the feminine. It seems safe to say this ambivalence did not diminish as a result of the sexual politics of the past three decades. Against this larger social and cultural backdrop, the contributions of this section chronicle a variety of male encounters with women and the feminine, organized broadly around four word-images: loving, losing, leaving, and longing.

We begin—where else?—with Mom, the woman upon whom we depend for life. She is also the woman whom it is said we must leave to affirm our masculinity. We can forget about trying to get away from our mothers, writes New York psychologist Paul Olsen, author of *Sons and Mothers*. "The connection will be there, hour after hour, day after day," even though, Olsen adds, a man's mother seems often to have the power to divorce *him*. As if nodding in agreement, French playwright Eugene Ionesco follows with brief remarks entitled, "The Day My Mother Gave Me Away," recalling the moment his mother released him to his wife-to-be. For the psychologist Carl Jung, matters are not so simple, at least for American men. In an excerpt from *C. G. Jung Speaking: Interviews and Encounters*, he argues that the "American man isn't ready for real independence in woman. He only wants to be the obedient son of his mother-wife." David Ordan's curiously compelling short story, "*Any Minute Mom Should Come Blasting Through the Door*," exposes a boy's guilt about his mother's death, and her continuing presence in his relationship with his father.

Literary critic Antony Easthope's essay, "The Madonna and the Whore," from his book *What a Man's Gotta Do*, offers revealing insight into classic male double standards toward female sexuality. In "The Fear of Women," San Francisco psychoanalyst Wolfgang Lederer similarly probes the complexities of men's response to *woman*, "the Other." As if to corroborate their theories, novelist Henry Miller admits to being perplexed by the difficulties he experiences when he follows his pattern of first *idealizing* women, and then *annihilating* them. Showing no traces of Miller's misogyny, the great Irish poet William Butler Yeats follows, nevertheless, with words of caution toward falling in love, from one who "gave all his heart and lost."

In "Sunday in the Park," Bel Kaufman, author of *Up the Down Staircase*, offers a convincing glimpse of a man scorned by his wife for refusing to fight for his son's honor—or for his own. Is the husband an example of Robert Bly's "soft male"? Was he wrong to walk away? Should he have slugged his wife for humiliating him? Only if he wanted to double his grief, say counselors Edward Gondolf and David Russell in their essay, "Man to Man: Abuse Isn't Worth It."

Men's movement leader Shepherd Bliss portrays a love that grew from his realization that "Making Love in Spanish Differs." Hermann Hesse, author of the classics *Siddhartha* and *Magister Ludi*, tells of the desire evoked in him by a woman he viewed from a distance but never met. Detective story writer Raymond Chandler ("Remembering Helga") reveals his enduring love for his late wife, followed by "This Ripening Fruit," writer Malcolm Muggeridge's reflections on the beauty of his wife's pregnant form.

California musician and artist Brian Knave, in "The Hard Facts of Jealousy," offers an ode to the scattered delights and frequent griefs of extramarital affairs. Frequent *New Yorker* contributor Arturo Vivante brings a very different voice and point of view to the same theme in his pungent short story "Can-Can."

That we men should find ourselves attracted to many women at once may corroborate the premise of psychologists John A. Sanford and George Lough, namely: that *she* is personified in many forms in every man. In an essay from their book *What Men Are Like*, these authors explore feminine archetypal forces, or "goddesses," that are active in the dark recesses of the male mind.

· · · · · · ·

40 · YOU CAN'T DIVORCE YOUR MOTHER

PAUL OLSEN

The mother-son relationship is usually a subtle interaction, between letting go and grasping—and that is what makes the process and the understanding of it so infinitely complex.

They are having a quarrel, the young man in his middle thirties and his mother. He is in the morass of a complicated and angry divorce, and something about the way he has been describing it, his feelings of helplessness, of being attacked, of being extracted from, has caused his mother to launch an assault on his wife. And he resents it because it makes him feel like a fool. She is telling him that she has always known that the woman he married was "beneath him," a manipulator—

and that he would not heed his own mother's advice to reject her before they married.

She becomes relentless and he explodes with anger, tells her that, as with his wife, it might be best if they don't see each other for a while. He can't bear the fighting; he needs some kind of comfort and all he gets is criticism. It might be best if they put some distance between them.

Summoning a strange, almost deadly calm, she replies, "You think you can do that, do you? You think you can deal with me the same way you dealt with your wife? You can just move away, not see me, not talk to me, as if I were just another person in your life? Well, let me tell you something, my dear: you can divorce anyone you please but you'll never be able to divorce your mother. It isn't possible. We're the same flesh, the same blood. You can think a divorce is possible, but it's not. Only a fool could ever think he can divorce his mother. *It just isn't possible.* Even if you tried with every ounce of strength you have—it just isn't possible."

The same flesh, the same blood—and saying that, she strikes the chords of a truth beyond refutation, and the chords are so loud, so deep, that no reply will make any sense whatever. She is right; a man can *think* that a divorce from his mother is possible, but when he lives it out, tries to act on it, he finds it is impossible, that the memories and thoughts will cease only momentarily, that the connection will be there, hour after hour, day after day, beating and pulsing within his body as if they were after all connected with the same blood, the same flesh, not metaphorically but in hard reality—a symbiosis, an odd kind of twinship, a Siamese joining of organs and membranes, thoughts and perceptions.

A man must attempt to grow out of the infantile aspects of this relationship, but he cannot divorce his mother, though she seems often to have the power to divorce him.

A man, but a very special man, a man who seems to have risen above his mundane humanness, transcending it to a position of godliness: only such a man can strip his queen-mother of some of her attributes—but the divorce of *mother and son* can never be effected. A mythic Egyptian Horus, betrayed by his mother Isis, who works against the independent judgment and accomplishment of her son, is able to seize the crown from her head and deny her rank—but that event took place in a world of gods and goddesses, and a man would have to become a god in order to see so clearly and stand free of the bond that keeps him imprisoned in an infantile state.

There can be years of separation, years of silence, and the bond will not be weakened by one thread. It is the fantasy, the dream, and the wishing within man, that thinks he can pry free; but something inside him also says that this total freedom is not possible—that no real divorce, whether by design or by the inevitability of death, will ever make a profound break in a bond established in such a powerful, dynamic way. Men may try to deny the bond, to pretend that it has no power, attempt to diminish its importance—and be condemned to live out a lie. Because denial is flight and running away avoids the self-confrontation necessary for growth and awareness.

When a man attempts to flee his mother, he closes down; he attempts to substitute emotional awareness with physical distance—an absurd confusion of functions. He runs in terror and rage instead of pausing to understand that freedom from his dependency is a task of the inner life precisely because he is dealing with emotional and psychological factors, not with physical imprisonment—although he may *feel* that physical nearness to his mother is toxic. He must also realize that his emotional liberation requires a balance of the "good" as well as the "bad." In other words, a man must come to realize that the positive aspects of his self-identity have been achieved not only *despite* his mother's influence but also largely *because* of it. As one of my colleagues expresses it: "A mother often provides the very material of rebellion and insight while she appears to be hanging on. Someday she may appreciate it, or she may never know about it at all."

> Speaking of her relationship with her son, a mother says, "I'm sixty-seven now. That's a lot of life, but I'm glad I got here because for the first time in all these years the storm is over. We seem to know each other now, and I'm not exactly sure how it happened.
>
> "Oh, I can recollect moments, sharp, painful moments. Like the way I told him to go to hell, that he was nothing I'd ever wanted him to be, and that it was obvious that *I* wasn't what he wanted *me* to be. And I said that I could live with it, and if he couldn't it was just too bad. 'Do what you want,' I told him, 'but just stop blaming me. Just do what you want to.'"
>
> She is a sculptress now, a very good one, a talent that bloomed after the death of her husband. She points to an unfinished piece of stone and says, "Like that. It's raw stuff and you must make something of it, not attack it. Your life is something you need to forge, to create, to find. You can't do it by smashing away at it or running from it.
>
> "Well, he must have done something about it. He doesn't have to thwart me anymore. He's lost his need to hurt me and blame me, and I've lost my need to make demands on him. And that's the core of it."

James Joyce, one among many writers, struck the theme resonantly in *Ulysses*, where the young artist Stephen Dedalus is incessantly reminded by his friends that he refused to kneel and pray at the bedside of his dying mother. But this, too, is symbolic; the new young god divesting his mother of her queenship. And it is a wish; there is no evidence that Joyce ever did such a thing in the reality of his nonartistic life, in the other reality of mundane earthly existence.

There is, indeed, little evidence that any man has ever done such a thing, or would—unless he had lost some sort of basic humanity, unless he were crazed with rage or found that his survival depended upon such a refusal, his survival in that case being the crucial necessity to remain sane.

The woman was right; a man cannot divorce his mother.

There are certain "reasonable" explanations why this can't be done—but they are explanations put forth in the framework of a "logic" that is grotesquely far removed from the actual event, the actual meaning. For example, men are too guilty to effect the divorce, afraid of some sort of retaliation; or, on the "mature" side of the coin, too responsible, too unwilling, as good people, to deny the needs of their mothers. And all this will have an intellectual, rational cast to it—yet, on closer scrutiny, we see that they are merely following what they have been taught to believe, trained to believe, as they have been conditioned by verbal means, by the eternal verities and values communicated to us in a daily series of lectures and sermons.

And very little of it will hit the mark.

A man spends most of his life running away from his mother's world through the pursuit of his masculine toys: he plays sports, jocks around in locker rooms, buys cars, spends his time learning how to wheel and deal financially, becomes sexually aggressive—all those driven activities that may turn a man into a parody. He can become intellectualized, using the "clean," "analytic," "logical" forms of thought and behavior to identify himself with "maleness," abandoning the intuition, sensitivity, and feeling that he defines as "female." And to cement his necessary avoidance of anything that may bring him closer to a way of being defined as feminine, society has provided him with a fear of homosexuality. To be tender is to be queer, to touch another man is to be queer, to kiss another man is to be queer—to be, that is, quintessentially feminine.

That is how far he wishes to travel from his mother. But he does it at the cost of incredible damage and waste: he buries at least half his life, lays to rest at least half his potentiality as a full human being—and will live the rest of his life in conflict, like a self divided, like a socially acceptable schizophrenic. His so-called maleness always at war with his unconscious, with what is hidden from him, with what he does not know about the deeper regions of himself—but which always gets expressed in one way or another.

Or if he is a psychotherapist he lassoes his unconscious like some wild animal, interprets it (rightly or wrongly is of no importance), and thereby gains an illusory control over it: a kind of rape of the psyche.

But the running away does no good: like Heracles he will finally fall into the oblivion of the mother sucking him back into his unawareness. It was Jung who said that mother is a symbol of the unconscious—and Jung may have been quite correct. And this is what happens to a man when he avoids a confrontation with the mother inside him, the mother absorbed into him by that original swallowing and blending of flesh.

This is what happens so often when a man retires after years of "masculine" work: he sinks back into a dependency, into the pull of the mother inside him, and he becomes like a child "looking for something to do," looking without finding because he has never once in the course of running from his inner life paused to discover what riches are within—because the within is what he cannot see, cannot "think" about or "reason" about, and so must fear. Marriage can die right here, because he is surrounded only by women— the woman inside, the darkness, the woman outside, his wife, who tries to mobilize him but who is suddenly seen as a dictator.

The woman was right: a man cannot divorce his mother. He can only discover who she is, how she is separate from him—and come to appreciate what she has given him.

But he cannot run away from her forever. Because like Heracles, like the protagonist of John O'Hara's *Appointment in Samarra*, he will run exactly to the place where he will become overwhelmed, where he will die in his own darkness.

In a moment when his guard is dropped a man can experience something new:

> "I never made love before," he says. "I just screwed. But when it happened, it was like nothing I'd ever experienced before. I think I must have blacked out for a second, and all I was aware of was some kind of incredible warmth, my whole body was filled with it, and I didn't want to leave her or roll away from her. I wanted to get closer to her, very close. I could feel the warmth of her body against mine, soft and gentle, and for the first time in my life I stayed in a woman's arms and fell asleep."

What he does with that experience only time will tell. He can deny it in the morning. Or he can enter it fully and never again feel the need to run away.

· · · · · · · ·

41 · THE DAY MY MOTHER GAVE ME AWAY

EUGENE IONESCO

When I had told my mother that I was going to get married, she went to see my fiancée, and when the latter opened the door to her, my mother looked at her for a moment, although she had known her for quite a long time, as though she had an unfamiliar person in front of her . . . a friend, the daughter of a friend, who was also a stranger, was becoming in some unexpected fashion her closest relative, as it were a daughter . . . as it were another herself, someone she had been expecting from the beginning, whom she had foreknown, whom she did not recognize, and at the same time whom she seemed to have known since the beginning of time: the person chosen by fate, whom she was compelled to accept and yet had chosen. This was the princess, her heiress, soon to become queen in her stead. My future wife returned my mother's gaze; my mother had tears in her eyes but was restraining her emotion, and her quivering lips expressed a feeling beyond words. . . . At that moment my mother gave up her place, and gave me up too, to my wife. This was what my mother's expression said: he is no longer mine, he is yours. What silent injunctions, what sadness and what happiness, what fear and hope, what renunciation there was in this expression! It was a dialogue without words, in which I had no part, a dialogue between one woman and another.

• • • • • • •

42 · AMERICAN MEN AS SONS OF THEIR WIVES

C. G. JUNG

I study the individual to understand the race, and the race to understand the individual. I ask myself, What influence has the building of America had upon the American man and the American woman of today? I find that it is a good subject for the student of psychoanalysis.

There is only so much vital energy in any human being. We call that in our work the Libido. And I would say that the Libido of the American man is focused almost entirely upon his business, so that as a husband he is glad to have no responsibilities. He gives the complete direction of his family life over to his wife. This is what you call giving independence to the American woman. It is what I call the laziness of the American man. That is why he is so kind and polite in his home, and why he can fight so hard in his business. His real life is where his fight is. The lazy part of his life is where his family is.

When men are still in the barbaric state they make women their slaves. If, while they are still barbaric by nature, some influence makes them see that they dare not treat women as slaves, then what do they do? They do not know yet how to love something which is equal to themselves. They do not know what real independence is, so they must kneel down before this slave and change her into the one thing that they instinctively (even when they are barbarians) respect: they change the slave idea into the mother idea. And then they marry the mother-woman. And they respect her very much, they can depend upon her. They need not be her master. In America your women rule their homes because the man has not yet learned to love them.

I made many observations on shipboard. I notice that whenever the American husband spoke to his wife there was always a little melancholy note in his voice, as though he were not quite free; as though he were a boy talking to an older woman. He was always very polite and very kind, and paid her every respect. You could see that in her eyes he was not at all dangerous, and that she was not afraid of being mastered by him. But when any one told him that there was betting going on he would leave her, and his face became eager and full of desire, and his eyes would get very bright and his voice would get strong, and hard, and brutal. That is why I say his Libido, his vital energy, is in the game. He loves to gamble. That is business today.

It takes much vital energy to be in love. In America you give so many opportunities both to your men and women that they do not save any of their vital force for loving. This is a wonderful country for opportunity. It is every-where. It spreads out. It runs all over the surface of everything. And so the American mind runs out and spreads over the whole country. But there is a dark side of this. The people of America do not have to dig deep for their own life. In Europe we do.

In Europe we have many divisions. Take my own little country of Switzerland. In Switzerland we must be Swiss, because we won't be German, and we won't be French, and we won't be Italian. And the people of Germany feel the same way. But in America you can be anything. In my country I have not as many opportunities given to me. Therefore I dig deeper and deeper in order to find my own life. In America you think you are concentrated because you are so direct, because you like your men who have only one idea at a time. I find that you distrust a man if he has two ideas. But if he has only one, you give him every chance to launch his enterprise. I do not feel that you care for those things that are profound. You can so easily distract yourself. And any-thing that you find unpleasant you bury so quickly at once in your uncon-scious mind.

The American husband is very indignant when he comes to me for treat-ment for neurasthenia or nervous breakdown, and I tell him it's because he is brutal on one hand and prudish on the other. You have in America the wooden face, just as they have it in England, because you're trying so hard to hide your emotions and your instincts. In Europe we have many little outlets for our emotions. We have an old civilization, which gives us a chance to live like men and women. But in England, even a hundred years ago, the people were still the conquering race that had been colored by the savage instincts of the original inhabitants of the British Isles. The English had to conquer the Celt, and the Celt lived a few hundred years ago in almost savage conditions.

In America you are still pioneers, and you have the great emotions of all adventurous pioneers, but if you should give way to them you would lose in the game of business, and so you practice the greatest self-control. And then this self-control—which holds you together and keeps you from dissolution, from going to pieces—reacts upon you and you break down under the effort to maintain it.

That is what I mean by psychoanalysis. The search back into the soul for the hidden psychological factors that, in combination with physical nerves, have brought about a false adjustment to life. In America just such a tragic moment has arrived. But you do not know it is tragic. All you know is that you are nervous, or, as we physicians say, neurotic. You are uncomfortable. But you do not know that you are unhappy.

You believe, for instance, that American marriages are the happiest in the world. I say they are the most tragic. I know this not only from my study of the people as a whole, but from my study of the individuals who come to me. I find that the men and women are giving their vital energy to everything except to the relation between themselves. In that relation all is confusion. The women are the mothers of their husbands as well as of their children, yet at the same time there is in them the old, old primitive desire to be possessed, to yield, to surrender. And there is nothing in the man for her to surrender to except his kindness, his courtesy, his generosity, his chivalry. His competitor, his rival in business, must yield but she need not.

There is no country in the world where women have to work so hard to attract men's attention. There is in your Metropolitan Museum a bas-relief that shows the girls of Crete in one of their religious dances about their god in the form of a bull.[1] These girls of 2000 B.C. wear their hair in chignons; they have puffed sleeves; their corseted waists are very slender; they are dressed to show every line of their figures, just as your women are dressing today.

At that time the reasons that made it necessary to attract men to themselves in this way had to do with the morals of their country. The women were desperate just as they are today, without knowing it. In Athens four or five hundred years before Christ there was even an epidemic of suicide among young girls, which was only brought to an end by the decision of the Areopagus that the next girl who did away with herself would be exhibited nude upon the streets of Athens. There were no more suicides. The judges of Athens understood sex psychology.

On Fifth Avenue I am constantly reminded of that bas-relief. All the women, by their dress, by the eagerness of their faces, by their walk, are trying to attract the tired men of their country. What they will do when they fail I can't tell. It may be that then they will face themselves instead of running away from themselves, as they do now. Usually men are more honest with themselves than women. But in this country your women have more leisure than the men. Ideas run easily among them, are discussed in clubs, and so here it may be that they will be the first ones to ask if you are a happy country or an unhappy country.

It may be that you are going to produce a race that are human beings first, and men and women secondarily. It may be that you are going to create the real independent woman who knows she is independent, who feels the responsibility of her independence, and, in time, will come to see that she must give spontaneously those things that up to now she only allows to be taken from her when she pretends to be passive. Today the American woman is still confused. She wants independence, she wants to be free to do everything, to have all the opportunities that men have, and, at the same time, she wants to be mastered by man and to be possessed in the archaic way of Europe.

You think your young girls marry European husbands because they are ambitious for titles. I say it is because, after all, they are not different from the European girls; they like the way European men make love, and they like to feel we are a little dangerous. They are not happy with their American husbands because they are not afraid of them. It is natural, even though it is archaic, for women to want to be afraid when they love. If they don't want to be afraid, then perhaps they are becoming truly independent, and you may be producing the real "new woman." But up to this time your American man isn't ready for real independence in woman. He only wants to be the obedient son of his mother-wife. There is a great obligation laid upon the American people—that it shall face itself—that it shall admit its moment of tragedy in the present—admit that it has a great future only if it has courage to face itself.

· · · · · · ·

43 · ANY MINUTE
MOM SHOULD COME
BLASTING THROUGH THE DOOR

DAVID ORDAN

Mom died in the middle of making me a sandwich. If I had known it was going to kill her, I never would have asked. It never killed her before to make me a sandwich, so why all of a sudden? My dad didn't understand it, either. But we don't talk about it too much. We don't talk about it too much at all. Sometimes we try. Sometimes it's just the two of us at dinner, and things are almost good.

But only sometimes.

Most of the time it's different. Most of the time I do things like forget to leave her place out at the table. And then we don't know what to do. Then we don't even try to talk. Three plates. Three glasses. The kitchen shines. A bright, shiny kitchen, Mom used to say. And there we are—my dad, her place, and me. And any minute Mom should come blasting through the door, all bundles and boxes, my big winter coat squaring her off at the shoulders and hips, her face smiling and wrinkled like a plant.

I should have known better.

I should have known about these things.

Come on, Mom, what do you say? Is it going to kill you to make me one sandwich? Is it really going to kill you? Remember how you used to play with me? Remember? And then I snuck up behind her chair, undid her curlers, and ran my fingers through her hair until she said all right already, what kind did I want? Then she stood up, turned to my dad, and opened her bathrobe so he could get a peek just to see if the old interest was still there. But I don't think it was. What? he said. He hasn't seen this before? Make the sandwich, he said. And he let his body melt like pudding into the easy chair.

That was it. That was the last thing he said to her. Mom turned up the TV, went into the kitchen, and the next thing we knew, she was calling out for help.

Well, my dad didn't know what was going on anymore than I did, so he got up from his chair, trudged across the room—making sure to scrape his feet on the carpet all the way so he could really shock her good this time—and that was it. Mom was dead on the floor of the kitchen, her bathrobe open at the waist.

And I thought, Well, there's Mom dead, what now? No one thinks about that. No one thinks about what happens after you find your mother dead like that, all over the kitchen floor. But I'm telling you, that's when the real fun starts. That's when you have to try mouth-to-mouth on her—on your mother, for God's sake— knowing that if she does come around she'll spit up in your face, because that's what happens, but praying for it, anyway, because if she doesn't, then it's all over. That's when you've got to call an ambulance and wait for them to throw a sheet over her head so they can take her away from you. That's when you've got to sit there and watch them put their hands all over her body and know they'll never believe you even tried to save her. That's when the neighbors see the flashing red light in your driveway and wonder what kind of rotten son you are that you couldn't save your mother. That's when you've got your whole life to live, and all it's going to be is one excuse after another for why you didn't save her. What do you do? We didn't know, so my dad poured her on the couch, and we waited. We waited and watched TV.

It was on.

But like I said, we don't talk about it too much. How can we? Mom was the talker. That's what she used to say. She used to say, "Boys, what would you do without me?" And here we are, without her. My dad and I wouldn't know how to talk to each other if you paid us, so we don't even try. Not much, anyway. What am I going to say? How's your love life? What's it like to sleep alone? He doesn't want that. He doesn't want that at all. He wants me out of the house. But he doesn't really want that, either, you know. What would he do then? Six rooms can be too many if you're not careful. I tell him this at dinner sometimes. I tell him how much he needs me. How much he cares. But he doesn't care. He cares about the kitchen, the robe, the things I did to try to save his wife. My hands. Her body. My lips. Her mouth.

"Tell me," he says, "is that really how you want to remember your mother?"

. . . .

44 · THE MADONNA AND THE WHORE

ANTONY EASTHOPE

'Dynasty,' ABC Television, since 1980

Blake Carrington, a self-made man, is an oil tycoon based in Denver, Colorado, and has a fortune estimated at $200 million. In 1954 he married Alexis Morell (Joan Collins) with whom he had three children, Adam, Fallon, and Steven. Following her adultery in 1965 they were divorced. Alexis was given a generous financial settlement on condition that she did not visit the children. In 1980 Blake married his secretary, Krystle Jennings (Linda Evans). Accused of manslaughter, also in 1980, he was convicted largely on the testimony of Alexis.

Machinations by Blake's one-time friend, Cecil Colby, led in 1981 to Blake coming close to financial ruin and also to an explosion in which he temporarily lost his sight. In 1982 Alexis married Cecil Colby, who died immediately afterwards leaving her a controlling interest in his company, Colbyco, and instructions to destroy Blake. In the same year Krystle discovered her previous divorce was not valid, nor was her marriage to Blake. Alexis offered her a million dollars to leave Blake for good. However, in 1983 Krystle remarried Blake. In 1985 she had a daughter, Krystina Carrington.

Meanwhile, as chairman of Colbyco, Alexis has become the only woman to succeed in the oil business. In 1984 she persuaded Rashid Ahmed to double-cross Blake in a deal over South China oil, and in consequence Blake lost half his fortune. Alexis has since married Dex Dexter, and rediscovered her long-lost daughter, Amanda.

> Every woman is a whore except
> my mother who is a saint.
>
> ITALIAN SAYING

Out of the tradition of Victorian melodrama, television has developed a genre all of its own, soap opera, a form perfectly adapted to present a sense of the family and the relations between men and women. At present [1986] the most popular soap in the world is *Dynasty*. This is watched regularly by one hundred million viewers in more than 70 countries. In Britain it collects an audience of 11 million. It may seem surprising that British television cannot produce glossy, escapist soap opera about immensely rich people and that as a result we have to make do with the mundane realities of *Coronation Street* and *Crossroads*. There is a good reason for this. In a British context the very rich would have to be either aristocratic, lords and ladies, or commoners who had made good. Either way a large chunk of the audience would turn away from them. And that, no doubt, is why, as Rosalind Coward points out in her book *Female Desire*, the story of the Royal Family is the longest-running soap opera in Britain. Only they can appear to be above both class and money.

ALEXIS AND KRYSTLE

The contrast between Alexis and Krystle is at the center of *Dynasty* and its success. In fact the cover photograph of *Dynasty, the Authorized Biography of the Carringtons* demonstrates this very well. Blake Carrington, in a dinner jacket, stands between Alexis, wearing black, and Krystle, wearing turquoise, while all three look at the camera and the viewer. Blake, therefore, is posed as able to choose between and have at his command both women. They represent the two great types of categories into which women are divided by the masculine myth. The opposition between Krystle and Alexis can be named in all kinds of ways—as Love Sacred and Profane, as Agape and Eros, platonic love and sexual love, as love versus desire, or, at its crudest, in the American phrase, the difference between "nice girls" and "easy lays."

Together, Krystle and Alexis make up a pair of opposites. Krystle is ash blonde, Alexis brunette. She had blue eyes, Alexis has greeny brown. Krystle's large mouth typically parts into a "sweet" smile, while Alexis tends to pout and has what the *Authorized Biography* rightly names as "inviting lips." Krystle's fringe tends to give her no brow, and so, by implication, little brain; Alexis has a full brow barely covered by curls. The two types are opposed also in terms of sensual and pure, worldly and unworldly and, of course, work and home. Krystle's name suggests the translucence of crystal while the other has a man's name inside it, Alex-is. The biography unerringly summarizes the difference between them in the appropriate clichés. Krystle is "an American Aphrodite, good as she is beautiful." Alexis personifies Kipling's observation that "the female of the species is deadlier than the male." Both types relate to a man, Blake Carrington.

The meaning of each stereotype, the "good girl" and the "bitch," is repeated and repeated with little change through a long series of events. Basically they are opposed as active to passive. In terms of sexual drive, Alexis says yes and Krystle says no. In terms of narcissism Alexis follows her self-interest while Krystle submits to the interests of others. It is easier to list the men Krystle has turned down than the ones Alexis has made love with. In 1980, when her marriage to Blake was going through a sticky patch, Krystle was tempted by Matthew Blaisdel but turned him down. In 1981 she didn't even notice Nick Toscanni's passion for her and in 1983 she was again tempted but refused Mark Jennings, who was her first husband.

Alexis seeks to dominate Blake Carrington and her own children in a way that sometimes brings her into conflict with the law. She succeeded in having Blake convicted of manslaughter by testifying in court to his violence; she tried to buy off Krystle. She went along with her son Adam when he tried to poison Jeff Colby and she has schemed with Rashid Ahmed to ruin Blake. Thinking that Kirby Anders, as the daughter of a servant, is not a good enough match for her son Adam, she tells her a family secret that had been kept from her, and Kirby at once leaves. The attempts by Alexis to get rid of Krystle have twice brought the two women to physical violence. It is significant that both occurred only when Krystle felt her maternal interests were being threatened. One fight took place in 1982 at Alexis's studio when Krystle thought Alexis had purposely fired a rifle that scared her horse and caused her miscarriage. The re-match took place, mainly in a lily pond, in 1983, because Krystle thought Alexis was implicated in the departure of her grandson Danny from the Carrington mansion. In these melodramatic scenes the opposition between the two types is vividly dramatized.

THE DOUBLE STANDARD

Just as Alexis and Krystle both stand in relation to Blake Carrington, first wife and second, so the two types are a masculine product and projection on to the world of masculine fantasies. As always, for psychoanalysis the difference between the sexes originates in the different paths they follow past the mother. Female heterosexual desire begins with the mother, moves to the father, transfers to the bridegroom; male heterosexual desire begins with the mother and transfers, without any mediating figure, to the bride. This is what lies behind the masculine polarity between the madonna and the whore.

Male sexual feeling has both an affectionate and a sensual side. The affectionate current springs from the little boy's first object, the mother. Later, however, especially at puberty, a second sensual current develops, aimed at an adult woman. However, the second cannot but follow the model for the first. In ideal circumstances, the sensual current will take over from the affectionate one. If it doesn't, or doesn't completely, this is because desire has got stuck or fixated on the first object, the mother. In consequence the man can only desire women who do not recall the incestuous figure forbidden to him. His feeling polarizes between love and desire. In its most acute form this would mean he was impotent with the woman he loved and could only feel sexual desire for other women.

Perhaps the opposition might be so extreme that he could only desire someone who was as far opposed for him to the image of the mother as a prostitute might be. Of those who experience this Freud remarks sadly, "Where they love they do not desire and where they desire they cannot love." But he also notes that the condition touches most men in some degree. Its source lies with the proximity between the mother and the bride in the pathway of masculine development. And this goes some way to explain how masculinity tends to approach the feminine in terms of two opposed categories.

But psychoanalysis alone does not go far enough. Other societies, even other patriarchal societies, have interpreted the opposition very differently or hardly felt it at all. Freud himself suggests that the double standard has taken on a much more fierce quality in Western culture since the establishment of Christianity. Whereas the ancient world placed very few barriers on the fulfillment of sexual drive, Christianity made a name for itself by doing just that. The condemnation of sexual desire in Christianity encourages at the same time an idealization of sacred love and precisely the figure of the mother, the Madonna. And the pattern is intensified in bourgeois culture, after the Renaissance. As work and home become ever more separated, culture marks off the woman at home as ever more perfect. She is idealized as wife and mother, in the phrase of the Victorian poet, Coventry Patmore, "an angel in the house." The more this saint has to be loved, the more other women will be desired.

Hence the perfect reproduction of a Victorian stereotype in Krystle and Alexis. For all the seeming independence of Alexis, she is not what the *Authorized Biography* calls her, "a world-class woman who is totally in control of her life." In fact, all her independence and ruthlessness is not for herself but for a man. It is an attempt to regain Blake Carrington in some way. So both she and Krystle are women for men, images in the dominant culture.

As a masculine construction the double standard cuts both ways. It is never unambiguous that Krystle is to be preferred to Alexis. Because she is an object of desire, Alexis is clearly more interesting, more attractive than Krystle, who seems in contrast nice, dull, and maternal. Equally, Krystle, can be used as a stick to beat Alexis, because in her sexual desire is active and appetitive. The double standard blames women either way and is able to build up considerable amounts of aggression against them—for being both too nice and too desirable, for saying no and for saying yes. As Joan Collins summed it up in an interview, "Alexis is only called a bitch because she's a woman; if a man did what she does, they wouldn't think of it that way."

· · · · · · ·

45 · THE FEAR OF WOMEN

WOLFGANG LEDERER

The Mothers! How it strikes my ear!
What is the word that I don't wish to hear?

GOETHE

Of all the concerns that occupy men's minds, the relationship between the sexes is the most basic and important: and also the most intricate, perplexing, and elusive. Throughout the ages, philosophers, writers, and psychologists have, each from their own particular point of view, elaborated various aspects of it, stating truths as they saw them; and in the process they have commonly contradicted not only each other, but also themselves. The truth, it seems, is full of paradoxes, and evades precise definition.

However, while we cannot tell how these things really *are*, we can with some certainty describe how they *seem*: for in each culture area there does prevail a more or less dominant concept of women as seen by men. In our Western culture, which reached its clearest definition during Freud's lifetime and which today, in spite of much dilution and adulteration, still largely follows the basic values of his time—in this our Western culture men have seen women variously as charming or boring, as busy homemakers or emancipated discontents, as inspiring or castrating; but throughout, and in spite of everything, still basically and always as "the weaker sex." Whether dominated, tolerated, despised, adored, or protected, in any case they are to be "the Other," the appendage and foil for "the Lord of Creation," man.

This ill accords with the awareness, never lost sight of, that man *needs* woman; or with the full and popular recognition of maternal importance in childhood. Yet the myth of the "weaker sex" has to such extent slanted the perception of Western man that he must, to this day, consider any fear of women as unmanly and hence unacceptable. He has, in fact, so solidly sold himself on being superior, that he can take great pride in granting women "equality": a magnanimous pretense, implying that she is inferior to man, but that she can be helped to his level—presumably because she will never become a true competition or threat.

And yet—in the unashamed privacy of our consulting rooms we do from time to time see strong men fret, and hear them talk of women with dread and horror and awe, as if women, far from being timid creatures to be patronized, were powerful as the sea and inescapable as fate.

What do they say? Or rather: what do they resentfully confess? A brief sampling will do: A lawyer races his sports car home, lest his wife accuse him of dawdling. A pilot cannot get married, because he is nauseated by womanish toilet smells, which recall his mother's sanitary napkins. A student shudders at the hair on his girl's arms, and an engineer is morbidly fascinated and repelled by varicose veins and what he has learned to call "fatty necrosis" on women's legs. A full-sized man has nightmares that his wife, in bed, will roll on him and crush him. A car salesman, single, is afraid to be roped in, and a wine merchant, married, is afraid of being kicked out, by their respective women. One professor complains that he can never understand his wife, nor predict what she will do next; another suffers from what he feels to be his wife's superior and dominant practical efficiency. A young father anxiously evades his daughter's budding breasts, and an old son clings trembling to breasts long dry, and feels himself an obedient prisoner of wilting arms. Some men cannot resist extramarital seductions, others cannot seduce their own wives to make love, and many cringe because they cannot bring their wives to climax.

A student with a long-delayed adolescence complains of shattered friendships and married friends: "Women are poison to friendship—it's a shock to me to see those guys—they might as well be in jail or dead." And a married man: "A woman's anger—a woman's anger is to be feared because she can throw the man out of the house. She can also kill him. She can not only cut off his balls but she can kill him: that's what my mother did to my father—from the day she kicked him out of the house to the day he lay on the slab he steadily went downhill."

So it goes. So, and in a thousand other ways. Man, confronted by woman, does seem to feel, variously, frightened, revolted, dominated, bewildered, and even, at times, superfluous.

We are living in a very enlightened age. We live by reason—and therefore we know less about woman than almost any other age.

Oh, of course, we know more about her chemistry and physiology, her glands and her hormones and her cycles; we know more about the feeding and care of her body, so that she, always sturdier than man, is today more healthy and beautiful and long-lived than ever. We also know a good deal more about embryology and the care of the mother and the child—pre-, inter-, and post-partum; and, in short: the proposition "woman" has never been so securely in hand.

Provided, that is, we are talking of the body only. When it comes to the psychology, and, worse still, to interpersonal relations between the sexes, then things seem to be every bit as mysterious as ever. In fact, it would seem that we have "forgotten" more than we permit ourselves to know.

We have forgotten, or tried to forget, how much we are in awe of woman's biological functions, her menstruating and her childbearing, and how much we abhor the smelly fluids of her organicity, the many secret folds and wrinkles of her inevitable decay. We are trying to deny her threat to our manhood, her serpent's tongue, and the sharp teeth in her two bloody mouths. We refuse to believe in the lure of her depths, and the infinite demandingness of her void. We belittle her sexual challenge and deride, uneasily, her fighting strength: the edge of her cruelty we sheathe in silence.

Thus we diminish her power, to reduce her importance. For we should like, with a shrug of the shoulder, to dispense with her, should she prove difficult. Whereas in truth—and this too we try to forget—we need her, and depend on her altogether: for she is the shipyard in which we are built, and the harbor that is our base and strength, and the territory we live to defend; and she is the hearth, and the salvation from the dumb misery of the beast and from the icy loneliness of the mind.

And what is the penalty for our suppressions and repressions?

This time we know the answer: all the mechanisms of defense, all the denials and displacements and projections and rationalizations and sublimations and what have you—they altogether do not protect against symptom formation and maladaptation.

So we do not fear woman? Then why so attracted to the complicated substitutes, to the love of men and boys and little children and what not else? Then why the rapists and the wife-beaters and all those who are potent only with a woman defective or somehow inferior? Why the elusive bachelor, the absentee husband, and the ivory-tower hermit? Then why no more taming of the shrew, and why the obedience to Mom, ruling the pecking order of the roost while hatching her golden moneybags?

No, it will not do. We must admit and face our fear of woman—and as therapists make our patients admit and fact it—the way the heroes of old faced it and, facing it, conquered fear and woman and the monsters of the unconscious deep, of night and death.

What then: are we all to be heroes?

Why not—since there is no choice? For each of us the task is laid out from the beginning, from birth; we all run essentially the same obstacle course. We each must learn to escape her seductive embrace, and yet return to her; we must destroy the teeth in her vagina, and yet love her potently and tenderly; we must defeat the amazon in order to protect her; we must drink sustenance and inspiration from her dark well, and yet not drown in it; and we must cater to her insatiable needs, and not be destroyed by them; we each must define ourselves as men in opposition to woman as nature, and yet not lose our humanity in frigid isolation.

How do we say this to our sons? How to our patients?

Aye, there's the rub.

Whether is pedagogy, or in therapy, we cannot teach but what we know; and so, having learned to analyze and exorcise within ourselves all manner of terrors and devils, it would behoove us first of all to become once more our own confessors, and to admit and label, without shame or evasion, the fear of woman in our own hearts. After which, it may be extirpated, or overridden, or ignored, or at least taken into frank consideration, according as we are able.

Then, when it comes to our sons, we need few words: but may teach through conduct and example, which always have been the most cogent and lucid preceptors. And when it comes to our patients, we again need few words: but able to spot within them the many and varied excuses and self-deceptions behind which the fear of woman commonly takes cover, we may point them out and call a spade a spade, in whatever language will serve. "You are not truly considerate of your wife, you are afraid of her."—"You are not really sparing your mother's feelings, you are afraid to tell her the truth."—"You are not bored with the wife of your youth, but you are afraid to admit to her new sexual wishes, afraid to demand of her new intellectual growth, afraid even, in front of her, to let your hair down and to act as young and foolish as you sometimes still feel" . . . and a thousand variations on this theme.

Of course: to know that one is afraid—that does not make him unafraid. But it is a good beginning. There's many a John-a-dreams, who, once called pigeon-liver'd, will, like Hamlet, bestir himself to action, and quickly, too: and I have seen several such, long hung-up, get un-hung with most gratifying effect. For others, it is true, the awareness of their fear frightens them more; and there, it must be basic therapy to question, whether fear needs to be feared, and whether to proceed in spite of it could not be both possible and beneficial. Nothing is so therapeutic as an act of courage, not matter how small; and in private as in political life, major revolutions can start with a trifling rebellion.

It all sounds rather martial—somewhat like the din of Theseus and his Greeks beating back the Amazons on the slopes of the Acropolis. It sounds like a constant, never-ending struggle—and it is. And yet—the so-called "war between the sexes" was never just that; far from being destructive, there has come of it, of its demands and tensions and ever-changing vicissitudes, all that we are proud of in human history. It would be foolhardy indeed to try to fix, as of here and now, what man's or woman's role should be; that woman should "stay home," or should not stay home, should be superior or subordinate or equal or whatever. Nor will it do, as has been done, to depict her either as a victim of nature,[1] or of maltreatment and dastardly subjugation by man,[2,3] or both;[4] or to find her naturally superior but tricked into subjugation.[5]

In the course of history man has, since those first heroic victories, attempted many a defense against woman; during the Dark Ages, he tried to banish femininity; during the Middle Ages, through the inquisition, he sought himself to devour the all-devouring Kali; since then, woman has been 3the toy of the Rococo, the doll (Ibsen's Nora) of the bourgeoisie. The proletariat, out of brotherly love, mass-produced denim-blue female comrades shorn of all feminine appeal.[6] Each social system, in its own way, tried to limit her magic.

And today—today our defensive stratagem is the cry for equality. And in promoting loudly woman's equal status, we fondly hope that she will thereby feel promoted, and not just kicked upstairs. For under the cloak of "equal rights" we attempt to deny the specifically feminine. To make woman equal means: to deprive her of her magic, of her primordial position; and means further: to deprive Shiva of Shakti, and Man of his inspiration.

In fact, men and women were never equal, but each unique in their own way. The difference between them is, to quote Erickson, "A psychobiological difference central to two great modes of life, the paternal and the maternal modes. The amended Golden Rule suggests that one sex enhances the uniqueness of the other; it also implies that each, to be really unique, depends on a mutuality with an equally unique partner.[7]

Call it, then, a partnership, or call it a battle—it comes to the same thing. In either case, it is a fluid, dynamic interplay of forces, a constant readjustment, a gravitating around a common center that will permit of no definitive escape.

Woman, anyway, has no use for freedom: she seeks not freedom, but fulfillment. She does not mean to be a slave, nor unequal before the law; nor will she tolerate any limitations in her intellectual or professional potential: but she does need the presence, in her life, of a man strong enough to protect her against the world and against her own destructiveness, strong enough to let her know that she is the magic vessel whence all his deepest satisfactions and most basic energies must flow.

As to the man, what he most wants of woman is that she should make him feel most like a man. This is a big demand, and no woman can fill it all the time. In marriage, dissatisfactions are built in: no wife can ever be maternal, sexual, and intellectual in just the right proportions to suit her husband's needs. And in no two generations does the masculinity of man, the femininity of woman, take quite the same form, serve quite the same ends. There are, no doubt, big modulations still to come, considering that, on a scale never before encountered in history, woman's central function—fertility, and man's central function—aggressivity, have each become a lethal threat to the survival of the race.

But whatever the balance will be—it will not result from equality, nor from fear: but from the highest possible perfection of the respective uniqueness of man and woman.

· · · · · · ·

46 · "And then I Annihilate Them"

HENRY MILLER

Men always say, "The women *I* select." I say *they* select us. I give myself no credit for selecting. Sure, I ran after them, I struggled, and all that, but I can't say, "Oh, that's gonna be mine. Now that's the type I want and I'm gonna get it." No, it doesn't work that way.

. . . I do think women find it difficult to live with me. And yet, you know, I'm the easiest person in the world. But it turns out there is something tyrannical in me. And maybe my critical side comes out very strongly when I live with a person, whether man or woman. I have a great sense of caricature. I discover quickly one's foibles, one's weaknesses, and I exploit them. I can't help it.

That's the kind of person I am. I start out by putting women on a pedestal, by idealizing them, and then I annihilate them. I don't know if what I say is exactly true—but it does seem to work that way. And yet I remain friends with them, all of them except one woman, warm friends. They write me and tell me they love me still, and so on. How do you explain it? They tell me they love me for myself, but they can't live with me.

· · · · · · ·

47 · NEVER GIVE ALL THE HEART

W. B. YEATS

Never give all the heart, for love
Will hardly seem worth thinking of
To passionate women if it seem
Certain, and they never dream
That it fades out from kiss to kiss;
For everything that's lovely is
But a brief, dreamy, kind delight.
O never give the heart outright,
For they, for all smooth lips can say,
Have given their hearts up to the play.
And who could play it well enough
If deaf and dumb and blind with love?
He that made this knows all the cost,
For he gave all his heart and lost.

· · · · · · ·

48 · SUNDAY IN THE PARK

BEL KAUFMAN

It was still warm in the late-afternoon sun, and the city noises came muffled through the trees in the park. She put her book down on the bench, removed her sunglasses, and signed contentedly. Morton was reading the *Times Magazine* section, one arm flung around her shoulder; their three-year-old son, Larry, was playing in the sandbox: a faint breeze fanned her hair softly against her cheek. It was five-thirty of a Sunday afternoon, and the small playground, tucked away in a corner of the park, was all but deserted. The swings and seesaws stood motionless and abandoned, the slides were empty, and only in the sandbox two little boys squatted diligently side by side. *How good this is,* she thought, and almost smiled at her sense of well-being. They must go out in the sun more often; Morton was so city-pale, cooped up all week inside the gray factorylike university. She squeezed his arm affectionately and glanced at

Larry, delighting in the pointed little face frowning in concentration over the tunnel he was digging. The other boy suddenly stood up and with a quick, deliberate swing of his chubby arm threw a spadeful of sand at Larry. It just missed his head. Larry continued digging; the boy remained standing, shovel raised, stolid and impassive.

"No, no, little boy." She shook her finger at him, her eyes searching for the child's mother or nurse. "We mustn't throw sand. It may get in someone's eyes and hurt. We must play nicely in the nice sandbox." The boy looked at her in unblinking expectancy. He was about Larry's age but perhaps ten pounds heavier, a husky little boy with none of Larry's quickness and sensitivity in his face. Where was his mother? The only other people left in the playground were two women and a little girl on roller skates leaving now through the gate, and a man on a bench a few feet away. He was a big man, and he seemed to be taking up the whole bench as he held the Sunday comics close to his face. She supposed he was the child's father. He did not look up from his comics, but spat once deftly out of the corner of his mouth. She turned her eyes away.

At that moment, as swiftly as before, the fat little boy threw another spadeful of sand at Larry. This time some of it landed on his hair and fore-head. Larry looked up at his mother, his mouth tentative; her expression would tell him whether to cry or not.

Her first instinct was to rush to her son, brush the sand out his hair, and punish the other child, but she controlled it. She always said that she wanted Larry to learn to fight his own battles.

"Don't *do* that, little boy," she said sharply, leaning forward on the bench. "You mustn't throw sand!"

The man on the bench moved his mouth as if to spit again, but instead he spoke. He did not look at her, but at the boy only.

"You go right ahead, Joe," he said loudly, "Throw all you want. This here is a *public* sandbox."

She felt a sudden weakness in her knees as she glanced at Morton. He had become aware of what was happening. He put his *Times* down carefully on his lap and turned his fine, lean face toward the man, smiling the shy, apologetic smile he might have offered a student in pointing out an error in his thinking. When he spoke to the man, it was with his usual reasonableness.

"You're quite right," he said pleasantly, "but just because this is a public place. . . . "

The man lowered his funnies and looked at Morton. He looked at him from head to foot, slowly and deliberately. "Yeah?" His insolent voice was edged with menace. "My kid's got just as good right here as yours, and if he feels like throwing sand, he'll throw it, and if you don't like, you can take your kid the hell out of here."

The children were listening, their eyes and mouths wide open, their spades forgotten in small fists. She noticed the muscle in Morton's jaw tighten. He was rarely angry, he seldom lost his temper. She was suffused with tenderness for her husband and an impotent rage against the man for in-volving him in a situation so alien and so distasteful to him.

"Now, just a minute," Morton said courteously, "you must realize. . . . "

"Aw, shut up." said the man.

Her heart began to pound. Morton half rose; the *Times* slid to the
ground. Slowly the other man stood up. He took a couple of steps toward
Morton, then stopped. He flexed his great arms, waiting. She pressed her
trembling knees together. Would there be violence, fighting? How dreadful,
how incredible. . . . She must do something, stop time, call for help. She
wanted to put her hand on her husband's sleeve, to pull him down, but for
some reason she didn't.

Morton adjusted his glasses. He was very pale. "This is ridiculous," he
said unevenly, "I must ask you. . . . "

"Oh, yeah?" said the man. He stood with his legs spread apart, rocking a
little, looking at Morton with utter scorn. "You and who else?"

For a moment the two men looked at each other nakedly. Then Morton
turned his back on the man and said quietly, "Come on, let's get out of here."
He walked awkwardly, almost limping with self-consciousness, to the sandbox. He stooped and lifted Larry and his shovel out.

At once Larry came to life; his face lost it rapt expression and he began to
kick and cry. "I don't *want* to go home. I want to play better, I don't *want* any
supper, I don't *like* supper . . . " It became a chant as they walked, pulling
their child between them, his feet dragging on the ground. In order to get to
the exit gate they had to pass the bench where the man sat sprawling again.
She was careful not to look at him. With all the dignity she could summon,
she pulled Larry's sandy, perspiring little hand, while Morton pulled the
other. Slowly and with head high she walked with her husband and child out
of the playground.

Her first feeling was one of relief that a fight had been avoided, that no
one was hurt. Yet beneath it there was a layer of something else, something
heavy and inescapable. She sensed that it was more than just an unpleasant
incident, more than defeat of reason by force. She felt dimly it had something
to do with her and Morton, something acutely personal, familiar, and
important.

Suddenly Morton spoke. "It wouldn't have proved anything."

"What?" she asked.

"A fight. It wouldn't have proved anything beyond the fact that he's bigger than I am."

"Of course." she said.

"The only possible outcome," he continued reasonably, "would have
been—what? My glasses broken, perhaps a tooth or two replaced, a couple of
day's work missed—and for what? For justice? For truth?"

"Of course," she repeated. She quickened her step. She wanted only to
get home and to busy herself with her familiar tasks; perhaps then the feeling,
glued like heavy plaster on her heart, would be gone. *Of all the stupid, despicable
bullies*, she thought, pulling harder on Larry's hand. The child was still
crying. Always before she had felt a tender pity for his defenseless little body,

the frail arms, the narrow shoulders with sharp, winglike shoulder blades, the thin and unsure legs, but now her mouth tightened in resentment.

"Stop crying," she said sharply. "I'm ashamed of you!" She felt as if all three of them were tracking mud along the street. The child cried louder.

If there had been an issue involved, she thought, *if there had been something to fight for. . . . But what else could he possibly have done? Allow himself to be beaten? Attempt to educate the man? Call a policeman?* "Officer, there's a man in the park who won't stop his child from throwing sand on mine. . . . " The whole thing was as silly as that, and not worth thinking about.

"Can't you keep him quiet, for Pete's sake?" Morton asked irritably.

"What do you suppose I've been trying to do?" she said.

Larry pulled back, dragging his feet.

"If you can't discipline this child, I will." Morton snapped, making a move toward the boy.

But her voice stopped him. She was shocked to hear it, thin and cold and penetrating with contempt. "Indeed?" she heard herself say, "You and who else?"

· · · · · · ·

49 · MAN TO MAN: ABUSE ISN'T WORTH IT

EDWARD W. GONDOLF AND
DAVID M. RUSSELL

We want to talk to you, *man to man.* No beating around the bush or fancy lingo; just some hard facts we men must face. A lot of us are abusive—often in ways we don't even realize. We put women down, we control them, we physically hurt them. Often we don't mean it. Often we're unaware of our effect on them. We may brush it off as no big deal. Or we may think they had it coming. We may think, like Charlie, that abuse is natural or expected.

"Something Snaps"

Charlie has been a conscientious furniture sales representative for some twenty years. He is also the devoted father of four children, two of whom are in college. He and Mary, his wife, have had their "tense times," but only in the last few years has he ever hit anyone. One day he slapped Mary and gave her a black eye. Since then he has been physically abusive again and again.

Charlie asks, "Why? Why? It just seems automatic. Something snaps and— wham—I go off like a gun." He recalls recently throwing a bowl of chili at Mary, and swinging at her. "She knows I don't like chili cooked with those kind of beans. But I still shouldn't have hit her. I know that is the one thing you don't do. My father drummed that into me. You never hit a woman. I mean, that is about as low as you can go."

In recent years, the occasional outbursts worsened. Charlie started breaking Mary's favorite china and other possessions. Finally, his wife went "on a vacation" and sent the children to stay with a relative, leaving Charlie to fend for himself.

Charlie admits that he has some rigid attitudes that can lead to angry confrontations. He believes, for instance, that children should obey their parents, "especially in this time of confusion and doubt." So, if his younger daughter does not do the dishes when he tells her to—right after dinner—or leaves her room messy after being told to clean it up, "I let her know what I think about it. That's my duty. Someone has to keep them in line."

Charlie also explains that he feels he must always be on top of his work. "There are the end of the quarter reports to be completed, a new sales representative to train—who doesn't know what he is doing—and my wife's mother is in poor health." He sighs, "It does start to wear on a guy after a while." As the tensions mount so does Charlie's sense of responsibility. "Whenever Mary empties her basket of problems, I feel I have to fix them all."

In thinking about his style, Charlie says, "I admit I'm a perfectionist. If you're going to do something you might as well do it right. Why have the bricks out of line or a nail bent if, with a little more effort, you can do it right? I know Mary or the children offer to help me sometimes, but it isn't always worth it because I'm so demanding. I realize I should be a little more patient, but it's hard."

As he reexamines his abusive incidents, Charlie recalls that he "had just had it." When asked why he didn't do something about his feelings before they turned to violence, he explains, "I should not have to tell people that I'm fed up. They should have enough sense to know that they are out of line." He does not talk specifically about his wife without prodding. Rather than implicate her in the abuse, he criticizes her homemaking:

"I give Mary all sorts of things, too much in fact. I let her decorate the house the way she wanted and gave her the money she needed. I was giving, giving—and she was fretting about little things."

As Charlie realized, abuse is no good—for us or them. If it hasn't caught up with you yet, it is going to sooner or later. Many men we know who have been abusive find themselves deserted and alone, despised by their wives or lovers and children, shamed by their neighbors. More and more, men who abuse are even ending up in jail. Our society is starting to get tough with those who abuse.

ABUSE ISN'T WORTH IT

When we abuse women, we destroy those whom we love. We harm women much more than we ever realize. We hurt them physically because we don't know our own strength. We hurt them emotionally because we don't know the impact of our words and actions. We hurt their self-esteem, their will, their love.

We also hurt our children. They will probably become emotionally crippled because of our abuse. Even more frightening, it's very likely that they will grow up to be abusive like their father and have troubled relationships of their own.

Do we want this for ourselves or for our loved ones? More and more men are saying *"No!"* They are trying to do something to stop their abuse. We think you might want to join them.

STOPPING THE ABUSE

You can stop your abuse. Although it isn't easy, it can be done. If you accept the challenge, we know that you will appreciate the results. While gaining more control over your behavior—which is itself a good feeling—you may even discover a world of new friendships and better relationships. This may sound like a puffed-up promise. Nevertheless, it is a possibility—one we think is worth working for.

Our first goal is to help you stop any behavior that even approaches violence—especially any grabbing, pushing, pulling, shoving, hitting, or hair pulling. These are not only harmful, they are against the law. The ultimate goal to work toward is staying *stopped*. We have to begin to change not just our behavior, but ourselves, in order to do this.

There are some practical steps you can take—steps that will help you stop yourself from being violent. Remember, though, they are not an end in themselves. Don't use them like a crutch. They are merely a safety precaution—something like putting handcuffs on for the moment.

The most common safety precaution—one you can start using right now—is taking *time out*. The idea of *time out* is for you to leave the house and cool off before you become abusive. It is a deal that you must work out with your wife. Use it to help you both, never as a way to manipulate or get back at her. Here are the procedures for taking a *time out*. You should review them with your wife.

1. Identify a "cue" that trouble is coming (usually a physical sign expressed by a tightening chest, clenching of your hands; or a feeling that you must control her).

2. Give a T-sign with your hands to show you need to take a TIME OUT as soon as you feel that cue.

3. Let your wife know that you need a time out to get control of your behavior. Let her know how much time you need to calm down.

4. Depart without slamming the door or making any further comments.

5. Walk briskly (it's better not to drive) while thinking about the *Self-Talk* statements below. Call a friend. Don't drink.

6. Return at the end of your stated time limit and admit at least one error you made before leaving. (If an argument develops, take another *time out*, or agree on a later time to discuss the matter.)

Some programs, instead, require men to develop a "responsibility plan." In this approach, the men establish, with their wives, several alternatives to violence—what the husband and wife can do if the man is abusive. We think it's a good idea to move toward such a negotiated plan, one that goes beyond *time out*. Meanwhile, it is important that you establish a means to interrupt the abuse before it starts. *Take time out . . . and be safe.*

USING POSITIVE SELF-TALK

We are our own worst enemy. Over and over again we say defeating things to ourselves: "I can never change," "It isn't worth it," "I don't need any help," "I can't change until she does." Our mind keeps rehearsing past events and building mountains out of molehills. We store up burdensome resentment and keep convincing ourselves how we have been wronged. If you think about it, the process is almost like self-hypnosis. The best way to avoid hypnosis is to refuse it.

Many programs recommend talking to ourselves positively, to check the negative thoughts. It's a matter of having faith that we can and will be better than what we think. We all have abilities that lie largely untapped. Assert some of those to yourself—once a day when you get up—and especially when taking a *time out*. Here is a list of "can's" you might say to yourself:

1. I can change.

2. I can learn new ways of thinking and acting.

3. I can show my feelings in nonabusive ways.

4. I can ask for help when I need it.

5. I can ask for what I want but know that I cannot always get it.

6. I can tell people when I cannot fulfill their expectations of me.

7. I can reject stereotypes of how I am "supposed" to be.

8. I can take responsibility for my actions.

9. I can show my strength by choosing *not* to abuse someone.

These "can's" may appear to be way beyond your reach. If so, you may want to think beyond your own limits and will. Some people choose to contact that "strength" through a groups of caring people; some through nature.

Some self-help programs such as Alcoholics Anonymous, encourage their members to open themselves up to spiritual power. Whatever religion or name you might try to put on it, there is a power beyond our individual efforts that harmonizes and improves life. It's that power that gives us the potential, courage, and strength to change.

· · · · · · · ·

50 · MAKING LOVE IN SPANISH DIFFERS

SHEPHERD BLISS

"Where are you staying?" The cinnamon-shaded Spanish nurse inquires. "In a hotel in Las Ramblas," I answer, referring to Barcelona's promenade, down which everyone strolls, night and day. *"Puedes quedar en mi casa* (You're welcome to stay in my home)," she offers.

Hospitality to strangers remains strong in Spain and other Mediterranean cultures. Thinking she probably lives with a large family, I feel her invitation to be gracious and probably not sexual. After all, we had just met a couple of days before at a conference. But, I wonder, what is the message in her invitation? And what do I feel in response to her initiative? And what do I do?

I decline. After all, I am here in Barcelona—beautifully suspended between the Mediterranean Sea and two majestic mountains—for professional, rather than romantic, reasons. I had been invited to the Eighth Congress of Humanistic Psychology to offer workshops on the men's movement; men and women from over a dozen countries attended my presentation.

Assumpta smiles at my hesitation, then suggests dinner together, which I gratefully accept, basking in the golden glow of her skin and her radiant, outgoing presence. Barcelona exudes beauty—human and panoramic. Its air is charged with the sea's connective moisture, its views incredible, and its art among the best in the world. The streets bristle with activity; people live outside, invite you on *paseos* (strolls), or to the musical fountain. The afternoon meal is quite social and can take hours, followed by a *siesta* (nap), during which the entire city closes down. With its Catalan culture, Barcelona has long been a European crossroads where people gather.

As Assumpta and I walk to my hotel after dinner, she takes my hand and holds it tenderly. "Another Latin custom," I think to my Anglo self, noticing that many are holding hands and gently touching each other. The first verbal initiative had been hers, then physical initiative. Now she is looking—deep black eyes—at me very warmly: visual initiative. I love it when women take initiative.

We hear the sad and florid strains of *cante jondo*—deep song—which is part Moorish, part Oriental, part Gregorian, part Jewish, and very gypsy. It evokes my longing. Assumpta is also very *gitano* (gypsy); she crackles with irrepressible enthusiasm. Assumpta was literally clicking castanets when I first met her, adding high notes to the low tones I was playing on my drums.

Still not fully understanding what is happening, I remember those typical Anglo-Latin conversations—where the Latin moves closer, to feel comfortable, and the Anglo backs off, also to feel comfortable. I have prided myself in not being a typical Anglo, but am I backing off? Or is she really coming forward? Something mysterious, beyond my comprehension, seems to be happening.

A part of me melts by the attention. I also keep some professional (Anglo?) distance. Where are my defenses? Perhaps back home in California. What are the rules here? Assumpta reaches up, extends herself, gives me a light kiss, in the middle of my confusion, and departs, *"Hasta mañana* (See you tomorrow)."

I stand for a while as she walks off, alone, down Las Ramblas. It is past midnight. We have just finished dinner, which began at 10 P.M., the typical dinner time here. The streets are full of people; it is a Wednesday night. This culture is quite distinct. Who will I be here?

I took the risk of sending this essay to Assumpta. Her response was immediate, strong, thoughtful and full of the passion that drew us together originally. "A beautiful declaration of love—a public statement of what we have expressed privately," was how she described the essay. She was so moved that we arranged to meet again, after not having seen each other for half a year.

Assumpta's memory of our first evening together was amazingly similar to mine. She added (in my rough translation from her Spanish), "The gaze which we exchanged made me feel very close to you—so much in the eyes. Simply looking was a deep experience of rich emotion for me. In those first moments I did not feel as much sexual attraction as tenderness and the desire for fusion."

Looking into Assumpta's eyes, holding her hand, my mind goes back 40 years to Panama and my childhood. I remember the black panthers, boa constrictors, and three-clawed sloths in the jungle outside our backyard. During Panama's rainy season it pours almost every day, usually at the same time. A sensual naturalness and wholeness exists to the trees and wild creatures, which I miss in urban America's more artificial environment. In Latin America's rural areas people are more a part of the scene of animals and plants, rather than separate from nature. I remember Panama's dark, attractive people. Their melodic Spanish language entered my soul forever.

"Don't ever go into that jungle again," my stern military father loudly commands, restraining me from the lush expanse that comes up to the fence in our backyard. I remember the Panama Canal Zone, where I was raised, as a moist, dark place full of tropical plants and wild animals. My little friend Gordie and I would crawl through the bamboo in search of excitement. Something ancient was fulfilled as we penetrated the opening reeds.

Full of four-year-old boldness, I curiously respond to my towering father, "Why can't I go into the jungle?" My giant, khaki-clad father seems to get even bigger, "Because the wild animals might eat you alive." He adds, "Or the headhunters might get you." My eyes get wider as he goes into his room, returning with a bag from which he deliberately pulls out a sight I will never forget—a shrunken head, "You'll end up like this."

Gordie and I never returned to that wilderness beyond the fence, except in our imaginations. The sight of that ugly, tiny head terrorized me and remains embedded in my memory.

Years later I returned to Panama and asked a Panamanian historian, "How are your headhunters doing?" He laughed. "You must have been raised in the Canal Zone." I marveled, "How can you tell?" He noted, "Because the headhunter fiction is what military parents use to control their children's natural curiosity. We are a dark people and the jungle is a wilderness, but our people are not headhunters."

Fear of the wilderness (including sexual wilderness), as well as racism, were what my controlled military family was teaching me by the headhunters fabrication. "Stay away from animals and wild things," was their message, including that vital, refreshing animal instinct within this boy—which so frightened my adult parents. "You might get hurt." Deep inside me there is a story that seeks to block my natural impulse of going toward the otherness of dark, and the beckoning rain forest.

I had been lured by the moist Latin jungle, and restrained by my cautious Anglo parents. Today I echo the lament of that great Spanish poet Federico Garcia Lorca, "Give me back/ the soul I had as a boy,/ matured by fairy tales,/ with its hat of feathers/ and its wooden sword. . . . "

My eyes continued to incline toward the beauty and otherness of Spanish and my eyes towards olive-colored skin. That darkness and otherness have become part of my erotic preferences. My adult passions include "the life of the mind" (the motto of the University of Chicago, where I did my doctoral studies) and relating to dark women. My desire reaches equally toward the eros of books and women, seeking connections with both.

Assumpta is not really my "type"—young, not well enough organized, short—let me count the many ways I can talk myself out of a deep connection. But there she is, standing in front of me, looking at me with such open eyes. Then touching me . . . hugging me . . . kissing me. I love the ways in which she takes initiative. Her shamelessness. "*Me de las ganas* (I have the desire)," she would say. Responding to her opens me to places that I have not felt for years.

Assumpta's earthiness, a characteristic of Spanish women, draws me to her. She is both exuberant and introspective. She carries Spain's *sol* and its *sombra*—sun and shade. She is bright and deep. Spain is Western Europe's wildest country, and Assumpta is one of its daughters. Spain's bread—rough and unrefined—is symbolic of the qualities its people retain and is some of the best bread I have ever tasted. "My initial feelings toward you were very primitive," Assumpta revealed. "They had no logic or room for reason. I was very impulsive—driven by an instinct of great pleasure and affection with a mixture of feelings."

"Trust your body," I whisper to myself. "Trust your heart," I add. "You'll not be hurt," I reassure myself, "And if you are, you can mend." I'm out of my element. I don't know where I am. Who I am. What I'm saying. It comes from my mouth—but such strange sounds—this Spanish. So many ways to speak of love—*amor, carino, te amo, te gusto, to quiero*. In Spain people are forever giving each other *besos* (kisses) on both cheeks and *abrazos* (embraces). I don't know where I am. Who I am. I don't even know how to get anywhere from here. I feel goal-less. Yet not rootless or without ground.

As I recall Assumpta's *abrazos* I associate them with the embrace of another Latin friend—Gilberto Madrid, a Chicano elder with our men's drumming group The Sons of Orpheus. A big man, he has a special way of drawing some of the younger men in our group—such as Guillermo Ortiz and myself—into his elder's *abrazo*. My capacity to connect with Assumpta, as well as with other women, is aided by the men's movement. My brothers support me in my explorations of male models of feeling and being—beyond shame and judgment. I played one of Assumpta's songs to members of the Sons—who responded by making a tape of our drumming, singing, and playing around for her in various languages. We invited her to visit in California, which for various reasons has not yet happened. Living in California, I realize how fortunate I am to be in a multicultural and multilingual environment, which engages various distinct parts of me. There are certain feelings, as well as gestures, that I have only in Spanish, aspects of me that emerge only when I am in the Spanish language or a Spanish culture.

Making love in Spanish is different than in English. It differs by approach, sound, pause, memory, expectation, and body closeness. Spanish words often end in vowels, which merge, whereas English words conclude frequently in consonants, which end. Spanish has a romantic legacy that has infused its words with passion less available in the more precise and logical English. Spanish and American modes of lovemaking are quite distinct. Spanish flows like a river, whereas English tends to be more orderly. Spain absorbed many cultures, some of which conquered her, whereas England dominated many peoples and lands. Their respective languages bear the imprints of those economic and political differences.

Yet part of what Assumpta says to me has a ring of female universality. "The woman will ask the man many times if he needs her, desires her, loves her. The woman wants proof of love to confirm that man's love feelings; the man expresses his love at times in ways which the woman does not understand. Women want evidence that the love is reciprocal and at the same level. At times the codes of communication between men and women are so distinct that lovers believe that the love does not exist and that it was all a marvelous illusion, a desire, a dream." She later adds, "The masculine message does not always conform to the feminine form and desire for communication."

Hearing this, I relax, knowing that Assumpta understands something that is essential to better relations between the sexes, which could be described not in terms of "the opposite sex" but as "the other sex." When women expect men to communicate like and be like women, they are bound to be disappointed, and vice-versa. The differences, especially in modes of communicating, can be quite significant, as well as interesting. A radical otherness distinguishes the sexes—which can bring us much pleasure, confusion, and sometimes pain and even misery.

One of the things Assumpta and I struggle about—sometimes playfully—is closing doors, both literally and metaphorically. I like the boundaries that closed doors provide, such as on bathrooms. Then I can have my privacy and not hear the sounds that can interrupt my writing. Assumpta does not like such boundaries—which can block her feminine flow. So she tends to go around opening doors; I tend to go around closing them. We are sometimes like a comic act—the European, Latin woman with her customs and the Anglo, American man with his, following each other around. People must wonder about us. At times our differences draw us together; at other times they separate us; often they are just comic, which sometimes we are able to perceive. She opens, perhaps inviting me in, which sometimes I accept, other times closing, retaining my boundaries, which have served me long—for better or worse.

The dance continues—sometimes with joy, other times with unmet longing and even sadness. Is this enough? I feel she wants more—an introvert's eternal dilemma: people always seem to want more than we offer. "These are my limits," I often feel. I am not always proud of them; but I have survived. They have protected me.

Thinking/feeling about sexuality, that pleasure gives way to longing. I left—Chile, Barcelona, and many other sides of sexual pleasure. All left behind, though somehow kept inside as well. Will I ever touch again, as deeply? I remember Barcelona's streets—narrow, loud, and full of people. Cars rushing by. And Assumpta's tiny, clean apartment at the top of the hill. Moments of deep relaxation and profound communication. Touching, and being touched.

· · · · · · ·

51 · BEAUTIFUL HAPPY DREAM WOMAN!

HERMANN HESSE

The first small town on the southern side of the mountains. Here the true life of wandering begins, the life I love, wandering without any special direction, taking it easy in sunlight, the life of a vagabond wholly free. I am much inclined to live from my rucksack, and let my trousers fray as they like.

While I have having a drink of wine in a garden, I suddenly remembered something Ferruccio Busoni once said to me. "You look so rustic," that dear man said to me with a touch of irony the last time we saw each other—in Zurich, not so long ago. Andrea had directed a Mahler concert, we sat together in our usual restaurant. I was delighted once again at Busoni's bright pale spiritual face, at the alertness in the most glittering enemy of philistines we still have with us.—Why does this memory come back?

I know! It's not Busoni I remember, or Zurich, or Mahler. They are just the usual tricks of memory when it comes to uncomfortable things; then harmless images thrust too easily into the front of the mind. I know now! With us in that restaurant sat a blond girl, shining, her cheeks glowing, and I never said a word to her. Angel! All I had to do was look at you, and it was suffering, it was all my delight, oh how I loved you for that whole hour! I was eighteen years old again.

Suddenly everything is clear. Beautiful, brilliantly blond, happy woman! I don't even know your name. For a whole hour I was in love with you, and today, on the sunny street in this mountain town, I love you again for a whole hour. No matter who has ever loved you, he never loved you more than I do, no man ever granted you more power over himself, unqualified power. But I'm condemned to be untrue. I belong to those windy voices, who don't love women, who love only love.

All of us wanderers are made like this. A good part of our wandering and homelessness is love, eroticism. The romanticism of wandering, at least half of it, is nothing else but a kind of eagerness for adventure. But the other half is another eagerness—an unconscious drive to transfigure and dissolve the erotic. We wanderers are very cunning—we develop those feelings which are impossible to fulfill; and the love which actually should belong to a woman, we lightly scatter among small towns and mountains, lakes and valleys, children by the side of the road, beggars on the bridge, cows in the pasture, birds and butterflies. We separate love from its object, love alone is enough for us, in the same way that, in wandering, we don't look for a goal, we only look for the happiness of wandering, only the wandering.

Young woman, fresh face, I don't want to know your name. I don't want to cherish and fatten my love for you. You aren't the end of my love, but its awakening, its beginning. I give this love away, to the flowers along the path, to the glitter of sunlight in my wine glass, to the red onion of the church tower. You make it possible for me to love the world.

Ah, what silly chatter! Last night in my mountain hut I dreamed about that blond girl. I was out of my mind in love with her, and would have given up all I have left of life, together with the joys of wandering, only to have her beside me. I have been thinking about her all day today. For her sake I drink my wine and eat my bread. For her sake, in my little book I make my sketches of the small town and the church tower. For her sake, I thank God—she is alive, and I got my chance to see her. For her sake, I'm going to write a song, and then get drunk on this red wine.

And sure enough: my first peace of heart in the serene south belongs to my yearning for a luminously blond woman on the other side of the mountains. How beautiful, her fresh mouth! How beautiful, how silly, how magical—this poor life.

· · · · · · ·

52 · REMEMBERING HELGA

RAYMOND CHANDLER

She was the beat of my heart for thirty years. She was the music heard faintly at the edge of sound. It was my great and now useless regret that I never wrote anything really worth her attention, no book that I could dedicate to her. I planned it. I thought of it but I never wrote it. Perhaps I couldn't have written it. Perhaps by now she realizes that I tried, and that I regarded the sacrifice of several years of a rather insignificant literary career as a small price to pay, if I could make her smile a few times more.

. . . I wasn't faithful to my wife out of principle but because she was completely adorable, and the urge to stray which afflicts many men at a certain age, because they think they have been missing a lot of beautiful girls, never touched me. I already had perfection. When she was younger she used to have sudden and very short-lived tempers, in which she would throw pillows at me. I laughed. I liked her spirit. She was such a terrific force fighter. . . . And she always won, not because she deliberately put on the charm at the tactical moment, but because she was so irresistible without even knowing it or caring about it.

. . . For thirty years, ten months, and four days, she was the light of my life, my whole ambition. Anything else I did was just the fire for her to warm her hands at. [From letters by the author after his wife's death.]

· · · · · · ·

53 · THIS RIPENING FRUIT

MALCOLM MUGGERIDGE

It was at this time that Kitty first became pregnant. I found the whole process utterly wonderful; her stomach gradually swelling up, and the thought that out of our fleshly gyrations, beautiful and hilarious and grotesque all in one, should come this ripening fruit, this new life partaking of us both, and breaking out of its cocoon—her womb—to exist separately in the world. I had seen death, now I was to see birth. A white stomach rounding out, and inside it something growing, moving, living. It gave a point to every touch and caress and heave and groan; like print in a foreign language, laboriously spelled over, until suddenly it says something, and one understands. How beautiful are the Magnificats, the songs of birth! How desolate and ultimately disastrous and destructive is the pursuit of Eros for its own sake! The sterile orgasm; the bow passed across strings and no music coming, the paddle dipped in the water and no movement following.

. . . .

54 · THE HARD FACTS OF JEALOUSY

BRIAN KNAVE

When my lover and I came together we were each ecstatic to have found a sexually tolerant mate, one who would allow extracurricular intercourse. Neither of us had ever known such a freedom, though we had both lustfully hoped for it. Transfixed with our advanced understanding, we considered this tolerance the irrefutable assurance that ours was true love—"I love you enough to let you do what you want." We swore off jealousy and moved under the same roof. We knew, of course, that monogamy was easier, but wasn't it an abomination of true love? We hoped to make Eros and Agape into the same thing. Amanda Ziller (*Another Roadside Attraction* by Tom Robbins) was our model: "A strange spurt of semen," she says, "is not going to wash our love away." So that was our creed—until now. Lately one of those strange spurts of semen is no longer a stranger. It is too familiar, it comes from the same guy every week or so. I know the smell and it sometimes makes me sick.

In quantum physics I learned, intellectually, the basic instability of All Things, the irrevocable Flux of the Universe. Of course I already knew that all things change, but Heisenberg's Uncertainty Principle confirmed it for me. One day I was looking out a window at the pavement below, trying to visualize the atomic reality of the asphalt. It's just energy, I told myself, solid only in relation to my corporeal form, which is also energy. If I jump, I'll simply mingle my atoms with those of the asphalt. I didn't test the theory, but I did return home with the conviction that jealousy is a lie. If nothing is eternally solid—eternally *there*—I reasoned, then it's a lie to possess something. We own nothing, not even the cells and atoms of our bodies. So I realized that love is not merely eternal, but exists *outside* the Spacetime/Energymatter system we inhabit. At that profound moment I could have walked in on one of my girlfriend's extracurricular lovemaking sessions and handled it gracefully, perhaps with no malice at all. That's what mental transcendence can do for you.

A friend tells me that jealousy is simply one of the human emotions, that we should never repress it. Sometimes—when it's convenient—I believe him, but I also imagine that jealousy might be one of the unnecessary by-products of human evolution. I grant that in Pre-Dawn man it may have served some function, but I can't think what function it serves today, other than being a key ingredient in the recipe for violence.

But it matters little where jealousy originated—I have to deal with it now. I entered my relationship with the understanding that promises are essentially lies. No one can guarantee fidelity. Many people pretend to, but then they fornicate on the side and are forced to lie—"the truth would hurt her." At least my lover and I communicate. When she comes home carrying a strange spurt of semen we talk about it, or at least try to. And you're damned right it hurts, it hurts worse than anything in the world. And I don't repress it, no, I go into a nonviolent but very aggressive rage. Than I get over it until the next time. But what's the threat? I know she loves me, I really don't think she intends to replace me with that other guy. *Can* a strange spurt of semen wash our love away? How about several strange spurts? I curse Amanda Ziller for being fictional—she couldn't be like that in real life. I bet even Tom Robbins is a jealous god. But what about the pornographic film stars I've read about? One famous porn queen has been happily married for thirteen years, and her husband directs many of her films. They claim they're not at all jealous. Now here's a man who regularly watches his wife getting screwed by other men and he can handle it. That bothers me, intrigues me, because I'm certainly not that advanced. Or is that advanced? Maybe he's just used to it.

I do have the right to ask my girlfriend to stop carousing, but she says then she'll resent me—which could rapidly deteriorate her love for me, she implies. When she's out doing it I start feeling like I should be doing it too, not to get back at her, but simply to keep up (though I do want her to get a taste of her own medicine). Of course it's not like I can go out and get laid every time she does. Who will deny that a woman has an easier time getting picked up than a man?

If humans were incapable of loving two or more persons at one time, the problem would be more than half solved, though I suppose worse problems would follow. But love really does exist outside of space and time. Indeed, I am still in love with most every lover I've had, and even some I haven't had. If I were to make love to any them, my current lover would be jealous. But she would not *want* to be jealous. Most couples we know profess monogamy while one partner or the other hops from bed to bed. My lover and I admit we are fallible from the start. We know that genitals can talk as loud or louder than promises. So we don't fool ourselves. And we hope that neither of us takes undue umbrage of our mutual promiscuity tolerance. But it's impossible to draw the line between what is or isn't permissible. We're at the stage that we detest jealousy (note that the word contains *lousy*), but we still succumb to it at times. We tolerate extracurricular sex, but still cringe and cry when we find out about it.

· · · · · · ·

55 · CAN-CAN

ARTURO VIVANTE

"I'm going to go for a drive," he said to his wife. "I'll be back in an hour or two."

He didn't often leave the house for more than the few minutes it took him to go to the post office or to a store, but spent his time hanging around, doing odd jobs—Mr. Fix-it, his wife called him—and also, though not nearly enough of it, painting—which he made his living from.

"All right," his wife said brightly, as though he were doing her a favor. As a matter of fact, she didn't really like him to leave; she felt safer with him at home, and he helped look after the children, especially the baby.

"You're glad to be rid of me, aren't you?"

"Uh-huh," she said with a smile that suddenly made her look very pretty—someone to be missed.

She didn't ask him where he was going for his drive. She wasn't the least bit inquisitive, though jealous she was in silent, subtle ways.

As he put his coat on, he watched her. She was in the living room with their elder daughter. "Do the can-can, mother," the child said, at which she held up her skirt and did the can-can, kicking her legs up high in his direction.

He wasn't simply going out for a drive, as he had said, but going to a café, to meet Sarah, whom his wife knew but did not suspect, and with her go to a house on a lake his wife knew nothing about—a summer cottage to which he had the key.

"Well, good-bye." he said.

"Bye," she called back, still dancing.

This wasn't the way a husband expected his wife—whom he was about to leave at home to go to another woman—to behave at all, he thought. He expected her to be sewing or washing, not doing the can-can, for God's sake. Yes, doing something uninteresting and unattractive, like darning children's clothes. She had no stockings on, no shoes, and her legs looked very white and smooth, secret, as though he had never touched them or come near them. Her feet, swinging up and down high in the air, seemed to be nodding to him. She held her skirt bunched up, attractively. Why was she doing that of all times *now*? He lingered. Her eyes had mockery in them, and she laughed. The child laughed with her as she danced. She was still dancing as he left the house.

He thought of the difficulties he had had arranging this *rendezvous*—going out to a call box; phoning Sarah at her office (she was married, too); her being out; his calling her again; the busy signal; the coin falling out of sight, his opening the door of the phone box in order to retrieve it; at last getting her on the line; her asking him to call again next week, finally setting a date.

Waiting for her at the café, he surprised himself hoping that she wouldn't come. The appointment was at three. It was now ten past. Well, she was often late. He looked at the clock, and at the picture window for her car. A car like hers, and yet not hers—no luggage rack on it. The smooth hardtop gave him a peculiar pleasure. Why? It was 3:15 now. Perhaps she wouldn't come. No, if she was going to come at all, this was the most likely time for her to arrive. Twenty past. Ah, now there was some hope. Hope? How strange he should be hoping for her absence. Why had he made the appointment if he was hoping she would miss it? He didn't know why, but simpler, simpler if she didn't come. Because all he wanted now was to smoke that cigarette, drink that cup of coffee for the sake of them, and not to give himself something to do. And he wished he could go for a drive, free and easy, as he had said he would. But he waited, and at 3:30 she arrived. "I had almost given up hope," he said.

They drove to the house on the lake. As he held her in his arms he couldn't think of her; for the life of him he couldn't.

"What are you thinking about?" she said afterwards, sensing his detachment.

For a moment he didn't answer, then he said, "You really want to know what I was thinking of?"

"Yes," she said, a little anxiously.

He suppressed a laugh, as though what he was going to tell her was too absurd or silly, "I was thinking of someone doing the can-can."

"Oh," she said, reassured. "For a moment I was afraid you were thinking of your wife."

· · · · · · ·

56 · THE GODDESSES AND MASCULINE PSYCHOLOGY

JOHN A. SANFORD AND GEORGE LOUGH

The goddesses are particularly important for an understanding of feminine psychology, but they are also important for understanding masculine psychology. While the gods portray those archetypes that can directly shape a man's ego, the goddesses portray those archetypal powers that influence a man from the unconscious. Their effect on a man is more subtle but no less profound than that of the masculine archetypes. In fact, in some men in whose psyches the feminine plays an especially important role, the feminine powers may be the dominant powers. We have already seen, for instance, that in the case of a musician or other kind of artist the Muses personify determining archetypal influences. In similar fashion, while a man like General George S. Patton of World War II fame may have been a devotee of Ares, god of war, a Dr. Zhivago is a true son of Aphrodite.

Even a brief resume of the major goddesses of Greece will give us helpful insights into the psychology of the feminine in a man. We have already considered the Muses, so we will begin with Aphrodite.

Aphrodite was the goddess of the rapturous love-embrace, of union with the beloved, and of the bringing of life to fruition. It was said by Hesiod that when the god Cronus avenged himself on his father Uranus, Uranus' male member fell into the sea. White foam swirled up from the spot where Uranus' phallus floated on the water and out of the foam emerged Aphrodite. When Aphrodite came to shore, the earth bloomed, and Eros and Himeros, the gods of love and longing, escorted her joyfully to the place of the gods. Hesiod says that Aphrodite's "portion of honor among men and gods is girlish babble and deceit and sweet rapture, embraces, and caresses."[1] She became the goddess who stirred all living creatures to make love and be fruitful. Only Artemis, Athena, and Hestia could restrain her charms; all others, divine and human alike, were under her power, so surely could she ensnare and enchain them with her charms. She manifested herself in blooming gardens, which were often consecrated to her. The rose was sacred to her, as was the apple tree. The love that she inspired was no respecter of the sanctity of marriage, and under her influence a man or woman might shatter the most honorable and sacred vows for the sake of the beloved. Aphrodite was accompanied by a retinue of lesser goddesses including the three Graces, and, especially, Aidos, whose name means shame, modesty, and reticence. Not all was beauty in her eyes, however, and Aphrodite also reveled in the strife and quarreling that so often accompanies lovemaking. She could also be cruel, especially to women, whom she sometimes inspired with an impossible love for an unsuitable man. Those who spurned her felt her wrath. Hippolytus, for example, was a young man so devoted to Artemis that he paid no heed to Aphrodite. She was so offended at his negligence that she changed herself into a monster, and so frightened the horses of Hippolytus that they dragged his chariot to destruction and him to an untimely death.

When Aphrodite stirs a man she fills him with the longing for love. He is driven by the archetypal energy that she symbolizes to seek union with the beloved. If the man is particularly unconscious she will be experienced on the lowest, most grossly lustful level. On the highest level she will be the power urging him to union with the Divine. If he denies this energy in himself it will torment him all the more, manifesting itself perhaps in sexual obsessions, anxiety, or depression. In some men Aphrodite represents the most important archetype in the psychology. Such men gravitate toward, and love, the world of the feminine. They may be devoted to the graceful and beautiful side of life and shun that which is harshly masculine. As we have mentioned, they are the Dr. Zhivagos of this world for whom love, beauty, and relationships are the truly compelling things of life. This does not mean they are not masculine men, only that their masculinity is enlisted in the service of love rather than of war or power, science or craft.

Hera was the wife of Zeus and the queen of heaven. She resided on Mount Olympus where she presided in regal fashion over the banquets of the gods. She was not so much mother, however, as queen and matriarch. She was fiercely jealous of Zeus' frequent amors with mortal women and once implored Aphrodite for the loan of her golden girdle, which gave to the wearer an irresistible power in love. Yet basically her province was not love, the love-embrace, and passion, but the sanctity of marriage as an honorable and necessary social institution. She personifies that archetype that brings forth, guards, and protects all the social institutions that give cohesiveness to the social order and enshrine and perpetuate the highest of social values.

A man in whom Hera prevails as an archetypal power of the feminine will be drawn toward the social order and its preservation. For instance, he might become a clergyman who is devoted to the church, caring for her and her enshrined values protectively and lovingly. The institution of marriage will be important to him because of the values that it nourishes and cherishes, although his actual relationship with his wife, while correct and supportive, might lack intimacy and depth. He might well be a political conservative in his desire to protect and perpetuate the world of established values. His devotion will be to the collective order of things, rather than to the personal, to social concerns and values rather than to the individual soul.

Artemis was the goddess of free, virginal nature, with its shining brilliance and enchanting, awe-inspiring wildness. Hers was not the maternal side of nature, but its purity and remoteness, and also its harshness and cruelty. Hers were the clear air of the mountain tops, the untouched depths of virginal forests, the remoteness of flower-strewn meadows, and the sparkling clarity of clear streams and springs. She was the mistress of that which is pure, that which delights and enchants, but also that which is dangerous. She was the uniting principle that weaves together all the multitude of natural forms into a sublime whole. Wild animals were sacred to her, especially the lion and the bear. Indeed, she was called "the Lady of the wild beasts."[2] She was the goddess of distance and the vast and fascinating ranges of mountains were her special province. The migratory bird was thus an appropriate symbol for this goddess who, like Hermes, called men to distant journeys and was a good companion to travelers. Because of her chasteness she was immune to the power of Aphrodite and her passion. She was devoted instead to athletes and presided over the athletic competitions of ancient Greece.

Men in whom Artemis is predominant are likely to be constant and faithful but somewhat remote in their relationships. Their special province in relationship is not the world of sexuality and desire but that of firm, strong companionship. They will have a love for the wilderness and may make good members of environmental organizations with a passionate, holy zeal in their defense of untouched nature. A man like John Muir is an excellent example of this type of man. For him, wilderness is sacred, and its destruction a violation of all that was holy; he simply could not understand that other men (in whom there were different archetypes) could see wilderness only as something to be subdued. Such men may also have a mystical bent, a far-seeing inner vision that often gives them deep insight. The long-distance runner, content in his contemplative solitude, rejoicing in the chaste strength of his body, will likely have Artemis running beside him.

Demeter was the earth mother goddess whose passion and function was to nourish all living creatures. Hers also was the province of love, but for the child more than for the lover. Hers was the elemental or primitive feminine world, and hers was the power that caused the earth to bear fruit and the crops to grow. Like Aphrodite and Artemis she also had her dark and dangerous side, for she could devour the children to whom she gave birth, and could also neglect her divine task of bringing the earth to fruition. Indeed, when her daughter Kore was abducted by Hades, king of the underworld, she was so stricken with grief that she neglected the earth and its needs. Winter then came, and the whole earth became cold; life retreated, and nothing grew. Only when her daughter was restored to her half of the year did she relent. Spring then came, and flowering, blooming summer.

A man in whom Demeter is a strong influence will have a way with children, will be a faithful and devoted father, a protector and nourisher of all that is young and helpless. While Hera guards the sanctity of home and marriage, Demeter guards the young child, and a man who serves the archetype of Demeter will likewise serve all that needs his caring nourishment. A clergyman might turn this nourishing energy to his congregation, a politician to the city, a psychotherapist to a client, a doctor to a patient, a gardener to the seedlings in the garden, a farmer to his fields. Wherever helpless living creatures need a helping hand the man with Demeter in him will be drawn to fill the need.

Hestia is the goddess of hearth and home, but for its own sake, not simply as a place in which the children live. She is the least known of the goddesses, and indeed there is little to be told about her, but that in itself reveals her character. For Hestia is content to lead a simple and even invisible life. In a man she is that instinct that draws him away from the world and back to the safety and nourishing comfort of hearth and home. Here he is content for a while to enjoy the simple pleasures of warm fires at night and the snug comfort of home as a nest. Under the influence of all that Hestia represents he puts aside, at least for a while, his urge to fame or desire to make an impression on the world. If she is an especially strong influence in a man he may live a life known only to a few, yet will find this not a lack of fulfillment but a comfort and a joy.

Athena, like Artemis, was a virgin goddess. She was not born from a woman's womb but sprang into life from the head of Zeus himself, fully grown, and arrayed in warlike armor. For Athena was a warrior goddess. However she did not relish war for the sheer love of combat as did Ares, but waged war coolly, employing strategy, and inspiring warriors with courage. She particularly excelled in wars in defense of that which was noble and sacred, and was justly acclaimed for this by the Athenians, who named their city after her. In Homer's *Iliad*, the brawling Ajax was a son of Ares, but the clever Odysseus was the favorite of Athena.

Athena's province is intelligence and wise counsel, practical understanding, and thinking things through. She is a creative and constructive goddess who inspires men and women to creative achievement. From her comes culture. The joiners learn their art from her, the smiths also, and the potters, indeed all those who engage in artistic handicraft. Her special animal is the owl, symbol of wisdom and the capacity to see even in the darkness. Nothing pleases her more than the emergence in a man of greatness, consciousness, and heroic action. In a man, Athena personifies the capability for a larger than usual life; he will tend toward the heroic, and will be inventive and inclined to cultural achievement. While not prone to begin strife, he will be a man to be reckoned with should conflict be unavoidable.

We hope this brief resume of the most important goddesses of Greece, with descriptions of how they live on today in a man's psyche as archetypal influences, will give some idea to the scope and importance of the archetypes and particularly the feminine archetype in a man's psychology. However, our discussion brings up another point for which Jung's psychology has sometimes been criticized: that it divinizes the psyche.

For instance, Jung sometimes uses the word *numinous* to describe the archetypes. The word numinous was coined by Rudolph Otto to describe the idea of the holiness of God.[3] Some critics of Jung say that by using the word numinous to describe the psyche Jung in divinizing it, and setting it up in the place of God.

The psyche does not take the place of the transcendent God, but it is a fact that the archetypes produce in us fascinating, awe-inspiring, and emotionally gripping effects, and that these are the qualities of numinosity as described by Rudolph Otto. The archetypes *act* like divinities, which is why they were personified as divine beings in an age in which mythology anticipated psychology. Jung does not make the psyche into a divinity; it is the psyche itself that is numinous. The numinosity of the psyche is attested to by the effect on us of a nightmare. For at least a brief time after we awaken from a nightmare we are all believers.

· · · · · · ·

PART 6

THE TALL ONE CALLED FATHER: PSYCHOLOGICAL, MYTHIC, RELIGIOUS, AND PERSONAL REFLECTIONS

I do not want my children to have a monolithic memory of me. . . . On the contrary, I would like them to know the vulnerable man that I am, as vulnerable as they and perhaps more so.

GEORGES SIMENON

We were not like father and son, my father sometimes said, we were like buddies. I think my father sometimes actually believed this. I never did. I did not want to be his buddy; I wanted to be his son. What passed between us as masculine banter exhausted and appalled me.

JAMES BALDWIN

INTRODUCTION

. . . .

The title of this section comes from a satirical television vignette of a few years ago. His back to the viewer, a man walks pensively, barefoot, shoes in hand, along a solitary California beach. A male voice, effecting Hallmark Card nostalgia against a backdrop of sentimental elevator music, is heard wistfully recalling childhood memories of family outings that included "a tall man we called dad." The irony is flawless: the viewer is led to accept the premise that this now-adult son remembers primarily that *back then* there was usually another man present called father, who was simply "tall." The spot ends with the man wandering into the distance as the music fades.

Back then . . . wandering . . . distance . . . fades. These images capture the spirit of contemporary reflections on the father–son relationship, especially recollections of fathers by sons. It's a fact that almost all the great fiction and plays about fathers and sons are written by sons. Ours is a literature, notes the political scientist Harold Isaacs, "in which writers across the generations have tried to deal with the experience of wrenching free from their fathers or have written sad or tender memoirs about what their fathers were like as they finally came to remember them."

The opening selections here offer just such reflections. We begin with "For My Father Who Never Made It to Paris" by San Francisco writer Phil Cousineau, author of *The Hero's Journey: The Life and Work of Joseph Campbell*. Next, North Carolina novelist David Guy ("Of God, and My Father: A Memoir") remembers sleepless childhood nights, concerns about God's existence, and the disease that would take his father's life. Armenian mystic G. I. Gurdjieff talks about the important things he learned from his father, and novelist/poet James Dickey recalls the final moments of his father's life. San Francisco writer Michael Shorb offers "My Father's Garage on Christmas Night," a poem that appeared in *The Sun*. From his autobiography *Childhood of the Magician,* Hermann Hesse recalls his father as belonging neither to "the world of the idols . . . nor to the workaday world of the city."

Robert Bly, in a final excerpt from my interview with him, says that the deep longing for father in modern culture reflects, in part, the Industrial Revolution's removal of fathers from home life. Northern California psychotherapist Thomas Steele, in an essay written for this volume, extends Bly's thoughts: "Not only is the father either physically or psychologically absent from our homes and family life . . . but our philosophers and theologians have started to pronounce him gone from our mythological and religious lives as well." Steele explores the story of Abraham and Isaac as a meditation on initiation, infanticide, and primal tension between the "Great Father" and the "Son of Promise." In "Mentor as Father," taken from his book *Finding Our Fathers: The Unfinished Business of Manhood,* Massachusetts psychologist Samuel Osherson argues that for many men, "the experience of trying to separate from their fathers colors their relationship with mentors, making separation and rejection critical components of the mentor-mentee dynamic."

Jungian analyst James Hillman's short, provocative essay ("Fathers and Sons") urges skepticism toward the widespread assumption that men don't get the fathering they need. The cry to be fathered is typically based on an idealized image of father, says Hillman, who argues that "deficient" (abusive or absent) fathering constitutes a valuable initiation into a man's sense of darkness, loss, grief, and shadow. "The commonality—and commonness—of shared shadow can bond father and son in dark and silent empathy as deep as any idealized companionship," Hillman concludes.

Nor Hall offers an equally fresh perspective in a brief excerpt from *Broodmales,* a wonderful book focusing on the folk customs of *couvade*—"brooding" or "hatching"—in which a man takes on the specific sexual and emotional events of a woman's body so that her experiences become his. The father "becomes pregnant, writhes in labor, nurses the child, suffers postpartum fatigue—in short, is a male mother," writes Hall, a St. Paul, Minnesota, psychotherapist.

Lou Becker, a community organizer from rural Georgia, closes this section with a moving selection entitled "An Older Father's Letter to His Young Son," which originally appeared in an anthology called *New Men, New Minds: Breaking Male Tradition.* Now that so many sons have begun to call out to their lost fathers, I hope more fathers will follow Becker's example and speak from their hearts to their sons—before they are lost, too.

. . . .

57 · FOR MY FATHER WHO NEVER MADE IT TO PARIS

PHIL COUSINEAU

For my father who never made it to Paris
I meet friends late at night in smoky cafes
To drink frothy cappuccino and listen
To Coltrane sax solos on old jukeboxes,
And talk of the wounds
Of fathers and sons.

For fathers and sons
Who never returned home,
I reach down for words to express my grief,
Like an emergency ward surgeon groping
For stray shrapnel in the flesh
Of bleeding loved ones.

For all the words never found between men,
The buried burning words slowly infecting us,
I drop quarters in no-name bar telephones
To call suicidal friends, distraught fathers,
Lone wolf sons who howl at the indifference of the moon,
And offer the round table of brotherhood.

For all the tumors caused by sorrow,
And all the ulcers formed by anger,
For all the nightmares wrought by rage,
And all the emptiness carved by despair,
I probe friends and family
For healing stories.

For my father and all fathers
Who never saw Paris,
One friend listens, reveals,
Reaches in an open wound,
Finds a piece of gold shrapnel,
Cashes it in for airfare,
Takes his father to the Left Bank.

So the healing
Can begin.

· · · · · · ·

58 · OF GOD AND MY FATHER: A MEMOIR

DAVID GUY

When I was ten years old I passed through a period when I could not sleep. Probably the first sleepless night was an accident, or perhaps the first two, but I began to worry about them, and soon I couldn't sleep at all. Long before bedtime I would start feeling anxious, and however tired I might have been all evening, by the time I was ready for bed I was awake and alert. In my anxiety I would go to my parents, trying to laugh, make light of it all, and they would laugh with me, aware of my worries and wanting not to add to them. We would laugh at my comic arrival in their bedroom, at ten o'clock, eleven, eleven-thirty, at twelve; when it got that late they would say, "Oh David, are you *still* awake?" and I could see the concern behind their smiles, and perhaps a trace of annoyance, as they let me come with them into their bed, and promised that if I were too tired the next day, I would not have to go to school.

My memories of my father are vivid from those years. I particularly remember the long, hot summer evenings, when we would have opened every window and door, trying to catch a breeze (my father announcing its arrival with a shout like a command: "Feel the breeze"); by the late evening it did get cool, and quite comfortable, as we sat reading in the living room. He would still be wearing a white shirt, rumpled by then, from work, and an old pair of khaki pants that he relaxed in. He did not smoke at the office—I think he felt a doctor shouldn't smoke in front of his patients—but in the evening would take some cigarettes from my mother's pack and smoke them between the hours of his nap (he always took a nap after dinner) and his late bedtime. He had a can of beer beside his chair, which through the evening must have been two or three cans; he was not a heavy drinker, but would have a drink before dinner and those several beers afterward. My father sitting with several buttons of his shirt open, so the thick graying hair of his chest showed; his light occasional sips from the beer; the three or four long, quiet exhalations of smoke from his lungs (when I later took up smoking, I would try to duplicate exactly those sounds); the rustling sound as he turned a page—I sat on the couch less to read than to be enveloped in that atmosphere. I was too old, by then, to sit with him in his chair, feel the warmth of his breath on my head, smell the faint odor of his sweat, but being just a few feet away was almost as comforting.

Those nights when I could not sleep I began to ask the unanswerable questions. I don't remember whether my sleeplessness was a result of the anxiety they caused me, or whether, already awake, I stumbled upon those questions that were to cause me so much anguish. At first they did not exist in my mind as questions, simply an attempt at comprehension: I was trying to understand eternity, and I could not. I would picture endless blackness, like the utter darkness I had experienced once in the depth of a cavern; I would imagine myself moving through it with no end to my movement. I would try to imagine existing with no expectation for tomorrow, next week, next year, or the end of time, because there would be none, only an endless present. I would try to understand how God could exist with no beginning to his existence, how there could be an existence with no beginning, and then, by analogy, would try to conceive of my own life with no end, but I couldn't do it; I would imagine myself, in that eternal blackness, thinking, "But it all must have started sometime, so it must sometime be going to end," and if it all did end sometime—the universe, God, everything—what would be there in its place? What had been there before it began?

It may be that I was just afraid of dying, that I had suddenly discovered death—certainly the thought of eternal non-being terrified me—but somehow I was equally afraid of eternal life. What I could conceive of it—an existing with no particular purpose, goal; a thousandfold anxiety at its indeterminate future—seemed impossible, incredible, grotesque, an existence no one could want to lead.

Great thinkers have said that of all the eternal possibilities, endless life on this mortal Earth would be the worst. Yet, I also think that in those days what I most wanted was an assurance that my life as it existed then would infinitely continue, that there would be one after another of those quiet summer evenings with my father.

I finally took my fears to him, late on one of those nights when I couldn't sleep. I have calculated: he died when I was sixteen, and I was told then that he had known of his illness for more than six years. I was experiencing those fears at the same time he had discovered the disease in his body that was to kill him. I can remember my mother telling me of his long silences in those days just after he had been to the doctor; she had to wait several days for him to tell her what was wrong. I have often wondered if, by coincidence, I was asking him those questions at the worst possible time.

I remember his first reaction, a laughing, quizzical concern, as if he were amazed I had brought those things up. I don't remember exactly how he answered me. I don't remember, either, that what he said particularly set my mind at rest; there was a long period when I could only get to sleep in bed with my father and mother. But I do remember something he told me, and perhaps it was the most important thing, just because it is what I have remembered through all the years.

He must have sensed my solitude. For as I tried to imagine eternity, I did not envision a physical location, and therefore did not picture anyone around me. I knew that eternal life was to be spent in communion with God, but I didn't know what that involved, what activity could last through eternity. I pictured only myself, in endless space and time, and the answer my father offered me—not as a little story you tell your son to allow him to sleep, but as a belief so much a part of him that it came naturally to his mind (if he had believed there was no eternal life I think he would have said that)—was that I was not alone, that I lived in the presence of God. It's odd as I think of it: he didn't say that I would some day live in the presence of God; in a way he wasn't answering my questions at all. But he said that when we are young we are unaware of God's existence, of any existence, in fact, but our own; as far as we are concerned, the universe revolves around our being. It is only as we grow— perhaps he said if we grow—that we discover we are not the center of things, that the core of existence lies elsewhere, and, inasmuch as we continue to grow, we move out from concern with ourselves, try to center our existence in that core. The whole process of growth, in fact, involves that moving out from ourselves. Inasmuch as we grow at all we are involved in a search for God.

Those few words—it took him only moments to say them—did not

make the universe any smaller or simpler for me. I have no memory of immediately putting what he said into practice. I doubt that I really understood it; I
had never thought of God in anything even remotely like those terms. But it
must have impressed me. It is what I have remembered through all the years,
even more than my fears.

Those fears have not disappeared. It seems the nature of human existence
that, no matter how well we once explain them away, they do return, because
they are not rational concerns. I still sometimes envision the darkness, feel the
leaden weight of eternal time. But I think of my father, facing death straight
on, devoting even his last days to his family, patients; I think of my wife, son,
friends, the many lives that I touch just by being alive; I think of God, in an
infinite universe, calling others into being that He might love them—just as,
by loving, even we can call others into being. And my fears are not dispersed
(I must learn to live with the fears within me always), but I do see a shadow, a
hint, of the nature of eternal life.

· · · · · · ·

59 · WHAT I LEARNED FROM
MY FATHER

G. I. GURDJIEFF

My father had a very simple, clear, and quite definite view on the aim of human life. He told me many times in my youth that the fundamental striving of
every man should be to create for himself an inner freedom toward life and to
prepare for himself a happy old age. He considered that the indispensability
and imperative necessity of this aim in life was so obvious that it ought to be
understandable to everyone without any wiseacring. But a man could attain
this aim only if, from childhood up to the age of eighteen, he had acquired
data for the unwavering fulfillment of the following four commandments:

First—To love one's parents.

Second—To remain chaste.

Third—To be outwardly courteous to all without distinction, whether
they be rich or poor, friends or enemies, power-possessors or slaves, and
to whatever religion they may belong, but inwardly to remain free and
never to put much trust in anyone or anything.

Fourth—To love work for work's sake and not for its gain.

My father, who loved me particularly as his firstborn, had a great influence on me.

My personal relationship to him was not as toward a father, but as toward an elder brother; and he, by his constant conversations with me and his extraordinary stories, greatly assisted the arising in me of poetic images and high ideals.

．．．．．．．

60 · A FATHER'S DYING BEAUTY

JAMES DICKEY

Long deathwatch with my father. Nothing in his wasted and lovable life has ever become him so much as when he moved close to death. It is astonishing to understand that one's father is a brave man: very brave. The only thing he worried about was my seeing him in that condition. He cannot ever understand, whether he lives or whether he dies, how much better he looked with his arms full of tubes, with one of those plastic hospital things in his nose, and the rest of it, than at any time I have ever seen him before. He was a man up against an absolute limit, and he was giving as well as he got and he was afraid of nothing in this world or out of it. God bless that man. No matter how I came from him, I hope that it was in joy. For the end is courage.

．．．．．．．

61 · MY FATHER'S GARAGE ON CHRISTMAS NIGHT

MICHAEL SHORB

Back after all these years and older,
The silence better, more like
Friendship, two neighbors
Rooting for the same team.
Rafters are filled with the detritus
Of mutual lives: a tent we used

For camping at the lake, a punching bag
No one hits now, my sister's furniture.
And your workbench is piled higher
Than ever with a hundred
Accomplished or forgotten
Repairs and adjustments,
Power sander and soldering iron askew,
A wood box filled with broken things
Waiting to be renewed.

This is what you ended up with.
A garage domain, a world of certain things,
Perfect fits. I don't question it anymore.
Perhaps, half lost in worlds of ideas
And perplexions of beauty, I even envy
This yoga of wood and metal tightly joined,
Of things held down by nuts and bolts.

Admiring this platter you once fashioned,
Quail in flight on smoky plastic, I praise
It perhaps too much, or awkwardly, meaning
A hundred other appreciations left unspoken,
Meaning to say you weren't what I thought,
That you never understood the anger
Of your sons, the drugs, the grasping
For roads. America has nothing
    to do with this.

There's just the two of us, looking
More alike than we realize, feeling
What we don't know how to say.

· · · · · · ·

62 · MY FATHER WAS DIFFERENT

HERMANN HESSE

My father was different. He stood alone, belonging neither to the world of the idols and of my grandfather nor to the workaday world of the city. He stood to one side, lonely, a sufferer and a seeker, learned and kindly, without falseness and full of zeal in the service of truth, but far removed from that noble and tender but unmistakable smile—he had no trace of mystery. The kindliness never forsook him, nor his cleverness, but he never disappeared in the magic cloud that surrounded my grandfather, his face never dissolved in that childlikeness and godlikeness whose interplay at times looked like sadness, at times like delicate mockery, at times like the silent, inward-looking mask of God. My father did not talk to my mother in Hindu languages, but spoke English and a pure, clear, beautiful German faintly colored with a Baltic accent. It was this German he used to attract and win me and instruct me; at times I strove to emulate him, full of admiration and zeal, all too much zeal, although I knew that my roots reached deeper into my mother's soil, into the dark-eyed and mysterious. My mother was full of music, my father was not, he could not sing.

. . . .

63 · FATHER HUNGER IN MEN

ROBERT BLY

KEITH THOMPSON:
Underneath most of the issues we've talked about is the father or the absence of the father. I was moved by a statement you made in *News of the Universe* that the love-unit most damaged by the Industrial Revolution has been the father-son bond.

ROBERT BLY:
I think it's important that we not idealize past times and yet the Industrial Revolution does present a new situation because as far as we know, in ancient times the boy and his father lived closely with each other, at least in the work world, after age twelve.

The first thing that happened in the Industrial Revolution was that boys were pulled away from their fathers and other men and placed in schools. D. H. Lawrence described what this was like in his essay, "Men Must Work and Woman as Well." What happened to his generation as he describes it, was the appearance of one idea: that physical labor is bad. Lawrence recalls how his father enjoyed working in the mines, enjoyed the camaraderie with the other men, enjoyed coming home and taking his bath in the kitchen. But in Lawrence's lifetime the schoolteachers arrived from London to teach him and his classmates that physical labor is a bad thing, that boys and girls both should strive to move upward into more "spiritual" work—higher work, mental work. With this comes the concept that fathers have been doing something wrong, that men's physical work is low, that the women are right in preferring white curtains, and a sensitive, elegant life.

When he wrote *Sons and Lovers*, Lawrence clearly believed the teachers: he took the side of "higher" life, his mother's side. It was not until two years before he died, when he had tuberculosis in Italy, that he began to realize it was possible that his mother hadn't been right on this issue.

A mental attitude catches like a plague. "Physical work is wrong." And it follows from that that if father is wrong, if father is crude and unfeeling, then mother is right and I must advance upward, and leave my father behind. Then the separation between fathers and sons is further deepened when those sons go to work in an office, become fathers, and no longer share their work with their sons. The strange thing about this is not only the physical separation, but the fact that the father is not able to explain to the son what he's doing. Lawrence's father could show his son what he did, take him down in the mines, just as my own father, who was a farmer, could take me out on the tractor, and show me around. I knew what he was doing all day and all the seasons of the year.

In the world of offices this breaks down. With the father only home in the evening, and women's values so strong in the house, the father loses the son five minutes after birth. It's as if he had amnesia and can't remember who his children are. The father is remote, he's not in the house where we are, he's somewhere else. He might as well be in Australia.

And the father is a little ashamed of his work, despite the "prestige" of working in an office. Even if he brings his son there, what can he show him? How he moves papers? Children take things physically, not mentally. If you work in an office, how can you explain how what you're doing is important, or how it differs from what the other males are doing? The German psychologist Alexander Mitscherich writes about this situation in a fine book called *Society Without the Father*. His main idea is that if the son does not understand clearly, physically what his father is doing during the year and during the day, a hole will appear in the son's perception of his father, and into the hole will rush demons. That's a law of nature; demons rush in because nature hates a vacuum. The son's mind then fills with suspicion, doubt, and a nagging fear that the father is doing evil things.

This issue was dramatized touchingly in the 1960s when rebellious students took over the president's office at Columbia looking for evidence of CIA involvements with the "university." It was a perfect example of taking the fear that your father is demonic and transferring the fear to some figure in authority. I give the students all the credit they deserve for their bravery, but on a deeper level they weren't just making a protest against the Vietnam War, they were looking for evidence of their father's demonism. A university, like a father, looks upright and decent on the outside, but underneath somewhere you have the feeling that he's doing something evil. And it's an intolerable feeling that the inner fears should be so incongruous with the appearances. So you go to all the trouble to invade the president's office to make the outer look like the inner, to find evidence of demonic activity. And, then, naturally given the interlocking relationships between establishments, you do discover letters from the CIA and demonic links are found! But the discovery is never really satisfying, because the image of the demons inside wasn't real in the first place. These are mostly imagined fears: they come in because the father is remote, not because the father is wicked. Finding evidence doesn't answer the deep need we spoke to in the first place—the longing for the father, the confusion about why I'm so separate from my father, where is my father, doesn't he love me, what's going on?

KEITH THOMPSON:

Once the father becomes a demonic figure in the son's eyes, it would seem that the son is prevented from forming a fruitful association with *any* male energy, even positive male energy. Since the father serves as the son's earliest role model for male ways, the son's doubts will likely translate into doubts toward the masculine in general.

ROBERT BLY:

It's true, the idea that male energy, when in authority, could be good has come to be considered impossible. Yet the Greeks understood and praised that energy. They called it Zeus energy, which encompasses intelligence, robust health, compassionate authority, intelligent, physical, healthy authority, good will, leadership—in sum, positive power accepted by the male in the service of the community.

The Native American understood this too—that this power only becomes positive when exercised for the sake of the community, not for personal aggrandizement. All the great cultures since have lived with images of this energy, except ours.

Zeus energy has been disintegrating steadily in America. Popular culture has destroyed it mostly, beginning with the "Maggie and Jiggs" and "Dagwood" comics of the 1920s in which the male is always foolish. From there the stereotype went into animated cartoons, and now it shows up in TV situation comedies. The young men in Hollywood writing these comedies have a strong and profound hatred for the Zeus image of male energy. They believe that they are giving the audience what it wants or simply that they're working to make a buck, whereas in fact what they are actually doing is taking revenge on their fathers, in the most classic way possible. Instead of confronting their father in Kansas, these television writers attack him long distance from Hollywood.

This kind of attack is particulary insidious because it's a way of destroying not only all the energy that the father lives on but the energy that he has tried to pass on. In the ancient tradition, the male who grows is one who is able to contact the energy coming from older males—and from women as well, but especially male spiritual teachers who transmit positive male energy.

KEITH THOMPSON:

I find in your translations of the poems of Ranier Maria Rilke, as well as in your own most recent book of poems, *The Man in the Black Coat Turns,* a willingness to pay honor to the older males who have influenced you—your own father and your spiritual fathers. In fact, in the past few years, you seem to have deliberately focused on men and the masculine experience. What inspired this shift in emphasis away from the feminine?

ROBERT BLY:

After a man has done some work in recovering his wet and muddy feminine side, often he still doesn't feel complete. A few years ago I began to feel diminished by my lack of embodiment of the fruitful male or the "moist male," I found myself missing contact with the male—or should I say my father?

For the first time, I began to think of my father in a different way. I began to think of him not as someone who had deprived me of love and attention or companionship, but as someone who himself had been deprived, by his mother or by the culture. This process is still going on. Every time I see my father I have different and complicated feelings about how much the deprivation I felt with him came willfully and how much came against his will—how much he was aware of and unaware of. I've begun to see him more as a man in a complicated situation.

Jung made a very interesting observation; he said that if a male is brought up mainly with the mother, he will take a feminine attitude toward his father. He will see his father through his mother's eyes. Since the father and the mother are in competition for the affection of the son, you're not going to get a straight picture of your father out of your mother. Instead, all the inadequacies of the father are well pointed out. The mother tends to give the tone that civilization and culture and feeling and relationship are things that the mother and the son and the daughter have together. Whereas, what the father has is something inadequate. Still, maybe brutal, unfeeling, obsessed, rationalistic, money-made, uncompassionate.

So the young male often grows up with a wounded image of his father— not necessarily caused by the father's action, but based on the mother's observation of these actions.

I know in my own case I made my first connection with feeling through my mother, she gave me my first sense of human community. But the process also involved picking up a negative view of my father and his whole world.

It takes a while for a man to overcome this. The absorption with the mother may last ten, fifteen, twenty years, and then, rather naturally, a man turns toward his father. Eventually, when the male begins to think it over, the mother's view of the father just doesn't hold up.

Another way to put all this is to say that if the son accepts his mother's view of his father, he will look at his own masculinity from a feminine point of view. But eventually the male must throw off this view and begin to discover for himself what the father is, what masculinity is.

· · · · · · · ·

64 · FATHER INITIATION
WHEN FATHERS ARE ABSENT

THOMAS R. STEELE

Now the story of Abraham has the remarkable property that it is always glorious, however poorly one may
understand it; yet here again the proverb applies, that
all depends upon whether one is willing to labor and
be heavy laden.

SØREN KIERKEGAARD[1]

We live in an era of absent fathers. The father is either physically or psychologically absent from our homes and family life in increasing numbers, and
our philosophers and theologians have started to pronounce him gone from
our mythological and religious lives as well. "God is dead!" said Nietzsche
just over a century ago, and the reverberations of his pronouncement have
continued until the present day.[2] In fact, one can characterize the past 200 or so
years as a relentless slaying and eradication of the father wherever he is found.
Our Enlightenment belief in progress and enthusiasm for finding knowable
fixed laws has rendered the lawmaker, or father, obsolete. The father has thus
become the expendable parent.

It is difficult to know just what to make of such a situation except to say
that it is now increasingly the norm that when a man looks within his own
soul he will at some level find an absent father. If instead of resisting this fact
we accept it, then we can use this perspective to help unravel a difficult paradox that faces modern men. The paradox involves a transition, perhaps we
should say an initiation, into the realm of the fathers even if they are absent. In
contrast to rites in which adolescent boys are initiated into the community of
men, I am speaking of the transition of the mature man into his own unique
existential individuality—a father initiation.

Stories about father transformation are rare, so when we find one we are
well-advised to take special care to listen. The story of Abraham and his
sacrifice of Isaac on Mount Moriah is such a story. From the perspective of
Isaac, the story resembles the typical initiation rite of the young man through
separation, ordeal, and return. However, it is the change in Abraham that distinguishes this story. He starts the journey to Mount Moriah as the father of a
great nation, but returns as the father of faith. It is this change in the father
that will be our focus.

I suggest not looking at the story of Abraham and Isaac as a story about the relationship between fathers and sons. There are enough of these already. As psychologist James Hillman notes, it is the splitting of the father-son relationship between the generations that perpetuates this cultural wound in men. It cannot be healed in that form.[3] Rather, we will look at the story as it applies to the father and son as they are found within the individual psyche. From this point of view, Abraham can be seen as any man who tries to reconcile within himself the demands of the Great Father (the Lord) and the Son of Promise (Isaac). When we psychologize a story in this way we must remember that we are not telling the true (that is, de-mythologized) version, having somehow solved its mysteries like a riddle. Rather, we are telling a version that opens its issues to everyday life. Where it goes from there is its own business.

> Now the Lord said to Abraham, "Go forth from your country, . . . And from your father's house, To the land which I will show you; And I will make you a great nation, . . . And in you all the families of the earth shall be blessed." (Gen. 12 : 1–3[4])

This is quite a heady deal! However, if we look past the exciting possibilities presented we see some important features of the father/son relationship as it relates to our inquiry. First, we see what we have dimly suspected all along: The absent father carries within him an absent son. The Great Father appears as an authoritative voice that contains within his words a verbal image of the Son of Promise.[5] We could call this the father's son, which, in contrast to the mother's son, has a particularly masculine developmental course.[6] Second, we see that even though they appear they are still, in a sense, absent—without body. It is precisely Abraham's willingness to embrace them both, in this unsplit form, that opens his ordinary life to its heroic dimensions.

I would argue that calls to specific destinies are not limited exclusively to mythical figures, but that we all heed such calls. The heroic period of a man's life begins when he embraces and acts upon the call to achieve his own unique place in society. Whether that call is to be a business and family man, an artist, or a political reformer, they are all valid social roles, with a history, and as such are sanctioned by the fathers. It is usually the hope of a future promise that fuels a man's efforts to seek out and master his vocational role and achieve the position that he hopes will allow his promise to come to fruition. We could say that it is every man's task, after his adolescent initiation, to make this cultural adaptation.

But Abraham has a problem. Like so many couples today, Abraham and his wife Sarah are infertile. Like a knight errant, Abraham wanders and waits. In times of doubt the Great Father unwaveringly holds fast to His end of the deal and deepens it with renewed promises, rituals of covenant, and name changes. Yet both the Great Father and the Son of Promise remain absent, unseen. Whether our call has been to some great task or to the equally grandiose "simple life," there comes a time when the distance between the promise that inspires our efforts and our actual reality causes us to stop and reconsider. Perhaps it is at these times that we lose heart and sink into bitter resignation, or look for a new promise—a new career, a new wife, a new hope to recharge our lives. But Abraham remained true both as a son to the Great Father and as a father to the Son of Promise.

Now we get to the heart of the story. Finally the promise comes to fruition. Sarah conceives a son. Abraham is a proud and beaming father and raises Isaac dutifully to the age of puberty. It is perhaps one of the most satisfying moments in a man's life when he has finally "made it" in whatever form his own Great Father and Son of Promise have laid out. But we must be careful here to note that only the Son of Promise has been made visible, embodied, and it is just here that the story takes a twist.

> Now it came about after these things, that God tested Abraham, and said to him, "Abraham! . . . Take now your son, your only son, whom you love, Isaac, and go to the land of Moriah, and offer him there as a burnt offering on one of the mountains of which I will tell you." (Gen. 22 : 1–2)

It is here that most of us leave the story of Abraham, and who can blame us? We have worked too hard to bring our Son of Promise to a visible, tangible form to imagine answering such a call. With the call to infanticide the story becomes heavy laden. The fact that Abraham goes on forces us to consider some crucial questions. Surely it must have dawned on Abraham, as it does on us, that the heroic period of our lives in some subtle way is profoundly unsatisfying. Abraham's promise of being the father of a great nation hollows out as soon as he realizes that he will be long dead before the promise is fulfilled. In fact, in the story he does not even get to see his grandchildren. He could cut his losses here by refusing the call. And yet he goes on.

To understand this situation at all we must reinvestigate a man's relationship to his vocational role.[7] In primitive societies the elder men, who represent the fathers, wound and draw blood from the boys they initiate. In this way they communicate that the ancestors have a claim on their lives, which are no longer solely theirs. They have a duty to the cultural order and its social roles. The fact that the fathers wound but do not kill bears witness to the restraint of that claim. In our society these wounds stay open and can deepen dangerously during the heroic phase of life.

The fact that our capitalistic economy and international power posturing thrive so well on men's heroic energy usually obscures the fact that this phase of life is supposed to be limited. There are so many intoxicating incentives, power accessories, and remediations for tired heroes that we seldom get a chance to see the invitations to father initiation that await us. We see only the paths of heroes, anti-heroes, and losers. Yet, while the bright light of heroism shines, the infanticidal father remains in the shadows, deepening our wounds to mortal levels. I would argue that Abraham's willingness to sacrifice Isaac is not an act of infanticide but his willingness to reveal that the infanticidal father was there all along. We are just beginning to make this move in our own culture.

Splitting the father/son relationship leads to unresolvable conflict. Fathers continue to ask for blood, and sons continue to give it while fighting to get enough elbow room for their own sons to be born. For Abraham the split is between the absence of the Great Father and the presence of the Son of Promise. However, the resolution of that conflict takes an unpredictable twist. It seems as if the son is to be returned to his absent state as Abraham draws the knife. It is at this moment, when the infanticidal Great Father incarnates, that the mystery is revealed. At the critical moment there is a doubling of both the Great Father and the Son of Promise. From the Great Father comes the angel of mercy who restrains Abraham, and from Isaac there appears a ram caught in the bushes. And it is the ram who is to be sacrificed.

This whole situation turns on Abraham's willingness to embody and make visible the Great Father in his infanticidal form. I would contend that it is only when the absent Great Father is in some way humanized that he becomes aware of his infanticidal nature and restrains himself. Neither Isaac nor Abraham cry out for mercy nor is there any hedging about what is taking place. It is all laid bare. In this way, the Great Father enters the human arena and sees what obedience to his laws is costing. Until then it is a archetypal situation and, as such, it is compulsively driven by blind instinct. The sacrifice of the ram (that is, the animal instinctuality of the father/son relationship) frees both Abraham and Isaac to live their separate human destinies. But this release cannot happen until both are fully present.

> Abraham I cannot understand: in a certain sense I can learn nothing from him except to be amazed. (Kierkegaard[8])

The psychoanalyst Peter Blos has noted that the infanticidal father often lies at the rock bottom of his male patient's psychic wounds.[9] The issues involved tap into the deepest levels of emotion. Bringing this dynamic to consciousness is so difficult because restraint comes from the father himself and not from our pleading with him. It seems that in an era of absent fathers, such as ours, this aspect is exaggerated and compulsively driven. Such a situation amplifies and extends a man's heroic phase of life far beyond what is necessary or healthy. If this were not the case, then stories about drawing near to the infanticidal father would be wildly irresponsible and we would be better off to leave them alone.

It is no accident that Kierkegaard titled his book on Abraham *Fear and Trembling*. Who can read it without being shaken to the bones? However, it leaves us with a mystery. Since father initiation involves a return of individuality, it must be uniquely different for each person. Abraham's ordeal was specifically his own. Although we can use his example to open questions, no one can describe or predict in what form our own call to Mount Moriah may take. It seems to require a faith in one's own inner calling and a willingness to labor and be heavy laden.

. . . .

65 · MENTOR AS FATHER

S A M U E L   O S H E R S O N

It was with my mentor that I first recognized the unfinished father issues in my own life. For many men the experience of trying to separate from their fathers colors their relationship with mentors, making separation and rejection critical components of the mentor-mentee dynamic.

I actually wasn't all that interested in mentors when I started my research on men's lives. I talked at length to men about mentors, but that seemed to be more because *they* wanted to than because I did. Older, more senior men weren't relevant to the younger generation coming of age; gray, bland creatures, demanding and unsympathetic—so my conceit went. There I was, still distancing my own father, trying to act as if *he* were unimportant. That act chagrins me, now that I realize how much I depended on mentors for their love, indeed sought them out, and how angry I would be when they wouldn't give me what I wanted.

The day I went to see my mentor to tell him I was taking a year off, I felt absolute dread. It was at a time when I needed space and time away from my academic and research responsibilities. The hardest person to explain my planned absence to was the director of my department, whom I shall call Robert. Leaving would hurt his feelings, I feared. There seemed to be an unspoken obligation to be there. Separating and rejecting seem very hard to sort out at that point. And, too, I was scared to let go of him.

It was a gray early October day when I went over to the department to tell Robert of my plans for the year.

As I stepped off the subway and walked down toward the hospital building where our department was housed, my chest began to tighten. The place looked somber and depressing. Its presence diminished my plans for the year. Given so much suffering in those wards, why try to sort out my pain at all? I felt like a coward abandoning the field of battle.

At the departmental lunch, surrounded by other colleagues, including Robert, all of us munching on our brown bag lunches, I had a failure of nerve. I avoided telling them that I would hardly be around and finessed the topic when it came up. I found part of myself subtly aborting my carefully thought-out plan for the year. I almost started volunteering for *more* work when it was offered. Would I supervise some new psychiatrists? "How about lectures for a new course that needs your help, Sam?" "Sam, let's meet regularly to write that grant proposal we've talked about."

"Maybe, maybe," I found myself mumbling. "Let me think about it."

By the time I got home to dinner that night I was a total ball of what we call "stress" these days. My wife Julie asked me how my day had been.

"Okay I guess. Went over to the department. Staff lunch. Saw a lot of people." I gave voice to my disguised terror. "There's a lot going on over there. I'm thinking of doing some supervision, maybe writing that grant proposal."

There was a plea for help in those offhand comments. In my roundabout way I was silently asking, "Is it okay for me to say NO to all this? I need some support, or my whole year will be thrown away in these commitments I don't want!"

"Gee, Sam," Julie came through. "Don't you think you've got enough scheduled? Aren't you going to leave yourself some time?"

Tears formed in the back of my eyes when she said that, verbal proof of her faith in me, proof that she was on my side. It was more than I could say for myself. Her reply was like a beam of warm light, and in its warmth I could see the self-defeating part of myself that all day had been piling on the work, burying the hope of a calmer, more reflective, joyful year of self-discovery.

Where was the origin of my ambivalence? I could not get the face of my mentor, Robert, out of my mind. He had been smiling at me when I met him in the corridor before the lunch, a puff of smoke rising from his pipe. He was glad to see me. I in contrast felt like the carrier of a dirty secret: I was abandoning him. We would not be spending days together, doing our work together in the same old way.

He sits in his office busily at work, smoking his pipe, thinking, being careful, precise, and orderly.

He was too precise and restrained for me. All I felt was a need to get away, and that felt like abandonment. It was impossible to justify, and I couldn't explain.

For the last five years I had met with him once a week. We analyzed data, then sat around and talked. In my time of need, eight years ago, he was there for me. Feeling dead-ended in a university teaching job, dimly aware that I *had* to find something else, I began desperately writing fellowship and grant proposals.

Then, at the suggestion of a friend, I went to see Robert. We hit it off immediately. My grants to study the adult development of men were funded. Robert was interested, and soon I was working with him in his department. In contrast to my graduate school and junior faculty experience, where encouragement had been meagerly dispensed, as if there were a critical worldwide shortage, with Robert everything became good, more than good enough. Things I said in our talks became nuggets, treasures to be examined and thought out. Robert found my work fascinating. He is an eminent man in the field. Now I was working and studying with him as an equal. His confidence in me was a heady experience. The way he valued me was food and drink I couldn't get enough of. Yet suddenly it felt as though I had to get distance from him.

By an unlucky stroke of fate, that year he was in crisis too. His wife was deathly ill, budget cuts jeopardized his research, and I felt *his* need of *me*.

I wanted to be a good son for him, the good son everyone told me I already was for him. His wife confided that I'm his friend, that he talks at home about what we say at the office. Colleagues, worried about him, ask me how he's doing with all the troubles in his life.

And how is he doing? He's *doing* it: Takes care of his wife, applies for grants, sits patiently in his office, trains more scientists, meets with students, goes to all the meetings demanded of him. How can he do it? Doesn't he want to scream, cry, shout, destroy a few buildings? Where are his feelings? I couldn't stand being around that patient, aching silence.

Robert just endures! His silent message to me was that this is the fate of men, to swallow their emotions, rise above them, and get on with the work.

And in the depths of my soul I realized that to show my love for this man, to be the good son we both want me to be, I'd have to follow his example. We would have to spend the year sitting around and talking about *data*.

Does *he* want to be taken care of? I would wonder. Does anyone take care of him these days? No. He looked haggard and drawn, and seemed not to notice it himself. I would look at him, see so much unacknowledged pain, and feel a terrible sadness. To live with someone who needs caring but will not accept it is a terrible, brutalizing thing. I wanted to talk about what it is like to have a wife dying, about how to ask for and get caring. How do you accept such misfortune? His answers would have been very significant, given that I idealized this man so.

Could I have said that to him? It felt impossible, as if taboo. I wanted to care for him, hold him, comfort him, but he made that impossible and I felt my own wish to care suspect—the pain too overwhelming and foreign. How do you comfort a father? How do you deal with a wife's dying?

Few pains in life are as intense as the recognition that you want to befriend someone and there's only one way to do it: Give yourself up.

He was in the "armor mode" stage of personal crisis in his life, taking care of his wife, so ill at home, keeping her as long as possible out of the hospital. This caring man just wanted to "get through." Yet how do we do that?

There is a deeper prohibition: *We will not talk about my experience of this.* I submit it is absolutely terrifying to have someone you love in jeopardy and not be able to find out what is going on within that person. And I submit too that this is routine for sons with fathers, and carries over to men's experience of mentors and work.

The day he told me of his wife's illness, Robert made the prohibition clear. He knocked on my door and asked if we could talk for a few minutes. Sitting heavily in the lounge chair in a corner, he came directly to the point:

"Ruth has cancer."

As we talked, he would answer any question I had. She had a recurrent history of it; this wasn't the first incident. Yes, it looked bad, but they were hopeful. He would tell the rest of the staff. He might have less time around the office than he had hoped. Any question he'd answer—except the most important.

"What's this all like for you?" I asked.

He waved his hand as if to dismiss the question. "It's tough, tough, but . . ." His eyes looked right at me, beseeching, "you understand." What did I understand? That a man doesn't need support when tragedy hits? That I had nothing in the way of deeper caring to offer? That I should not look for holding and caring when I was in pain?

The anger I felt at Robert may have lain in the obligation I felt, the sense of being valued only in terms of what I provided to my mentor. If I lived up to what he wants of me, he'll love me; if I try to be different, he will be enraged. The feeling men speak about of being "smothered" in a relationship reflects the feeling that our personality will disappear under the weight of another.

I believe my mentor got solace from my being there; we both seemed to me to have derived deep satisfaction and relief from my being like a son. Yet there was oppression in that demand, which can never be talked about, perhaps the same oppression women have identified as the objectification they experience from husbands and men as "just sex objects," or with mothers when they feel loved as adults only when they are "finally married." So too for sons.

We want to meet that obligation to endure in silence, to distance ourselves from our feelings and get the job done. The prohibition against talking of it leaves us all holding onto the obligation and trying to get away from it.

I went ahead with my year off, but we couldn't talk together about why I was doing it. What became a productive year was split off from him, filled with accusations of betrayal and rejection on both sides, with unfortunate consequences that were to take years to work out.

Those feelings about a mentor were surely "inappropriate." They may seem so particularly for people who don't like it when adult life gets muddied up with unfinished sadness from childhood. We do need to distinguish how the mentee approaches the mentor. When the mentee comes to the mentor as a needy little boy in search of an all-knowing, all-loving father, both men are put in a difficult position: The mentor may feel angry, constrained, and confused (without being sure why, since the parental overtones to the relationship are often hard to see), while the mentee will easily feel disappointed, guilty, and angry. When both mentor and mentee feel comfortable enough with their feelings, values, and identity—and with each other—to express themselves honestly and to explore relatively openly their mutual vulnerabilities and strengths, there is less difficulty. Clearly that happens in some mentoring relationships, but we must understand that the issue of male vulnerability becomes highly charged for both mentor and mentee from their own relationships with their fathers.

The question is not, Is it "right" to seek parenting from mentors? Given the male experience, it often may be inevitable. The derivation of the word mentor is instructive in this regard. Mentor was Odysseus' trusted counselor under whose disguise the god Athena became the guardian and teacher of Telemachus in his father's absence. Sons will need those transitional male figures to consolidate their identity as men; the price we pay is that father–son dynamics will reappear where we least expect it. Rather than working to keep it out of the relationship, both young and old might do better learning how to tolerate vulnerability better.

During my time away from the department I felt for months like a bad son, and a terrible question shadowed me: How did I ever abandon my father?

· · · · · · ·

66 · FATHERS AND SONS

J A M E S   H I L L M A N

This desire in the father to kill the child we ignore to our peril, especially since psychoanalysis descends from fathers. If this myth is foundational to depth psychology, then infanticide is basic to our practice and our thought. Our practice and our thought recognize infanticide in the archetypal mother, its desire to smother, dissolve, mourn, bewitch, poison, and petrify. We are aware that inherent to mothering is "bad" mothering. Fathering too is impelled by its archetypal necessity to isolate, ignore, neglect, abandon, expose, disavow, devour, enslave, sell, maim, betray the son—motives we find in biblical and Hellenic myths as well as folklore, fairy tales, and cultural history. The murderous father is essential to fathering, as Adolf Guggenbühl has written. The cry to be fathered so common in psychological practice, as well as the resentment against the cruel or insufficient father so common in feminism—whether as cruel or insufficient ruler, teacher, analyst, institution, program, corporation, patriarchy, or God—idealize the archetype. The cry and the resentment fail to recognize that these shadow traits against which one so protests are precisely those that initiate fathering.

This because: first, they kill idealization. The destructive father destroys the idealized image of himself. He smashes the son's idolatry. Whenever, wherever we idealize the father, we remain in sonship, in the false security of a good ideal. A good model, whether kind analyst, wise guru, generous teacher, honest chief, holds these virtues of kindness, wisdom, generosity, and honesty fixed in another, projected outside. Then, instead of initiation, imitation. Then the son remains tied to the person of the idealized figure.

Second, the terrible traits in the father also initiate the son into the hard lines of his own shadow. The pain of his father's failings teaches him that failing belongs to fathering. The very failure fathers the son's failings. The son does not have to hide his share of darkness. He grows up under a broken roof that nonetheless shelters his own failings, inviting him, forcing him, to be dark himself in order to survive. The commonality—and commonness— of shared shadow can bond father and son in dark and silent empathy as deep as any idealized companionship.

Third, the terrible traits in the father provide a countereducation. How better bring home a true appreciation of decency, loyalty, generosity, succor, and straightness of heart than by their absence or perversion? How more effectively awaken moral resolve than by provoking moral outrage at the father's bad example?

· · · · · · ·

67 · BROODMALES

NOR HALL

A Congolese Bantu sits stone still in front of his expectant wife's hut. All the cords and knots of his clothes have been cut so that when he rises he will be as naked as the child coming in. "Hatch as hatch can," as James Joyce says. This is how the father does it.

To make its way into the world, new life needs an opening. Infancy wants a tender reception. The man who goes to lie in the hammock next to the hut makes a receptive curve of himself to welcome the child. He unties knots and cords, opens doors and windows, unbraids hair, frees tethered animals, unfastens the moored boat. Everything bound up is freed so that energy can flow. This release is especially critical at the time of birth. Things need to be undone. The father needs not to go about business as usual, needs not to get things done, but rather to leave work undone, to brood rather than be busy.

In the beginning the Spirit of God "brooded over the face of the deep" in order to bring the first day out of darkness into light. As a great bird would hatch a cosmic egg, the Spirit settled its intent upon that which was not-yet-created. Such settling of intent upon us is often prelude to a creative emergence. To be brooded over is to be completely covered by an extraordinary concentration of warmth that waits for the slightest stirring in the depths. It is a gathering of energy that is nonforceful even though it has purpose. Its purpose is not to penetrate—which is unusual for the spirit regarded as masculine—but to bring forth. This intention to bring forth is powerful in the way of roiling black thunderheads gathering electricity to themselves or those majestic laboring clouds of Milton's that rest upon the mountain's breast. Brood force is as intense as the storming God and as soft as the under-belly of a hen. It is very heavy, but will not break an egg.

A mother with this brood awareness knows when a sleeping child stirs to the need of cover. The body so recently come from her own, where covering was accomplished merely by the child's dwelling *in utero,* feels like an extension of herself. A father, likewise, in the beginning, needs to spread himself out as if spreading his wings for cover (rather than for flight). Ainu fathers in northern Japan sit wrapped and still by the fire in the same room with the newborn. The brood male conserves his heat to pass it on to his child. Couvade customs recognize that children need warmth from their fathers, especially small children who need to be covered because they cannot take cover. They need to be brooded over, surrounded by thoughts, enveloped by the heart's heat, made the focus of concentrated energy that is not invasive. Our language locates the feeling of "cherishing" in the Old English *bredan* which means "to actively warm" or "direct the heat of the body towards."

Brooding turns ominous when it hovers without cherishing—as in the cases where fathers hurt their wives and children. Brooding turns morbid when it loses its object. Someone in a "brown study," for example—or shades deeper, a "black mood"—is so self-absorbed that his energy concentrates into an impenetrable field. Dark brooding establishes distance between people regardless of proximity. Roland Barthes describes that blackening of mood that will occur in relationships as "a faint black intoxication." The cloud that moves over the landscape of two of us is the thought "I am missing something." It is another covert symptom of couvade reported by women who sense their partner's emotional absence increase in proportion to their pregnancy. In these cases "the object lost" to the darkly brooding man is his wife. She is lost to him because her energy has shifted into the brooding mode that has internal life (that is, rather than his life) as constant focus.

Recent studies of the father's role in all aspects of childbirth identify four possible directions for his "pregnancy career" to take. In one, he denies the pregnancy, abandons the woman, and leaves to establish an alternate identity. In the second, he regards the pregnancy as his wife's responsibility and his place as peripheral. He may help if asked. Third, the father develops a special bond with the fetus and shares the pregnancy experience. And fourth, he claims total identification with the fetus, sometimes to the exclusion of the mother's role, and attempts to cut her off from everyday activities.

Boundaries between these possibilities blur a bit in the psyche where no man's repertoire is limited to a single part. The fact that customs of couvade seem to chart a man's course through a continuum of involvement represented by these too distinct, yet recognizable, roles suggests that we read between the lines to discern the arc of a plot. Most men will know the feeling of each of these courses at different times, in either their wives' pregnancies or as partner to their own creative process.

Couvade customs that are enacted primarily at the birth of the first child have as their aim the preparation of the man for becoming a father. Once he goes through the structural shift that thoroughly rearranges his sense of himself around a child's soul, he who was separate is no longer. Observances in the first stage of pregnancy require that a man give up his ordinary activities. In order to learn how to brood in the woman's way, he is cut off from the male world. He lays his hatchet in the arm of a tree and sticks his hunting spears into the ground. He can no longer be careless. If he fishes, someone else has to make the hooks or his child might have a harelip. If he is a builder, another man must drive the stakes into the soil. All violent moves, including riding a horse too hard, jumping from rooftop to rooftop, or climbing rocks, are to be avoided. It is because such actions "cause" miscarriage as Dawson's anthropologists report, or is it that the deliberate, daily exercise of care on the part of the father perceptibly attunes him to the body as carrier?

In practicing couvade, the male makes himself wombly. An initiated aboriginal man made womanly by sub-incision can imitate the womb's ability to open. Zeus, in the mythology of the Mediterranean, opened his own thigh in order to carry his unborn son. He did it with the loud cry of the father ringing out: "O Come child, enter this my male womb!" Then he bore the child God Dionysus in this makeshift prenatal chamber, which he closed with golden clasps.

A child emerging from such a father hold is called "twice born"—once from the mother and once from the father. As is the convention in patriarchal Christianity, the mother is mortal, of the earth and matter, and the father is immortal, belonging to the realm of overhead, "heavenly" bodies and metaphor. Tradition has it that one part needs to be grounded and the other lifted. In other eras it is the man who is grounded and the woman elevated. Either way, the child borne by the awareness of both is designated special, gifted, divine—a child of Earth and Starry Sky.

• • • • • • •

68 · AN OLDER FATHER'S LETTER TO HIS YOUNG SON

L O U   B E C K E R

Dear Jacob:

When I was a little boy, as you are now, my daddy—your grandpa—died. For a long, long time, I thought that he had done that on purpose, and I guess I thought that he did it just to get away from me. I didn't know why he wanted to, but that's the only reason I could think of for him leaving me. I tried to remember him, but I never could. I knew what he looked like, from pictures, but I couldn't *remember* him. I couldn't remember if he hugged me and kissed me; couldn't remember his voice, or his smell, and how he tasted when I kissed him. I missed him a lot, but I was also very angry at him for going away forever. So when I grew up, I thought that it was a good idea to try to be a person who didn't love other people a lot, because if you love someone a lot and he or she goes away forever, it hurts so much. But as I got older I discovered that you can't just *choose* to not love other people; if you love them, well, you just *love* them, that's all. But do you know what else I discovered? I discovered that you can *pretend* that you don't love other people, and you can make it very hard for them to love *you*. You can make up a lot of reasons why people *shouldn't* love you. You can pretend that people don't need you to hug them a lot, and talk to them about how you're feeling or about how *they're* feeling, and share private things. You can pretend that you don't ever feel like crying, because if someone sees you cry then that person might decide to make you cry by hurting you. You can pretend that you could live in a tree house, all by yourself, and be happy there because no one could hurt your feelings, or not like you, or go away forever and you wouldn't be able to remember them. I pretended all that stuff to your sisters and their momma, and to my momma and sisters, and I even pretended it to *your* mom for a long time.

But then something happened to me, and slowly I began to change. You know how when spring is just beginning and we see our daffodils start to change? First the stem gets green, and then the buds appear, still wrapped tight in their leaves. And then some morning, almost like magic, the yellow blossoms are there when we go outside. That's sort of how I was. My life had a new spring, and very slowly I began to change, too. I began to feel like a daffodil; just as the daffodil *knows* that it wants to open itself to the hugs and kisses of the sun and rain, and to give its pollen to the bees and its color and shape and smell to people to make them feel good about things starting to grow again after a brown winter, I also wanted to be like that. I wanted to open *myself*—to love and be loved, to grow, to *be* beautiful and to *feel* beautiful, to give myself because I had good things inside me to give to other people. Our daffodils act like they love us because they open up to us and give us pleasure and do their own natural things. They don't pretend that they're *weeds;* they don't hide their blossoms and their pollen so people and bees can't share them. They open up and grow because that's what daffodils are *for:* for loving the rain and sun, for loving the bees' hairy legs and tiny feet, for loving being cared for and needed and loved just as they are.

My spring began when you were born. That was the first warm day after my long brown winter: Even though it was cold and snowing that day, it was the beginning of my spring. I had pretended for so long that I could be alone that it wasn't easy for me to change. I had forgotten how to be loved, so I had also forgotten how to be loving. And at first I still pretended. I pretended that you needed me because you were so little and couldn't do things for yourself. I pretended that I wouldn't love you too much, because you might go away. I pretended that you shouldn't love me because *I* might go away—and that anyway you *wouldn't* love me because there wasn't much about me to love.

But I was wrong. For the nearly five years that you and I have been together, we have loved each other as hard as we could. Why do you suppose that is? Some of it, I think, is because I've been lucky enough to get to take care of you all day every day. When your sisters were little, I went away to work every day, so I didn't get to be with them all the time. And when I *was* with them I guess I thought I was supposed to *teach* them things, and be the one who knew everything. That was just more pretending, though. I never spent much time finding out what they knew so I imagined that they—and all little people—probably really didn't know very much at all.

With you, however, I just let myself be loved. And that made all the difference. Because you loved me, slowly I began to imagine that I could be loved. So I stopped hiding and pretending, and loved you back. I let you be my teacher. I learned to sing because if I sang like a crow you didn't make fun of me. I learned to cry because we sometimes cried together about the same thing. I learned to listen, because you had lots of things to say that we needed to think and talk about. I learned that the most important thing I had to do while we were together was to *be* with you and to *do* things with you. Work and play got to be the same thing: When we worked together building something, what we built wasn't very important, but the fun we had doing it together *was* very important. When we play baseball it really doesn't even matter if we hit the ball; what matters is that we're having fun with each other. I guess that learning new things with you has been the most fun of all: One minute neither of us knows a certain thing, and the next minute we both know that new thing at exactly the same time!

I wanted you to know all this stuff for two reasons. First, if when you're big you decide that you'd like to be a daddy, I hope you'll remember that the best part of that is to arrange it so that you can be with your child all day. If you can do that, if you're anything like me, you'll find that your special loving muscles get bigger and bigger and stronger and stronger, and you'll almost explode with love, like a big pudding!

The second thing is that even though I tell you that I love you, and we snuggle a lot, and sit on laps, some day I'll be gone, and you might wonder why, or be angry, the way I used to be. If that happens, I want you to be able to unfold this paper and sort of listen to me while I tell you this special story about myself, and about how your magic turned me into a beautiful daffodil.

I love you very much.

Dad

PART 7

. . . .

WAYS OF MEN AT WORK

The [Horatio Alger] hero did not aim at success but at succeeding—that is, at character formation and "self-improvement." . . . The self-made man is the true American monster. . . . He must ever be tinkering, improving, adjusting; starting over, fearful his product will get out of date, or rot in the storehouse.

GARRY WILLS

Without work all life goes rotten. But when work is soulless, life stifles and dies.

ALBERT CAMUS

INTRODUCTION

· · · · · · ·

Whosoever would be a man must also be a nonconformist. This proverb from Ralph Waldo Emerson's classic essay "Self-Reliance" captures the essence of masculinity prior to the conforming, standardizing atmosphere of the mid-twentieth-century industrial world. If the Emersonian male succeeded or failed as an individual, the post–World War II male found himself in a different situation: "expected to accept the company line because the company, with all its collective wisdom, really knew what was best." (writes Joe L. Dubbert in *A Man's Place: Masculinity in Transition*)

That this development marked a fundamental shift in masculine identity is indicated in a revealing statement by sociologist Talcott Parsons:

> It is perhaps not too much to say that only in very exceptional cases can an adult man be genuinely self-respecting and enjoy a respected status in the eyes of others if he does not "earn a living" in an approved occupational role. *(Personality in Nature, Society and Culture,* 1949)

However, Robert S. Weiss disagrees in "The Importance of Work," from his book *Staying the Course.* Weiss says he is not so certain that work itself is essential for self-esteem and peer respect. Other important factors include whether a man has reached an age that entitles him to retire with honor, and "whether he has available to him a different kind of valued community—a religious community or a voluntary organization—that offers not only membership but also a mission that would give meaning to his life."

John Lippert ("Sexuality as Consumption") takes us to his workplace, where he asks why he and his fellow autoworkers assume that "we really do face that factory alone," rather than as compatriots who share common struggles and aspirations. "I was struck by the kind of role sexuality plays in mediating the relationships of people in the factory," he reports.

In "A Rescued Farm" from his book *The Gift of Good Land,* distinguished essayist, novelist, and poet Wendell Berry makes clear that a man's dream of making something valuable with his own hands did not die with Emerson or with the birth of the Industrial Revolution. Here we meet Wallace Aiken, an Ohio foundry worker who, in his spare time, restored an abandoned strip mine into a working farm. Next to Berry's account I have placed Massachusetts poet Georges Bajenaru's lyrical poem "The Man of the Fields" because I enjoy imagining Wally Aiken as the farmer Bajenaru imagines working "the deeply plowed land,/ Where his ancestors have kneeled/ Guarding this land for two thousand years."

Finally, in an excerpt from *Fire in the Belly: On Being a Man,* philosopher Sam Keen reflects on the love he feels for his work and on his recurring suspicion that within his very passion lurks something driven. Keen asks: "In working so much have I done violence to my being?" May this question echo through all cars equipped with telephones, fax machines, and lap-top computers.

· · · · · · · ·

69 · THE IMPORTANCE OF WORK

ROBERT S. WEISS

What would go wrong with a man's life were he simply to walk away from work? Is work essential as a basis for self-esteem and security?

The answer is, it depends. It depends on whether the man is old enough to be honorably retired or is still in the age range where working is what a man does. And it depends on what else, besides working, there is in which he could invest his energies, especially whether he has available to him a different valued community—a religious community or a voluntary organization—that offers not only membership but also a mission that would give meaning to his life.

Few men in the age range in which men expect themselves to be productive can find another basis for self-esteem that serves as well as valued work. Furthermore, place at work is critical for establishing place in the larger society. To judge the social position of a man just met, we ask, as soon as good manners allow: "What do you do?" In response, men provide job titles. Young men perhaps may supply the name of the firm for which they work, if that carries more weight. And a man whose occupation is truly impressive—a neurosurgeon, say—may choose modestly not to name it, although he will keep it in mind, as a poker player might his hole card. But these are variations on the theme; in general, occupational title locates a man's social place.

So closely linked are social place and what a man does at work that a man without adequate work will tend to withdraw from social life and may question the legitimacy of his functioning as a husband and father.[1] The distress produced by an absence of adequate work diffuses everywhere within a man's life.

Representative samples of American men have been asked, in several studies conducted over the past thirty years, whether they would go on working if they did not have to work for a living. Nancy Morse Samelson and I used the following phrasing in a 1955 study: "If by some chance you inherited enough money to live comfortably without working, do you think that you would work anyway or not?" Eighty percent of the men who responded said yes, they would keep on working.

The percentage of men who said they would continue to work did not vary greatly by the kind of work they were doing. It was not much higher among professionals and managers than among those whose jobs were monotonous or low in status, closely supervised, unpleasant, or dangerous. And though few assembly-line workers or laborers said they would go on working at the same jobs if they had the money to quit, most said they would go on working.

Asked why they would continue to work even if they didn't need the money, only three percent of men said that it was because they enjoyed their work. Most said they needed something to do. They wanted to keep occupied. Yes, they could watch television or take long walks or build an addition on the house. But none of these are occupations in a social sense, in the sense that provides place in the society.

One of the men we interviewed for the present study, a contrast case of a special sort, actually did not have to work to earn a living. Mr. Taylor's family had been wealthy for several generations, and when Mr. Taylor was still an adolescent his grandfather had died, leaving him a large trust fund. From then on Mr. Taylor was able to live well on its income alone. And he did.

Mr. Taylor had been a good student at prep school, an honor graduate of his Ivy League college, and successful as a graduate student in a field that was both intellectually demanding and glamorous. But despite possesion of an advanced degree, he was unable to find an acceptable job.

> I felt I was going to go and get a fine job and work hard and become a really productive member of society. I was very confident. I had several good things in line. I was offered one position which, if I look back on it now, I probably should have taken. But it was a lesser position than they'd advertised. I said, "Look, I'm sorry, I'm not interested in the lesser position. I came here for the one that you advertised." And then it was a long period without a job.

As time went on and Mr. Taylor remained unemployed, he became desperate for a job. Undoubtedly, had he not had his trust fund he would have found work in another field. He could have gone into a building trade; he had done much of the work required in remodeling his home. But as things were, Mr. Taylor preferred to continue to look for work in his field. And yet positions in his field were scarce. In addition, employers may have been put off by a résumé without substantial employment; at first only a year without employment after leaving school, but then two years and, every year, one year more.

Mr. Taylor lost confidence in himself. His efforts to find work became sporadic.

It wasn't like all of a sudden somebody walked up to me and said, "Oh, by the way, you are no longer employable." That's not the way it happened. It was a slow, steady erosion of confidence, of that feeling of positiveness.

Mr. Taylor turned to psychotherapy.

The psychiatrist couldn't deal with the fact that I had enough money that I could make my own choice. He felt that that was robbing me of the necessity and that that was the problem. What he thought was I didn't really want a job, I wanted to be a coupon clipper. And that was just totally wrong. Not having a job was eating me up. It was destroying me from inside. And it still does, to a great extent.

Mr. Taylor resented the thought that he would be content to be a coupon clipper, a member of the idle rich, a noncontributor. Perhaps Mr. Taylor should have described himself as an investor. That might have done the trick, if he could have convinced himself that it was a valid occupation. But he had given years to training in another field, and he would not relinquish that investment in self.

Mr. Taylor was not actually idle. He had done all the contracting for remodeling his house and much of the actual labor. But that wasn't a contribution to a larger enterprise, nor was it work in the field in which he had trained. Before the remodeling was completed, he had lost interest in it.

Mr. Taylor gave a good deal of time to volunteer work, especially as a member of the board of trustees of a local charity.

I have outside activities. I'm on the Shelter Board and I put in a lot of time, more time than my wife likes, on the telephone. But you have to look into yourself for the rewards rather than toward a job situation in which you accomplished a goal or got a big bonus, or things like that. You don't get those kinds of returns.

Mr. Taylor found volunteer work helpful but ultimately unsatisfactory. Although his contributions as a volunteer were valued, he was not a full member of the community of work. He lacked the place that would have been his had he been employed. One indication of his lack of place was that he had no obligations; other people did not count on him. Had he received income from his work, he would have had responsibilities. He would, to begin with, have been expected to show up. But as it was, people at work had to be ready to do without him.

As a volunteer, Mr. Taylor was removed from the usual organizational rewards and penalties, from promotion, salary increases, and bonuses. But that meant he was a nonparticipant in much of the life of the organization. Furthermore, the recognitions of worth that are so important to paid members of an organization were unavailable to him.

Nor did service as a volunteer provide a basis for occupational identity. It is an inadequate response to "What do you do?" to say, "I'm on the Shelter Board," or "I help raise money for charity programs."

You have to cast away what is, in our society, a major element of self-definition. You have to throw that out the window and say, "Well, I'm not going to be a lawyer, fireman, Indian chief, whatever." The loss of that is something that I suppose you have to grieve to some extent.

Mr. Taylor envied the other men in the loose network of friends and former fellow students who served as a sort of reference group for him. He felt like an oddball, a man without a place.

I went to dinner last night and there were a bunch of people who I had been to school with or who were associated with the school. And I'll never lose the pain of thinking, "My God, here are all these people walking around who have good jobs and are working in these various places. And I so much wanted this. And I just didn't seem to be able to make it happen for some reason or other." And that is very painful.

In short, though income without work will enable men to sustain themselves materially, it leaves them unable to sustain themselves socially. Perhaps, if a man's contemporaries are also without work, he may find a place in a community of the leisured—though this is far from certain. But when a man's contemporaries are workers, to be without work is to be marginal. And insofar as a man's feelings of worth are based on his valuation by others, worklessness leads to feelings of worthlessness.

· · · · · · ·

70 · SEXUALITY AS CONSUMPTION

J O H N   L I P P E R T

I work at a Fisher Body plant over in Elyria, Ohio. And so I spend about sixty hours each week stacking bucket seats onto carts. I used to spend all my time here in Oberlin as a student. But I had to give up that life of comfort as it became financially impossible and as it became psychologically and politically a less and less satisfactory alternative. I still try to remain rigorous about my intellectual growth, though, and so I still take a few courses here at the college. Such a schizophrenic role is at times hard to bear psychologically, and the work load is often staggering. But such a dual lifestyle also gives me something of a unique perspective on both Oberlin and Fisher Body. I feel this perspective is a useful contribution to this conference on men's sexuality.

One of the things that really surprised me when I went to work for Fisher Body is that it really is hard to go to work every day. I don't know why that surprised me. At first I thought that everyone around me was pretty well adjusted and that I was still an irresponsible hippie at heart. But then I found that just about everyone I know at the plant has to literally struggle to go back to work every day. Again I was surprised, but this time also encouraged, because I made the very casual assumption that I could look to the people around me for help in facing the strain of that factory. But I soon found that there is nothing "casual" about this kind of support; it is incredibly difficult to find. I have lots of friends now, from all over Northern Ohio and from all different kinds of cultural backgrounds. But most of these relationships seem based on a certain distance, on an assumption that we really do face that factory alone. At first I had to look to see if it was my fault, to see if there was something in me that made it hard to have nurturing relationships with the people I work with. I soon found out that it is my fault, but that it is part of more general phenomena. I began to explore these "phenomena" as completely as I could: this exploration became an essential part of my struggle to go to work every day.

In trying to look at these barriers between me and the people around me, I was struck immediately with the kind of role sexuality plays in mediating the relationships of people in the factory. I spend much time working with men in almost complete isolation from women. I soon found out that instead of getting or giving nurture to these men that I was under intense pressure to compete with them. We don't seem to have any specific goal in this competition (such as promotions or status, etc.). Each member of the group seems concerned mainly with exhibiting sexual experience and competency through the competition. Past sexual history is described and compared in some detail: as a newcomer, I was asked to defend my sexual "know-how" within a week of joining the group. Also, we try to degrade each other's sexual competency verbally, through comments like, "Well, why don't you introduce your wife to a *real* man," or "Well, I was at your house last night and taught your wife a few things she didn't know." But it is important to note that none of what happens between men in the plant is considered "sexuality." That remains as what we do with (or to) our women when we get home. And so even though homosexuality is generally considered to be some kind of disease, most men are free to engage in what seems to be a pretty basic need for physical intimacy or reassurance. This can be expressed very simply, through putting arms around shoulders or squeezing knees, but it can also become much more intense and explicit, through stabbing between ass cheeks or pulling at nipples. But all of this physical interaction occurs within this atmosphere of competition. It takes the form of banter, horseplay, thrust and parry seemingly intended to make the need for such physical interaction seem as absurd as possible. But even through this competition, it is easy to see that many, many men enjoy this physical interaction and that they receive a kind of physical satisfaction from it that they just don't get when they go home.

My relationships with women seem somehow equally distorted. Entry of women into the factory is still a relatively recent event, at least recent enough so that contact between men and women is still unique and very noticeable. Much occurs before words are even spoken. Like every other man there, I discuss and evaluate the physical appearance of the women around men. This analysis is at times lengthy and involved, as in "She's pretty nice but her legs are too long in proportion to the rest of her body." Of course this evaluation goes on in places other than the factory, but here it seems particularly universal and intense. Perhaps a reason for this intensity is that the factory is an ugly place to spend eight or ten hours a day, and attractive people are much nicer to look at.

I guess I really do get some sort of satisfaction from engaging in this analysis. But there is an incredible gap between the kind of pleasure I get when I sleep with someone and the kind of pleasure I get when I see someone attractive in the shop. And yet I behave as if there is some connection. Many men are completely unabashed about letting the women know they are being watched and discussed, and some men are quite open about the results of their analysis. Really attractive women have to put up with incredible harassment, from constant propositions to mindless and obscene grunts as they walk by. Men who call out these obscenities can't actually be trying to sleep with the women they are yelling at; they are simply making the women suffer for their beauty.

In this attack they are joined by some older men who just don't like the thought of working with women. Many women have been told they ought to leave the factory and get a husband, and then they are told in some detail what they have to do to get a husband! It is really difficult for women to work in that factory. In many cases women have merely added eight hours a day of boredom and frustration in the factory to eight or more hours a day of housework and childcare at home. And they have to contend with this harassment on top of all that.

But women are getting more secure in the factory. More and more now, men who are particularly offensive in this harassment are responded to in kind, with a flippant "Up your ass, buddy!" In any case, by the time I get close enough to a woman to actually talk to her, I feel like a real entrepreneur. By that time I've already completed my analysis of the woman's physical appearance, and in the beginning of the conversation we are both trying to find out the results of the analysis. And to reinforce this feeling of entrepreneurship, when I get back to the men I'm working with, I get all kinds of comments like "Did you tap it?" or "Are you going to?"

But one thing that really amazes me about my sexuality at the factory is that it has a large effect on my sexuality at home. I first began to notice this when, in the first week, I began to feel an incredible amount of amorphous and ill-defined sexual energy at the moment I left the plant. This energy makes the drive home pretty exciting and it influences my behavior the rest of the day. I often think something like, "Well, I have two hours before I go back to work, and it would really be nice if I could get my rocks off before then." I found that dissipating this sexual energy really does make it easier to go back. Also, I began to notice that my sexuality was becoming less physically oriented (as in just being close to someone for a while) and more genitally oriented (as in making love and going to sleep). Also, as household chores were becoming more formidable while working, I began to ask people who came into my house—and for some reason, especially my sexual partners—to take more responsibility in keeping the place fixed up.

In trying to understand how my sexuality was being influenced by the factory, this relationship between sexuality at home and at work became an important clue. Working is much more than an eight-hour-a-day diversion; it influences everything I do. If I'm not actually working I'm either recuperating or getting ready to go back. Because I confront this fact every day, it's not hard for me to imagine the changes in my sexuality as essentially in response to the fact that I have to go to work every day.

Now there is an important contradiction in this "I go to work." When I'm at work, I'm not really "me" any more, at least in some very large ways. I don't work *when* I want to; I don't work *because* I want to; I don't work *at* something I'd like to be doing. I don't enjoy my job; I feel no sense of commitment to it; and I feel no satisfaction when it's completed. I'm a producer; my only significant role is that I make money for Fisher Body. Now Fisher Body values me highly for this, and at the end of each week they reward me with a paycheck that is mine to consume as I like. But notice: I have to spend a large part of that check and much of my time off in preparation for my return to my role as producer. To a large extent, I don't consume so that I can feel some satisfaction or something like that. Now I consume so that I can go back to work and produce. And that part of my consumption that I actually do enjoy is influenced by my work in that what I enjoy has to be as completely removed from my work as possible. I build elaborate and often expensive systems (such as families, stereos, or hot rods) into which I can escape from my work each day. And this is as true of my sexuality as it is true of the music I consume for escape each day, the car I consume to get back and forth, or the soap I consume to wash the factory's dirt off me when I get home.

There is an important adjunct to this: the specifically asexual or even antisexual nature of the work I do. For the last three months my role as producer has consisted of stacking bucket seats on carts. That's it; nothing more and nothing less. Many parts of me are stifled by this type of work; we've all read about the monotony and so on. What is relevant here is that whatever dynamic and creative sexual energy I have is ignored for eight hours each day and at the end, is lost.

I hope that by now a picture is beginning to emerge that explains much of what is happening to me sexually as a function of this split between my role as producer and my role as consumer. What is the nature of this picture? The essential conflict is that in my role as producer, much of what is organic and natural about my sexuality is ignored for eight hours each day and at the end lost. I have to spend much of the rest of the day looking for it.

But notice: already I have lost much of what seems such a basic part of me. My sexuality is something that is no longer mine simply because I am alive. It is something that I have to look for and, tragically, something that someone else must give to me. And because my need to be sexually revitalized each day is so great, it becomes the first and most basic part of a contract I need to make in order to ensure it. The goal of this contract is stability, and it includes whatever I need to consume: sex, food, clothes, a house, perhaps children. My partner in this contract is in most cases a woman; by now she is as much a slave to my need to consume as I am a slave to Fisher Body's need to consume me. What does she produce? Again: sex, food, clothes, a house, babies. What does she consume for all this effort?—all the material wealth I can offer plus a life outside of a brutal and uncompromising labor market. Within this picture, it's easy to see why many women get bored with sex. They get bored for the same reason I get bored with stacking bucket seats on carts.

But where did this production/consumption split originate and how does it exert such a powerful influence over our lives? The essential conflict is that we really do have to go to work and we really do have to let our employers tell us what to do. There's nothing mysterious about this. People who will not or can not make a bargain similar to the one that I have made with Fisher Body are left to starve. If we are unable to convince ourselves of this by looking around this room or this college, we need only expand our observation slightly. Furthermore, Fisher Body and other employers have spent decades accumulating bureaucracies and technologies that are marvelous at producing wealth but that leave us with some awfully absurd jobs to perform. We have no say in deciding the nature of these jobs; they are designed only from the point of view of profit maximization.

But to question the economic power of Fisher Body is to question most of what is to our lives essential and leads us to an intellectual tradition that most of us find repugnant. But if we are to have an adequate look at our sexuality we must begin with these observations: that our society is largely influenced by two relationships that are universal in our society: *that as producers we are forced into roles that we cannot design and that ignore our sexuality precisely because it is an unprofitable consideration, and that as consumers our sexuality becomes a pawn in our need to escape from the work we do and our need to return to work each day refreshed and ready to begin anew.*

Now what is the power of the conclusion we have just made? It is a conclusion that was reached through the exploration of day-to-day experience, but at this point it is an intellectual abstraction that leaves much out. For instance, it doesn't consider important influences of family and school on sexuality. At this point, the conclusion is general enough to apply equally well to blue- and white-collar workers (the main conflict is that we really do have to go to work). The conclusion doesn't attempt to explain every detail of the life of every worker. It does, however, attempt to describe a certain dynamic to which those lives respond and certain boundaries within which those lives occur. This conclusion is necessary for us in this conference if only from the point of view of intellectual clarity; we can hardly proceed unless we are aware that we as men and the college as an institution play a particular kind of economic role in society. Enough self-awareness to include the discussion of sexuality is a form of consumption that is simply not available to the mass of the people in our society. And it is to their time spent as producers that we owe our own extravagant consumption.

But what is the political significance of the conclusions we have reached? That is, can our discussion of sexuality affect the evolution of Fisher Body's power over us? For today, the answer seems no, that for today Fisher Body is incredibly strong because, like myself, the majority of people who work for it are basically committed to their jobs. But we need only consider individual survival for a moment to see that it can only be sought in the long run in a collective consciousness that is capable of challenging the power Fisher Body has over our lives. And this is why we need to confront our sexuality; because our sexuality is based on competition among men and at best distorted communication between men and women, it will make building that collective consciousness an incredibly difficult task.

In a short time we in the United States will feel the need for that collective consciousness much more sorely than we feel it today. The Third World is in revolt and the U.S. economy is in the midst of an economic collapse that rivals the collapse of the Thirties in proportions. As a result, we face massive unemployment in this country and the awesome prospect of battles between different groups of people fighting for the "privilege" of working for Fisher Body. If people see that it is only Fisher Body that can gain from such a battle, they may decide not to fight it. And if people see that a victory for Fisher Body means inevitably a return to a lifetime of alienation and oppression inside offices and factories, they may decide to fight instead for the right to control their own lives.

• • • • • • •

71 · A RESCUED FARM

WENDELL BERRY

At least since the early sixties, when strip mining became so extensive and destructive that it could no longer be ignored, there has been an almost continuous public effort to "regulate" it, and to "reclaim" the land afterwards. And there have been a lot of ideas, public and private, for using this reclaimed land. There has, I grant, been some success: there is a lot more regulation and reclamation now than there was fifteen years ago. But there is also a lot more strip-mined land than there was fifteen years ago; the government machinery necessary to regulate and reclaim is a lot bigger and more expensive than it was fifteen years ago; and no strip-mined land, however regulated and reclaimed, is as good as it was before—and, in human time, it is not going to be as good.

As for the ideas for using this land, I believe that nearly all of them have failed to materialize. My own opinion is that these ideas have been thought up too far from the strip mines. When the thinkers have got to the abandoned benches and spoil banks, the prospect has looked paralyzingly dismal, and they have looked for something easier to think about. At present, the principle user of exhausted strip mines is Nature, who is trying to grow weeds and bushes on them. Most of the human work done on strip mines—both to make and to unmake them—is still done by people who work for absentee owners and absentee governments, and who will not have to live with the consequences of their work.

I have often wondered what sort of human (as opposed to industrial or official) intention might finally turn toward these wasted places. And I had no answer until several months ago I received a letter from Wallace Aiken of East Palestine, Ohio: "The past several years I have been trying to reclaim some strip-mined land. I have a big bulldozer I use for this." The letter said "several years"—it wasn't written out of a pipe dream—and it contained information that suggested that this man knew what he was doing.

I replied by asking if I might come to see his work. The restoration of ruined land is a subject of great importance now in our country, where ruining land has been so lucrative and respectable a business, and I thought Wallace Aiken's methods and the extent of his success might therefore be of interest. But I also wondered what manner of man might, on his own, put "several years" into the reclamation of a strip mine. Mr. Aiken said that he would be pleased to show his farm and his work.

Wally Aiken is employed as a grinder in a foundry. He works the second shift so as to have the mornings free to work on his farm: "I'd rather be tired for their work than for mine." He lives with his mother on the outskirts of East Palestine in a good house built by his grandfather in 1912 for $1,500. There is a family memory of a nearby hillside on which the townspeople pastured their milk cows, the children coming out night and morning to drive the cows home for milking. Now the hillside has been "developed," the hilly farmland beyond has been strip mined, and the children, having no cows to bring home, contract the sophistications of TV.

Wally's farm is half a mile from his house. Outside town you leave the backdrop and climb a steep haulroad corduroyed with railroad ties. At the top of the hill is a concrete block building surrounded by mowed lawn, a vegetable garden, big stacks of sawed firewood, and a machinery shed. From the hilltop you look down a long stretch of green hillside in a landscape grown over with trees and bushes. This opening is Wally Aiken's farm. Even from the height you can see that it is a restoration project, for the grass cover varies in density from one place to another, and at the far end of the opening Wally's enormous orange bulldozer sits in the midst of a patch of newly graded bare earth.

The block building was once the clubhouse of a local ham radio group. Wally was a member, and when the group split up he bought the clubhouse and the two acres of hilltop that went with it. That was his start in farming. Before that he had no agricultural experience.

For a while he raised hogs in pens now weed-grown on the slope below the clubhouse. But the next real step in his development as a farmer came when the adjoining forty-two acres came up for sale at a sheriff's auction. Wally bought it for $750—about $18 an acre. At the time he thought simply that it looked like a cheap way to own some land.

The land had been stripped for coal "on several different occasions in the past forty years." Wally, who is now thirty-two, has "no real idea what the place looked like before." What he had was a "farm" with a "surface like ripples on a pond"—the "ripples" being six to twelve feet high and covered with trees, bushes, briars, and vines. To walk across it would have been no casual undertaking. Nevertheless, it somehow got to be a farm in Wally's mind. All he had to do was correct the mayhem and negligence of his predecessors— a project, I think, that would have daunted a civil engineer—much less a would-be farmer who had never run a bulldozer.

He was a long way from farming. But he found the old bulldozer—an Allis-Chalmers HD 19—bought it for $2,500, rebuilt the engine with the help of a more experienced friend, and started making his farm.

Though he has used the technology of the strip miners and some of their know-how, his methods have been opposite to theirs. They made rubble out of a farm. His aim has been to make a farm out of the rubble. To begin with, he wasted nothing. Before he started in with the bulldozer, he took out all the firewood and fence posts. The land was unquestionably a mess, but Wally's initial accomplishment seems to have been to respect it as it was; he would waste no part of the mess that he could see a way to use. And now that he has smoothed them out, he feels a "certain nostalgia toward those humps and undulations of earth." Clearing the land, he says, "gave me the first opportunity to come to know it." But he came to know it in the process of changing it. Now that most of the grading has been done, it no longer looks like the same place, and he has had to begin a new acquaintance with it.

The grading starting in 1975, and that involved a sort of solitary apprenticeship as a bulldozer operator. The worst part of it, Wally says, was that from the driver's seat it is virtually impossible to see what you're doing: "I remember the first time I pushed dirt . . . I'd push ten feet or so, then hop down and look around front to see what I'd done." He still seems a little awed to think that so large a machine has to be run so much by guess—but that, he says, is the way you run it. "I'll always remember that old bulldozer roaring away and me sitting there trying to do something with it, and learning to guess."

It is hard to imagine how you would undo the damage of big machines except by a big machine, and so Wally has necessarily reconciled himself to the bulldozer. But he remains in a kind of conflict with it too. It is a powerful generalizer, and tends, just by its size and power, to work against his own governing impulse to take care of things, pay attention to details. It is too easy to be lazy when you are on the dozer: "It'll move anything. It's hard to save a log or a tree. I have to keep telling myself: 'Get off of this thing.'"

Wally has had a lot of dirt to move, a lot of uphill pushing, and the work has gone slowly. One plot of about an acre required 170 hours to backfill and grade. But now, in the sixth summer of the work, a small farm is, sure enough, appearing where the "ripples" of the old spoil banks have subsided beneath the dozer blade. Wally doesn't know exactly how many acres he has recovered, but it looked to be somewhere in the neighborhood of ten—which, added to the several acres of unstripped land on the property, will indeed make up a little farm, with plowland, pasture, and woodland, that will provide a subsistence and a modest surplus to sell.

Once the bulldozer work is finished on a given plot, Wally does what he calls the "groundwork"—picks up the larger stones, the tree branches, and the roots. And then he prepares a seedbed. This phase of the work needs to be carried out in haste: "The fewer trips the better." He sows rye along with a mixture of grasses and legumes: timothy, orchard grass, tall fescue, red clover, alfalfa, birdsfoot trefoil. The seed is put in with a cultipacker—which, he says, produces far better stands than he got before he bought it.

Once the seed is in the ground, Wally likes to cover it with a mulch of spoiled hay or manure. One year he hauled and spread eighty-five pickup loads of manure. When I visited Wally's place he showed me mulched and unmulched seedings in adjoining strips. The mulched strips were remarkably better.

But to give an idea of the way Wally thinks about his work and does it, I will quote his description of one of his problems:

> Since I was filling against a hillside, the finished grade was a slope. I knew I had to get some cover established as quickly as possible. I skipped picking up the stones, etc., and disked it lightly, then planted my grass-legume mixture. I then went over the whole thing with a cultipacker. I next spread out several hundred bales of spoiled and low-quality hay I bought. Well, it didn't rain, and it didn't rain, but the seedlings sprouted anyway just from the moisture in the ground. Weeks went by and still no rain. Then came hurricane Frederick. It rained and rained. I was afraid to look at my future pasture, but finally did. I was surprised to see that it had fared pretty well, considering the volume of rain we had had. It had washed in places, to be sure, but the damage was small. The washes were quickly filled with more hay. I think the hay mulch was the real lifesaver in this instance. The grass and legumes made several inches of growth before winter came.

My walk across Wally's remade farm began at a plot reclaimed the previous year. There was a good deal of bare ground showing through a stand of grasses and legumes that were obviously struggling for a roothold. And so I began in doubt. How would this pale mixture of subsoil and gravel ever support a sod? Who, after so much work, could be encouraged by this result? By the time we reached the oldest of the reclaimed plots, my doubts were gone. The ground was covered everywhere by a dense, thriving stand of pasture plants comparable to the best you would see anywhere. And underneath the sod was a brown, duffy layer of humus, where topsoil was building again. I was impressed to see that this layer was already thicker under a six-year-old soil than it was under the thirty- or forty-year-old thicket growth on the spoil banks.

And so the evidence is there. Wally Aiken is doing what he set out to do; he is making a farm out of the spoil left years ago by people who turned good land into money and smoke, in contempt of everything that might come after them. That they have had human successors at all here, where their destruction is bewildering and depressing, and in a nation where the care of such land is a mixture of bad habit and shoddy policy, is itself a kind of wonder. Wally Aiken has become their successor and their correction because, he says, "It is nice to have something to devote oneself to, to care about and be a part of." And his work has mended both the ruined land and (in himself at least) the human greed and folly that ruined it.

Why has he done it? I can only take him at his word—for what he has done is not "practical" or "economical," as things are now reckoned, and certainly not easy. He has done it out of devotion to a possibility once almost destroyed in his place, and now almost recovered. He has had a few things in his favor: the land is not too steep or too rocky, the soil is apparently rich in the necessary minerals, and he has had no trouble with acid drainage from the coal seams. But at the start that possibility lay as much in the mind and character of Wallace Aiken as in his land. The work, he says, has been satisfying all along, but "the final satisfaction will come when the place can produce, support animals, have fences, and begin to resemble some sort of agricultural operation. This is the goal I work toward."

· · · · · · · ·

72 · THE MAN OF THE FIELDS

GEORGES BAJENARU

He harnesses himself to the day's carriage of light
And the dawn swallows him up in the fields until he disappears.
He likes to caress the field as if he were a lover
In the crystal clear sleep, when the night starts to unravel.

Eternal clock in the calendar of time, the man of the fields
Carries within him the time of the entire country
And takes it up higher in the large circle of the horizon
Where his parents have passed through in layers for centuries.

And his word is as simple as a heavy stone
That rolls over the deeply plowed land,
Where his ancestors have kneeled
Guarding this land for two thousand years.

His longing wanders over furrows, and the bird can feel him . . .
In his chapped hands the seed comes into life.
And the entire field acknowledges him every morning
As it would a God that foretells the abundance.

. . . .

73 · AT WHAT PRICE?

S A M   K E E N

I am lucky to have work that fits skintight·over my spirit. I hardly know how to separate work from self. Even when I subtract the long hours, the fatigue, the uncertainties about money, the irritation of having to deal with a million nit-shit details, the long hours in the limbo of jet planes and airports, the compromises I have to make, the sum is overwhelmingly positive. I don't know who I would be without the satisfaction of providing for my family, the occasional intoxication of creativity, the warm companionship of colleagues, the pride in a job well done, and the knowledge that my work has been useful to others.

But there is still something unsaid, something that forces me to ask questions about my life that are, perhaps, tragic: In working so much have I done violence to my being? How often, doing work that is good, have I betrayed what is better in myself and abandoned what is best for those I love? How many hours would have been better spent walking in silence in the woods or wrestling with my children? Two decades ago, near the end of what was a good but troubled marriage, my wife asked me: "Would you be willing to be less efficient?" The question haunts me.

PART 8

. . . .

KEEPING MALE COMPANY: THE SPIRIT AND SOUL OF MEN TOGETHER AS MEN

Many people believe that men in hazardous
occupations have friends, but usually, when the
danger passes, so does the *active being* of friendship; it is replaced by a warm shared nostalgia. True,
friendship may sometimes arise in all such contexts,
but it is finally independent of them. Friendship is
its own context.

STUART MILLER

The weakness of (the women's liberation) movement
lies, surely, in its unstated insistence that men should
come forward with rational reasons why, in some
situations, they prefer the company of their own
gender . . .

WILLIAM F. BUCKLEY, JR.

INTRODUCTION

· · · · · · ·

A man is getting a haircut. Three men are sitting along the wall across from him. One of them, Charles, tells of hunting for deer the day before with his hungover son. Without warning, one of the others takes strong exception to something Charles says. The mood in the barber shop turns suddenly ugly; a fight seems likely. One by one the men leave, except for the man in the barber chair and Bill, the barber. The room is silent. The barber turns his client in the chair to face the mirror, puts a hand to either side of his head, and then runs his fingers through his hair, slowly, as if he is thinking of something else. Later, the man remembers that day: "Today I was thinking . . . about the calm I felt when I closed my eyes and let the barber's fingers move through my hair, the sweetness of those fingers, the hair already starting to grow."

The preceding events take place in Raymond Carver's short story "The Calm," which appears in the author's final collection entitled *Where I'm Calling From.* I love the way Carver, one of America's most gifted fiction writers, shows in a story what is harder to tell in an essay: how men's relationships with other men so often seem to travel an interface between competition and caring, one emerging immediately after, from, or with the other, reflecting a characteristic tension between polarities. Call the polarities what you will: attraction/repulsion, eros/alienation, acceptance/rejection, desire/hostility. I suspect that beneath them all lies a more fundamental split in the male psyche, between an impulse to love and a fear of that impulse.

In a passage from *Inter Views,* his book-length conversation with Laura Pozzo, James Hillman sees *homoeros,* the attraction of like to like, both as an essential aspect of and a threat to male friendship. He says that friendship demands "that you let yourself take in the other person, let your imagination be stirred by thoughts, approaches, feelings that shake you out of your set ways." In "The Old Pal Network," San Francisco *Chronicle* columnist Gerald Nachman talks about a different yet quite classical threat to male friendship: marriage. "To a bachelor, anyone's marriage threatens to break up the act," Nachman writes. "It's more fun being single with someone else who's also flying solo."

"Lies," by Pennsylvania poet Christopher Bursk, is a lyrical account of particular assumptions that men carry about themselves and other men, assumptions that provide a sense of necessity for particular choices and actions. Listen next to J. Glenn Gray's moving account of the secret attractions men find amid the horrors of war: "The delight in seeing . . . the delight in comradeship . . . the delight in destruction." The narrator in "The Rebels" (from comedian Jonathan Winters' poignant and delightfully strange collection of short fiction, *Winters' Tales*) tells how he and three fellow Vietnam veterans built a lasting bond around their war injuries.

"Men Together in Group Therapy," by Atlanta psychotherapists Louis W. McLeod and Bruce K. Pemberton, speaks of men bonding to explore, among other things, "how they use anger to control, dominate, and avoid issues of intimacy, helplessness, fear, and potency." Terrance O'Connor ("What Is a Man Without His Sword?") describes the decidedly mixed feelings that nearly kept him from attending a different kind of all-male event: a weekend gathering with Robert Bly and Michael Meade. "I like to have control of my little world. I know that I will not be in control there," O'Connor admits to himself while debating whether to go. "Can I trust a group of strange men?"

Another man asks a similar question in "A Man Needs a Lodge," a short essay of mine that appeared in a 1986 issue of *Utne Reader.* "The lodge door opens wherever and whenever men ask questions about their feelings, their relationships, and what it is that hurts or haunts them," I wrote. "This is the path of living our wounds—not refusing their dark energies, their veiled gifts, the opaque depressions that somehow open to new depths of soul."

I'm pleased to close this section on men in relationship with men with one of my favorite pieces: "The Cliff" by Charles Baxter. Originally appearing in the author's book *The Harmony of the World,* this short tale of a boy's apprenticeship to an unlikely sorcerer reveals something new to me each time I enter its images, especially the image of a young male protégé understanding "the dirty purposes of flight."

· · · · · ·

74 · LOVE IN MALE FRIENDSHIP

JAMES HILLMAN

LAURA POZZO:
There is always a homosexual component in friendship. . . . It depends on how you regard homosexuality. If you see it as a perversion or if you see it as a sexual, a Venusian moment, or an erotic moment, that engenders friendship.

JAMES HILLMAN:
Oh! in that sense, of course, there is a homosexual component in friendship. A friend is someone you want to be physically close with—eating, fishing,

sitting around. Doing things together. Even talking is a physical reality. Look at all the talking going on in the Socratic dialogues! Homosexuality has been reduced to men putting their penises through toilet walls—utterly imperso-nal pickups, autonomous genitals. Homosexuality is far more than this; it is homoerotics, the eros between men, between women, or between "likes"—similars, familiars, sames. Homoerotics has become confused with autoero-tics, but autoerotics can appear in heterosexuality just as it does in homo-sexuality. . . .

There was an old Jungian analyst, a very remarkable man, John Layard, who gave me a great deal of love, of friendship, and he was always breaking down and looking for an analyst, especially among younger men because he claimed that Jung hadn't understood and wouldn't even try to understand homoeroticism. So he wanted to do some analysis with me—and I refused because I wanted to keep our relationship as a friendship. Again I valued love or friendship more than analytical consciousness. Our connection was work-ing in the friendship archetype; it seemed wrong to shift to another archetypal pattern. There is a kind of collaboration of psyches that goes on in friend-ship—not necessarily that the friends actually work together on the same or similar projects but the psyches collaborate, affect each other, move each other. The friend enters your imagination and fertilizes it: that is some of the homosexuality in friendship. Men patients who are quite closed in on them-selves are very resistant to the homosexual advances and attractions that ap-pear in their dreams. Usually these images are interpreted as proof of latent homosexuality and therefore the patient's closedness is seen as a result of his latent homosexuality. But this has it backwards because the homosexual ad-vances made to him by the psyche are precisely the healing that could open him up to taking in another spirit, being penetrated, opened. Homoeros can move you out of closedness; it doesn't have to make you more closed.

Friendships are so hard to maintain because they continually demand ac-cessibility, that you let yourself take in the other person, let your imagination be stirred by thoughts, approaches, feelings that shake you out of your set ways. I am more angry and more intolerant—I mean I rage and shout more at my friends and with my friends than I do with anyone else. But this is only one tiny aspect of friendship. It is far more complicated than that—even the eros that moves through archetypal psychology, . . . is a kind of communal friendship. All I want to get over is the value of these kinds of love—homo-eros, friendship—and point up that the culture has always recognized that im-portance from the Greeks through the Renaissance and the romantic move-ments and that they are just not paid the right attention in psychology today.

LAURA POZZO:
You were mentioning other aspects of love, less personal. Were you meaning mystical love or religious love, Western or Eastern, spiritual or physical?

JAMES HILLMAN:
I was probably thinking of something much closer at hand. I meant love that is fixated to pairing, coupling, the dyad, the delusion of reciprocity, you call it. A third has to come in. Love itself makes this move. It brings in the triangle, and that's the importance of jealousy: it makes you awfully conscious of the third. Just look at this interview: the interview itself is a kind of love. It is moving the psyche back and forth as a third thing is being explored, the interview. It would not work if there were not a love going on as we work. And what is that love? Is it love for each other? We don't know each other. But there is a reciprocity somewhere, although it is not just between the two of us . . . there is a reciprocity in regard to what is happening. So it is the *interview*—not our relationship—the *object* of our love: a work, a forming, a making. You see, love is not a phenomenon of the person, love is a phenomenon of the spirit and it stirs the soul and generates imagination.

· · · · · · ·

75 · THE OLD PAL NETWORK

GERALD NACHMAN

I'm losing a friend in a few months. He's not dying or moving to Europe. Worse. He's getting married.

This is not a generous view, I concede, but then his is a serious breach of faith, a callous breaking of single ties. Some bachelors view married life as the enemy—not for ourselves, necessarily, but always for our friends. Ever since college, I've felt it's rather rude of old buddies to get engaged without first consulting me.

I pretend to be delighted for them, and in a vague way, I am. It's me I'm unhappy about—or rather, *us*. We had a nice thing going; why louse it up?

Married women look upon bachelors as members of the underground. It's well known that certain wives won't allow their husbands to associate with single men, for fear we may be catching, silent carriers of a virulent strain of wildness or, more dangerously, well-being.

They suspect we sit around whispering in the ears of innocent husbands, leading them down the garden path, like the fox luring Pinocchio—whose song, "I've Got No Strings on Me," is the bachelors' national anthem.

Less discussed, though, is the feeling among single men of being sold down the river when a friend decides to throw him over (not him, *them*— buddyhood) for a mere wonderful woman.

Most couples maintain unwed friends as surrogate singles, sort of faithful retainers they keep around to hear how the other half lives. They're Upstairs, with the *au pairs* and baby buggies, while we, Downstairs, are called upon to report in with amusing and scandalous tales of life among the squalid dating class.

When an old friend, even a woman, marries, I take it personally, as a subtle rebuke to a way of life we not only once shared but secretly, silently championed.

I admit to feeling dark treasonous pangs whenever a close friend crosses over to the married side, never to be heard from again, at least not in quite the same way.

A good friend who marries is still around, halfway, but without the private jokes, conspiratorial winks, and last-minute pizza dinners. Now when I visit, we must meet in committee. All plans need to be cleared, seconded, and written in triplicate.

A man I know who lives with someone complains he feels guilty if he sees me, or any man, more than twice a week. Once OK, twice is borderline OK, three times and he detects a definite cooling trend at home. When we go to a movie, I feel like his mistress.

Recently, one old friend got married, and now another is mulling it over. I'm not into male bonding, . . . but one of the simpler, non-swinging joys of single life is its bachelor camaraderie.

To a bachelor, anyone's marriage threatens to break up the act. It's more fun being single with someone who's also flying solo. This is the old clubhouse mentality, where girls are appreciated and tolerated but not allowed in because they get in the way of more important things, like baseball, Jewish princess jokes, and general boorishness.

Every so often, I meet for lunch with two recently remarried friends—one man, one woman—who always ask whom I'm seeing, have stopped seeing, is not seeing me, etc. Innermost secrets are divulged.

With the woman, it's the same, but with the man it's different than when he was one of us, a member in good standing of The Boys. Oh, he's interested, but when he asks what's happening, it's almost as if he's inquiring about my folks. Indeed, his advice now takes on a faintly parental tone.

I politely inquire into his married life, but my heart's not in it, and he knows it. Marriage isn't as sexy, at least not to outsiders, or maybe just too complex to get into. Babies are beyond my comprehension. He soaks up all the lurid details of singlehood while I smile weakly at junior's latest rejoinder.

It gives men a feeling of strength (warmth, anyway) to meet regularly and swap the talk of buccaneer bachelors. I don't mean a night out with the guys: no bowling, poker, or saloons. Guys in groups terrify me. I just mean the jolly one-on-one banter and *bonhomie* of my loyal unmarried brothers.

Among single men, one's company, two's a crowd.

· · · · · · ·

76 · LIES

CHRISTOPHER BURSK

My son and I kiss the same woman goodbye.
We are meeting thousands in the dark Capitol.
This is the first lie:
that I wish to bring peace to anyone
beside those with me now in the lamp's small territory.

Soon we'll be marching down a wide street
    ending in flags
and marble—and dawn, huge, and official,
turning the white stone glistening.
We shade our eyes, march into the dazzle
as if light were another kind of government.

This is the second lie:
that the men inside the building hate the light,
have been hurt so deeply they'd have the world hurt.
With them are my father, my brother,
gentle, considerate men,

and though I love them, I rise with others
    against them.
This is the third lie:
that we have weapons they don't—a love for children,
a concern for the planet.
My boy and I welcome the sun
    on the backs of our necks,
we need it there
as we walk into the darkness between buildings.
The police wait for us.
Soon they'll raise their arms and bring down
the shadows we expect.

This is the fourth lie:
that these men like to wield the darkness.
The fifth lie: that they have chosen to.
Mother and wife, the person we love
    most in the world,
has sent instructions:

keep away from the violence.
This is the sixth lie: that we can.
The seventh: that we wish to.
We move closer to the damage, lurk in its shade
as if hearing the screams

seeing the blood, we might understand.
The eighth lie is that we do.
We'd thought by walking in great sunlit masses
before those who began this war
we might end it. We lift the sun in our hands

as if to show the men in small groups
    gathering at the windows
there is another government.
The ninth lie is that they do not know this,
are not grateful like us for free passage on the earth,
the sun's generosity.

The tenth lie is the hardest.
That we are in no danger from these men,
that you are in no danger, my son,
from the faithful, the earnest, from friend, brother,
or father.

· · · · · · ·

77 · THE ENDURING APPEALS
OF BATTLE

J. GLENN GRAY

Millions of men in our day—like millions before us—have learned to live in war's strange element and have discovered in it a powerful fascination. The emotional environment of warfare has always been compelling; it has drawn most men under its spell. Reflection and calm reasoning are alien to it. I wrote in my war journal that I was obsessed with "the tyranny of the present"; the past and the future did not concern me. It was hard for me to think, to be alone. When the signs of peace were visible, I wrote, in some regret: "The purgative force of danger which makes men coarser but perhaps more human will soon be lost and the first months of peace will make some of us yearn for the old days of conflict."

Beyond doubt there are many who simply endure war, hating every moment. Though they may enjoy garrison life or military maneuvers, they experience nothing but distaste and horror for combat itself. Still, those who complain the most may not be immune from war's appeals. Soldiers complain as an inherited right and traditional duty, and few wish to admit to a taste for war. Yet many men both hate and love combat. They know why they hate it; it is harder to know and to be articulate about why they love it. The novice may be eager at times to describe his emotions in combat, but it is the battle-hardened veterans to whom battle has offered the deeper appeals. For some of them the war years are what Dixon Wecter has well called "the one great lyric passage in their lives."

What are these secret attractions of war, the ones that have persisted in the West despite revolutionary changes in the methods of warfare? I believe that they are: the delight in seeing, the delight in comradeship, the delight in destruction. Some fighters know one appeal and not the others, some experience all three, and some may, of course, feel other appeals that I do not know. These three had reality for me, and I have found them also throughout the literature of war.

War as a spectacle, as something to see, ought never to be underestimated. There is in all of us what the Bible calls "the lust of the eye," a phrase at once precise and one of the widest connotation. It is precise because human beings possess as a primitive urge this love of watching. We fear we will miss something worth seeing. This passion to see surely precedes in most of us the urge to participate in or to aid. Anyone who has watched people crowding around the scene of an accident on the highway realizes that the lust of the eye is real. Anyone who has watched the faces of people at a fire knows it is real. Seeing sometimes absorbs us utterly; it is as though the human being became one great eye. The eye is lustful because it requires the novel, the unusual, the spectacular. It cannot satiate itself on the familiar, the routine, the everyday.

This lust may stoop to mindless curiosity, a primordial impulse. Its typical response is an open-minded gaping at a parade or at the explosion of a hydrogen bomb. How many men in each generation have been drawn into the twilight of confused and murderous battle "to see what it is like"? This appeal of war is usually described as the desire to escape the monotony of civilian life and the cramping restrictions of an unadventurous existence. People are often bored with a day that does not offer variety, distraction, threat, and insecurity. They crave the satisfaction of the astonishing. Although war notoriously offers monotony and boredom enough, it also offers the outlandish, the exotic, and the strange. It offers the opportunity of gaping at other lands and other peoples, at curious implements of war, at groups of others like themselves marching in order, and at the captured enemy in a cage.

However, sensuous curiosity is only one level of seeing. The word "see," with its many derivatives, like "insight" and "vision," has an imaginative and intellectual connotation that is far more expansive than the physical. Frequently we are unable to separate these levels of seeing, to diminish the outer from the inner eye. This is probably no accident. The human being is, after all, a unity, and the sensuous, imaginative, and intellectual elements of his nature can fuse when he is absorbed. Mindless curiosity is not separated as much as we like to believe from what art lovers call the disinterested contemplation of beauty. The delight in battle as a mere spectacle may progress almost insensibly to an aesthetic contemplation or to a more dominantly intellectual contemplation of its awfulness. From the simplest soldier who gazes openmouthed at the panorama of battle in his portion of the field to the trained artist observing the scene, there is, I believe, only a difference of degree. The "seeing" both are engaged in is for them an end in itself before it becomes a spur to action. The dominant motive in both cases appears to be neither the desire for knowledge, though there is much that is instructive in the scene, nor the need to act, though that, too, will become imperative. Their "seeing" is for the sake of seeing, the lust of the eye, where the eye stands for the whole human being, for man the observer.

There is a popular conviction that war and battle are the sphere of ugliness, and, since aesthetic delight is associated with the beautiful, it may be concluded that war is the natural enemy of the aesthetic. I fear that this is in large part an illusion. It is, first of all, wrong to believe that only beauty can give us aesthetic delight; the ugly can please us too, as every artist knows. And furthermore, beauty in various guises is hardly foreign to scenes of battle. While it is undeniable that the disorder and distortion and the violation of nature that conflict brings are ugly beyond compare, there are also color and movement, variety, panoramic sweep, and sometimes even momentary proportion and harmony. If we think of beauty and ugliness without their usual moral overtones, there is often a weird but genuine beauty in the sight of massed men and weapons in combat. Reputedly, it was the sight of advancing columns of men under fire that impelled General Robert E. Lee to remark to one of his staff: "It is well that war is so terrible—we would grow too fond of it."

Of course, it is said that modern battles lack all the color and magnificence of spectacle common to earlier wars. John Neff, in his valuable study entitled *War and Human Progress,* makes much of the decline in our century of the power and authority of what he calls "the claims of delight." In earlier times men at war, he points out, were much more dominated by artistic considerations in the construction of their weapons. They insisted on the decorative and beautiful in cannons, ships, and small arms, even at the obvious expense of the practical and militarily effective. Then, artists of great skill and fame worked on weapons of war, and gunsmiths took great pride in the beauty of their products. The claims of beauty, Neff believes, have had to give way more and more to materialistic and pragmatic aims in this century of total warfare. When I remember some of the hideous implements of battle in World War II, it is hard indeed not to agree with him. Standardization and automatization of weapons have frequently stripped them of any pretense to beauty.

This, though, is only one aspect of battle and of modern war. What has been lost in one realm is compensated for in another. War is now fought in the air as well as on land and sea, and the expanse of vision and spectacle afforded by combat planes is hard to exaggerate. Because these powerful new weapons usually remove those who use them further from the gruesome consequences of their firing, they afford more opportunity for aesthetic satisfaction. Combat in the skies is seldom devoid of the form, grace, and harmony that ground fighting lacks. There are spectacular sweep and drama, a colorfulness and a precision about such combat that earlier centuries knew only in a few great sea battles. It is true that the roar of fighting planes can be unpleasant in its assault upon the ears, and their dives upon their victims for strafing or bombing can be terror-inspiring. But the combatant who is relieved from participation and given the spectator's role can nearly sate the eye with all the elements of fearful beauty.

I remember most vividly my feelings while watching from a landing boat, on the morning of August 25, 1944, the simultaneous bombardment of the French Riviera by our planes and by our fleet of warships. We had come relatively close to the targets under the cover of darkness. As dawn broke and the outline of the coast appeared, thousands of us watched motionless and silent, conscious that we would be called upon to act only after the barrage and bombing were over. Then we saw the planes, appearing from nowhere, and in perfect alignment over their targets. Suddenly, fire and smoke issued from huge cannon on our ships, and the invasion had begun. Our eyes followed the planes as they dived into the melee of smoke and flame and dust and emerged farther down the coast to circle for another run. The assault of bomb and shell on the line of coast was so furious that I half expected a large part of the mainland to become somehow detached and fall into the sea.

When I could forget the havoc and terror that was being created by those shells and bombs among the half-awake inhabitants of the villages, the scene was beyond all question magnificent. I found it easily possible, indeed a temptation hard to resist, to gaze upon the scene spellbound, completely absorbed, indifferent to what the immediate future might bring. Others appeared to manifest a similar intense concentration on the spectacle. Many former soldiers must be able to recall some similar experience. However incomprehensible such scenes may be, and however little anyone would want to see them enacted a second time, few of us can deny, if we are honest, a satisfaction in having seen them. As far as I am concerned, at least part of that satisfaction can be ascribed to delight in aesthetic contemplation.

As I reflect further, it becomes clear, however, that the term "beauty," used in any ordinary sense, is not the major appeal in such spectacles. Instead, it is the fascination that manifestations of power and magnitude hold for the human spirit. Some scenes of battle, much like storms over the ocean or sunsets on the desert or the night sky seen through a telescope, are able to overawe the single individual and hold him in a spell. He is lost in their majesty. His ego temporarily deserts him, and he is absorbed into what he sees. An awareness of power that far surpasses his limited imagination transports him into a state of mind unknown in his everyday experiences. Fleeting as those rapt moments may be, they are, for the majority of men, an escape from themselves that is very different from the escapes induced by sexual love or alcohol. This raptness is a joining and not a losing, a deprivation of self in exchange for a union with objects that were hitherto foreign. Yes, the chief aesthetic appeal of war surely lies in this feeling of the sublime, to which we, children of nature, are directed whether we desire it or not. Astonishment and wonder and awe appear to be part of our deepest being, and war offers them an exercise field par excellence. As I wrote:

Yesterday morning we left Rome and took up the pursuit of the rapidly fleeing Germans. And again the march was past ruined, blackened villages, destroyed vehicles, dead and mangled corpses of German soldiers, dead and stinking horses, blown bridges, and clouds of dust that blackened our faces and filled our clothes. . . . Later I watched a full moon sail through a cloudy sky . . . saw German bombers fly past and our antiaircraft bursts around them. . . . I felt again the aching beauty of this incomparable land. I remembered everything that I had ever been and was. It was painful and glorious.

* * * * * * *

78 · THE REBELS

JONATHAN WINTERS

It wasn't that we had known one another all our lives, because we hadn't. It just seemed that way because we did have one thing in common: we had been in a war and we were all badly wounded. Although we were from different parts of the country and in different outfits—army, navy, marines—we were all discharged from the same VA hospital. We had labeled ourselves the Rebels. I was Hawk, an airborne. Sergeant had lost both hands trying to detonate a land mine; Gunner was blinded by an explosion on a patrol boat in the Mekong Delta, Vietnam; and last, but not least, Bronco, a marine first sergeant, had been deafened in both ears by heavy bombardments on his bunker on the DMZ in Vietnam. Why were we rebels? Not just because we'd been hit badly, it was *how* we handled our disabilities. For instance, Hawk, who had nothing left below his wrists, spent six days a week going to a local beauty parlor getting his fingernails done on his plastic hands. As for Gunner, blind, he would go from one optometrist to another, places where they fitted you for glasses and go through all kinds of different tests. Bronco, the deaf marine, wore two hearing aids and was always going into places like record shops or the Radio Shack and making the salesmen turn everything up "so he could hear it."

We four men now shared an apartment. We were often asked by our parents, friends, sweethearts, "What are you going to do with your lives?" And our answer was, "We gave half of our lives to our country, the rest belongs to us. We want to be rebels. We don't want to conform anymore."

. . . .

79 · MEN TOGETHER IN GROUP THERAPY

LOUIS W. MCLEOD AND
BRUCE K. PEMBERTON

The decision to lead an all-male therapy group was a logical extension of our friendship. We met at a party and spent several hours talking about ourselves, our mutual friends, and our beginning practices of psychotherapy. We learned that both of us had recently experienced an increase in the number of men we were seeing in therapy and speculated about the reasons. Sitting together, we began to realize we had met in each other a man with whom we could share, trust, and risk.

After such an intense sharing, we were ready to play. Entering a room where people were dancing, we discovered everyone in pairs, including some women. With a little bit of wine and feeling quite safe, we began to fast-dance together. We were laughing, enjoying ourselves, and thinking ourselves quite smart when suddenly the record changed to a slow song by Johnny Mathis. Looking at each other we knew it was a moment of truth. Finally one of us said, "What the hell!" After some awkwardness over who would lead, we slow-danced for the first time with another man. One of us closed his eyes, put his head on the other's shoulder, and followed his lead. The experience of slow-dancing with each other became very important in our relationship and later in our work with men. It was a great relief to dance with someone our own size, to lean on and be supported by a partner, and to share the responsibility for leading and constantly being alert. Slow-dancing with another man symbolizes many issues confronting men today: following as well as leading, being receptive as well as active, letting go as well as being in control, facing homophobia as well as our attraction to other men, and acknowledging competitiveness as well as cooperative efforts. Our developing relationship with each other led us to speculate about the many men who yearn for a qualitatively different relationship with other men. As a result, we helped form a peer-support system for men called the Atlanta Men's Experience.

For two years, we were in a weekly male peer-support group. We learned the value of peer support in which men socialized and helped each other outside the group. That experience challenged many of our notions of the traditional coed therapy group. At the same time the limitations of a leaderless men's group led us to imagine what a men's therapy group might be like. An increasing number of men were calling us about the Men's Experience and male support groups. As we talked to these men we began to understand that some were looking for therapy and we regretted not having a men's therapy group to offer.

In the fall of 1978 we decided to begin a men's therapy group. Our first step was to conduct individual interviews. We explored with each man the appropriateness of his being in a men's therapy group. With our own clients, we explored the transference issues that would emerge from seeing one's therapist in an intimate relationship with other men. We also explained the basic structure of the group. Particularly helpful was our insistence that the men know each other by first name only. We discouraged contact outside the group so the men could relate as "intimate strangers." We asked for a four-month minimum commitment. We knew that many men had difficulty with commitments involving intense emotions and intimacy. Holding participants to this commitment was a crucial factor in helping a number of men through the initial stages of the group. We find men are less likely to drop out early in a group if women are present to provide basic support and nurturance. Another requirement was returning for a minimum of four times to say good-bye after deciding to leave the group. Many men do not end relationships well. Staying to say good-bye afforded each man the opportunity to acknowledge and experience his sadness in leaving, express any unresolved anger, and share his warmth and caring for the other men.

We held the first group in January 1979, and continued meeting weekly until the fall of 1984. The average length of group membership was two years. In the first meeting we asked men to choose a partner, talk about their fathers, and then introduce each other by sharing impressions of the other man's father. Our goal was to create an early bonding experience through talking about fathers; and connecting with one another provided many men with a "buddy" during the group's initial growing pains.

To enhance our effectiveness as leaders we met an hour before the group for supper and 30 minutes afterwards to debrief. During the debriefing we took turns writing our responses to three questions:

1. What is the state of our relationship and how do we doing as co-therapists?

2. What are we learning about a men's therapy group and where do we see this group in its development?

3. What is the development of each individual man and what needs to happen for him next week?

Prior to each group, we took five minutes to read the previous week's notes. This allowed us to move from the social experience during supper to preparing for the group.

WHAT WE LEARNED ABOUT OURSELVES AS CO-THERAPISTS

Doing a men's therapy group has been a very nourishing experience. We nourished each other in our pregroup connection while eating together. Experiencing men exploring their relationships with each other deepened our own relationship. During the last five years we have consistently regarded Monday nights as the most personally rewarding part of our practice.

Our relationship became a model for the group of how two men could relate. Over the years, we became comfortable in sharing our own relationship dynamics and began to disagree and fight openly in the group. Several men talked of how important it was to see us resolve our differences. For men who were mostly locked in competitive stances with the other men in their lives, we demonstrated how men can love, disagree, and reconnect.

In any intimacy, regardless of gender, male/female roles will exist. As the group evolved, members would assign maternal/paternal, feeling/action, and female/male roles to us as co-therapists. Very early the group assigned these roles and talked quite directly of experiencing one of us (Bruce) as initiating, talking more, interrupting, leading, and so forth ("You seem like the father"); and the other (Louis) as supportive, reflecting, summarizing, listening, and so forth ("You seem like the mother"). We suspect that initiative and integrative functions have evolved from primitive or archetypical images of the masculine and feminine. In our groups not only did these roles get assigned to the two male leaders but they also shifted between us over the years depending upon how we functioned in the group.

In our own relationship we were working hard to become more equal and were beginning to integrate our individual masculine/feminine aspects. Bruce, who had been most active in the group, was working at being more receptive. Louis, who had provided the more supportive function, was working at being more confrontive. The relationship of trust and friendship resulted in our ability to experiment with new behaviors and to risk making mistakes in the group. Early in the group Bruce confronted one group member even to the point of becoming careless. While Louis reported later an internal sense of discomfort, he neither protected the client nor confronted Bruce. We both agreed that we eventually lost that client from the group in spite of his generally having had a good experience. However, as Louis became more confrontive with Bruce and as Bruce listened and accommodated to Louis, the group experienced a shift in the roles, viewing Louis "as the father" and Bruce "as the mother." Four years after the early confrontation, Bruce faced a group member with some anger that surprised even him. Louis was prepared to intervene if there was a need. The client, who was quite shocked, later reported how Louis's manifest presence gave him protection and enabled him to stay in a powerful connection with Bruce during and after the confrontation.

Finally, both of us worked through many residuals of homophobia in our relationship. In this society, any two men being intimate will have to confront the issue of attraction and homophobia at some point in their relationship if they are to deepen the trust and caring. We found that our relationship affirmed our heterosexuality rather than threatened it. Modeling our comfort with intimacy and acknowledging the sexual aspect of any loving relationship allowed group members to explore their own fears and questions concerning their masculinity and sexuality. This issue is perhaps the most difficult for a men's therapy group to confront and explore. It is not surprising therefore, that it took a number of years for this to become a focal issue in the group.

Steve sought therapy after an unsatisfactory six months with another male therapist, "I thought if I told him enough information about myself, then he would tell me what to do. I also did not feel close to him." Steve's initial goals included resolving issues about his sexual orientation, being less judgmental about himself, and becoming more intimate with other people. He was involved in a relationship with a woman, had had platonic and sexual relationships with women before, but was afraid he might be homosexual because of his attraction to other men and early feelings of being "different sexually." After 1 ½ years of individual therapy, he joined the men's therapy group. Steve found that the group enabled him to explore his relationships with other men at a deeper level.

Initially he focused on his troubled relationships with women and explored openly his attempts to be sexual *and intimate* with the same woman. It was only after much trust had developed in the group that Steve risked talking about his sexuality and his concerns about his attraction to men.

He wondered openly, "Am I gay?" His initiative sparked other men to look at doubts about their own sexual orientation and attraction to men as well as to explore previous homosexual experiences. The support Steve received from the group allowed him to experiment sexually with men outside the group. His sexual relationships with women were also enhanced. A key element in his experimentation was the support for exploration that came from other men.

WHAT WE LEARNED ABOUT THERAPY GROUPS FOR MEN

1. When women are present in a group, men automatically "play" to the women. When men and women are together, men focus on the relationship: How am I doing? Am I scoring? What does she think of me? In the men's therapy group the men first explored their intrapersonal dynamics and later their interpersonal relationships. Without women present, competitiveness was diminished.

2. In a coed group males tend to turn to women for nourishment. In the men's therapy group we modeled nourishment and intimacy between two men as well as with each individual man. As a result, the men in the group began to see each other as sources for support and nourishment. Often men in the group began to establish intimate relationships with other men outside the group. With women present, men seldom identify another man as a primary source of nourishment and support.

> Men often see themselves bonded in intimacy with women and bonded in competition with men. Therefore, men most often turn to women for support when in pain and most often self-disclose with women about their vulnerability. Two problems arise from this practice. First, women are much more skilled at self-disclosure and yearn for a partner who can be open and vulnerable. More and more, women are openly admitting their withdrawal from men who are unable to share feelings, emotions, and secret fears. Yet as the man "breaks down" and becomes more open, the woman experiences a bind, since she has been taught to seek a strong partner who will provide for her. This dilemma means she will often stop the very process of his being more vulnerable that she encourages in the man.[1]

In a men's therapy group men do not need to compare themselves nor compete with women, who are often more experienced at identifying and expressing feelings. As men begin to identify and express feelings at their own pace, a camaraderie and excitement grows into a self-perpetuating process.

3. Male/male intimacy is also one step in understanding and deepening male/female relationships. Intimate sharing and sexuality often become confused when men establish relationships with their women.

> There is nothing inherently wrong with support and sexuality being mixed in the same relationship; but, for most men, warm, close feelings call for a sexual advance. Few men have learned that sexual feelings can be enjoyed, acknowledged, and not acted upon, in the service of intimacy. Being vulnerable, open, experiencing pain, joy, closeness, and comfort with a woman often becomes sexualized by men. Thus, the man is moved to initiate (sexually) just when he could get most from being receptive (support, nurturance).[2]

In a men's therapy group men come to appreciate a nonsexualized inti-mate relationship with other males. This provides the experience and idea that intimacy can be separated from sexuality with women. In the group men often expressed their relief and enjoyment in establishing nonsexual friend-ships with women for the first time. At the same time, many men experienced a more integrated intimacy with their *sexual* partners.

4. In many circles it is the prevailing notion that men are more comfort-able with their anger and rage than they are with their sadness and tears. Our experience is that anger, rage, sadness, and tears are equally difficult for men. Men tend to express a form of intellectualized anger whenever they begin to feel helpless. Most men in this society are inadequate in expressing anger and rage in the service of intimacy. It is interesting to note that the treatment of choice for physically abusive males is the all-male support group in which they explore how they use anger to control, dominate, and avoid issues of in-timacy, helplessness, fear, and potency.

Often men display their intellectualized anger through sarcasm, put-downs, temper tantrums, demands for perfection, and so forth. These men are ter-rified of their anger. They fear any strong expression of anger might lead them to be the abusive, murderous, out-of-control male stereotype.

Anger and rage evolve predictably as an issue in a men's therapy group. For the man who is initially afraid his anger will become uncontrollable and consume him, a men's therapy group provides an immediate reassurance that he cannot overpower the group. In the group it is easy to provide limit-setting structures where the man can fully experience his rage in a safe setting.

We still live in a society in which most men have an internal prohibition against feeling, expressing, and getting support for their sadness. That pro-hibition has been perpetuated and continues to be enforced by males in this society (fathers, bosses, politicians). In the men's therapy group, men slowly begin to explore ways they block their expression of tears. It is a unique expe-rience for men to receive support, holding, and acceptance of their sadness from other men.

5. Leading a men's therapy group is fun. We have led this group for over five years. The personal learnings and enjoyment of working with men have become a high point in the week for each of us. Prior to this experience, nei-ther of us could imagine a men's therapy group being as personally stimulat-ing as a coed group. We now feel that a men's therapy group has a uniqueness, power, and potency for the male therapist that cannot be replicated in any other group. Being with men as they grow and relate intimately to each other is unique and invigorating.

· · · · · · · ·

80 · WHAT IS A MAN
WITHOUT HIS SWORD?

TERRANCE O'CONNOR

I am thumping my way around the drum section of the House of Musical Traditions. The brochure in my pocket reads, "A Day for Men with poet Robert Bly and storyteller and drummer Michael Meade." It encourages the participants to bring hand drums. Is this ridiculous? I've never played a drum in my life. Am I really considering buying one for a one-day conference: Yes. Yes, I am. I select an inexpensive bongo and allow myself to feel a little boy's excitement.

For some time I've been feeling that it's time for a men's movement. Maybe this is it. As a therapist I have been concerned about how isolated my male clients are from other men, and how this makes them too emotionally dependent on women. I see that the lives of my male friends and colleagues follow a similar pattern. The old gang of fiercely bonded adolescent young adult male friends slowly broke into isolated family units. Perhaps we kept some of these friendships, but most faded. We made new friends, but not as quickly as the old ones moved away or changed or died. But even those of us fortunate enough to have a number of close men friends have lost that wonderful sense of tribe. I have been keenly aware of these losses. I am ready for a day for men.

I ride there with a new friend. On the way we talk about growing up as men and our relationship to our fathers. Later I see that this is what always happens. When men get together to talk about being men, the first issue is always fathers. Almost to a man, we were isolated from our fathers, who were also isolated from other men. It is the common wound, the emptiness we all carry. My friend and I discover that we both have alcoholic fathers and I tell him about a pivotal incident in my life. I was struggling in my first year of high school. My father had just given me holy hell for the scores I had received on a standardized test. I felt terrible. In my room I went over the results again and again. These kinds of test results were new to me. Suddenly a ray of hope. They needed to be converted. I was astonished. In percentiles, my scores were in the nineties. Reprieved! Vastly relieved, I rushed out to show my father. He took the paper, looked at it in silence and handed it back to me. "Then why in hell don't you get better grades?" he yelled. It was a dagger in my heart. When would I ever learn? Never a word of love. Never a word of praise. Back in my room, teeth and fists clenched, eyes brimming, I said a prayer: "Dear God, never, never, never, let me grow up like that son of a bitch."

We park and enter the building. At the registration table in the hall, we can hear the drums through the closed doors. I have never heard such drumming. It sounds primitive. We walk through the doors and are enveloped by drumming. We are early, but there are well over a hundred men here already, about a third of whom are drumming: Native American drums, bongos, African drums. I am bathed in this energy. Beneath my arm, the skin of my drum vibrates in resonance with its brothers.

Men are milling about by the coffee table. The trickle through the door is becoming a stream, the throbbing drumbeat is overwhelming. I take a seat near the back. I put my drum between my knees and prepare to join the chorus. This is new. I look about shyly. All around me men are glancing about, with shy, mischievous grins. We are little boys who have stumbled upon a wonderful secret. We are men in the first blush of rediscovering the harmony of our hearts in the beat of a drum.

Four hundred men have come. Four hundred men in search of a common thread. It feels like a homecoming. Meade tells a story that ends in a dilemma: kill the king, or kill the father. The crowd is divided into two groups: regicide on the left, patricide on the right. The groups argue with one another. A man on the right stands above the rest on his chair. "Kill the bastard. Off with his head!" he screams. "No! Never kill your father," someone on the left screams in return. Waves of emotion crash back and forth. A man in the middle who has joined neither group shouts out, "I will kill no one. I will break my sword." Bly jumps in with a caution. "What is a man without his sword?" he asks. Meade challenges those of us who have not chosen; he questions our courage. I am unfazed. I think that the king is my future, and I will not kill that. Yet it is dawning on me that I have killed my father too many times already. He is a ghost. Can't I just let him fade? Bly has a good point about the sword. I will hold on to the sword. I will not fear my own power. I am not sure what all of this means, but I am bathing in the tides of male energy.

An announcement is made that a sign-up sheet is available for those who are interested in creating an ongoing men's meeting. A few weeks later about fifty of us gather in the hall of a local church. This is the birth of the Men's Council of Greater Washington. What do we want? We want to drum. We want to dance. We want to talk, to make friends. We cannot agree on any structure or purpose. It is too early. We debate, argue, dance, drum. We begin to make friends. We resolve to evolve.

At this monthly meeting, some of us decide to create more intimate support groups. In a few weeks I am sitting on the rocks overlooking the waterfall at Great Falls Park with seven other men, talking about what we want from one another, what we have to give. Above the roaring falls there is an air of quiet excitement. In the smaller group our sense of isolation begins to break down immediately. We are hungry for support. We begin to lay out our fears and our personal dilemmas as if we were laying down armfuls of wood we have carried for too long. As the weeks go on, our cares roll out. Thump, thump, our loads released. Some of us cry, perhaps for the first time in front of other men. The themes repeat: love, work, Dad. It is amazing not to be alone with this. An exhilaration begins to rise with the realization that we are experiencing a trust and understanding that is different than any we have experienced with women. It has something to do with intimacy without fear of dependence, ferocity without fear of destruction.

But it is not smooth or easy. We question whether there is too much hard-edged male energy and not enough gentleness. There is a struggle for direction, leadership. One of the men wants to take us to loftier realms of spiritual enlightenment. This requires his leadership but not his emotional vulnerability. The rest of us see a need to go inward, downward. Finally, he leaves the group. Yet there is freedom for fierce confrontation that is quite productive. Ben, who is sitting on my right, is talking about his relationship with women. His tone is haughty. Someone comments on this.

"Yeah," he admits, "I guess I've got my nose up in the air a bit."

"Well," I put in, "that is a gentle way of saying it."

"Why," he asks, "what would you say?"

"That you are an imperious asshole."

He winces. The group roars.

"Takes one to know one," someone yells over the laughter. We all nod. It is a moment of truth. As a group we have acknowledged our arrogance as our primary defense.

There is a week-long men's conference with Robert Bly, Michael Meade, the psychologist James Hillman, and tracker John Stokes. I registered a long time ago, and now I regret it. I can't afford it. I am too busy. I really need time to myself rather than being pressed together with one hundred men for a week. I call the day before to see if I can get out. Too late. Now I must admit that I am just plain scared. But what am I afraid of? Forced intimacy, competition, being judged and found wanting, being dominated by a group? All of the above. I like to have control of my little world. I know that I will not be in control there. Can I trust a group of strange men?

We are divided into groups of eight who eat, sleep, and meet together. Our first instructions are to share our vulnerabilities rather than our accomplishments. Eight strange men sit in a circle in the forest and lay them out: fears of aging, body image, career crisis, marital problems, death of a father. I wonder if this intimacy is too fast, but my fear has been reduced a little.

We have left one world and entered another. Morning to night we are busy in large or small groups: conflict resolution, mask making, animal dancing, drumming, sharing. The eight of us are bunked together in a primitive cabin. I snuggle down in my sleeping bag and stare into the darkness. The pouring rain provides a background for the masculine symphony of belches, snores, and farts. Is this genetic, or what? I chuckle, but I miss the sweet, soft femininity of my wife.

As the week unfolds, bright and dull moments are blended into the larger fabric. Animal dancing with John Stokes stands out. I can imagine looking at a video tape of a bunch of men growling like bears or hopping about like kangaroos. Out of context, it would look supremely ridiculous, a quarry for those who would throw stones. But when Stokes, who has lived among the aborigines of Australia, takes on the form of an animal, he *becomes* the animal. Men have imitated and taken on the spirit of nature for far longer than they have lived in cities and protected their egos with cynicism. There is an awareness this week that male energy has broken away from its roots in mother earth and is creating devastation on the planet. There is a call to reconnect, to align with nature.

And there is sharing. Sometime during the week nearly every man stands and bares his heart to the group. The pain is breaking through. The burdens of isolation are dropped. Most of the sharing is about fathers and grandfathers, but some is of a more immediate nature. One construction worker, a man in his fifties, stands up and tells us that in all his life he had never let another man get physically close to him. This morning in mask making his partner had touched his face with gentle fingers, and, here he chokes up, "and I liked it." He bursts into tears. He is immediately surrounded by comforting men.

In this group, the older men, the elders, are given special respect. They are given seats in the front row as places of honor and to make them protectors of the younger men. The eldest, a man in his seventies, turns spontaneously to the group one day and tells us, "If I cannot protect you with my body, I will protect you with my spirit." We accept this as a blessing. All ages of men are appreciated. One afternoon, after an intense gathering, the doors to the meeting house burst open and a man in his mid twenties flies out and down the hill, discarding clothes as he goes. He hits the pier naked and running and dives off the end. A group of middle-aged men watch silently as he swims furiously across the cold, October lake. "Well," one says finally, his voice filled with admiration, "there goes the youngest."

By the end of the week I am deeply struck by the many forms of male beauty: Stokes as a deer, cocking his head to hear a noise in the forest; Hillman tap dancing; Meade's smiling eyes and compelling drumming that invites us deeper into the forests of the mythical world; Bly, his silver locks like solar flares, arguing fiercely with the intense young man with lightning eyes and jet black beard—warmth through friction. Big roaring bears of men, fierce flying falcons of men, deep diving trout of men. Gentle men, angry men, laughing men, men lounging naked on the pier, shaving at the sinks, peeing in the woods. Men gathering leaves for masks, men gathered in council around the fire, men hugging, men howling, men crying, men dancing, singing, drumming, men sitting alone in the moonlight, men wearing masks, men taking masks off. Men, men, men, men, men. Have I been so competitive that I have missed all this beauty? Is it me, or is it them, or is it us?

It is a year and a half since the first monthly meeting of the men's council. Tonight I have brought my son. The council has evolved and grown. At this meeting there are more than 130 men, nearly half of whom are here for the first time. In the time for free sharing, most of the men do not speak to the evening's topic, but rather they speak in mourning about their fathers. Given the number of new men this is no surprise. When I stand up to share, I do relate my comments to one theme of tonight's program: the wasteland. I speak to the role of the men's movement in creating something other than a wasteland on the planet. Then, looking at the faces of the new men all struggling with the same old issues, I sense a unique opportunity. "As I am standing here," I say, "I suddenly realize I have an opportunity that I don't think I will pass up. I came here tonight with my son, Sean." My voice cracks, and my eyes tear up. I put my hand to my chest and gulp some air. "This is hard for me," I continue. "Sean just finished his first semester of college. Two days before the semester began, he broke both of his legs. He spent most of the semester in a cast to his hip, dragging himself around a big campus on crutches. He just got his report card. He got a 4.0. And I want to say, "Sean, I'm proud of you, and I love you.'" I sit down to loud applause. Someone behind me strokes the back of my head. A few seats down, Sean has tears in his eyes.

A man gets up to say how important it is for elders to acknowledge younger men. A couple of other men take turns speaking, and then, to my surprise, Sean stands up. "I didn't think I would speak here tonight," he started, "but when my dad spoke, well, I had to say something too. He hasn't always had it easy. He had some tough times growing up. He didn't get much support from his father. He went through a difficult divorce . . . from my mother, and he's taken some risks. He's created a good private practice, and he's writing and speaking out on things that really matter to him, and I just want to say" he turns to me, "I'm proud of you, Dad." If there is a dry eye in the house it isn't one of mine. After the meeting, a number of men come up to congratulate both of us. On his way out the door, Ben, from my support group, stops to thank Sean for his sharing. Then he grabs me and hugs me. "I love him too," he tells Sean.

It is the last hour of the last day of the week-long conference. My small group has decided to lift each person. We start with the largest. He is a big man, but the seven of us have no trouble lifting him high over our heads. I am the last. I fall backward without hesitation. I am surprised. I had anticipated the jolt of being caught, the force of being lifted. The sensation is not like that at all. The moment I stop supporting my own weight I am swept up, weightless. My descent and ascent are one. I rise as gently as a cloud. My arms and head hang down. I am utterly relaxed. I have literally never felt so supported in my life.

. . . .

81 · A MAN NEEDS A LODGE

KEITH THOMPSON

Opening the door is easier than Roxanne imagined it would be, as is walking out into the humid morning air. Gary sits there, says nothing, watches her go. Both know she won't be living in that house again. He knows their ten-year marriage has been getting "weird" (his word), but he doesn't believe Roxanne would ever just leave. Now, she's gone. He folds his clenched hands onto the kitchen table and stares, numbed, through streaked glass at the neighbor's vacant backyard.

Weeks pass. Roxanne files for divorce. Gary gets stoned. The divorce is granted. Gary stays stoned. His friend Dave suggests that Gary join his group of men who get together one night each week to talk about problems with work, tensions with women, hassles with their kids, anxieties about money and status, doubts about living, and, occasionally, fears of dying.

"Spill my guts to complete strangers? You've *gotta* be kidding," Gary responds with icy contempt. Dave keeps insisting, Gary keeps refusing. Finally Dave gives up trying, decides to leave Gary alone for a while. Not long thereafter, Gary has a vivid dream of drowning in quicksand in the midst of a huge city where passersby cannot hear his screams. "Okay, I'll come, I'm ready," he tells Dave.

At first Gary listens to other men's stories. "I assumed from the start that my own problems were probably stupid and trivial, so I just shut up." By the end of the second meeting he's talking. About Roxanne. About women. About "how women are." His voice fills with an anger he tries to control. The man next to him leans over and whispers, "You don't have to swallow your feelings. Not here." Gary looks momentarily dumbfounded, then thinks to himself: "Right." He stops swallowing it long enough to let out a bellowing roar, one that lifts him off his chair and onto trembling legs.

Looking around the room, expecting rejection, he's surprised to see supportive smiles. Sinking back into his seat, he feels warm energy running up his spine. "That's all for now," he says, finally laughing at himself. Other men laugh with him and a rich silence fills the room. For the rest of the evening he listens to others talk about what's going on in their lives. By the end of the meeting, he has had a striking realization: He's not the only one who pretends to have it all together most of the time. Other men have similar griefs!

In nearly every culture, the lodge—as a mythic image, a metaphor, and often a physical place—has been associated with certain qualities of men being men together. In traditional cultures the sweat lodge is where songs and prayers are offered all through the night. Other lodges, like my father's, feature the sounds of billiard balls and poker chips. When Ralph Cramden and Ed Norton or Stan Laurel and Oliver Hardy needed time to get themselves out of trouble, especially with their wives, they invariably headed for the lodge.

Although sweat lodges, Elks and Rotary gatherings, and men's rap groups don't serve precisely the same functions, they do tend to share some rather enduring ideas: Refuge. Sanctuary. Privacy. Friendship. Camaraderies. Brotherhood. As a physical location, the lodge provides retreat from concerns about money and work, family pressures, and responsibility to roles prescribed by what Jung called "the collective."

And a place to get away from women. Not because women are wrong, or the enemy, but because they are, in fact, women, and men are men. Contrary to the misguided assumption that the complete eradication of gender differences somehow adds up to equality, men and women continue occasionally to need time away from one another in the company of their own gender.

As Gary discovered, when the male lodge takes the form of a men's talk group, it can become a context for the naming of male wounds—wounds that often fester because men don't talk about them. Another power of the male lodge—whether as actual physical place, mythic motif, mode of conversation and presence, or simple pleasure of friendship—is that it allows men to develop feeling judgments and values of their own, and to establish patterns of relationship unconstrained by the notion that women are the rightful arbiters of "true" feeling. Because intimacy and feeling are defined in our culture as "feminine," male intimacy is often seen not as *different* from women's, but as defective when *compared* with women's. In James Hillman's phrase, feeling in our culture is "overdetermined" by women:

"First of all mothers, next sisters and aunts, grandmothers and teachers, and then childhood lovers exert their influence over the development of the feeling function in men and women." Notice that Hillman is not blaming women, nor am I. Rather, it seems evident that the feeling-as-feminine equation places impossible burdens upon women as well as men.

Men's therapy groups, poker clubs, fishing cabins, pool halls, ski condos, rain-or-shine running partnerships, pre-work espresso meetings, men working together on cars, books, or trail clearings: all have been known to invoke the lodge archetype without much notice. Perhaps the lodge can be said to exist in any context allowing a group of men to be real together: sometimes in silence, other times in words—especially words that help work through some of the gnarled stuff that keeps old wounds from forming scar tissue, and thus from healing.

I don't mean to suggest that your average Moose Lodge is a place where men can be found sitting around "exploring their woundedness" (not even in California). Even for men to get together *as men* is to call forth one of the deepest woundings of all: armored, isolated masculinity, "the loneliness of the male body" (philosopher Don Hanlon Johnson's apt phrase). One of the enduring factors in "making a lodge" is the indirect presence of the wound in the very stipulation that, "at least for this time we gather together apart from every other identity we carry at any other time—provider, father, husband, lover—in this place we gather as *men*."

This shared understanding is in itself a way of getting on speaking terms with wounds specific to being male, a process quite different from the subtle and solitary bragging that often underlies our overly heroic "spiritualized" versions of defeat and failure. ("It was good for me—I've learned many lessons.")

Where, then, is the lodge for men today? How does one get there?

The lodge door opens wherever and whenever men open to their feelings, to soul bonds with other men, to what it is that hurts or haunts them, to what they love and value in male company. This is the path of living our wounds—not refusing their dark energies, their veiled gifts, the opaque depressions that somehow open to otherwise hidden depths.

I'm not suggesting that we shift from Rambo's denial of pain to Sartre's idealizing it. Rather, I'm searching for words and images to connect the sufferings of male spirit with confidence, as in *confiding:* with entrusting to fellow men the knowledge of private wounds.

The task of lodge-building doesn't require us to stop talking to women; only that we start talking to each other. "Man to man," as my father, and every father, has at one time said. The way of the lodge.

. . . .

82 · THE CLIFF

CHARLES BAXTER

On the way out to the cliff, the old man kept one hand on the wheel. He smoked with the other hand. The inside of the car smelled of wine and cigarette ashes. He coughed constantly. His voice sounded like a version of the cough.

"I used to smoke Camels unfiltered," he told the boy. The dirt road, rutted, dipped hard, and the car bounced. "But I switched brands. Camels interfered with my eating. I couldn't taste what the Duchess cooked up. Meat, salad, Jell-O: it all tasted the same. So I went to low tar. You don't smoke, do you boy?"

The boy stared at the road and shook his head.

"Not after what I've taught you, I hope not. You got to keep the body pure for the stuff we're doing."

"You don't keep it pure," the boy said.

"I don't have to. It's *been* pure. And, like I say, nobody is ever pure twice."

The California pines seemed brittle and did not sway as they drove past. The boy thought he could hear the crash of the waves in front of them. "Are we almost there?"

"Kind of impatient, aren't you?" the old man said, suppressing his cough. "Look, boy, I told you a hundred times: you got to train your will to do this. You get impatient, and you—"

"—I know, I know. 'You die.'" The boy was wearing a jacket and a New York Mets cap. "I know all that. You taught me. I'm only asking if we're there yet."

"You got a woman, boy?" The old man looked suspicious. "You got a woman?"

"I'm only fifteen," the boy said nervously.

"That's not too old for it, especially around here."

"I've been kissed," the boy said. "Is that the ocean?"

"That's her," the old man said. "Sometimes I think I know everything about you, and then sometimes I don't think I know anything. I hate to take chances like this. You could be hiding something out on me. The magic's no damn good if you're hiding something out on me."

"It'll be good," the boy said, seeing the long line of blue water through the trees. He pulled the visor down lower, so he wouldn't squint. "It'll be real good."

"Faith, hope, charity, and love," the old man recited. "And the spells. Now I admit I have fallen from the path of righteousness at times. But I never forget the spells. You forget them, you die."

"I would not forget them," the boy said.

"You better not be lying to me. You been thieving, sleeping with whores, you been carrying on in the bad way, well, we'll find out soon enough." He stopped the car at a clearing. He turned the key off in the ignition and reached under his seat for a wine bottle. His hands were shaking. The old man unscrewed the cap and took a long swig. He recapped it and breathed out the sweet aroma in the boy's direction. "Something for my nerves," he said. "I don't do this every day."

"You don't believe in the spells anymore," the boy said.

"I *am* the spells," the old man shouted. "I invented them. I just hate to see a fresh kid like you crash on the rocks on account of *you* don't believe in them."

"Don't worry," the boy said. "Don't worry about me."

They got out of the car together, and the old man reached around into the back seat for his coil of rope.

"I don't need it," the boy said. "I don't need the rope."

"Kid, we do it my way or we don't do it."

The boy took off his shoes. His bare feet stepped over pine needles and stones. He was wearing faded blue jeans and a sweatshirt, with a stain from the old man's wine bottle on it. He had taken off his jacket in the car, but he was still wearing the cap. They walked over a stretch of burnt grass and came to the edge of the cliff.

"Look at those sea gulls down there," the old man pointed. "Must be a hundred." His voice was trembling with nervousness.

"I know about the sea gulls." The boy had to raise his voice to be heard above the surf. "I've seen them."

"You're so smart, huh?" the old man coughed. He drew a cigarette out of his shirt and lit it with his Zippo lighter. "All right, I'm tired of telling you what to do, Mr. Know-It-All. Take off the sweatshirt." The boy took it off. "Now make a circle in the dirt."

"With what?"

"With your foot."

"There isn't any dirt."

"Do like I tell you."

The boy extended his foot and drew a magic circle around himself. It could not be seen, but he knew it was there.

"Now look out at the horizon and tell it what I told you to tell it."

The boy did as he was told.

"Now take this rope, take this end." The old man handed it to him. "God, I don't know sometimes." The old man bent down for another swig of wine. "Is your mind clear?"

"Yeah," the boy said.

"Are you scared?"

"Naw."

"Do you see anybody?"

"Nope."

"You got any last questions?"

"Do I hold my arms out?"

"They do that in the Soviet Union," the old man said, "but they also do it sitting on pigs. That's the kind of people they are. You don't have to hold your arms out. Are you ready? Jump!"

The boy felt the edge of the cliff with his feet, jumped, and felt the magic and the horizon lifting him up and then out over the water, his body parallel to the ground. He took it into his mind to swoop down toward the cliffs, and then to veer away suddenly, and whatever he thought, he did. At first he held on to the rope, but even the old man could see that it was unnecessary, and reeled it in. In his jeans and cap, the boy lifted himself upward, then dove down toward the sea gulls, then just as easily lifted himself up again, rushing over the old man's head before flying out over the water.

He shouted with happiness.

The old man reached down again for his wine.

"The sun!" the old man shouted. "The ocean! The land! That's how to do it!" And he laughed suddenly, his cough all gone. "The sky!" he said at last.

The boy flew in great soaring circles. He tumbled in the air, dove, flipped, and sailed. His eyes were dazzled with the blue also, and like the old man he smelled the sea salt.

But of course he was a teenager. He was grateful to the old man for teaching him the spells. But this—the cliffs, the sea, the blue sky, and the sweet wine—this was the old man's style, not his. He loved the old man for sharing the spells. He would think of him always, for that.

But even as he flew, he was getting ideas. It isn't the style of teenagers to fly in broad daylight, on sunny days, even in California. What the boy wanted was something else: to fly low, near the ground, in the cities, speeding in smooth arcs between the buildings, late at night. Very late: at the time the girls are hanging up their clothes and sighing, sighing out their windows to the stagnant air, as the clocks strike midnight. The idea of the pig interested the boy. He grinned far down at the old man, who waved, who had long ago forgotten the dirty purposes of flight.

. . . .

PART 9

THE LAST SEASON: MEN GROWING OLDER

But, dear Josephine, do you still think of me now as I think of you?

Wherever you are today, do you sometimes wonder, as I do, whether your view of the world is merely a matter of getting old? Or has the world changed that much for you, too?

MELVIN L. MARKS

Old men love to give advice to console themselves for not being able to set a bad example.

LA ROCHEFOUCAULD

INTRODUCTION

. . . .

For males of the Samburu tribe of East Africa, masculine initiation takes
place at the onset of puberty—but not only then. According to State University of New York professor of anthropology David D. Gilmore, in *Manhood in
the Making:* "Samburu males must pass through a complicated series of age-
sets and age-grades by which their growing maturity and responsibility as
men in light of these tribal values are publicly acknowledged." Gilmore adds
that the male life cycle is advanced and celebrated through colorful rituals.

Initiation into and celebration of elderhood, tragically, is almost unim-
aginable in our modern/postmodern world. What a grievous loss to our culture's soul that those elder males most in a position to teach young males, by
virtue of living a long life, are not called upon to say and show what they
know. Like the Japanese, we could venerate our elders as national treasures;
unlike the Japanese, we do not. Is it really so hard to imagine that many of the
grizzled, dehydrated old men sleeping on sidewalk grates at night could have
something of value to tell 12-year-old boys about the kinds of choices they
will have to make?

Two weeks before this book went to press, I mentioned to a group of
thoughtful, playful, and wise men (ages 55–75) that I was editing a volume of
writings "on what it means to be a man." Their instantaneous response,
partly in jest but mostly not, still rings in my ears: "Why, *we* know what it
means to be a *man*! You should ask *us*—us old guys who've been *around*!"
There was not a hint of bragging or condescension in their words or gestures.
They wanted *me* to know that *they* knew what being a *man* was all *about*. I
didn't doubt that they did, either. I wanted to ask them to tell me their secrets
but they were in a rush to get to the nearby state park where they intended to
walk eight miles to the epicenter of the recent California earthquake. It was
enough, apparently, that they knew that I knew that they knew.

Luckily for all of us, Yale University professor Daniel Levinson did not
neglect to ask. For over ten years he and his research team examined the lives
of forty men in detail to find out what it means to be an adult male. The opening selection, "Late Adulthood," is from Levinson's groundbreaking study of
the male life cycle, *The Seasons of a Man's Life*. In "On Becoming an *Adult
Sports Fan*," author Don Lessem describes how, slowly and with time, he has
come to see the humanity behind his sports heroes and to cheer their efforts
no less than their accomplishments. In "Sex After Sixty," literary critic Edmund Wilson finds himself approaching sex and love in the same spirit as
Lessem's mid-life approach to baseball: the old fanaticism is gone . . . but
not forgotten. "We may still desire, touch rapture, we still may be left as if

drunken with the aftermath of love. . . . Yet sex has come to seem more irrelevant to the other things that occupy our minds," Wilson writes. From a slightly modified perspective, William Butler Yeats finds himself looking all day upon a lady's beauty and sighing, "O would that we had met/ When I had my burning youth." The poet indicates that he almost believes his title to be true: "Men Improve with the Years."

Jim Warters takes a similarly qualified view of the period after a man's work years have ended. In "Retired," the author draws on his memories of personal confusion and relief at retiring early and unexpectedly, to suggest that most men are "ill-prepared for this major life event and its effects on their self-concepts, their emotions, and their primary relationships."

The final two contributions are among my favorites. I love Frost's "The Road Not Taken" because it speaks to a sensibility—choices made and not made—that grows particularly poignant not only at the end of a man's life but also at the end of any phase, voyage, or endeavor (an anthology about men and masculinity, for instance). And I love Hesse's "Saying Good-Bye" because it so beautifully speaks to *leaving* . . . anyone, anything, at any time. Both are accounts of men at peace with themselves, which is as good a definition of the deep masculine as I have heard.

· · · · · · ·

83 · LATE ADULTHOOD

DANIEL J. LEVINSON

In the early sixties middle adulthood normally comes to an end and late adulthood begins. The character of living is altered in fundamental ways as a result of numerous biological, psychological, and social changes. This era needs to be recognized as a distinctive and fulfilling season in life. It lasts, we believe, from about 60 to 85.

Middle and late adulthood, like the other areas, are not demarcated by a single universal event. Various marker events, such as illness or retirement, may highlight the end of middle adulthood and shape the transitional process. The late adult transition lasts from about 60 to 65. It exists for the same kinds of reasons as the midlife transition, though the specific content is different.

At around 60, there is again the reality and the experience of bodily decline. As I've mentioned, there is statistically a gradual decline starting at about 30 and continuing its inexorable course over the remaining years. A man does not suddenly become "old" at 50 or 60 or 80. In the fifties and sixties, however, many mental and physical changes intensify his experience of his own aging and mortality. They remind him that he is moving from "middle age" to a later generation for which our culture has only the terrifying term "old age." No one of these changes happens to all men. Yet every man is likely to experience several and to be greatly affected by them.

There is the increasing frequency of death and serious illness among his loved ones, friends, and colleagues. Even if he is in good health and physically active, he has many reminders of his decreasing vigor and capacity. If nothing else, there are more frequent aches and pains. But he is also likely to have at least one major illness or impairment—be it heart disease, cancer, endocrine dysfunction, defective vision or hearing, depression, or other emotional distress. He will receive medical warnings that he must follow certain precautions or run the risk of more serious, possibly fatal or crippling illness. The internal messages from his own body, too, tell him to make accommodations or major changes in his mode of living. Of course, men at around 60 differ widely. Some face a late adulthood of serious illness or impairment, while others lead active, energetic lives. However, every man in the late adult transition must deal with the decline or loss of some of his middle adult powers.

In addition, there is a culturally defined change of generation in the sixties. If the term "middle-aged" is vague and frightening, what about our terminology (and imagery) for the subsequent years? The commonly used words such as "elderly," "golden age," and "senior citizen" acquire negative connotations reflecting our personal and cultural anxiety about aging. To a person in the twenties, it appears that passing 30 is getting "over the hill." In the thirties, turning 40 is a powerful threat. At every point in life, the passing of the next age threshold is anticipated as a total loss of youth, of vitality, and of life itself.

What can it mean, then, to approach 60 and to feel that all forms of youth—even those seemingly last vestiges remaining in middle age—are about to disappear, so that only "old age" remains? The developmental task is to overcome the splitting of youth and age, and find in each season an appropriate balance of the two. In late adulthood the archetypal figure of age dominates, but it can take various forms of the creative, wise elder as long as a man retains his connection to youthful vitality, to the forces of growth in self and world. During the late adult transition, a man fears that the youth within him is dying and that only the old man—an empty, dry structure devoid of energy, interests, or inner resources—will survive for a brief and foolish old age. His task is to sustain his youthfulness in a new form appropriate to late adulthood. He must terminate and modify the earlier life structure.

Once again the ending of an era brings the culmination of the strivings that were important within it. In late adulthood a man can no longer occupy the center stage of his world. He is called upon, and increasingly calls upon himself, to reduce the heavy responsibilities of middle adulthood and to live in a changed relationship with society and himself. Moving out of center stage can be traumatic. A man receives less recognition and has less authority and power. His generation is no longer the dominant one. As part of the "grandparent" generation within the family, he can at best be modestly helpful to his grown offspring and a source of indulgence and moral support to his grandchildren. But it is time for his offspring, as they approach and enter middle adulthood, to assume the major responsibility and authority in the family. If he does not give up his authority, he is likely to become a tyrannical ruler—despotic, unwise, unloved, and unloving—and his adult offspring may become puerile adults unable to love him or themselves.

In his work life, too, there will be serious difficulties if a man holds a position of formal authority beyond age 65 or 70. If he does so, he is "out of phase" with his own generation and he is in conflict with the generation in middle adulthood who need to assume greater responsibilities. It sometimes happens that a man in his seventies or older retains a pre-eminent position in government, religion, business, or other institutions. Names come quickly to mind: Mao Tse-tung, Chou En-lai, Churchill, Ben-Gurion, Gandhi, de Gaulle, and John D. Rockefeller. But, even when a man has a high level of energy and skill, he is ill-advised to retain power well into late adulthood. He tends to be an isolated leader, in poor touch with his followers and overly idealized or hated by them. The continuity of the generations is disrupted. The generation in middle adulthood suffers from powerlessness and conformism, while the generation in early adulthood suffers from the lack of innovation, moral support, and tutelage they need from their immediate seniors.

Some men can retire with dignity and security as early as 50, others as late as 70. Within this range, the age at which a man retires from formal employment, and especially from a position of direct authority over others, should reflect his own needs, capabilities, and life circumstances. After "retirement" in this specific sense, he can engage in valued work, but it now stems more from his own creative energies than from external pressure and financial need. Having paid his dues to society, he has earned the right to be and do what is most important to himself. He is beyond the distinction between work and play. He can devote himself in a serious-playful way to the interests that flow most directly from the depths of the self. Using the youthfulness still within him, he can enjoy the creative possibilities of this season. Financial and social security are the external conditions for this freedom of choice. We are just beginning to learn how to create facilitating environments for development in early and middle adulthood so that more men will have the internal resources for meaningful work-play in their later years.

A primary developmental task of late adulthood is to find a new balance of involvement with society and with the self. A man in this era is experiencing more fully the process of dying and he should have the possibility of choosing more freely his mode of living. Without losing his love of humanity, of his own tribe, and of his self, he can form a broader perspective and recognize more profoundly our human contradictions, creativity and destructiveness. Greater wisdom regarding the external world can be gained only through a stronger centering in the self. This does not mean that a man becomes more selfish or vain. Just the opposite. It means that he becomes less interested in obtaining the rewards offered by society, and more interested in utilizing his own inner resources. The voices within the self become, as it were, more audible and more worthy of his attention. He continues to be actively engaged with the voices and realities of the external world, but he seeks a new balance in which the self has greater primacy.

If a man creates a new form of self-in-world, late adulthood can be a season as full and rich as the others. Some of the greatest intellectual and artistic works have been produced by men in their sixties, seventies, and even eighties. Examples abound: Picasso, Yeats, Verdi, Frank Lloyd Wright, Freud, Jung, Sophocles, Michelangelo, Tolstoy. Countless other men have contributed their wisdom as elders in a variety of counseling, educative, and supporting roles in family and community.

In Sigmund Freud's late adulthood, passionate vitality was in constant struggle with morbid pessimism. Ernest Jones, in his great biography, divides Freud's life into three segments that correspond to the eras presented here. Volume 1, *The Formative Years and the Great Discoveries: 1856–1900*, carries Freud through his mid-life transition and his shift from neurology to psychoanalysis. Volume 2, *Years of Maturity: 1901–1919*, covers the years of middle adulthood from age 44 to 63. During this time Freud sought to establish psychoanalysis as a clinical specialty, a scientific theory and a movement that would strongly influence the academic and psychiatric world. He was totally engaged in this struggle.

Volume 3, *The Last Phase: 1919–1939*, describes his late adulthood. During this era Freud's creativity took new forms. He turned 60 in 1916, and World War I was an intrinsic part of his late adulthood transition. Again we see a convergence of societal history and individual development: as Freud was leaving the peak years of his middle adulthood, the Western world was starting its transition out of an age (dominated by the imagery of reason, science, gradual and continuing progress toward the good society) that had existed for over two hundred years. He had to deal with his own decline as well as the decline of the culture to which he was so ambivalently committed. His previous scientific and clinical interests continued, but they were overshadowed by his growing concern with philosophical-religious issues and with the origins and fate of human civilization.

Late adulthood is an era of decline as well as opportunity for development. Erikson's final ego stage occurs in this era. It begins at about 60, and its key polarity is Integrity *vs.* Despair. As a man enters late adulthood he feels that he has completed the major part—perhaps all—of his life work. His contribution to society and to his own immortality is largely completed. He must arrive at some appraisal of his life. The developmental task is to gain a sense of the integrity of his life—not simply of his virtue or achievement, but of his life as a whole. If he succeeds in this, he can live without bitterness or despair during late adulthood. Finding meaning and value in his life, however imperfect, he can come to terms with death.

To gain a genuine sense of integrity, a man must confront the lack of integrity in his life. During the late adult transition, everyone at times has a sense of utter despair. This always has some basis in actuality as well as in irrational self-accusation. He feels that his life has been of no value to himself or others, that its good qualities are far outweighed by the recurrent destructiveness, stupidity, and betrayal of the values he holds most dear. Worst of all, the damage is done: there is no further opportunity to right the balance.

Whatever our values, we cannot live up to them fully. In the end, we must effect a reconciliation with the sources of the flaws and corruptions in our lives. The sources are multiple: they are in ourselves, in our enemies and loved ones, in the imperfect world where each of us tries to build a life of integrity. Making peace with all the enemies in self and world is an important part of this task. To make peace in this inner sense does not keep a man from fighting for his convictions; but it does enable him to fight with less rancor, with fewer illusions, and with broader perspective.

LATE LATE ADULTHOOD

More people are now living into the eighties and beyond, but very little is known about development in those years. It is obviously an oversimplification to regard the entire span of years after age 60 or 65 as a single era. Given the lack of research data, we can only speculate about this concluding segment of the life cycle. The following hypothesis is offered mainly as a point of departure to stimulate further work on this issue. We suggest that a new era, late late adulthood, begins at around 80.

Most men who survive to enter their eighties are suffering from various infirmities and at least one chronic illness. The process of aging is much more evident than the process of growth. The life structure usually contains only a small territory, a few significant relationships, and a preoccupation with immediate bodily needs and personal comforts. Under conditions of severe personal decline and social deprivation, life in this era may lose all meaning. Under more favorable conditions, however, there is psychosocial development as well as senescence.

What does development mean at the very end of the life cycle? It means that a man is coming to terms with the process of dying and preparing for his own death. At the end of all previous eras, part of the developmental work was to start a new era, to create a new basis for living. A man in his eighties knows that his death is imminent. It may come in a few months, or in twenty years. But he lives in its shadow, and at its call. To be able to involve himself in living he must make his peace with dying. If he believes in the immortality of the soul, he must prepare himself for some kind of afterlife. If not, he may yet be concerned with the fate of humanity and with his own immortality as part of human evolution. Development is occurring to the extent that he is giving new meaning to life and death in general, and to his own life and death in particular. If he maintains his vitality, he may continue to be engaged in social life. He may provide others an example of wisdom and personal nobility.

Above all, he is reaching his ultimate involvement with the self. What matters most now is his final sense of what life is about, his "view from the bridge" at the end of the life cycle. In the end he has only the self and the crucial internal figures it has brought into being. He must come finally to terms with the self—knowing it and loving it reasonably well, and being ready to give it up.

. . . .

84 · ON BECOMING AN *ADULT* SPORTS FAN

DON LESSEM

Like some hung-over, deflowered cheerleader, I think hazily about the time I lost my innocence—in my case, the capacity to root.

I envy the devout and the oblivious, for whom that magical time still exists. Yet I'm happy to have recently rediscovered a love of watching sports. It's another sort of rooting, less fanatical, more—I shudder to use the word—*adult* in its scope and temperance.

It's easy to bemoan the lost innocence of sports fanaticism, harder to find the moment when the light began to fail. As a sometimes sports reporter, in Boston, I've had more than ordinary opportunity to see athletes up close and personal, under a glare that would make any mortal look unappealing.

No grimmer moment comes to mind than what I witnessed at a Fenway Park batting practice several seasons ago. Erstwhile Red Sox left fielder Jim Rice grabbed a *Boston Globe* sportswriter by the neck and shoved him up against a railing for comparing Rice's matador defense to that of the Orioles' "Disco" Danny Ford.

Nothing was as disappointing as my first visit to the lavish Red Sox locker room. The Sox were filtering off the field after a narrow and dispiriting (to me, at least) mid-season loss. The unfolding scene was a routine one, yet an affront to all my well-tended myths. One by one, the overweight men trudged in and undressed, joking with cheery adolescent crudeness about zits, broads, and beer. Only one, muscular shortstop Rick Burleson, pounding his locker in frustration, displayed the physique and temperament I had imagined of a professional. I turned in search of left fielder Carl Yastrzemski, a paragon of fitness among older athletes. Unable to locate him, I inquired of a clubhouse man who sat on a nearby stool, his back to me: gray, shirtless and slope-shouldered, puffing a cigarette in silence. Yaz smiled back.

Among other early brushes with not-so-greatness was an attempted interview with then-neophyte Mets pitcher Ron Darling. Just a few years before, I'd visited a modest, articulate Darling, fresh out of Yale, in a bandbox minor-league stadium and had written glowingly of his poise, his scholarly and athletic attainments. Now I stood a supplicant before his locker while he tried to convince me he was second baseman Wally Backman, razzed a teammate for wearing a K-Mart suit, fretted over the state of his Vuitton bags, and exchanged raunchy reminiscences of the previous night's bar pickups with Darryl Strawberry.

The last time I hoped for extraordinary character in an athlete was when I arranged to interview a reinvigorated Bill Walton of the Celtics. I went into it hurting for a gifted and sensitive athlete who'd been badgered for his lifestyle choices, beleaguered by insensitive management, tormented by injuries. What I found was a manipulative adolescent toadying to Larry Bird and looking to me for free meals.

It shouldn't matter that some—indeed, many—of the players (and nearly all of the owners) aren't any more fit, motivated, or virtuous than the rest of us. Together, men will be boys. Rich, pampered, sheltered, yet hounded, professional athletes dwell in a stunting, hothouse world of exploitation. If deeply rooted character traits have anything to do with their success, mean-spiritedness and aggression count as much as determination.

But it does matter to those of us who once worshiped them. Understanding, expecting, foibles in professional athletes makes those failings no less hard to confront because once upon a time, as with millions of other boys, the players were gods to me. Certain franchises were *my* teams. Sports was the religion, the drug, that sustained me through the awkward uncertainties of youth.

Over Wheaties, I took my morning fix of box scores from the *New York Times* (West Coast games too late to be noted). With my father's evening return from work came the *New York Post,* standings in large print (West Coast games included) and columns full of the gossip missing from Red Smith's literate observations.

I went to sleep with a transistor radio under my pillow, hoping for rain—the better to pick up wayward sound waves from Forbes Field, in Pittsburgh, or Baltimore's Memorial Stadium. And, if I could keep awake long enough, there came word of those Giants and Dodgers games that would remain a mystery in the minds and morning papers of my nearly-as-obsessed friends.

I shared these moments of private worship through all the rituals of the child-fan. Sports was the mortar that bound me to my peers, to the real world, and to the dream fields walked by our gods. We pressed sports into every nook of the suburban school day. Even as we struggled with elementary algebra, like idiots savants we talked standings and statistics, back to Hoss Radbourn.

We collected baseball cards, but not as shrink-wrapped commodities. Instead we memorized them, bent them, flipped them against walls, competing to win our heroes.

On the field we became them, or rather a ludicrous approximation of their mannerisms. The Cleveland fans twirled the bat as Vic Power did and crossed themselves à la Colavito, a radical gesture of affection in Jewish children. Also a rare one in the environs of New York, where one was more narrowly defined as a Yankees fan or a Yankees hater. I began as a Dodgers fan, when Johnny Podres beat the Yankees in the 1955 World Series. After the O'Malleys deserted Brooklyn, I transferred my affections to the next Yankee-killers, the Milwaukee Braves. I bought the glove Eddie Mathews endorsed, emulated the neck twitches of Felipe Alou. Mostly, I was No. 44, Henry Aaron, waving the bat, loping, blowing bubbles in right field.

Moreover, this entire sports pantheon was a singular link to the world of my hardworking father, a link fashioned over games watched on television, reinforced once a year at the ballpark and, best of all, tempered with his memories of games played long ago. Those athletes my father recalled were even more outsize: stick-legged Ruth; Honus Wagner, with hands the size of washboards; iron man Gehrig, pride of the Yankees.

We might have made our own memories of fathers and sons playing catch, but he was far off in a far-from-glamorous world of six-day work-weeks and long commutes. My older brother was the surrogate parent-pitcher in his absence. Instead, my father and I were fans of a common game, though at different times and with different heroes. If there was nothing magical about my father's real world, there was something special in the childhood dreams he'd reheat for me, and I took sustenance from them.

But in adult life, myths are harder to sustain. What we accepted as juveniles to be immutable truths proved illusory. Sex is not always great. Zucchini tastes good, Twinkies taste awful. High school seniors are not cool. Nuclear attack cannot be escaped by sitting under your desk.

My heroes turned out to have feet of clay, hearts of stone, heads of balsa wood. Mantle, it seems, was a carousing beaver-shooter, Cousy an insufferable know-it-all, Jim Brown a surly egotist. Aaron was a moody man who once battled teammate Rico Carty on a team flight and would eventually become a sharp-tongued, paunchy executive.

So? What I took to be blemishes on otherwise perfectly sculpted images I now see as inevitable imperfections in the mold. These guys are only human.

What changed? For one thing, me. I'm 38. I'm an adult now, most days. About athletes I think more and feel less. I root differently. The players look young. Now that I am older than almost all of them, I see pro athletes past and present in a kinder light. Strawberry may be the lead ham on a team of bad actors and an underachiever on the field, but I'm pulling now for the kid who has struggled with alcoholism and a fouled-up marriage.

It isn't so easy to muster sympathy for many other pros. But when I see a happily mediocre pitcher like Wes Gardner in the Red Sox doctor's office before a game, reading a newsletter for those who earn $250,000 and over, I don't curse his preoccupation with his prosperity. Rather, I appreciate his financial savvy. And I wonder, briefly, if he's considered income averaging on his tax returns, for in no more than a few years' time he will be an unemployed young man.

A modicum of concern is a long fall from daily doses of idolatry. There are millions of people more deserving and in need of sympathy, or my money, than Strawberry and Gardner and the thousands of other generously paid young men and women who play pro sports. But there are few with their athletic talents and accomplishments, few so fascinating to observe.

I root now like they play. I can't get psyched up for the everyday games, can't even recall when last I watched an entire baseball game before the playoffs, or the first half of a regular-season basketball game, unless it was a college game. Those I once skipped as inconsequential matchups of inferior players, jump-shooting over zone after zone. Now I am fascinated by the (unpaid, or rather modestly, illegally paid) players' rabid enthusiasm, equaled by their fans', for inconsequential matchups and jump-shooting over zones, under the ranting of martinet coaches.

If I can't muster anything near those players' and fans' intensity, emotional distance allows me to appreciate other aspects of the games. I train my eyes to look away from the ball, to see the block-outs under the hoop, the shoving in the line, the shifting of the infielders before the pitch. The backs who pick up the blitzes, the guards who fall back to seal off the fast break, the catchers who block the plate, now capture my fancy more than their hell-bent attackers.

Maybe because I'm the age of the coaches, not the players, I now savor all insights into the chessmanship behind all performances, even a Denver Nuggets free-for-all. (Though you'd never have guessed it from the resulting contest, plays were actually diagramed in the locker rooms at the last NBA All-Star Game.) Once I had no truck with strategic dissections, a view apparently thought to be common to all fans or else why would TV color men be so devoid of insights? Could John Madden have coached the way he babbles to Pat Summerall?

I'm still partial to Gene McCarthy's definition of a football coach: "Smart enough to understand the game, but not smart enough to lose interest in it." But I'm starting to like Allie Sherman's chalk talks before ESPN's Sunday-night NFL games more than the games themselves. I'm not yet convinced that how you stack your linebackers is more important to the outcome of a game than whether your psychopaths can beat up their psychopaths, but I'm willing to listen to the arguments.

I still marvel at spectacular athletic grace—a Barry Sanders cut, a Steffi Graf forehand winner, a Michael Jordan anything—just as I did as a child at Gale Sayers's jukes, Rod Laver's volleys, and Connie Hawkins's jams. But now I take much more interest in those who achieve with seemingly inferior skills, by dint of perseverance and plan—the graceless lunch-bucket players of my youth, utility men such as Joe Morrison of the football Giants and Phil Jackson of the Knicks, who were of relatively minor interest then. Now I prize effort above talent and welcome the triumph of determination. So I have come to admire the performances of guys like Kurt Rambis and Mike Boddicker, or of the Steelers and the Bruins.

In rare cases, I have the chance to apply my new rooting standard to the same performer I once cheered for other reasons. I'm hoping a humble, hardworking 40-year-old Mark Spitz will triumph in his comeback, even as I cheered his overwhelming talent and overlooked his overwhelming crassness two decades ago.

I'd hardly call Spitz a hero of mine, however. My new view of sports doesn't leave much room for idols, for turning deliriously drunk at victories, disconsolately sad at losses. Maybe this is growing up. Maybe watching other people play games, in any fashion, is a childish hobby. Certainly caring as much as an average Broncos fan does is not a sign of mental maturity.

But grown-ups can still have heroes. We just choose ours more carefully.

I have mine. In my living room, I toss pillows when they lose, exult when they win, just as I did for my teams thirty years ago. This team is a group of aging, sometimes chippy, relatively modestly talented professionals several years beyond their heyday: the Boston Celtics.

Their age, demeanor, and historic success are not what endear them to me—many other teams possess these criteria. But I've seen a little of these particular players off the court—not enough to make any pretense of really knowing them but enough to think of them as actual, likable individuals.

One can find the same multidimensional heroes in any big-league city. In fact I have, engendering a cross-team individual rooting pattern far more complex than the single-team adoration of my youth. In Houston, I've rooted lately for certain of the Rockets, from their compassionate coach, Don Chaney, to the men beating addiction and playing again with his help—John Lucas and Mitchell Wiggins.

As for the Celtics, I've seen enough to make me like them all. I've seen the grim Chief, Robert Parish, laughing, affectionately mocking his friend Dennis Johnson's prodigious butt. The Bird I think of is not the combative veteran, the cocky rube, or the guarded interview. Rather, he's the guy who wanted to play with my 3-year-old after practice, who softened her disappointment that he was Larry, not Big, Bird.

But it was Kevin McHale who, last year, gave me the most cause to reconsider my attitude about players and to rediscover my rooting interest. I'd gone to a Brookline gymnasium to interview him after a practice. As always, he was among the first to arrive, the last to leave, sweating through one-on-ones with backup center Joe Kleine. The contest ended, I approached, and McHale brusquely motioned me off.

I'd expected little more. Surliness is, I rationalized, a common, and justified, defensive reaction from a modern athlete. For some, like "Mo-no-talkin'" Moses Malone or stone-faced Steve Carlson (when he was a star; suddenly, on the downside, he became loquacious), it serves as a badge of distinction. Striking out with McHale, I got the newspaper fodder I needed from Johnson and Parish. The next morning, I received a message from McHale, courtesy of a *Boston Globe* basketball writer: He wished to apologize for his rudeness—he'd been troubled by a personal matter.

It was a small gesture of politeness on McHale's part but to me surprising. It was not, however, out of character for him, as I learned from subsequent courtside conversations, as he paused in those conversations to take his young childen to the bathroom or to comply with the latest team promotional demand.

Off the court, McHale may well have his problems, just as despite being an all-star he can be a black hole in the low post or overly enamored of his newly discovered three-point shot or a whining complainer à la Rick Barry ("a sissy motherfucker," in the words of one Rocket who'd fouled out trying to to guard McHale).

Maybe so. But McHale's also an open-faced, expressive, and gentle man. From his perspective, fan zeal is a bizarre, even unpleasant, phenomenon. "Fans don't see us as people," he told me. "They're amazed I have children, like I don't exist off the court." If fans consider athletes as people at all, their perceptions of them are all wrong, according to McHale. "They assume the best players are the best people. More often the greater the player, the bigger the jerk."

McHale became the player he is partly because he is six feet ten and coordinated, partly because he never was a fan. "As a kid, I played sports, I didn't have time to watch them." He roots for his few athlete friends now, and for those whose efforts he appreciates. "I like the Bruins because I can tell most of them are really playing hard," he says.

But for McHale, true heroes are found closer to home; Hibbing, Minnesota, that is: "My hero is my father, a good father who worked forty-two years for U.S. Steel. He did his job, took care of his family."

Perhaps it would be better to spend more time with everyday heroes or to reserve our hero worship, as John Lucas suggested, "for world leaders, not basketball players."

World leaders can't play ball, much as George Bush tries. And my father's work—dentistry—wasn't an appealing spectator sport. But I can appreciate effort in important, if unglamorous, realms such as managing the world or supporting a family. As McHale views his dad, so I now see my once-hardworking, now-retired father. I prefer to watch the Celtics work. But I'd rather get to know my father better than hang out with any of them (not that they are exactly begging to socialize with me). If being an adult fan has its limits, it allows for other pleasures or preoccupations, spending time with family among them.

One of my more enjoyable preoccupations, my daughter, the onetime 3-year-old unimpressed by Larry Bird, is now 8. She sleeps beneath a Celtics banner, stays up late listening to their games, and regrets she didn't use her time with Bird to get his autograph. I hope one day she'll want to know her father better. For now, she'd much rather know No. 33.

So on frozen New England nights, we sit side by side (she won't sit on my lap anymore), watching the Celtics, each in our own passing and enduring way.

· · · · · · ·

85 · SEX AFTER SIXTY

E D M U N D   W I L S O N

To one who has passed sixty, the exercise of the sexual function can hardly be made a cult or the longing for it give rise to extravagant idealization. The attainment of this satisfaction can no longer present itself as a supremely desired end, as it sometimes does in youth—when, however, we may not be aware that what we are aiming at is offspring more viable than we are. We have not arrived, at sixty, at the state of the aged Sophocles, who is made to say, in Plato's *Republic,* that he is glad to have escaped from a mad and cruel master. We may still desire, touch rapture, we still may be left as if drunken with the aftermath of love. We may even feel occasional symptoms of falling in love again, as we do those of some old ailment—gout or a sneezing from roses—to which we have become accustomed and which by this time we know how to cure. Yet sex has come to seem more irrelevant to the other things that occupy our minds, and we may sometimes push it away with impatience when we are busy with something else. . . . And at this time of life, in this state of mind, we can just begin to catch a glimpse of a world in which what we call love would be demoted to a place less important than it has occupied for our part of the world in the past.

· · · · · · ·

86 · MEN IMPROVE WITH THE YEARS

W I L L I A M   B U T L E R   Y E A T S

I am worn out with dreams;
A weather-worn, marble triton
Among the streams;
And all day long I look
Upon this lady's beauty
As though I had found in a book
A pictured beauty,
Pleased to have filled the eyes

Or the discerning ears,
Delighted to be but wise,
For men improve with the years;
And yet, and yet,
Is this my dream, or the truth?
O would that we had met
When I had my burning youth!
But I grow old among dreams,
A weather-worn, marble triton
Among the streams.

• • • • • • •

87 · RETIRED

J I M   W A R T E R S

There seems to be a tendency on the part of men, their families, friends, and society to view their future retirement in narrow, simplistic ways. It is going to be either some fantasy event (24 hours per day of fishing, golfing, or traveling) or else a sign of imminent death. The reality of retirement is far more complex.

I retired in 1983 at age 55 when my company eliminated the job I had had for the past 30 years. My personal response to retirement was a mixture of confusion and relief at the opportunity to escape a bad work situation. Other men's circumstances are different. Some leave work knowing their health is gone and they are dying. Others know they are no longer wanted and are allowed to save face by retiring. Still others stick it out until 65 (or 67 or 70), take their pension, party, and gifts—just as it is supposed to happen.

Although the circumstances surrounding retirement are unique to each person's work situation, there are developmental stages during retirement that I believe are common to many men. Retirement is the beginning or intensification of a major life passage that a good many men are totally unprepared for by their training, experience, or their male roles. Because men are socialized to define themselves in relation to their work, most are ill-prepared for this major life event and its effects on their self-concept, their emotions, and their primary relationships.

THE RETIREMENT PROCESS

The process of adjusting to my retirement turned out to be a series of emotionally charged steps. The initial phase of separation consisted of three parts, the first being imagining myself back at work. I would wonder what's going on at work (they'll never manage without me) and what I'd be doing at a particular time of day (fighting rush-hour traffic in the ice and snow). A second, more active response to retirement involved trying to hang on to elements of work life. It consisted of visiting work or calling co-workers or fellow retirees, nosing around for consulting jobs, having lunch, trading gossip, trying to still assert influence, etc. The third aspect of the separating process was more subtle, and concerned unresolved emotional issues I experienced during my last days at work. For example, I had to deal with the anger, hurt, and sadness at what was said or not said at the last meeting with my boss, the farewell party I never got, all the promised "carrots" I never received. It also included in some way my attempt to rewrite my work history. At some point during the process of separation, I became aware of, and had to begin coping with, a loss of identity. For the first time in 55 years, no program was laid out for me by others. I could no longer slot myself easily into society by means of my job title, company, or work history. Gone were the familiar benchmarks, rules, and structure that work had provided me. Without the distractions of a daily business/work life, I became aware of how guilt had become a substitute for joy in much of my life. I became more aware of a fear of vulnerability to and closeness with others. I also became aware of unfinished business with my father, scare and confusion about money, and some of the empty places in my life.

Then, at some point, I gradually experienced a critical new phase of grief and grieving. An important part of my life had ended and I could never experience (or change) it again. Fortunately, I let myself fully grieve this loss, and experienced the now familiar stages of denial and isolation, anger, bargaining, depression, and finally acceptance described by Elizabeth Kübler-Ross.

Where I find myself today is, I hope, the final phase, consisting of acceptance of self, as well as a search for a new identity. It is manifesting itself in how I live day to day and how I think about and plan for the future. There is overlapping in the above phases, and the work done in coping with retirement is not always neat and clean. It often involves getting stuck at a certain point in the process, overcoming the obstacle and moving on to the next stage. Some men deny that they need to readjust to retirement. For myself, I have come to trust the process, and trust myself.

Setting retirement aside for a moment, a maturing male faces other passages such as growing old and facing his own mortality. He begins preparing for death and may grieve for his lost youth and unfulfilled ambitions. Couple this with retirement, and each of these stages can be intensified to a painful level.

Retirement and the retirement process have a strong impact not only on the retiree but also on mates, family, friends, and the community. The first side effect that many people think of is the effect on the retiree's spouse or partner. Time structures get rearranged. His Time, Her Time, and Their

Time becomes mostly His Time and Their Time. Many couples are unprepared for and fear this shift. Also, the increased proximity often intensifies
latent or avoided relationship problems. Family roles are threatened and/or
changed. The partners can sometimes have conflicting fantasies about what
retirement will be like. Unless these issues are consciously tackled, often the
prevailing feeling is one of being scared: afraid that family members will
change or have to change, or afraid that the whole process is out of their control. In addition, money concerns evoke many practical and emotional responses, and are often accompanied by confusion and power struggles.

Changes in the family go beyond effects on the retiree's partner to include children and other dependent members. Changes include family time
structures, roles, expectations—family dynamics in general. Children seem
to experience fear and anger around the pressure for them to adapt to their
father's retirement. They are often unsure how to react to the perceived vulnerability on the part of the former breadwinner. Also, children get some
vivid firsthand experience of what it means to retire, which may cause them
to rethink their assumptions about their jobs and their own fantasies of
retirement.

Friends and the community are also affected by the retirement process.
Friends can be lost because of the retiree's lowered economic status, his with-
drawal from his social circle, or his moving to a retirement area. Because retirees aren't identified with their work roles, they can often become invisible
in their community.

The process of my retirement involved pains of loss, pains of transition,
pains of self-acceptance, and the shared pain of others in similar circumstances or those affected by my life. I can't, for the most part, label them "bad"
pains. They were (and are) more like birth pains—a birth into a new life.
Some of the pains I am currently labeling as "bad" are pains associated with
learned guilt. Guilt is unnecessary pain, and at the moment I seem to be stuck
with it.

The male roles of doer, provider, tough guy, game player, and controller
give a particularly male flavor to the problems of retirement. Some major difficulties seem to come from men's fear of being vulnerable and the male conditioning not to feel, give up, or admit defeat. When men stop viewing normal life changes as defeats, they will open themselves to the power they can
continue to have in their lives. Retirement can be a life-enhancing opportunity rather than a life-killing problem.

Retirement has led me to seek out other men in a new way. I've discovered the Pittsburgh Men's Collective and I'm actively making new male
friends. With the artificiality of the business world out of the way, I can experience men as supportive, vulnerable, and of interest in their own right. I am
surely still cautious in my opening to them. I've lost the structure of the work
world and find I miss it. But I also know I'm better off without that structure.
I've found new men willing to assist me to overcome my need to control, men
who support my attempts to establish a new, healthier structure.

. . . .

88 · THE ROAD NOT TAKEN

ROBERT FROST

Two roads diverged in a yellow wood,
And sorry I could not travel both
And be one traveler, long I stood
And looked down one as far as I could
To where it bent in the undergrowth;

Then took the other, as just as fair,
And having perhaps the better claim,
Because it was grassy and wanted wear;
Though as for that, the passing there
Had worn them really about the same,

And both that morning equally lay
In leaves no step had trodden black.
Oh, I kept the first for another day!
Yet knowing how way leads on to way,
I doubted if I should ever come back.

I shall be telling this with a sigh
Somewhere ages and ages hence:
Two roads diverged in a wood, and I—
I took the one less traveled by,
And that has made all the difference.

. . . .

89 · SAYING GOOD-BYE

HERMANN HESSE

This is the house where I say good-bye. For a long time I won't see another
house like this one. You see, I'm approaching a pass in the Alps, and here the
northern, German architecture, and the German countryside, and the German language come to an end.

How lovely it is to cross such a boundary. The wandering man becomes a primitive man in so many ways, in the same way that the nomad is more primitive than the farmer. But the longing to get on the other side of everything already settled, this makes me, and everybody like me, a road sign to the future. If there were many other people who loathed the borders between countries as I do, then there would be no more wars and blockades. Nothing on earth is more disgusting, more contemptible than borders. They're like cannons, like generals: as long as peace, loving kindness and peace go on, nobody pays any attention to them—but as soon as war and insanity appear, they become urgent and sacred. While the war went on, how they were pain and prison to us wanderers. Devil take them!

I am making a sketch of the house in my notebook, and my eye sadly leaves the German roof, the German frame of the house, the gables, everything I love, every familiar thing. Once again I love deeply everything at home, because I have to leave it. Tomorrow I will love other roofs, other cottages. I won't leave my heart behind me, as they say in love letters. No, I am going to carry it with me over the mountains, because I need it, always. I am a nomad, not a farmer. I am an adorer of the unfaithful, the changing, the fantastic. I don't care to secure my love to one bare place on this earth. I believe that what we love is only a symbol. Whenever our love becomes too attached to one thing, one faith, one virtue, then I become suspicious.

Good luck to the farmer! Good luck to the man who owns this place, the man who works it, the faithful, the virtuous! I can love him, I can revere him, I can envy him. But I have wasted half my life trying to live his life. I wanted to be something that I was not. I even wanted to be a poet and a middleclass person at the same time. I wanted to be an artist and a man of fantasy, but I also wanted to be a good man, a man at home. It all went on for a long time, till I knew that a man cannot be both and have both, that I am a nomad and not a farmer, a man who searches and not a man who keeps. A long time I castigated myself before gods and laws which were only idols for me. That was what I did wrong, my anguish, my complicity in the world's pain. I incresased the world's guilt and anguish, by doing violence to myself, by not daring to walk toward my own salvation. The way to salvation leads neither to the left nor the right: it leads into your own heart, and there alone is God, and there alone is peace.

A damp mountain wind drifts across me, beyond me blue islands of heaven gaze down on other countries. Beneath those heavens I will be happy sometimes, and sometimes I will be homesick beneath them. The complete man that I am, the pure wanderer, mustn't think about homesickness. But I know it, I am not complete, and I do not even strive to be complete. I want to taste my homesickness, as I taste my joy.

This wind, into which I am climbing, is fragrant of beyonds and distances, of watersheds and foreign languages, of mountains and southern places. It is full of promise.

Good-bye, small farmhouse and my native country. I leave you as a young man leaves his mother: he knows it is time for him to leave her, and he knows, too, he can never leave her completely, even though he wants to.

NOTES

. . . .

Chapter 10/Freestyle Initiations and the Quest for Male Validation/*Ray Raphael*

1. The historical relationship between the frontier spirit and the masculine mystique is explored in Joe L. Dubbert, *A Man's Place* (Englewood Cliffs, N.J.: Prentice-Hall, 1979); Mark Gerzon, *A Choice of Heroes* (Boston: Houghton Mifflin, 1982); Peter N. Stearns, *Be a Man: Males in Modern Society* (New York and London: Holmes and Meier, 1979); Joseph F. Kett, *Rites of Passage: Adolescence in America 1790 to the Present* (New York: Basic Books, 1977). In a sense, all historical works dealing with the social and psychological impact of the closing of the frontier are relevant to American conceptions of masculinity.

2. I use here the broadest possible terminology in order to give maximum leeway for the obvious comparisons with college fraternities.

3. This focus upon sexual imagery is reported in other fraternities as well: "In one, for example, pledges stand naked in front of an open fire in which branding irons are conspicuously heating. The pledges are blindfolded, told they will be branded, the branding irons are drawn from the fire and plunged, with a hiss, into a cold bucket of water as cold irons are jabbed against the buttocks of the candidates. Another fraternity strips pledges and ties bricks to their penises. Blindfolded, the pledges are told to throw the bricks without knowing the strings have been cut." (Garfinkel, *Man's World*, p. 104.)

4. At first glance, it might seem that the aura of secrecy contradicts the notion that initiations work best as public events. Ironically, however, secrecy is a sure indication of social importance. Secret societies utilize outsiders, from whom the secret is hidden, to cement bonds among insiders; secrecy gives special meaning to their shared symbols and events. In Georg Simmel's classic words: "The strongly emphasized exclusion of all outsiders makes for a correspondingly strong feeling of possession. For many individuals, property does not fully gain its significance with mere ownership, but only with the consciousness that others must do without it. The basis for this, evidently, is the impressionability of our feelings through *differences*. Moreover, since the others are excluded from the possession—particularly when it is very valuable—the converse suggests itself psychologically, namely, that what is denied to many must have special value." (*The Sociology of Georg Simmel*, trans. and ed. Kurt H. Wolff, [Glencoe, Ill.: Free Press, 1950], p. 332.) Simmel also notes how important it is that others are aware that a secret is present: "The sociological characteristic [of secrecy] is that the secret of a given individual is acknowledged by another." (Ibid., p. 330.)

Chapter 16/Ashamed to Be Male/*Francis Weller*

1. Blake, W., *The Portable Blake*. New York: Penguin Books, 1976.

2. Jung. C. G., *Modern Man in Search of a Soul*. New York: Harvest Books, 1933.

3. Kaufman, G., *Shame: The Power of Caring*. Cambridge: Schenkman Books, 1985.

4. Osherson, S., *Finding Our Fathers*. New York: Free Press, 1986.

Chapter 42/American Men as Sons of Their Wives/*C. G. Jung*

1. What Jung saw was apparently a copy of a fresco from Knossos, a new acquisition in the Hall of Reproductions. It is no longer on exhibition. The original fresco is reproduced in Arthur Evans, *The Palace of Minos at Knossos*, vol. 3 (1930), pl. xviii.

Chapter 45/The Fear of Women/*Wolfgang Lederer*

1. Beauvoir, S. *The Second Sex*.

2. Montagu, Ashley, *The Natural Superiority of Women*.

3. Hays, H. R., *The Dangerous Sex*.

4. Beauvoir, S. op. cit.

5. Montagu, A., op. cit.

6. Lederer, W., *Historical Consequences of Father-Son Hostility*.

7. Erikson, E. H., *Insight and Responsibility*, p. 235.

Chapter 56/The Goddesses and Masculine Psychology/*John A. Sanford and George Lough*

1. Walter F. Otto, *The Homeric Gods* (New York: Pantheon Books, 1979), p. 92.

2. Ibid., p. 83.

3. Rudolph Otto, *The Idea of the Holy* (New York: Oxford University Press, 1950).

Chapter 64/Father Initiation when Fathers Are Absent/*Thomas R. Steele*

1. Søren Kierkegaard, *Fear and Trembling*, translated by Howard & Edna Hong (Princeton, N.J.: Princeton University Press, 1983), p. 28. Much of this paper is a psychological reflection on Kierkegaard's seminal work in religious existentialism.

2. Friedrich Nietzsche, *The Gay Science*, translated by Walter Kaufmann (New York: Vintage Books, 1974), p. 181.

3. James Hillman, "Senex and Puer," in *Puer Papers*, edited by James Hillman (Dallas: Spring Publications, 1987). Hillman uses the terms Senex and Puer to denote the dynamic interplay of the opposites of the established man and the eternal youth as they appear in the psyche. I have chosen to use Great Father and Son of Promise for their simplicity.

4. All biblical quotes are taken from the *New American Standard* translation. The story of the life of Abraham can be found in Genesis Ch. 11:27 to 25:11.

5. A good account of the psychological relationship between speech and image as it pertains to the father/son relationship can be found in the work of J. Lacan. See for example, Jacques Lacan, *Écrits: A Selection* (New York: W. W. Norton, 1977).

6. Until recently most developmental psychology concerned only the mother/child relationship. The work of E. Abelin, M. Lamb, and K. Pruett, among others, has started to map out the importance of the father/child relationship.

7. See Charles Poncé, *The Archetype of the Unconscious and the Transfiguration of Therapy* (Berkeley: North Atlantic Books, 1990) for an investigation of the relationship between social roles, archetypes, and the psyche. Poncé argues that social institutions derive their compelling claims for adaptation through the incorporation of archetypal forces.

8. Kierkegaard, *Fear and Trembling*, p. 37.

9. Peter Blos, "Son and Father" in *Journal of the American Psychoanalytic Association* 32 (2, 1984), pp. 301–24. Blos, along with fellow psychoanalyst J. M. Ross, have broken the taboo about investigating the infanticidal father and its implications for masculine psychology.

Chapter 69/The Importance of Work/*Robert S. Weiss*

1. On the basis of a study of almost 700 men classified as "lower middle class" and "upper working class"—men who were clerks, salesmen, technicians, low-level managers, or employed in the building trades—Harold Wilensky writes: "Chaotic experience in the economic order fosters a retreat from both work and the larger communal life." Harold L. Wilensky, "Orderly Careers and Social Participation: The Impact of Work History on Social Integration in the Middle Mass," *American Sociological Review* 26 (August 1961): 521–39. A vivid statement of the importance of work to men is given by Robert Coles, "Work and Self-respect," *Daedelus* 105 (Fall 1976): 29–38. The importance of work even for men who are at the very bottom of the occupational ladder is documented by Elliot Liebow in Tally's Corner (Boston: Little, Brown, 1967).

Chapter 79/Men Together in Group Therapy/*Louis W. McLeod and Bruce K. Pemberton*

1. L. McLeod and B. Pemberton, "Men and Mental Health," in F. Crawford (Ed.), *Exploring Mental Health Parameters*, vol. 3 (Atlanta: Emory University, 1982), p. 267.

2. Ibid.

CONTRIBUTORS

. . . .

ANTLER was born in Milwaukee and grew up in Wauwatosa, Wisconsin. He earns a living reading his poems around America, trying to live up to Walt Whitman's invocation of the poet as "Itinerant Gladness Scatterer." He is the author of *Factory* and *Last Words*. Every year Antler spends two months alone in the wilderness.

GEORGES BAJENARU was born in 1938 in the village of Turari near Bucharest, Romania. After leaving Romania in 1980, he lived in exile for two years in the Federal Republic of Germany. He is the author of a book of poetry and prose in the Romanian language entitled *In Nobody's Shadow*. He makes his home in Belmont, Massachusetts.

CHARLES BAXTER writes: "My fiction usually concerns threatened realities." He is the author of two books of poetry: *Chameleon* and *The South Dakota Guidebook*.

LOU BECKER lives with his wife Jennie West and their son Jacob in rural central Georgia, where they helped co-found Eskenosen, Inc., a nonprofit organization that assists low-income people in organizing their communities.

WENDELL BERRY, one of America's most distinguished poets, essayists, and fiction writers, lives and farms with his family in Kentucky. His works include *The Gift of Good Land* and *The Wheel*.

SHEPHERD BLISS helps direct the Sons of Orpheus, a men's drumming troupe, and teaches men's studies and psychology at J.F.K. University and workshops in the United States, Canada, and Europe. He is especially interested in mythic and poetic approaches to men's work. A contributor to eight books, he lives in Berkeley, California.

ROBERT BLY, recipient of the National Book Award for *Light Around the Body*, is one of the outstanding poets and translators of our time and has been a major force in American poetry for over three decades. His most recent book, *Iron John: A Book About Men*, held number one on the *New York Times* bestseller list for several weeks.

CHRIS BRAZIER is an editor for *New Internationalist*, a British magazine that focuses primarily on world poverty.

CHRISTOPHER BURSK is a poet who lives in Langhorne Manor, Pennsylvania. He is the author of a book of poems, *Place of Residence*.

DAVID CALE was born and raised in England. He moved to New York in 1979. He has written and performed the shows *Smooch Music* (in collaboration with composer Roy Nathanson) and *The Redthroats*, for which he received a Bessie Award for Outstanding Creative Achievement.

RAYMOND CHANDLER, American detective story writer, was a leading exponent of the "tough" school of crime fiction. His fictional hero, Philip Marlowe, is the epitome of the hard-boiled, hard-hitting private eye.

ALLAN B. CHINEN is a psychiatrist in private practice in San Francisco and is on the Clinical Faculty at the University of California, San Francisco. He is the author of *In the Ever After: Fairy Tales and the Second Half of Life* and the forthcoming *Once Upon a Noon Time: Fairy Tales and the Psychology of Men and Women at Mid-Life.*

PHIL COUSINEAU is a free-lance writer, filmmaker, poet, and teacher. He is co-writer and associate producer of the award-winning documentary film, *The Hero's Journey: the World of Joseph Campbell*, author of its companion book, *The Hero's Journey: The Life and Work of Joseph Campbell*, and a collaborator with John Densmore on his autobiography, *Riders on the Storm: My Life with Jim Morrison and The Doors.* Cousineau is also author of the critically acclaimed epic prose poem, *Deadlines.* Currently, he lives in San Francisco, California.

SALVADOR DALI, born in Spain in 1904, was affiliated with a group called the Paris Surrealists, who sought to re-establish the greater reality of the subconscious over reason. His exploration of subconscious imagery as a painter and printmaker influenced a generation of artists and writers.

JAMES DICKEY is the author of several acclaimed books of poetry, including *Into the Stone and Other Poems*, and of a much admired first novel, *Deliverance.* In 1968, he became poet in residence at the University of South Carolina.

ANTONY EASTHOPE has taught in universities in England and the United States, and currently teaches English and cultural studies at Manchester Polytechnic in England. He has written *Poetry as Discourse*, on language and ideology in the poetic tradition, and is also the author of *British Post-Structuralism* and *Poetry and Phantasy.*

WARREN FARRELL is an author whose books include *The Liberated Man* and *Why Men Are the Way They Are.* He has been called "the Gloria Steinem of Men's Liberation."

ROBERT FROST, 1874–1963, was born in San Francisco and moved with his family to New England at the age of 11. He received four Pulitzer Prizes for poetry in 1924, 1931, 1937, and 1943. His poetry combines everyday language and commonplace images from his New England surroundings, yet hints of transcendental symbolic and metaphysical significance.

DOUGLAS GILLETTE, mythologist and cofounder of the Institute for World Spirituality, is co-author (with Robert Moore) of *King, Warrior, Magician, Lover: Rediscovering the Archetypes of the Mature Masculine.*

DAVID GOFF lives in the San Francisco Bay area where he works as a transpersonal therapist with men and pursues doctoral studies on existential community. His articles have appeared in a number of men's journals.

EDWARD W. GONDOLF is a research fellow at the Western Psychiatric Institute and clinic of the University of Pittsburgh, and professor of sociology at Indiana University of Pennsylvania (IUP). He is also affiliated with the Second Step Program for men who batter in Pittsburgh. Dr. Gondolf is the author of several books on domestic violence and many research articles on men who batter.

J. GLENN GRAY taught philosophy at Colorado College from 1948 until his death in 1977. He is the author of two widely acclaimed books: *The Warriors: Reflections on Men in Battle* and *The Promise of Wisdom*, which speaks to the philosophy of education.

GREG is a pseudonym for a young man whose personal account of coming to terms with his parents about being gay appears among many other such stories in *Like Coming Home: Coming-Out Letters*.

STEPHEN D. GRUBMAN-BLACK is an associate professor at the University of Rhode Island's College of Human Science and Services. His teaching experiences include work in gender role issues and workshops for men recovering from sexual victimization. He holds a Ph.D. in speech pathology from the State University Center at Buffalo.

G. I. GURDJIEFF, 1866–1949, was a mystic philosopher who founded an influential quasi-religious movement. Gurdjieff held that human life as ordinarily lived is practically indistinguishable from sleepwalking.

DAVID GUY is a novelist and essayist who lives in Durham, North Carolina. He has published four novels, most recently *The Autobiography of My Body*. His first novel, *Football Dreams*, concerned the death of his father. Others are *The Man Who Loved Dirty Books* and *Second Brother*.

RICHARD HADDAD co-founded Free Men, a national men's liberation organization in 1977. He has been speaking and writing on gender-role issues since 1977. From 1980 to 1984 he edited and published *American Man*, a men's issues periodical. He lives in Columbia, Maryland.

NOR HALL is a psychotherapist in private practice in St. Paul, Minnesota. Her books include *The Moon and the Virgin: Reflections on the Archetypal Feminine* and *Those Women*.

FREDERIC HAYWARD is executive director of Men's Rights, Inc. (MR Inc.), in Sacramento, California, and is a frequent speaker on gender issues.

ERNEST HEMINGWAY won the Pulitzer Prize for Literature in 1953 for his novel, *The Old Man and the Sea*, and the Nobel Prize for Literature in 1954. He also wrote such classics as *The Sun Also Rises, A Farewell to Arms,* and *For Whom the Bell Tolls*.

HERMANN HESSE received the Nobel Prize for Literature in 1946 for *Magister Ludi*, a fantasy about a community of men who devoted their lives to a formidable but utterly sterile project. His works include *Demian* and *Siddhartha*.

JAMES HILLMAN, representing the third generation in Jungian thought, is rapidly coming to be seen as one of the most original psychological thinkers in America today. Trained as a Jungian analyst, he calls himself an imaginal or archetypal psychologist, and his writings have captured the imaginations of novelists, poets, feminists, cultural historians, as well as his fellow analysts. He lectures widely and is the editor of the journal *Spring*. His books include *Suicide and the Soul*, *The Myth of Analysis*, *Re-Visioning Psychology*, *Anima*, *Loose Ends*, and *The Dream and the Underworld*.

ROBERT H. HOPCKE is a Jungian-oriented psychotherapist with a private practice in Berkeley, California, and cofounder of the Center for Symbolic Studies there. He is the author of *A Guided Tour of the Collected Works of C. G. Jung*, *Jung, Jungians, and Homosexuality*, and *Men's Dreams, Men's Healing*.

EUGENE IONESCO lived most of his life in Paris, where he gained reknown as a playwright who dramatized the absurdity of human experience and the futility of hope. His plays include *The Future Is in Eggs*, and *Chairs*.

DON HANLON JOHNSON is chair of the graduate program in Somatic Psychology and Education at New College of California and director of the Somatics Research and Education Program at Esalen Institute. He is author of two books and several articles on the body, and the forthcoming *Points of View: Body, Spirit, and Authority*.

C. G. JUNG, who died in 1961, one of the great personalities of our time, is probably best known as one of the founders of psychoanalysis. His reflections covered the full range of human problems and concerns of the modern soul. His overriding interest was the mystery of consciousness and personality, and their relationship with the great unconscious. His books include *Collected Works* (20 volumes), *Man in Search of a Soul*, and his popular autobiography, *Memories, Dreams, and Reflections*.

FRANZ KAFKA, 1883–1924, was one of the first writers to give literary expression to the existentialist plight of modern men and women. His works, including *The Trial*, *The Castle*, *Amerika*, and *The Penal Colony*, feature characters caught in a terrifying world beyond their control.

BEL KAUFMAN, granddaughter of the Yiddish author Shalom Aleichem, is the author of the best selling book, *Up the Down Staircase*. She is a teacher and frequent public speaker on the topic, "Don't flunk the teacher." Ms. Kaufman says: "I try to make my audiences laugh, think, and feel good about teachers."

SAM KEEN holds an M.A. from the Harvard Divinity School and a Ph.D. from Princeton University. His most recent book, *Faces of the Enemy*, was also a PBS documentary nominated for an Emmy Award. His other books include *Fire in the Belly*, *Apology for Wonder*, *To a Dancing God*, *The Passionate Life*, and

Loving Combat. He is a consulting editor and board member of *Psychology Today.*

AARON R. KIPNIS has taught numerous courses on archetypal psychology, gender reconciliation, and men's work, and is a frequent guest lecturer on gender issues at universities and institutes training new clinicians in psychology. He is a therapist at the Redwood Men's Center in Santa Rosa, California, and author of *Knights Without Armor: A Practical Guide for Men in Quest of Masculine Soul.*

BRIAN KNAVE, born in Johnson City, Tennessee, received his B.A. in English from East Tennessee State University and M.A. in Creative Writing from the University of California at Davis. Brian currently lives in Davis, California, where he writes, tap dances, plays drums and harmonica professionally, and teaches private music lessons.

DAVID KOTEEN is a writer and performer living just past the outskirts of Eugene, Oregon. He has fathered three sons. His story *Kusadasi* appeared in issue 177 of *The Sun.*

D. H. LAWRENCE, born to English working-class parents—a miner father and a mother with literary interests—remained gravely conscious of his "lowly" origins throughout his life. He secured his literary reputation in 1913 with the publication of *Sons and Lovers*, a compelling novel about emotional and family entanglements.

WOLFGANG LEDERER is a San Francisco psychiatrist whose book *The Fear of Women* is considered by many the definitive account of the pervasive ambivalence toward woman in both ancient and modern cultures. Dr. Lederer is a fellow of the American Psychiatric Association.

DON LESSEM writes mainly about dinosaurs. His articles have appeared in the *New York Times* and the *Boston Globe.* His books include *The Worst of Everything* and *At the Dinosaur Frontier.* He lives in Wabam, Massachusetts.

DANIEL J. LEVINSON, the principal author of *The Seasons of a Man's Life*, is professor of psychology in the Department of Psychiatry of the Yale University School of Medicine. He is the co-author of several books, including *The Authoritarian Personality* and *The Executive Role Constellation.*

JOHN LIPPERT was working at the Fisher Body plant in Elyria, Ohio, when he wrote the article that appears in this volume. He studied at Oberlin College.

GEORGE LOUGH earned his doctorate in counseling psychology from the University of Notre Dame where he studied under Morton Kelsey. He is a psychologist with a Jungian orientation who practices in Sherman Oaks, California, where he lives with his wife, also a psychologist.

NORMAN MAILER was born in Long Branch, New Jersey, in 1923. *The Naked and the Dead,* Mailer's post–World War II novel about men in battle, earned him accolades as a major new American writer. Today he makes his home in Brooklyn.

PETER MARSH is Senior Lecturer in Social Psychology at Oxford Polytechnic and is co-director of the Contemporary Violence Research Unit in Oxford University. In addition to *Tribes*, he has written *Rules of Disorder* and *Aggro: The Illusion of Violence*. He has also co-written *Gestures: Their Origin and Distribution, Aggression and Violence* and *Driving Passion: The Psychology of the Car*.

ROBERT AUGUSTUS MASTERS is the guide of Xanthyros, a Vancouver, British Columbia, community that he describes as "deeply dedicated to living a life of full-blooded Awakening." He is the author of *The Way of the Lover, Love Must Also Weep, Truth Cannot Be Rehearsed*, and *Blue Burns the Night, True Is the Light*.

CHRISTOPHER MATTHEWS is a nationally-syndicated political columnist and the Washington Bureau Chief for the *San Francisco Examiner*. Prior to serving in the U.S. Peace Corps as a trade development adviser with the government of Swaziland, he was a presidential speechwriter for former President Jimmy Carter and was a longtime senior aide to former House Speaker Thomas P. (Tip) O'Neill, Jr.

LOUIS W. MCLEOD is a psychotherapist in private practice in Atlanta, Georgia. He has worked with men in maximum security prison mental health units.

MICHAEL MEADE grew up in New York City, where he studied philosophy and literature. Today he teaches and speaks to groups, using stories, poems, and drumming to "help link the personal and the mythological." Robert Bly has called Meade, who lives with his family near Seattle, Washington, "one of the greatest teachers of men in the United States."

HENRY MILLER toured the United States in 1940 recording his impressions for a book he titled *The Air-Conditioned Nightmare*. His fiction, known for what Philip Rahv called "bohemian desperado," placed him in the class of D. H. Lawrence and James Joyce as a master of controversy.

EUGENE MONICK is a Jungian analyst practicing in Scranton, Pennsylvania, and New York City. He is a graduate of the Virginia (Episcopal) Theological Seminary. He received his doctorate from the Union Graduate School, and his Diploma in Analytical Pschology from the C. G. Jung Institute in Zurich.

ROBERT MOORE, professor of psychology and religion at Chicago Theological Seminary, is co-author (with Gordon Melton) of *The Cult Experience: Responding to the New Religious Pluralism* and general editor of the Paulist Press's Jung and Spirituality series. He is also co-author (with Douglas Gillette) of *King, Warrior, Magician, Lover*.

THOMAS MOORE practices archetypal psychotherapy in Dallas, Texas, and in Massachusetts. He is on the faculty of the Dallas Institute, International College, and he teaches archetypal psychology at Lesley College. His most recent book, *Dark Eros*, asks: "What poetic and imaginative powers lie at the base of torture, violence, and victimization?"

MALCOLM MUGGERIDGE, born in England in 1903, earned recognition for his stinging satires concerning organized religion, contraception, heart transplants, and egalitarianism. He also has written numerous plays, essays, and novels.

GERALD NACHMAN is a columnist and critic for the San Francisco *Chronicle*. His credentials include one marriage, one live-in arrangement, and 64,091 dates. He is the author of *Playing House* and *Out on a Whim*. He makes his home in San Francisco, California.

PABLO NERUDA was born in 1904, the son of a railroad worker. One of the greatest Spanish-language poets of all time, Neruda served as a member of the Chilean senate and as consul to Mexico. "I like the lives of people who are restless and unsatisfied, whether they are artists or criminals," he once wrote.

TERRANCE O'CONNOR is a psychotherapist in private practice in Silver Spring, Maryland.

PAUL OLSEN is a psychotherapist in private practice in New York City. In recent years he has expanded his work to include addictions, particularly alcoholism, and challenges of the creative process. In addition to publications in the area of psychology, he is the author of several critically acclaimed novels.

DAVID ORDAN received a Master of Fine Arts degree from Columbia University, and is the author of numerous short stories. He lives in Rochester, New York.

SAMUEL OSHERSON is a research psychologist and curator of Longitudinal Studies at the Harvard University Health Services. He received a Ph.D. in Clinical Psychology from Harvard and has held faculty positions at the Harvard Medical School, the Massachusetts Institute of Technology, and the University of Massachusetts. A practicing psychotherapist, he is the author of *Holding On or Letting Go: Men and Career Change at Midlife*. He lives in Cambridge, Massachusetts, with his wife and son.

BRUCE K. PEMBERTON lives with his wife Judy and two teenagers in Atlanta. He is in private practice as a psychotherapist and helped form the Atlanta Men's Experience, an ongoing support network for changing men.

RAY RAPHAEL teaches at the College of the Redwoods. He has been a homesteader, a civil rights activist, a Little League and Youth Soccer coach, and is father of two boys. His works include *Edges, An Everyday History of Somewhere*, and *The Teacher's Voice*.

RUMI was a thirteenth-century Sufi whose poems speak to soulful desire, longing, ecstasy, and grief.

DAVID M. RUSSELL is founder and former director of the Second Step Program for men in Pittsburgh, Pennsylvania. He works today as a spouse-abuse prevention counselor.

JOHN A. SANFORD is a psychologist living and practicing in San Diego, California. He is the author of many books, including *The Invisible Partners, Healing and Wholeness, The Kingdom Within, Dreams and Healing*, and *Between People*.

MICHAEL SHORB is a technical writer and editor from San Francisco, California. His poetry has appeared in *Michigan Quarterly, The Nation,* and numerous other publications. He is also a published author of children's stories, and is working on a historical novel.

TAV SPARKS is a therapist, lecturer, and writer living in Mill Valley, California. Formerly an addictions therapist, since 1985 he has led numerous workshops throughout the United States and Canada in Holotropic Breathwork TM and transpersonal approaches to recovery.

THOMAS R. STEELE is a psychotherapist in private practice in Chico, California. He is currently completing his doctoral dissertation on the psychological role of the father.

COOPER THOMPSON founded Resources for Change, a Cambridge, Massachusetts, organization providing training on masculinity, sex roles, and homophobia. He is a member of the National Council of the National Organization for Changing Men.

CÉSAR VALLEJO, one of Peru's greatest poets, was born in 1892 in a small mining town in northern Peru. Of Vallejo, John Knoepfle said: "He is at once the most immediate and isolated of poets, this man who is always talking to someone who cannot answer." Vallejo's books of poems include *Los Heraldos Negros* (*The Black Riders*) and *Deshojacion Sagrada* (*A Divine Falling of Leaves*).

MICHAEL VENTURA was born in New York City in 1945. Before becoming a columnist with the *Austin Sun* in Austin, Texas, in 1974, he "did everything—sold vacuum cleaners, flipped hamburgers, typed, hammered nails, poured concrete," educating himself voraciously on the way in the tradition of America's pre–World War II writers. He continues to write for the *L.A. Weekly* and lives in Los Angeles.

ARTURO VIVANTE is a writer who teaches in the writing program at Massachusetts Institute of Technology. He has published novels, plays, and short stories. His latest collection of short stories is entitled *Tales of Arturo Vivante*.

JIM WARTERS lives with his wife Nancy in Pittsburgh, Pennsylvania, where he attends classes at the University of Pittsburgh and enjoys the benefits of retirement.

ROBERT S. WEISS is Research Professor of the University of Massachusetts, in Boston, where he is director of the Work and Family Research Unit. He is also a lecturer in sociology in the department of psychiatry at the Massachusetts Mental Health Center, Harvard Medical School, where he was previously director of the Group for Research in Community Psychiatry. The author of *Marital Separation* and *Loneliness,* he lives in Brookline, Massachusetts.

FRANCIS WELLER is a licensed psychotherapist in private practice in Santa Rosa, California. For the past five years he has presented a public lecture series on healing the wounds of shame. He has been active working with men and exploring ways of restoring the masculine soul. He is married and a father.

JOHN S. WELTNER has a private practice of child, adult, and family therapy in Marblehead, Massachusetts.

FREDERIC WIEDEMANN is a clinical psychologist in Westlake Village, California. He has a private practice specializing in men's issues, and runs wilderness adventures and solos for men.

EDMUND WILSON established himself as a major American literary critic by attacking the detective story. *Cyprian's Prayer*, Wilson's allegorical play about a sorcerer's apprentice, was published in 1954.

JONATHAN WINTERS was born in 1925 in Dayton, Ohio. After serving with the marines in the South Pacific, he began his career as a disc jockey, and began making frequent television appearances in the Fifties. These led to his own network television programs, a distinguished career in the movies, and appearances as a nightclub and concert performer throughout the United States. He lives with his wife, Eileen, in Los Angeles.

WILLIAM BUTLER YEATS, 1865–1939, Ireland's greatest poet, spent his boyhood in the wild countryside of County Sligo. The title of his book of essays, *The Celtic Twilight*, has become proverbial. He received the Nobel Prize for Literature in 1923.

COPYRIGHTS AND PERMISSIONS

. . . .

Chapter 1 is an excerpt from "A New View of Masculinity" by Cooper Thompson. Copyright © 1985 Reprinted from *Educational Leadership*, 43, 4: 53–56, with permission of *Educational Leadership* and Cooper Thompson.

Chapter 2 is an excerpt from *Why Men Are the Way They Are* by Warren Farrell. Copyright © 1986 by McGraw-Hill Publishing Company. Reprinted with permission of McGraw-Hill Publishing Company.

Chapter 3 is an excerpt from "What Men Really Want: An Interview with Robert Bly," *New Age*, May 1982. Copyright © 1982 by Keith Thompson. Reprinted with permission of Keith Thompson.

Chapter 4 is an original essay created for this volume by Aaron R. Kipnis. Copyright © 1990 by Aaron R. Kipnis. Used with permission of the author.

Chapter 5 is an essay by Thomas Moore. Copyright © 1990 by Thomas Moore. Used with permission of the author.

Chapter 6 is an excerpt from "What Men Really Want: An Interview with Robert Bly," *New Age*, May 1982, with an additional passage not included in that interview. Copyright © 1982 by Keith Thompson. Used with permission.

Chapter 7 is an excerpt from "On Being a Man: An Interview with Michael Meade," *The Sun*, April 1989, Issue 161. Copyright © 1989 by *The Sun*. Reprinted with permission of *The Sun* and Michael Meade.

Chapter 8 is an excerpt from *King, Warrior, Magician, Lover* by Robert Moore and Douglas Gillette. Copyright © 1990 by Robert Moore and Douglas Gillette. Reprinted with permission of HarperCollins Publishers.

Chapter 9 is an excerpt from *Tribes* by Peter Marsh. Copyright © 1988 by Peter Marsh. Used with permission of Peter Marsh.

Chapter 10 is reprinted from *The Men from the Boys: Rites of Passage in Male America*, by Ray Raphael, with permission of University of Nebraska Press. Copyright © 1988 by the University of Nebraska Press.

Chapter 11 is excerpted from *Death in the Afternoon* by Ernest Hemingway. Copyright © 1932 by Charles Scribner's Sons, renewed 1960 by Ernest Hemingway.

Chapter 27 is an excerpt from an article that originally appeared as "Concepts and Overview of the Men's Liberation Movement" by Richard Haddad. Copyright © 1979 by Richard Haddad. Used with permission of Richard Haddad.

Chapter 28 is an excerpt from *The Secret Life of Salvador Dali* by Salvador Dali, published by the Dial Press. Copyright © 1942, 1961 by Salvador Dali.

Chapter 29 originally appeared as "The Sex Life" in *Redthroats* by David Cale. Copyright © 1989 by David Cale. Reprinted with permission of Random House, Inc.

Chapter 30 is a poem from *Last Words* by Antler. Copyright © 1986 by Antler. Used with permission of Antler.

Chapter 31 is an essay by David Goff that originally appeared as "Masturbation: Touching Oneself Anew." Copyright © 1990 by David Goff. Used with permission of the author.

Chapter 32 is an excerpt from *The Presidential Papers* by Norman Mailer. Copyright © 1960, 1961, 1962, 1963 by Norman Mailer.

Chapter 33 is an excerpt from *Like Coming Home: Coming-Out Letters* by Greg and His Parents, edited by Meg Umans. Copyright © 1988, published by Banned Books, an imprint of Edward-William Publishing Company, Austin, Texas. Reprinted with permission of Edward-William Publishing Company.

Chapter 34 is an excerpt from "We Need One Another," in *The Phoenix Papers: The Posthumous Papers of D. H. Lawrence*. Copyright © 1936 by Frieda Lawrence, renewed © 1964 by the estate of the late Frieda Lawrence Ravagli. Published by Viking Press.

Chapter 35 is an essay by David Koteen that appeared in *A Bell Ringing in the Empty Sky: The Best of The Sun*, Vol. II. Copyright by David Koteen. Used with permission of the author.

Chapter 36 is an article by Robert Augustus Masters taken from Issue #3 (Fall, 1990) of *Sacred Fire* (the quarterly journal of the Xanthyros Community). Used with permission of Robert Augustus Masters.

Chapter 37 is an excerpt from "Notes on Three Erections" in *Shadow Dancing in the USA* by Michael Ventura. Copyright © 1985 by Michael Ventura. Used with permission of the author.

Chapter 38 is an excerpt by Eugene Monick from *Phallos: Sacred Image of the Masculine* (Studies in Jungian Psychology by Jungian Analysts, no. 27), Inner City Books, Toronto, Canada, copyright © 1987. Used with permission of Inner City Books.

Chapter 39 is reprinted from *News of the Universe: Poems of Twofold Consciousness*, Sierra Club Books, 1980. Copyright © 1980 by Robert Bly. Used with permission of Robert Bly.

Chapter 55 is a short story by Arturo Vivante, as printed in *The London Magazine*, February/March 1972, Vol. 11, No. 6. Used with permission of the author.

Chapter 56 is an excerpt from *What Men Are Like* by John A. Sanford and George Lough. Copyright © 1988 by John A. Sanford and George Lough. Used with permission of Paulist Press.

Chapter 57 is a poem by Phil Cousineau. Copyright © 1985. Used with permission of Phil Cousineau.

Chapter 58 is an essay by David Guy, which appeared in *A Bell Ringing in the Empty Sky: The Best of The Sun*, Vol. II. Copyright by David Guy. Used with permission of the author.

Chapter 59 is an excerpt from *Meetings with Remarkable Men* (E. P. Dutton and Company, Inc.) by G. I. Gurdjieff. Copyright © 1963 by Editions Janus.

Chapter 60 is an excerpt from *Sorties: Journals and New Essays* by James Dickey. Copyright © 1971 by James Dickey.

Chapter 61 is a poem by Michael Shorb, which appeared in *A Bell Ringing in the Empty Sky: The Best of The Sun*, Vol. II. Copyright by Michael Shorb. Used with permission of the author.

Chapter 62 is an extract from *Autobiographical Writings* by Hermann Hesse, translated by Denver Lindley. Translation copyright © 1971, 1972 by Farrar, Straus and Giroux, Inc.

Chapter 63 is an excerpt from "What Men Really Want: An Interview with Robert Bly," *New Age* magazine, May 1982. Copyright © 1982 by Keith Thompson. Reprinted with permission of Keith Thompson.

Chapter 64 is an original essay created for this volume by Thomas R. Steele. Copyright © 1991 by Thomas R. Steele. Used with permission of the author.

Chapter 65 is an excerpt from *Finding Our Fathers: The Unfinished Business of Manhood* by Samuel Osherson. Copyright © 1986 by Samuel Osherson. Reprinted with permission of The Free Press, a Division of Macmillan, Inc.

Chapter 66 appeared in *Blue Fire: Selected Writings by James Hillman* (Harper and Row). All rights reserved. Used with permission of James Hillman.

Chapter 67 is an excerpt from *Broodmales* by Nor Hall. Copyright © 1989 by Spring Publications, Inc. Reprinted with permission of Spring Publications, Inc.

Chapter 68 is a letter by Lou Becker. Copyright © 1987 by Lou Becker. Used with permission of the author.

Chapter 69 is an excerpt from *Staying the Course* by Robert S. Weiss. Copyright © 1990 by Robert S. Weiss. Reprinted with permission of The Free Press, a Division of Macmillan, Inc.

ABOUT THE EDITOR

. . . .

KEITH THOMPSON is an independent scholar and journalist with a particular interest in the cultural imagination as expressed through art, religion, psychology, myth and folklore, mass media, and popular social movements. A consulting editor of ReVISION Journal, he is the author of the forthcoming book *Angels and Aliens: UFOs and the Mythic Imagination*. He makes his home on the central California coast.